TRAVELER

croatia

D1016793

San Mateo
Public Library

NATIONAL GEOGRAPHIC

TRAVELER

croatia

by Rudolf Abraham

National Geographic
Washington, D.C.

CONTENTS

Pages 2–3: Rab's towers loom over the Adriatic.
Opposite: Street musicians bring new life to Dubrovnik's old town.

TRAVELING WITH EYES OPEN

Alert travelers go with a purpose and leave with a benefit. If you travel responsibly, you can help support wildlife conservation, historic preservation, and cultural enrichment in the places you visit. You can enrich your own travel experience as well.

To be a geo-savvy traveler:

- Recognize that your presence has an impact on the places you visit.

- Spend your time and money in ways that sustain local character. (Besides, it's more interesting that way.)

- Value the destination's natural and cultural heritage.

- Respect the local customs and traditions.

- Express appreciation to local people about things you find interesting and unique to the place: its nature and scenery, music and food, historic villages and buildings.

- Vote with your wallet: Support the people who support the place, patronizing businesses that make an effort to celebrate and protect what's special there. Seek out local shops, restaurants, and inns. Use tour operators who love their home—who love taking care of it and showing it off. Avoid businesses that detract from the character of the place.

- Enrich yourself, taking home memories and stories to tell, knowing that you have contributed to the preservation and enhancement of the destination.

That is the type of travel now called geotourism, defined as "tourism that sustains or enhances the geographical character of a place—its environment, culture, aesthetics, heritage, and the well-being of its residents." To learn more, visit National Geographic's Center for Sustainable Destinations at *nationalgeographic.com/travel/sustainable*.

croatia

ABOUT THE AUTHOR

Award-winning travel writer **Rudolf Abraham** *(rudolfabraham.co.uk)* has explored many parts of the world, seeking out the remote and rarely seen gems of Europe, eastern Turkey, Central Asia, and Patagonia, but Croatia is his first love. Although a Londoner today, Abraham lived in Zagreb, Croatia's capital, around the turn of the millennium, and seldom spends long between return visits. Abraham is a trained photographer with a love of the great outdoors—the wilder the better—and he has a master's degree in the history of art. Croatia has the perfect combination for him of a varied landscape— the islands, wetlands, and mountain trails—age-old architecture, still thriving traditional culture and festivals, and a vibrant arts scene. Abraham's other books include *The Islands of Croatia, Istria, Walking in Croatia, The Mountains of Montenegro,* and *Torres del Paine.*

Charting Your Trip

Within a comparatively small area, Croatia has some of the best preserved medieval towns anywhere on the Mediterranean, as well as spectacular national parks and scenery, not to mention an archipelago with 1,200 islands.

How to Get Around

Croatia is a fairly small country, and getting around on the country's efficient public transportation network is a refreshingly straightforward affair. Domestic flights on the excellent national carrier, Croatia Airways *(croatiaairlines.com)*, are comparatively cheap and can get you from Zagreb to the coast in only half an hour or so. Reliable trains head east across Slavonia, west to Rijeka, and south to Split on the Dalmatian coast, with high-speed services to the latter destination. However, there is no railroad along the coast or north toward the Slovenian and Hungarian borders. Intercity buses are frequent, comfortable, and cover most major destinations, and local buses will get you around town or to a nearby sight. Some of the longer bus routes, such as Zagreb to Dubrovnik, can be a bit too long for comfort.

Many villages are a bit more remote and getting there on public transportation can be either impossible or a struggle. In these cases you would be better off renting a car—and there are plenty of car rental companies available. New freeways make driving between major centers a quick affair, although the main coastal highway (the Jadranska Magistrala) gets extremely busy during the summer months. Ferries are a wonderfully relaxing way to get to, from, and between most of the major islands—or down the length of the coast—and are also very cheap (although prices do rise considerably if you are taking a car aboard).

How to Visit

Despite the short distances involved, there is a huge amount to see in Croatia, and at the same time you may just find those sunny, café-filled medieval squares highly conducive to a long, lingering visit rather than speeding off to your next destination. Consequently, if you only

Statue of Grgur Ninski, Split

have a week in Croatia, you will have a more enjoyable time if you narrow your sights a little and concentrate on one or two areas rather than trying to see the whole country. Which areas you choose will of course reflect your own particular interest. Do you want to see the coast and islands, national parks and wildlife, the cities and museums, or historic architecture and ruins? Two possible itineraries follow, both of them cramming in a lot for a seven-day visit.

Zagreb, Istria, Zadar, & Split

The Croatian capital of Zagreb is arguably the country's most fascinating city, and you can easily spend a couple of days (or more) here before moving on to Istria, and northern and central Dalmatia.

Spend **two days** in the capital, exploring the old town on foot and visiting Gornji Grad, Kaptol, and Donji Grad (St. Mark's Square, the Cathedral, and the so-called "Green Horseshoe" of parks), along with some of the city's excellent museums (the Archaeological Museum, Ethnographic Museum, Modern Gallery, and Meštrović Atelier). Try to get to the bustling, colorful market (Dolac) one morning, and on **day three** head down to Pula in Istria (five hours by bus, or 40 minutes direct flight), and base yourself there for two more nights. Roam for the rest of the day around Pula's outstanding Roman ruins, then on **day four** make a day trip to Poreč (1.5 hours by bus) to see the Euphrasian Basilica with its dazzling sixth-century Byzantine mosaics. Allow yourself a bit more time in Pula in the evening. On **day five,** move on to Zadar (this will usually require two buses, changing at Rijeka, so you will save time driving this leg). Take the rest of the day to explore Zadar's old town, following Kalelarga down to the cathedral and the Church of St. Donatus.

On **day six** head for Split (three hours by bus), breaking your journey at Šibenik, if you have time, in order to see its extraordinary cathedral. Enjoy the rest of the day in Split, exploring Diocletian's Palace. On **day seven,** devote more time in Split, or make a trip to Trogir (30 minutes by bus) to see the cathedral there. Fly, bus, or take the high-speed train back to the capital, Zagreb.

NOT TO BE MISSED:

Catching one of Croatia's many public festivals and boisterous carnivals **18**

Exploring Zagreb, Croatia's vibrant, beating heart **56–85**

The amphitheater at Pula, one of the largest Roman arenas in the world **126–127**

Hiking on Velebit **182–183**

Diocletian's Palace in Split, a living Roman building **197**

Taking the trail through Plitvice Lakes National Park **230–231**

A morning spent walking the walls around Dubrovnik's old town **244–245**

Visitor Information

Croatia National Tourism Office (U.S.)
P.O. Box 2651, New York, NY 10108, croatia.hr, e-mail: info@htz.hr
Zagreb Tourist Information
Trg bana J. Jelacičać 11, tel 014 814 051 (free phone 0800 53 53), or Zagreb Airport, Pleso bb, zagreb-touristinfo.hr, e-mail: info@zagreb-touristinfo.hr
Split Tourism Information
Peristil bb, Split, tel 021 345 606, visitsplit.com, e-mail: turistinfo@visitsplit.com

Zagreb, Plitvice Lakes, Zadar, Split, Korčula, & Dubrovnik

This covers a bit more ground than the previous itinerary, with less time in any one place, and assumes early starts each day to get through everything.

Spend the **first day** in the capital, exploring the old town on foot and visiting Gornji Grad, Kaptol, and Donji Grad as per the previous plan. On **day two,** head for Plitvice Lakes (Plitvička Jezera) National Park with its stunningly beautiful travertine lakes and falls. This requires an easy bus ride, although driving would be better rather than waiting for onward bus connections the following day. On **day three,** continue to Zadar and enjoy your day in the old town, visiting the cathedral and the Church of St. Donatus. On **day four** continue to Split, and explore the spectacular living ruin that is Diocletian's Palace. Early on **day five** take the catamaran to Korčula, where you can occupy yourself wandering the streets of this beautifully preserved old town, the supposed former home of Marco Polo. On **day six,** take a morning bus to Dubrovnik, crossing to the mainland at the Pelješac Peninsula. During the afternoon and evening explore the old town of perhaps Croatia's most famous city, making sure you walk around the walls and visit the Franciscan and Dominican Monasteries. Discover more of Dubrovnik's old town the following morning **(day seven);** the morning's one of the better times to go up onto the walls. At the end of the day, fly back to Zagreb.

Croatian Currency

The Croatian currency is the kuna, usually written as kn and officially abbreviated as HNK. The kuna comes in banknote denominations of 5, 10, 20, 50, 100, 200, 500, and 1,000, and in coins of 1, 2, and 5. Each kuna consists of 100 lipa, of which there are coins in denominations of 1, 2, 5, 10, 20, and 50. The kuna is named for the pelt of the marten, an item widely traded in the medieval period and which was first recorded in this capacity in the town of Osor (on the island of Cres) in a document from 1018. Lipa is derived from the Croatian word for "lime tree." The kuna is a stable currency with about 5.6 kuna to one U.S. dollar. Croatia joined the EU in 2013, so within the next few years the kuna will probably be replaced by the euro.

If You Have More Time

If you have a few extra days or, even better, another week, you can cover a good bit of ground. Just staying for two extra nights in Zagreb allows you to embark on longer day trips to, for example, the baroque, 18th-century capital, **Varaždin** (1.5 hours by bus). The northern countryside in this area close to the Hungarian border is famous for vineyards and 16th-century Austrian castles. At the **Lonjsko Polje** wetlands (1.5 hours by car on the E70 and local roads), a huge population of nesting storks arrives every spring.

Alternatively, take the E70/A3 toward Osijek and Đakovo. After 125 miles (200 km), exit at Srendanci and continue 13 miles (22 km) on the E73/A5 to **Đakovo.** The town is famous for its Lipizzaner horses and the redbrick Cathedral of Sts. Peter and Paul (Katedrala Sv. Petra i Pavla) or take the wine route around nearby **Ilok.**

Another 35 minutes north on the E73 is **Osijek** on the Drava River (if you don't have a car, from Zagreb take the four-hour bus ride or five-hour train ride); Sts. Peter

As well as historic sites, Croatia offers numerous opportunities for adventure.

and Paul church here is Croatia's second tallest (295 feet/90 m). The next day, go north 5 miles (8 km) to the village of Bilge and the main gate to **Kopački Rit Nature Park,** where nearly 300 species of birds have been observed.

An alternative route for those with more time takes in Istria, east of Zagreb, then some island-hopping south from Split. En route to Istria, stop to hike into **Vražji Prolaz** (the "Devil's Pass") at **Skrad,** 1.5 hours south of Zagreb. Two hours farther along the A6/E61 and A8, reach **Istria** and spend the next day visiting the hill towns of **Motovun** and **Hum;** or travel 40 minutes to the eastern coast at **Rovinj** or the more southern **Pula** (these form a kind of triangle with Istria at the inland point).

On your third day, enjoy a mostly seaside, four-hour drive to Pag; head back north on the A8 and wrap around the tip of the Mediterranean Sea (A7/E61) to descend the coast opposite from the Istrian Peninsula (Route 8/E65). Take the Prizna-Žigljen ferry to reach **Pag** and have a dinner featuring local *Paški sir,* a salty, sheep's milk cheese.

On the fourth day, continue south on the A1 for the last two hours to **Split,** breaking for the hiking trails in **Paklenica National Park** or the scenery in **Krka National Park.** Devote the next three days—or however long you have!—to exploring by catamaran; sailing to nearby **Zlatni Rat** (on Brač island) or to the island of **Hvar;** or relaxing on the sand. For something more secluded, try **Vis** or **Kormiža.**

Driving in Croatia

Croatians drive on the right, and the speed limits are 31 miles an hour (50 kph) in built-up areas, 55 mph (90 kph) on open roads, 68 mph (110 kph) on major high-ways, and 80 mph (130 kph) on freeways. All drivers must have a reflective jacket in the car, and this must be worn if getting out of a vehicle on a major road. Croatia has some very new and very fast freeways *(autocesta)* operating on a toll system. Simply collect a ticket when you roll on and pay as you exit *(hac.hr).*

History & Culture

Nightlife on the Stradun, in the historic center of Dubrovnik

Croatia Today

Croatia is blessed with an outstandingly beautiful coastline, wonderful natural scenery, some exceptionally well preserved medieval towns, and a warm, sunny climate. That adds up to a heady combination of vibrant markets and sleepy fishing villages, architectural styles spanning millennia, and a thriving scene of folk arts and festivals.

As many as 5,000 years ago, Bronze Age cultures in what is now Croatia—or Hrvatska as Croats know it—were creating slender axe heads and beautiful pottery objects, living in thriving fishing and farming communities where they kept domesticated livestock. From the first century b.c., the Romans built flourishing trading ports and cities here,

marked by the precision stonework and monumental architecture that has lasted to this day. The fleeting medieval kingdom of Croatia in the 10th and 11th centuries was followed by some nine centuries of foreign rule, before the country's recent (and bloody) emergence from the former Yugoslavia as an independent state in the early 1990s.

Shaped by the Land

Though a comparatively small country, Croatia has remarkably varied landscapes and climate, from the scattered islands, rocky coast, and crystal clear waters of the Adriatic Sea to the spine of rugged limestone mountains of the interior and the rich agricultural land of the Slavonian Plain in the north. The parched, appearance of some of its long archipelago of islands (see pp. 210–223) contrasts markedly with the extensive wetlands beyond the mountains around the Sava and Danube Rivers, and the lush green forests, gurgling brooks, and cascading travertine waterfalls of its Plitvice Lakes (Plitvička Jezera) region (see pp. 228–231).

Croatia's coastline is extraordinarily beautiful and surprisingly long, running to 3,625 miles (5,835 km). Its length is a product of its many bays and inlets—and because of the large number of islands in the Dalmatian archipelago. There are more than 1,000 islands, most of them uninhabited and many virtually untouched by human hands.

The familiar Dalmatian cities with Romanesque bell towers and red-tile roofs on the coast and islands give way inland to elegant baroque (16th–17th century) and secessionist (late 19th century) architecture with a distinctly Central European feel. Meanwhile the capital and most populous city, busy Zagreb (see pp. 56–85), is a thriving cultural, administrative, and business center with high-rise apartment blocks and offices jostling for position with ancient churches, tree-lined avenues, and winding streets.

Croatia's climate is also varied. The brilliant sunshine and mild winters of the coast are exchanged for a more extreme continental climate in the interior, with much hotter

New and classic buildings stand side by side on Zadar's waterfront.

summers and a frigid winter landscape blanketed in snow. This dramatic change in climate and cultural legacy stems in part from the chain of mountains that, running parallel with the coast, have historically divided the Mediterranean zone from the continental landmass. Not until the Romans built five roads across the mountains, from the coast into the interior, in the first century A.D. were the two areas linked. In more recent times, the new motorway from Zagreb to Zadar (see pp. 170–176) still had to be bored at great expense through the mountains of southern Velebit in 2003. On another level, the landscape reflects the various cultural spheres under which the different areas have fallen—several centuries of Venetian rule on the coast and islands, and under the Habsburg monarchs in the interior—and later the coast as well.

Cultural Leader

Croatia is a nation immensely proud of both its cultural and natural heritage, from its literary tradition, which stretches back to the Renaissance, to the multitude of UNESCO World Heritage–listed cities and churches, as well as a national park. The first sites designated as such in 1979 were Diocletian's Palace in Split, Old Town of Dubrovnik, and Plitvice Lakes National Park.

Croatia's first university was founded in 1669 in Zagreb. Croatia's men of science have contributed to an explanation of the tides and rainbows, and its cities produced at least one Roman emperor. The Republic of Dubrovnik lead the continent with the establishment of a system of care for orphans, the elderly, and the sick by the 15th century; not to mention the establishment of one of Europe's earliest plans for fighting the plague. Slavery was abolished along this part of the Croatian coast in the 1400s before Columbus sailed to America.

Croatia's cultural heritage ranges from extraordinary Roman ruins (sometimes not so ruinous at all) and dazzling Byzantine mosaics inside Romanesque churches to Venetian-Gothic palaces, baroque castles, and entire medieval cities preserved with their original warren of streets and alleys.

The country's cultural heritage is matched by some truly outstanding natural scenery. The indented coastline and myriad isles and islets have become synonymous with Croatia's international image, but there are also thousand-year-old travertine cascades and some of the finest examples of karst landscapes—craggy peaks riddled with caves—you are likely to see anywhere. Croatia's museums and galleries are exceptional, both in terms of their fascinating, world-class contents and their sheer numbers. Some highlights include gallery collections of Croatian naïve art, exquisite medieval stone carvings, and some artifacts from the very dawn of human civilization in Europe.

Top 10 Croatian Phrases

Hello	Dobar dan
Goodbye	Do viđenja
Please can I have...?	Molim vas...?
Thank you	Hvala
Yes	Da
No	Ne
Sorry!	Oprostite!
Cheers! (as a toast)	Živjeli!
Pleased to meet you	Drago mi je
Do you speak English?	Govorite li engleski?

Presidential guards in Zagreb wearing traditional uniform—cravat included

Croatian Influence

Croatia is also the source of a few everyday things we take very much for granted. The groundbreaking work of scientist Nikola Tesla (1856–1943), born in a village in Croatia tucked away behind the Velebit mountains, laid the foundations for modern alternating current and commercial electricity, and many consider him the inventor of radio communications. The necktie, or cravat (from the word "Croat" or "Hrvat"), originated in a silk scarf worn by Croats, was adopted by fashionable members of the French royal court in the 17th century, and later metamorphosed into the standard item of business attire worn across the globe. And the fountain pen began life in 1907 as the brainchild of inventor Eduard Slavoljub Penkala (1871–1922) in Zagreb, where it was first produced, along with the world's first mechanical pencil, at the Zagreb Pencil Factory (Tvornica Olovaka Zagreb), which still exists.

> **Croatia's men of science have contributed to an explanation of the tides and rainbows, and its cities produced at least one Roman emperor.**

EXPERIENCE: Revel at Local Festivals

Croatia has no shortage of festivals, from small village celebrations to world-class events lasting several weeks. While many festivals are concentrated in the summer months and around Easter, chances are there will be something happening whatever time of year you choose to visit.

Festivals

Folk themes are central to many festivals in Croatia. The largest is Zagreb's spectacular **International Folk Festival** (msf.hr), held in July with much of it taking place in the main square. The **Brodsko Kolo** (brodsko-kolo .com), held in Slavonski Brod in June, is Croatia's premier folk-dance festival and has been going for some 50 years. Also held in June, the **Procession of the Ljelje** in the village of Gorjani (near Đakovo) is one of Croatia's most colorful festivals.

In July, Omiš holds its annual *klapa* (see sidebar p. 206) song festival, the **Festival of Dalmatian Klapa** (fdk .hr). This is a wonderful opportunity to hear performances of Dalmatia's traditional, hauntingly beautiful a cappella song. Đakovo's **Embroidery Festival** (Đakovački Vezovi) also takes place in July, an event that features (along with plenty of traditional embroidery), crowd-pleasing displays by the Lipizzaner horses for which the area is famous.

Children at Zagreb's International Folk Festival in July

Carnivals

Lent is a time of carnivals throughout predominantly Roman Catholic Croatia. The biggest and most spectacular of these is the **Rijeka Carnival** (ri -karneval.com.hr). Huge crowds line the streets to watch an endless parade of floats, dancing, and wild costumes.

On the last Thursday before Easter (Maundy Thursday) on the island of Hvar, a **Procession of the Cross** (Za Križen) takes place between the villages of Jelsa, Pitve, Vrisnik, Svire, Vrbanj, and Vrboska.

The island of Lastovo holds its own carnival for three days during Lent, the remarkable **Poklad Festival.** An effigy paraded around on a donkey is drawn down a 300-foot (91 m) rope and then summarily burned—an act meant to commemorate the miraculous destruction of a fleet of pirates, on their way to plunder the island.

August 15 (**Assumption Day,** or Velika Gospa in Croatian) is one of the country's largest feast days, marked by various celebrations including a pilgrimage across Medvednica from Zagreb to the church at Marija Bistrica, descending the stations of the cross.

Forged by War

The war that accompanied Croatia's secession from the former Yugoslavia between 1991 and 1995 is now frequently referred to as the Homeland War by Croatian sources. Croats also call the conflict the War of Independence or the Patriotic War. Serbians commonly have a different view of events and refer to the period as a civil war in Croatia, regarding the fighting as a conflict between Croats and Serbs. Most international opinion is that it was a civil war until Croatia's declaration of independence and an international war after that event. The majority of foreign observers also characterize the war as an act of Serbian aggression. However, neither side ever declared war.

Psychological Damage

The gruesome conflict haunted the country for several years in its immediate aftermath. Croatian casualties in the war are estimated at around 12,000 dead and missing, of whom nearly 6,800 were in the Croatian military. Around 35,000 people were wounded, many seriously. The conflict also destroyed nearly 180,000 dwellings and the infrastructure of a quarter of the new nation's economy. The conduct of the war eventually led to a number of cases before the International Criminal Tribunal for the former Yugoslavia, based in The Hague, the legislative capital of the Netherlands. Most of the indictments were made against members in the Serbian forces, but some, including charges of crimes against humanity, were laid against small elements of the Croatian army.

Today, some 20 years after the war, most Croatians want to put the past behind them and get on with their lives.

Today, some 20 years after the war, most Croatians want to put the past behind them and get on with their lives. Yet the country still bears many scars. The physical damage has been largely repaired, except on some landmarks, such as the shell-blasted water tower in Vukovar, which have deliberately been left in their ruined state to serve as sobering reminders. However, the social and psychological impacts will take longer to heal as minority communities inside Croatia and beyond its borders learn to live with the political settlement. If this seems at odds with the carefree experience of traveling on the coast, just walk into any cemetery in Slavonia and look at the number of gravestones marking the lives suddenly ended by the war.

People & Politics

Croatia has a population of 4.29 million according to the 2011 census, about 790,000 of whom live in the capital, Zagreb. Most of the population calls itself Croat (around 90 percent in the last census), while those calling themselves Serb make up less than 5 percent (8 percent less than before the war). The rest of the population is composed of several smaller minorities (including Bosnians, Hungarians, and Slovenians), each forming less than one percent of the total population. The dominant religion is Roman Catholic (86 percent), with 4.4 percent Serbian Orthodox and 1.4 percent Muslim. The GDP per capita was approximately $13,800 in 2012, and Croatia's total GDP in the same year $56.4 billion, the

Franjo Tuđman: Father of Modern Croatia

Everywhere you go in Croatia you will find references to Franjo Tuđman, a dominant figure during the difficult period of the 1990s. It was Tuđman who led the nation to independence and who is now regarded as the father of modern Croatia. Today, streets and squares, buildings and institutions throughout the country are named for him. Born in 1922, he joined the communist Partisans fighting against the occupying German forces in 1941. He rose through the ranks of the JNA (Yugoslav People's Army) to become one of the country's youngest generals in 1960.

Tuđman's nationalist sentiments eventually led to his disillusionment with the federal Yugoslav state. Retiring from the military, he became an academic in 1961.

Because of his views, he was expelled from the Communist Party in 1967 and was imprisoned as a dissenter in 1972 and 1981. In 1989, as Communist regimes across Eastern Europe began to disintegrate, Tuđman founded the nationalist HDZ (Croatian Democratic Union) party and was swept to power in free legislative elections in Croatia in 1990.

Tuđman led the country during the Homeland War and became Croatia's first president. His role in the war in Bosnia and Herzegovina, where Croatia gained virtual control of Croat-majority areas, led to some international criticism and an increasing tendency toward authoritarianism brought a decline in support for the HDZ at home and increasing diplomatic isolation abroad. Tuđman died in office in 1999.

highest of any country from the former Yugoslavia, including Slovenia, despite the fact that it, like Croatia, is also a member of the European Union (EU). Like other Western countries, Croatia has lost about 20 percent of its wealth during the recent downturn in the world economy. Unemployment had fallen to just over 13 percent in 2008, though that figure has risen since the economic downturn, and stood at more than 18 percent in 2013, and foreign debt remains comparatively high. Despite prices remaining reasonable for most foreign visitors, they remain high for locals, with an average gross monthly salary in Croatia somewhere in the region of $1,400 ($1,000 net).

Croatia is now a fully functioning parliamentary democracy. The nation's parliament is based on a unicameral, multiparty system.

Tourism is one of Croatia's greatest industries, while more than 60 percent of its exports (mainly machinery, chemical products, and other industrial goods and, to a much lesser extent, agriculture) are shipped within the EU, though a large amount of seafood is now exported to Japan. Slavonia is the great breadbasket of the country, its arable land producing wheat and other crops, whereas the harsh, rocky soil of the coast is better suited to olive trees and hardy grapevines.

Croatia is now a fully functioning parliamentary democracy. The nation's parliament (Sabor) is based on a unicameral (single chamber, in contrast to the United States), multiparty system. It has 153 elected members, each serving for a term of four years. The parliamentary speaker is elected from the members. Members are elected partly from single-member constituencies and partly under a system of proportional representation by universal adult suffrage. Six seats are reserved for Croats abroad and five for minorities, including Serbs, Hungarians, and Italians. The ceremonial president, who is directly elected for five years, appoints a prime minister, who chooses a council of ministers. This council commands a majority in the Sabor.

The two main political parties, by a very wide margin, are the right-wing nationalist HDZ (Croatian Democratic Union), which was in power in the late 1990s under Croatia's first president, Franjo Tuđman, and was reelected again in 2003, and the center-left SDP (Social Democratic Party), which was in power from 2000 to 2003.

The HDZ's Ivo Sanader, who resigned as prime minister in 2009, was succeeded by Jadranka Kosor, the first woman to hold this position in Croatia. The current prime minister is Zoran Milanović who was elected in 2011, and has been leader of the SDP since 2007. Croatia's long-standing former president, Stjepan Mesić was succeeded in February 2010 by Ivo Josipović.

The country is divided on an administrative level into 21 counties (called *županje*), each of which has an assembly of representatives elected by vote, serving four-year terms. The leaders of local government at the county level are *župan*.

Croatia joined NATO in April 2009. Its bid for European Union candidacy status was accepted in 2004. A modern and stable Croatia finally joined the EU in July 2013—"a testament," as Tánaiste (Deputy Prime Minister) of the Republic of Ireland Eamon Gilmore commented at Croatia's EU accession ceremony, "to its people's

Zoran Milanović, Croatia's prime minister when Croatia celebrated its admission into the European Union in 2013

determination to put a troubled period behind them and . . . an inspiration for its neighbours in the region."

Tourism

Croatia has been familiar with tourism since the mid-19th century, when Opatija in Istria became an eminently fashionable health resort for the wealthy Austrian elite. Later in the 19th century, Austrian businessman Paul Kupelwieser bought the Brijuni Islands and, within a relatively short time, converted them into a highly popular luxury health resort.

Croatia's Dalmatian coast became an extremely popular tourist destination during the 1970s and 1980s, particularly with German and Italian visitors, and provided a considerable source of wealth for the Yugoslavian economy.

The Homeland War had a catastrophic effect on tourism, effectively wiping the country off the map for several years. The results of the war included a shattered infrastructure and a legacy of shrapnel-scarred cities and wrecked hotels. Many hotels had been either shelled, used as barracks by the Serbian-controlled Yugoslav People's Army, or JNA, or requisitioned to house the thousands of refugees who had fled their homes in Slavonia, Bosnia, and elsewhere.

In the late 1990s, visitors began returning to an "undiscovered" independent Croatia (although NATO air strikes on Serbia in 1999 did little to encourage this), first in a steady stream and then in droves. Within the past 15 years, tourism has grown spectacularly, with more than 14 million foreign visitors arriving in Croatia in 2013 and contributing somewhere in the region of $9 billion to the economy just in the first nine months of that year alone. The extensive physical damage sustained during the Homeland War has since been painstakingly restored, nowhere more so than in the walled medieval city of Dubrovnik on the Adriatic, which was shelled relentlessly in 1991 and 1992, and gradually, the shattered baroque city of Vukovar on the Danube River near the border with Serbia.

The catchphrase of the Croatian National Tourist Board, "The Mediterranean as it once was," is not so far off the mark.

Today, Croatia has become one of the top 20 tourist destinations in the world, and the vacation industry accounts for about one-sixth of the country's economy. Although visitors are overwhelmingly lured to coastal Croatia during the summer months, this is a seasonal imbalance as inland ski resorts are attracting more winter visitors.

A wine grower harvests grapes at a vineyard on the Pelješac Peninsula.

In stark contrast to many other Mediterranean countries over the past 20 or 30 years, this increase in tourism has not generally been accompanied by rampant overdevelopment, and for the most part the Croatian Adriatic remains one of the most unspoiled stretches of coastline anywhere on the Mediterranean. The catch-phrase of the Croatian National Tourist Board, "The Mediterranean as it once was," is not so far off the mark. The dramatic increase in tourism has been accompanied by a boom in property buying by overseas investors, for whom Croatia still remains good value for money (not so for the locals, since this has served to push up housing prices beyond the reach of most Croats). While Croatia has catered to mid-level and luxury travel, increasing numbers of new hostels, smaller hotels, and campgrounds are now making the country an attractive destination for independent budget-minded travelers. ■

History of Croatia

Located at the crossroads of southern Europe, Croatia has a long history; Neanderthal bones discovered in a cave in northern Croatia show that the area has been inhabited for at least 130,000 years. More recent history has been one of a succession of foreign powers seizing the land, until at last a stable, democratic Croatia emerged in the latter part of the 1990s.

There is plenty of evidence of Neolithic civilization, especially around the banks of the Danube River. Many important finds have been made, including evidence of the Vučedol culture that dominated eastern Slavonia 5,000 years ago. During the Iron Age, the eastern Adriatic was inhabited by the Illyrians, a number of tribes of Indo-European origin who became increasingly powerful from around 400 B.C. They included the Histri, after which Istria is named; the Liburni, also from Istria and along the north Dalmatian coast; and the Delmatae, farther south on the coast and in the hinterland, another name that is still preserved today in the region's modern name. In the early fourth century B.C., the ancient Greeks began founding colonies on the Adriatic coast, initially at Issa—the modern town of Vis on the island of the same name—and then at Epidaurus (now Cavtat near Split), Pharos (Hvar), and Tragurion (Trogir), among several other places. The Celts also arrived in the region during the fourth century B.C., settling to the north along the middle Danube and in the Sava and Drava River Valleys.

> **Many important finds have been made, including evidence of the Vučedol culture that dominated eastern Slavonia 5,000 years ago.**

Invading Powers

Illyrian piracy—or at least, that was the reason given by the Romans—prompted Rome to launch a series of campaigns against her Illyrian neighbors in the second and first centuries B.C. Following those conflicts, Illyrian lands in what is now Croatia became the Roman province of Illyria, later divided into Pannonia and Dalmatia. The Romans established their provincial capital at the old Greek settlement of Salona (modern Solin, now a suburb of Split; see sidebar p. 203), with Pula, Zadar, and other settlements developing as important trading ports and cities. Among the most evocative remains of the Roman period in Croatia are the incredibly well preserved amphitheater at Pula (dating from the first century A.D.; see pp. 126–127) and the Diocletian's Palace at Split (constructed A.D. 295–305; see pp. 198–199).

Following the slow collapse of the Roman Empire in the West during the fourth century A.D., the region was ravaged by a series of chaotic and sometimes devastating invasions for the next two centuries. First the Huns from far to the east in Russia and the Goths from Scandinavia and around the Baltic Sea had taken control of

(continued on p. 28)

The Roman amphitheater in Pula

Medieval Croatia

During the second half of the ninth century, a time when much of Dalmatia was under Byzantine suzerainty and administered as a series of counties from Zadar, Croatia experienced a gradual increase in power and autonomy. This tendency was reflected in the emergence of Croatian dukes in positions of local rule and a move toward greater religious autonomy from Byzantium, as well as the adoption of the Glagolitic instead of Latin script by the local priesthood.

A page of 15th-century Glagolitic script. The oldest known slavic script first appeared in manuscripts around A.D. 1000.

The first half of the ninth century is also marked by a more widespread conversion to Christianity in Croatia from Slavic mythology, as well as the comparatively early appearance of Benedictine monasteries in the region.

Croatian Kings

The first person to be recorded with the title King of Croatia, in 925, was Tomislav, who is mentioned in a letter from Pope John X and whose equestrian statue stands before the main railway station in Zagreb. Details about Tomislav's reign remain sketchy (see sidebar opposite), though he successfully repelled the Hungarians in the north and appears to have been in conflict with Bulgaria (probably in support of the forces of Byzantium). He was succeeded in 928 by Trpimir II, then by Krešimir I in 935. Later in the tenth century, a certain Jelena (whose name is recorded in an epitaph from near Salona) ruled as a queen in her own right for several years.

The first known Croatian duke was Višeslav, who ruled from Nin in A.D. 800 while still acknowledging Byzantine sovereignty. Later in the same century, Trpimir ruled from the stronghold of Klis near Split around 852 (when his name is mentioned in a charter). Then, in around 880, Branimir, whose name is preserved in a number of Latin inscriptions from around this time, swore loyalty to Pope John VIII, assuming the titles Duke of the Croats and Duke of the Slavs.

Glagolitic Script

It was during this period that Grgur Ninski, Bishop of Nin—whose sculpture will be familiar to many from the back of Diocletian's Palace at Split (see p. 202)—attended the synods in 925 and again in 928, arguing for the use of Glagolitic (rather than Latin, which much of the Croatian population was unable to understand) in the liturgy. Nevertheless, the use of Glagolitic does not appear in manuscripts any earlier than about

1000, and the bishopric of Nin was actually abolished in 928.

It was not until the reign of Petar Krešimir IV (r. 1058–1074), however, that Croatia was unified for the first time as a single state, with Dalmatia wrested from Byzantine control and joined to Pannonian Croatia. Krešimir IV was succeeded by Zvonimir (r. 1075–1089), upon whom the title King of Croatia and Dalmatia was conferred by Pope Gregory VII.

During the reign of King Zvonimir, a donation of land to a church on the island of Krk was recorded on the famous stone now known as the **Baška Tablet** (Baščanska Ploča), the original of which is in the atrium of Zagreb's Academy of Sciences and Arts (see p. 77). The Baška Tablet is one of the earliest inscriptions in the Croatian language written in Glagolitic.

Foreign Rule

Following the death of Zvonimir, the country was ruled for a short period by Stephen II, whose death in 1091 effectively marked the end of the Croatian royal house (known as the Trpimirović dynasty, after its founder, Trpimir). It is often said that Zvonimir was actually murdered and that his dying curse upon his killers was that they should be forever ruled by foreign powers. As if by his word, Croatia was to see some 900 years of foreign rule before regaining its independence in the 1990s.

In 1091, King Ladislaus of Hungary invaded northern Croatia with the support of Zvonimir's widow (who was conveniently Ladislaus's sister), with the last pretender to the Croatian throne, Petar Svačić, defeated by Ladislaus's successor, King Koloman, in 1097 on Mount Gvozd (the modern Petrova Gora). In 1102, a treaty was signed between Croatia and King Koloman. The Hungarian Arpad dynasty inherited the rights of the Croatian kings, and a Hungarian *ban*, or governor, was installed.

Despite the Croatian dynasty's fleeting rule, the period has left a deep mark on the Croatian consciousness.

Despite the Croatian dynasty's fleeting rule, the period has left a deep mark on the Croatian consciousness. The period has also left a number of beautiful works of art, including two beautifully **carved stone panels** from the altar screen of Zadar's 11th-century Church of St. Domenica (Sv. Nedelja, which is no longer standing), with figures in arches before a seated ruler. They are now in Zadar's Archaeological Museum (see p. 173). Also surviving is the so-called **Baptistery of Višeslav** dating from around A.D. 800, now in the Museum of Croatian Architectural Monuments in Split (see p. 204), together with several richly **illuminated manuscripts.**

Tomislav, the First King of Croatia

The first Croatian king, Tomislav is regarded as father of the nation. Tomislav was duke of Dalmatia since circa 910. In 925, he united the duchy with Pannonia to create the kingdom of Croatia. His realm stretched to the present border with Hungary. He reigned as king of Croatia for only three years, until his death in 928. However, during this short time he built up the infant nation's forces, raising some 100,000 troops and commanding 80 ships in the Adriatic. Tomislav called an assembly at Split to reform the church in Croatia, but it insisted on retaining the use of Latin rather than Croat in the Mass. Nothing is known of the place or circumstances of Tomislav's death.

the land relinquished by the shrinking Roman Empire and launched repeated raids on the wealthy settlements in Dalmatia and the Balkans at large. In the following decades, the Visigoths and Ostrogoths, two of the main Goth tribes, learned a lot from their Roman foe, and a Romanized Visigothic culture developed in the Balkans close to the Danube River, a region that became the springboard for a full-scale assault on Rome. Alaric I, the Visigoth king, led his "barbarian" army all the way to Rome and sacked the once mighty city in A.D. 410. In the early seventh century, the Avars (another northern tribe) sacked Epidaurus, leaving its inhabitants to wander a few miles north and found a new city, Dubrovnik. The Avars also laid waste to Salona, whose inhabitants fled to the safety of Diocletian's Palace and have never left. The city of Split, which grew around the great palace, is now the second largest city in Croatia.

The First Croats

Slavs had begun migrating into the valleys of the Danube and Sava Rivers during the sixth century A.D. Originally from an area north of the Black Sea, they settled

The Church of St. Nicholas, where Croatian kings crowned in Nin were presented to their subjects

The Zrinski-Frankopan Conspiracy

Petar Zrinski (1621–1671), a member of one of the greatest Croatian noble families, became Ban (Viceroy) of Croatia in 1665. Through his marriage to Katarina, Zrinski was also the brother-in-law of Fran Krsto Frankopan (1643–1671), himself a member of one of the greatest Croatian landowning families. All three were accomplished poets. Following the treaty known as the Peace of Vasvár (1644), Austria effectively handed the Ottomans large areas of land belonging to Croatian and Hungarian nobles—and which the Croatian armies had been fighting hard to defend against the Ottomans in Austria's name. The two brothers-in-law became disillusioned and became the epicenter of a conspiracy against Austrian rule. When the plot was discovered, they traveled to Vienna to ask Emperor Leopold I for pardon, but instead were beheaded in April 1671 in Wiener Neustadt in Austria. Their remains were returned to Croatia in 1919 and their bones are now buried in Zagreb's cathedral.

in the Dinaric Alps and had reached the Adriatic by some time early in the seventh century. In 626, another Slavic people known as the White Croats were invited to move into the region by the Byzantine emperor, Heraclius, on condition that they fight against the troublesome Avars on behalf of Byzantium. Having successfully done the emperor's bidding, they settled in the area between the Adriatic coast and the Drava River, an area that was to take their name, Croatia. While this all sounds a little too perfect for an accurate account of historical events, there is evidence of another region named "White Croatia" located north of the Carpathian Mountains in southern Poland. This is thought to be the original homeland of the Croats and is confirmed by several medieval texts, including a ninth-century history written by the scholar Orosius for Alfred the Great of England.

> Toward the end of the eighth century, Holy Roman Emperor Charlemagne conquered both Pannonian and Dalmatian Croatia.

Toward the end of the eighth century, Holy Roman Emperor Charlemagne conquered both Pannonian and Dalmatian Croatia. All of Dalmatia, save one or two key cities, was formally handed over to the Frankish king in 812, although Byzantium regained control over Dalmatia in the second half of the ninth century. It was during this period that a number of Croatian dukes emerged as increasingly powerful figures in positions of local rule, which led in the 10th and 11th centuries to the so-called Trpimirović dynasty's brief period of rule over a unified medieval Croatia (see pp. 26–27).

Changing Hands

Kaptol, one of the two settlements that would later form the Croatian capital, Zagreb, is first mentioned in 1094, when it was made the seat of a bishop by the Hungarian king Ladislaus. A cathedral was built, only to be destroyed (along with much of the rest of the unfortified town) by the Mongols in the 13th century. Its neighbor, Gradec (modern Zagreb's Gornji Grad), developed into a fortified town and was declared a free city by King Bela IV of Hungary in 1242. Bela was himself pursued by the Mongols to the Adriatic coast, which they ravaged while he took refuge in Trogir.

Though nominally under Byzantine suzerainty, Ragusa (an early settlement that now forms the center of Dubrovnik) became an independent city-state in 990. It was forced to submit to an increasingly powerful Venice in the 13th century, however, which launched a series of attacks on the coastal cities and a number of the islands and, in 1202, enlisted the support of the forces of the infamous Fourth Crusade to sack Zadar.

Following the death of Bela in 1270, yet more coastal cities fell into Venetian hands. Ludovik I reestablished Hungarian control over Croatia in 1358, at which point the Ragusans cleverly agreed to pay an annual tribute to their new masters in return for almost complete autonomy, thus guaranteeing the future safety of their city from Venice. Later the canny Ragusans paid further tribute to the Ottomans, giving them free-trading status. This marked the beginning of the city's golden age, when it became enormously wealthy from trade, with extensive territories (see pp. 248–249). Following the death of Ludovik, Croatia passed to Ladislas of Naples, who, in 1409, sold Dalmatia to Venice, which would maintain its hold on the area for the next 300 years.

The late 16th century saw a turnaround in Ottoman fortunes, with a naval defeat at the Battle of Lepanto in 1571.

Ottoman Era

On June 28, 1389, St. Vitus's Day, the combined armies of Serbia, Croatia, and Bosnia were defeated by the Ottoman sultan Murad I at the Battle of Kosovo, an event that has since been elevated to the realm of collective folklore across the Balkans. This was followed by the fall of Constantinople in 1453, the conquest of Bosnia in 1463 and of Herzegovina in 1482, and in 1493 a last stand by the Croatian nobility was routed at the Battle of Krbavsko Polje in Lika. In 1526, the Ottomans defeated the Hungarians at the Battle of Mohács, and by 1529, Ottoman forces had laid siege to Vienna, the Austrian capital, turning the political and military landscape of southeastern Europe on its head for the next two centuries.

The late 16th century saw a turnaround in Ottoman fortunes, with a naval defeat at the Battle of Lepanto in 1571. The Croatians followed up with another victory, this time on land, at the Battle of Sisak in 1593. Austria established a military frontier (Vojna Krajina) across the north of Croatia and the Croatian hinterland, building and rebuilding forts (see pp. 92–93) and manning them with Croats, and settling the land beyond the frontier with Vlach communities from Romania. However, despite their defeat at the Battle of St. Gotthard in 1644, the Ottomans received favorable terms from Austria, and the Croats and Hungarians—who had hoped to drive the Ottomans out of their hereditary lands once and for all—were left bitterly disappointed. Two of the names most associated with the subsequent plot against Austrian rule are Petar Zrinski and Fran Krsto Frankopan (see sidebar p. 29).

Meanwhile, the Uskoks, locals displaced by the Ottoman advance in the Balkans, began their own campaign against the Ottomans. Initially based at the fortress of Klis (near Split) and then settling (with Austria's blessing) at the port of Senj on Kvarner Bay,

The turrets of a 14th-century fortress at Senj dominate the Adriatic coast.

they increasingly turned to piracy, targeting not only Ottoman but also Venetian shipping. Their raids eventually provoked open war between Venice and Austria, however, and following the peace treaty signed between the two in 1617, the Uskoks were forcibly disbanded and many of their leaders executed. Finally, with the Treaty of Karlovac in 1699, Ottoman territories in northern Croatia passed back to Austria.

National Awakening

The Venetian republic was extinguished with the arrival of Napoleon in 1797 and, by the Treaty of Campo Formio Dalmatia, was also transferred to Austria. However, any Croatian hopes of a unified Dalmatia and Slavonia were short-lived since the administrative division between the two was maintained. With Napoleon's incredible victory over the Austrians at Austerlitz in 1805, Dalmatia became part of Napoleon's Illyrian Provinces (Slavonia went to the Hungarians). Dubrovnik, weakened by the loss of its maritime supremacy as shipping routes moved away from the coast, was forced to invite Napoleon into the city to break a Russian blockade. In 1808, Napoleon abolished the Republic of Ragusa and incorporated it into the Illyrian Provinces. Following Napoleon's defeat in 1814, the Congress of Vienna returned Dalmatia to Austria.

The 19th century marked a period of national awakening for Croatia. The Illyrian Movement, formed by a group of young Croatian intellectuals, was a direct reaction to rising Hungarian nationalism and a response to years of suppression of the Croatian language by Croatia's Austrian and Hungarian masters, in favor of German and Hungarian. The movement gained momentum in the 1830s with the publication of Ljudevit Gaj's book on Croatian orthography (see sidebar this page), and in 1834, the first newspaper in the Croatian language was published. Its appearance prompted the Croatian parliament to call for the teaching of Slavic language in schools, though it met with fierce resistance from Hungary, and in 1843, the word "Illyrian" was outlawed.

In 1848, Croatia dispatched troops in support of Austria, led by Ban Josip Jelačić (see sidebar p. 67), to quell a Hungarian uprising, hoping in return to receive greater autonomy and the introduction of Croatian as the official language instead of Hungarian. However, once the revolution had been overturned successfully, with Russian help, Austria imposed strict new laws on both Hungary and Croatia, with German becoming the official language in schools and the Croatian flag banned.

Calls for a Croatia linked with Serbia, within the framework of Austrian rule, were led by Josip Juraj Strossmayer, Bishop of Đakovo (see sidebar p. 111), while those for an entirely independent Croatia were led by Ante Starčević and the Party of Rights. At the same time an increasingly distinct sense of a separate Orthodox (Serb) and Catholic (Croat) identity developed within Croatia, fueled to a large degree by the Orthodox and Catholic churches.

Ljudevit Gaj, Croatia's Beloved Poet

Renowned and influential Croatian poet Ljudevit Gaj (1809–1872) was the central figure in the Croatian Illyrian Movement of the 19th century, at a time when Croatian language and culture were heavily suppressed by Austria. His book on Croatian orthography, Kratka osnova horvatsko-slavenskog pravopisanja (Brief Basics of the Croatian-Slavonic Orthography, **published in 1830), laid the foundations for the modern Croatian script.**

World Wars

Following World War I (1914–1918), when it seemed as though her territory was being given away piecemeal to Italy following the secret Treaty of London, Croatia joined with Serbia to form the Kingdom of Serbs, Croats, and Slovenes, a parliamentary monarchy under Serbian King Peter I, later renamed the kingdom of Yugoslavia. However, the centralization of power in Belgrade and the closure of the Croatian parliament led to dissatisfaction in Croatia, with opposition led by Stjepan Radić of the Peasant Party, until he was shot dead in the Serbian parliament in 1928. A dictatorship followed under Peter's successor, Alexander I. As a reaction to this, the ultranationalist Ustaša movement was founded, committed to independence for Croatia at any cost. Alexander was later assassinated while in Marseille, in a plot devised by the Ustaša leader, Ante Pavelić.

Though Yugoslavia initially remained neutral in World War II (1939–1945), Prince Pavle (who had been governing the country in place of Alexander's successor, Petar, who was only 11 at the time of Alexander's assassination) was pressured into alignment with Hitler's Germany and Mussolini's Italy in 1941. A coup followed, annulling the agreement and placing the young Petar in power, to which Germany and Italy responded by invading Yugoslavia and bombing Belgrade. In Croatia, the Ustaša took power with the support of Hitler and Mussolini, setting up concentration camps (the most notorious at

Josip Broz Tito (center), the leader of the Partisans in 1943

Jasenovac) where thousands of Serbs, Roma (gypsies), and Jews, as well as Croats considered enemies of the fascist regime, were systematically slaughtered. Estimates of the number of dead vary wildly but are thought to be in the many thousands. Nevertheless, the Ustaša had only limited support within Croatia at large and were strongly opposed by many, not least those in the parts of Dalmatia that were handed to Italy.

Resistance to the German and Italian occupation was fought by the Četniks on the one hand (Serb royalists led by Draže Mihailović) and the communist Partisans on the other (led by Josip Broz Tito; see sidebar p. 94). The Četniks' actions included numerous massacres of Croatians, and at times, they actually collaborated with the Germans in their conflict with the Partisans. The Allies' initial support for the Četniks was transferred to the Partisans in 1943, with Fitzroy Maclean heading the British military mission to Tito.

Though Yugoslavia was a communist state, Tito broke ranks with Stalin's Russia in 1948, and his citizens enjoyed considerable freedom.

Following World War II, the Federal Republic of Yugoslavia was established in November 1945. It consisted of six republics (Serbia, Croatia, Bosnia, Montenegro, Macedonia, and Slovenia) and two autonomous provinces within Serbia (Vojvodina, with a large Hungarian population, and Kosovo, home to many Albanians), with Tito as its president. Though Yugoslavia was a communist state, Tito broke ranks with Stalin's Russia in 1948, and his citizens enjoyed considerable freedom. With each republic also governing its own internal affairs, Tito's policy of "Brotherhood and Unity" among the republics was remarkably successful. Dissatisfaction in Croatia stemmed from too many Serbs in the Yugoslav parliament and in high-ranking positions, and the channeling of money away from the wealthy Croatian republic to the poorer areas. This resentment came to a head in the "Croatian Spring" protests of 1971, which demanded greater civil rights for the Croatian people. The movement was ruthlessly suppressed. Tito's Yugoslavia courted great popularity on the world stage, and his funeral was attended by an enormous number of foreign diplomats, dignitaries, and heads of state.

Homeland War

Following Tito's death in 1980, problems within Yugoslavia that he had driven underground during his lifetime gradually rose to the surface once more, including both Serb and Croat nationalist aspirations. On June 28, 1989—600 years to the day from the defeat of Serbian and Croatian forces by the Ottomans at Kosovo Polje—the Serbian president Slobodan Milošević addressed a crowd of some one million supporters in Kosovo. In April 1990, against a background of the collapse

Bullet holes pockmark the streets of a neighborhood of Vukovar, in eastern Croatia.

of communism in Eastern Europe and a weak Soviet Union, Croatia held free elections, in which Franjo Tuđman and the HDZ were elected to power with 40 percent of the vote. Prompted by a media campaign emanating from Belgrade, which heralded the rebirth of the Ustaša, and mass dismissals of Serbs from the public sector in Croatia by the HDZ, Croatia's Serbs in the Krajina (the area around Knin) and eastern Slavonia demanded autonomy. They were supported by the JNA (Yugoslav People's Army), and in March 1991, a Serb unit took over the headquarters of Plitvice Lakes National Park. The resulting shoot-out with Croatian police claimed the first victims of the Homeland War in Croatia, from both sides.

> **A modern and stable Croatia finally joined the European Union in July 2013, becoming its 28th member state.**

In May 1991, following the deaths of 12 Croatian policemen in the village of Borovo Selo in Slavonia, and with Slovenia about to declare independence, Croatia held a referendum in which some 94 percent of the population voted in favor of Croatian independence from Yugoslavia. This independence was formally declared on June 25, 1991, the same day that Slovenia announced its own independence. The Krajina Serbs responded by proclaiming an independent Serbian state, the Republika Srpska Krajina, or RSK, with Knin as its capital.

The JNA entered Croatia and Slovenia in 1991, being ejected from the latter in a matter of days but in Croatia capturing around a quarter of Croatian territory within a period of three months. By the end of the year, thousands of Croats had been killed and more than half a million forced from their homes. In Slavonia, Vukovar was besieged and shelled relentlessly (see sidebar p. 119), and when the JNA entered the shattered ruins of the town in November, many of its survivors were massacred. Meanwhile, the JNA and Montenegrin militia also laid siege to Dubrovnik (see sidebar p. 247), drawing widespread media attention.

In 1992, United Nations negotiations under envoy Cyrus Vance led to a cease-fire and the deployment of a UN Protection Force. This was accompanied by the withdrawal of the JNA, but did not mark a return to prewar borders and did nothing to prevent a subsequent war in Bosnia. Croatian independence was finally recognized by the European Community in January 1992, and in May the same year, it joined the UN.

Over the next two years, Croatia retook some of the areas lost in 1991 and, in 1995, launched a series of major military offensives to recapture Slavonia and the Krajina. The RSK responded by shelling Zagreb. Fueled in part by the media in Belgrade, and in part by a number of attacks on civilians, some 200,000 Serbs, whose roots in the area stretched back centuries, fled. In December 1995, the Dayton Accord was signed, recognizing Croatia's international borders.

Following Tuđman's death at the end of 1999, the SDP was elected to power, with Stjepan Mesić as president and Ivica Račan as prime minister. The HDZ returned to power in 2003 with Ivo Sanader as prime minister. Sanader oversaw the extradition of several Croatian commanders accused of war crimes to stand trial at an international tribunal. In 2009, he was succeeded by Croatia's first female prime minister, Jadranka Kosor. Kosor was succeeded in 2011 by Zoran Milanović. A modern and stable Croatia finally joined the European Union in July 2013, becoming its 28th member state. ■

Arts & Culture

Croatia has a rich artistic, literary, and cultural heritage. This is well reflected by the number of sites in Croatia included on UNESCO's World Heritage List and List of Intangible Cultural Heritage—an impressive tally for a small country.

Architecture

Croatia has some outstanding architecture, spanning the centuries from Roman to Austrian secessionist of the late 19th century. The Romans of course were great builders, and as befits a country that was under their rule for several centuries and included the residence of one of their emperors, Croatia has some very fine ruins, built from blocks hewn from local limestone. Among the finest Roman monuments in Croatia are the amphitheater in Pula (the sixth largest in the world and incredibly well preserved), which dates to the first century A.D.; the Temple of Augustus, also in Pula, which was completed in A.D. 14; and Diocletian's Palace in Split, completed in A.D. 305 and built from stone from the island of Brač (the same stone that would later be used to build part of the White House).

While these and some other sites are well preserved, others are less so, having been toppled by earthquakes or plundered repeatedly for their stone. Much of the great amphitheater at Salona, for example, made its way into Venetian building works, while the base of the cathedral bell tower in Pula is composed largely of seats from the amphitheater. Even those sites of which nothing remains above the foundations often provide a fascinating insight into the organization of the Roman city, whether it be the production of olive oil or the luxury of former palaces. The most celebrated Byzantine monument in Croatia is without a doubt the Euphrasian Basilica in Poreč, which contains dazzling mosaics from the sixth century, easily comparable in quality to those at Ravenna in Italy and at Hagia Sophia in Istanbul, Turkey.

A number of early medieval (pre-Romanesque) churches survive in Croatia, usually small basilical constructions that closely follow Byzantine models. Examples of these include the ninth-century Church of the Holy Cross (Sv. Križ) in Nin and the tiny sixth-century Chapel of Mary Formosa (Sv. Marija Formosa) in Pula, all that survives of a much larger Byzantine building. One of the more unusual is the tall, circular Church of St. Donatus (Sv. Donat) in Zadar, which dates from the ninth century.

For many, Croatia's Romanesque architecture is synonymous with the exquisite stone-carved decoration and tall, elegant bell towers that form such a distinctive part

---

World Heritage Sites

Croatia has seven sites inscribed on UNESCO's World Heritage List, and several more have been submitted for future consideration.

- **Euphrasian Basilica, Poreč (p. 131)**
- **Cathedral of St. Jacob, Šibenik (p. 189)**
- **Diocletian's Palace, Split (pp. 198–199)**
- **Historic center, Trogir (pp. 205–207)**
- **Stari Grad Plain, Hvar (p. 220)**
- **Plitvice Lakes National Park (pp. 228–229)**
- **Old town, Dubrovnik (pp. 240–255)**

The floodlit Croatian National Theatre illuminates the Zagreb night.

Lions guard the entrance to the Cathedral of St. Jacob in the historic center of Šibenik.

of Croatian architecture on the coast and islands. The quintessential ensemble of Romanesque architecture is perhaps the town of Rab, with its four bell towers (albeit only three of them Romanesque), while other highlights include the wonderful cloister of the Franciscan monastery in Dubrovnik, with its slender double columns with individually carved capitals, and the magnificent 13th-century portal of the cathedral in Trogir.

> Croatia boasts several beautifully preserved baroque towns, in particular Varaždin's old center and Osijek's Tvrđava.

Renaissance architecture in Croatia does not get much more impressive than the Cathedral of St. Jacob (Sv. Jakov) in Šibenik, an outstanding building dating from the 15th and 16th centuries and built entirely from stone, without the use of any bricks. The east wall is decorated with a frieze of 74 sculpted portrait heads, each carefully observed and with highly realistic facial expressions.

A number of the architects and sculptors responsible for these buildings are known to have worked widely in Croatia during their lifetimes. Juraj Dalmatinac of Zadar, for example, who built the cathedral at Šibenik, also worked on buildings in Split, Dubrovnik, and Pag, while Nikola Firentinac, also of Šibenik cathedral fame, worked on the outstanding Ursini

Chapel in Trogir's cathedral. Others are known only from a single masterpiece that has survived to the present day, such as Radovan of Trogir (13th century), who was responsible for the breathtaking portal of the cathedral in Trogir.

Also familiar in towns and cities on the coast and islands are the Venetian palaces, built in Renaissance or Gothic styles. Their facades still line many town squares and include the Čipiko Palace in Trogir and the Hektorović Palace in Hvar.

Churches in Croatia like anywhere else have often been rebuilt and remodeled at various times over the centuries, but even some of the more drastic examples frequently maintain elements of the preceding structure, such as a wall or columns. Thus the 12th-century Cathedral of St. Mary (Sv. Marija) in Rab has a ciborium with three 9th- and 10th-century columns, while the 9th-century Church of St. Donatus (Sv. Donat) in Zadar contains bits of Roman masonry, including two temple altars in its walls.

Some of the systems of medieval fortifications in Croatia are particularly impressive, from single buildings (the Nehaj Tower in Senj) to whole towns (Dubrovnik) and even whole areas (the Ston district, on the Pelješac Peninsula). Over the centuries, Croatia was subject to the depredations of numerous other powers (for example the Venetians, Mongols, and Ottomans), and it fortified itself accordingly. Later, Austria established a military frontier across northern and central Croatia against the Ottoman advance, fortifying and refortifying numerous towns and castles.

Croatia boasts several beautifully preserved baroque towns, in particular Varaždin's old center and Osijek's Tvrđava. The main square in Samobor and the little-visited Karlovac are other fine examples. One of the finest baroque churches in Croatia is St. Catherine's (Sv. Katarina) in Zagreb's Gornji Grad.

Zagreb in particular has some outstanding secessionist architecture. The city owes its late 19th-century feel to the fact that many of its buildings were destroyed in an earthquake in 1880, following which an ambitious program of town planning saw large parts of the center converted into the elegant city we see today.

There is also some very beautiful traditional wooden architecture in the villages of Lonjsko Polje (where many of the houses are more than 200 years old) and the wooden churches of the Turopolje region (see sidebar this page).

Art

The single most important archaeological find from the Bronze Age in Croatia is the

The Wooden Churches of Turopolje

In the Turopolje region southeast of Zagreb are a number of remarkable wooden churches, most of them hardly ever seen by foreign visitors to Croatia. There are 13 in all, scattered throughout the region in villages that won't even appear on some maps, so you are advised to seek information and more detailed maps from the Zagreb County Tourist Board *(tzzz.hr)*. The earliest churches date from the mid-17th century. Others date from the 18th and 19th centuries, and some were built well into the 20th. Among the most interesting are the **Chapel of St. George** in Lijevi Štefanki (built in 1677, but moved to its present location in 1704) and the **Chapel of St. John the Baptist** at Buševec (late 17th century), while the most accessible is the **Chapel of the Wounded Jesus** near Zagreb's airport. Many of the churches are locked, so ask at the Zagreb County Tourist Office about who holds the keys.

so-called Vučedol Dove (probably actually a partridge), a three-legged pottery figurine from the Vučedol culture that flourished in eastern Slavonia around 4,500 years ago.

Roman art in Croatia includes a beautiful bronze head of a young woman from Salona, probably from the second century A.D., and some lovely floor mosaics, such as the third-century depiction of the punishment of Dirce on the floor of a villa in Pula, uncovered following a bombing raid in World War II. The real stars as far as mosaics go, however, are the sixth-century Byzantine ones in the Euphrasian Basilica in Poreč.

Some beautifully carved stonework has survived from the medieval period, often decorated with interlace patterns and figures influenced by Byzantine art, including the baptismal font of Višeslav and a beautifully carved stone tablet from the 11th-century Church of St. Dominica in Zadar.

An outstanding collection of Glagolitic missals is held by the National and University Library in Zagreb. Another is kept in the library of the Dominican monastery in Dubrovnik. Among the most celebrated Glagolitic missals is the *Misal po Zakonu Rimskog Dvora*, the earliest surviving printed Glagolitic missal (dated 1483, only 28 years after the Gutenberg Bible). Eleven copies survive, including one in Zagreb's National and University Library and one in the Library of Congress in Washington, D.C. Glagolitic missals in other collections include the Berlin Missal (dating from 1402, now in the Staatsbibliothek in Berlin) and the Roč Missal (15th century, now in the Austrian National Library in Vienna).

Croatian painters during the Renaissance period include Blaž Jurjev Trogiranin (ca 1412–1448), some of whose works can be seen in Trogir's town museum, and Juraj Julije Klović (1498–1578), also known as Giorgio Giulio Clovio, who worked in Renaissance Italy and is best known for his "Farnese Hours" (completed in 1546) and through a portrait of him by El Greco. Istria was the center of a remarkable fresco school in the 14th and 15th centuries. The extraordinary "Dance of the Dead" in the Church of St. Mary of the Rocks in Beram, near Pazin, is the best known fresco from this period. Dating from 1474, it is the work of one Vincent of Kastav.

The Modern Gallery in Zagreb (see p. 77) houses the finest collection of Croatian works from the 19th and 20th centuries. Modern sculpture is

A giant Easter egg decorated with naïve art is displayed in Zagreb.

Hlebine School of Naïve Art

The Hlebine school grew up around the village of Hlebine in Slavonia in the 1930s, encouraged by painter Krsto Hegedušić (1901–1975), who had studied in Zagreb. The first and most prominent artist of the school was Ivan Generalić (1914–1992), who was joined by Franjo Mraz (1910–1981) and Mirko Virius (1889–1943) among others. Themes range from scenes of traditional rural life and poetic realism to biblical subjects and psychological portraits. With the exception of Hegedušić, none of the Hlebine artists had any formal training, though some went on to receive considerable international recognition.

widely represented across Croatia, with outstanding pieces by many of the country's greatest sculptors standing in numerous towns and cities (in particular Zagreb, where it would be possible to construct a whole itinerary based around the city's public sculptures; see sidebar p. 62). Among the most important Croatian sculptors are Ivan Meštrović (1883–1962), one of the towering figures of 20th-century art in Croatia, whose colossal statue of Grgur Ninski stands at the back of Diocletian's Palace in Split, and Ivan Kožarić (b. 1921), whose sculpture of poet Antun Gustav Matoš sitting on a bench in Zagreb's old town is one of the most beloved sites of the capital (see p. 42).

Croatia has an excellent tradition of folk art, from the intricate handmade lace from the island of Pag (see sidebar p. 179) to the naïve school of painting that developed at Hlebine (see sidebar this page) and is showcased in Zagreb's Museum of Naïve Art. In 2009, a series of large Easter eggs painted in naïve style was installed on a number of Zagreb's main squares (including St. Mark's Square in Gornji Grad and Jelačić Square in the lower town), and toured several cities in Croatia and abroad.

An outstanding collection of Glagolitic missals is held by the National and University Library in Zagreb.

Literature

Croatia has a rich literary tradition stretching back to the Renaissance period, and its writers and poets are a constant source of pride and affection. The men and women of letters are commemorated all over the country in statues, which serve as a constant reminder of their achievements.

Foremost among Croatia's Renaissance writers is Marko Marulić (1450–1524), who was born into a noble family in Split and is often described as the father of Croatian Renaissance literature. Marulić is best known for his epic poem "Judita" ("Judith"), published in 1521. Petar Zoranić (1508–1543) is another Renaissance writer, widely credited as the author of the first Croatian novel, *Planine* (*The Mountain,* published 1569), in which he imbued the Velebit mountains around his native Zadar with myth and history in the tradition of Roman poet Ovid. Marin Držić (1508–1567), a Renaissance playwright from Ragusa (the Republic of Dubrovnik), is sometimes called the "Croatian Shakespeare." His most famous work is the comedy *Dundo Maroje*, published in 1551. His house in Dubrovnik is open as a memorial museum. Croatia's foremost baroque poet was Ivan Gundulić (1588–1638), also from Ragusa and best known for his epic poem "Osman."

Ivan Mažuranić (1814–1890), a poet, linguist, and politician, was a central figure in the Illyrian Movement (see pp. 31–32), whose hugely influential German-Illyrian dictionary was published in 1842. His best loved work is the epic poem "The Death of Smail-Aga," which recounts the story of the ambush of a tyrannical Muslim governor by Montenegrins as he went about collecting taxes. A member of the People's Party, Mažuranić also served as Ban of Croatia from 1873–1880. Petar Preradović (1818–1872), a poet and an officer in the Austrian army, was also strongly influenced by the Illyrian Movement.

Poet and novelist August Šenoa (1838–1881), whose statue stands on the corner of Stara Vlaška in Zagreb, was a local magistrate as well as senator of his native Zagreb during the great earthquake of 1880. His best known work is the novel *Zlatarevo Zlato (The Goldsmith's Gold)*, the setting of which revolves around Stone Gate (Kamenita Vrata; see p. 67), one of the old city gates to Zagreb's Gornji Grad. There is a statue of Dora, the daughter in *The Goldsmith's Gold,* beside Kamenita Vrata.

Antun Gustav Matoš (1873–1914), poet, critic, essayist, journalist, and writer of short stories and travelogues, was one of the central figures of the modernist

A teenager relaxes with the statue of poet Antun Gustav Matoš in Gornji Grad, Zagreb.

EXPERIENCE: Learn Croatian

Attending a Croatian language course in Croatia can be a great excuse to spend longer in one place, improving your language skills at the same time as getting to know an area in more depth than you could ever hope to when just passing through en route to your next destination. You will have the opportunity to practice what you have learned in the real world by going to the shops, using public transportation, or ordering in a café. You will also get the chance to meet and mix with the local population (particularly if you do not fall into the trap of socializing only with your fellow native-language speakers).

There are foreign language schools in Zagreb and elsewhere. They include **Lingua Grupa** *(linguagrupa.hr)*, **Vodnikova** *(vodnikova.hr)*, **Berlitz** *(berlitz .hr)*, and most famously **Croaticum** *(http://croaticum.ffzg.unizg.hr)*, the highly respected language school at the University of Zagreb. The **British Council** *(britishcouncil.hr)* in Zagreb is often a good place to start your search for a language school catering mainly to English speakers.

movement in Croatia, and remains one of the country's best loved writers. You will find a statue of Matoš on the edge of Zagreb's upper town, sitting on a bench in one of his favorite spots and contemplating the city below.

Vladimir Nazor (1876–1949) was a poet and politician. He fought with the Partisans during World War II and was the first president of Croatia under Tito's Yugoslavia. His best known work is *Pastir Loda (Loda the Shepherd),* which recounts the folk legends of his native Brač. Another influential Croatian poet of the early 20th century is Tin Ujević (1891–1955). Miroslav Krleža (1893–1981) is considered by many to be the greatest Croatian writer of the 20th century, celebrated for his complex and highly original use of language. A number of his works are available in English translation, including *Banket u Blitvi (The Banquet in Blitva)* and *Na Rubu Pameti (On the Edge of Reason)*. His house in Zagreb is open as a memorial museum (see p. 72).

Movies

The history of Croatian cinema began with propaganda movies made for the Ustaša during World War II, but by the early 1960s, Croatia was making a healthy contribution to the Yugoslav film industry. Recent Croatian films include *Ta Divna Splitska Noi* (*A Wonderful Night in Split,* 2004, directed by Arsen Anton Ostojić), *Put Lubenica* (*The Melon Route,* 2006, directed by Branko Schmidt), and the hard-hitting *Ljudožder vegetarijanac* (*Vegetarian Cannibal,* 2012, also directed by Branko Schmidt). Croatia also has a tradition of animation centered around the Zagreb animation school. One former pupil, Montenegrin Dušan Vukotić, won an Oscar for "Surogat" in 1963. If you want to catch Croatian cinema at its best, head for the Pula and Motovun film festivals in Istria (see p. 129). Animafest is an excellent festival of local and international animated film in Zagreb. ■

Animafest is an excellent festival of local and international animated film in Zagreb.

The Land & Wildlife

Croatia covers a land area of around 21,851 square miles (56,594 sq km), smaller in size than West Virginia. It stretches along the northeast Adriatic coast and, at its farthest extent, reaches inland to the Danube River. It is bordered by Slovenia and Hungary in the north, Serbia and Bosnia and Herzegovina in the east, and Montenegro in the south.

Croatia can be divided into several distinct regions, loosely defined as northern Croatia—which includes the capital, Zagreb—Slavonia, Kvarner, Istria, Lika, and Dalmatia. Slavonia is an area in the northeast extending toward the Danube, and bordered north and south by the Drava and Sava Rivers. Kvarner centers around a large bay on the northern coast with several large islands. Istria is a wedge-shaped peninsula at the northern end of the Adriatic. Lika is an area inland from the mountains that runs parallel to the coast. Dalmatia makes up the southern part of the country. It is divided between a bay-riddled coast, with an archipelago of islands, and a narrow—sometimes very narrow—hinterland between the coastal mountains and the Bosnian border.

Croatia's Adriatic coast remains the country's biggest draw for tourism. While undoubtedly busy during the summer months, it remains remarkably unspoiled—a place of idyllic islands, charming old towns, stunning architecture, and crystal clear waters. The Croatian archipelago encompasses somewhere in the vicinity of 1,200 islands, islets, and reefs, the figure varying somewhat depending on who's counting them. These range from large islands such as Cres and Krk (each around 250 square miles, or 405 sq km) to the tiny, scattered islets of the Kornati and Lastovo archipelagoes. Together, they bring the total length of Croatia's already highly indented coastline to approximately 3,625 miles (5,835 km). The islands are generally elongated, with their longest axis following the orientation of the coast. Croatian beaches are almost exclusively rocky, and only a very small handful can be described as sandy or fine shingle. Among the former are Vela Plaža on Krk, Rajska Plaža on Rab and Zlatni Rat on Brač.

The coast and many of the islands have suffered from progressive deforestation over the centuries, with the Republic of Venice in particular sourcing much of the timber for its fleet from Dalmatia, though as early as the 13th century the Republic of Dubrovnik placed restrictions on the sale of timber to foreign powers. This combined with overgrazing has led to extensive soil erosion, particularly noticeable

Outstanding Natural Monuments

- The travertine lakes and waterfalls of Plitvice Lakes National Park
- The limestone crags of Rožanski Kukovi in Northern Velebit National Park
- The gorge of the Krka River in Krka National Park in Dalmatia
- The wetlands of Kopački Rit Nature Park
- The sea cliffs and scattered islets of Kornati National Park

Hikers explore the rugged coast of Mljet Island.

Boardwalks take visitors through the heart of beautiful Plitvice Lakes National Park.

on islands in the north, such as Goli Otok (literally "Naked Island'") and Pag.

A chain of mountains (collectively part of the Dinaric Alps) runs parallel with the coast, neatly dividing it from the interior. With only a couple of exceptions—the Krka and Cetina Rivers, which break through the mountains in spectacular gorges to flow into the Adriatic—most river systems drain inland away from the coast. The Dinaric Alps contain several national parks and nature parks, and constitute the finest hiking area in Croatia. These mountains have numerous karst features, from cone-shaped dells and depressions to deep caves and elaborate underground drainage systems. Surface streams are rare, and rivers often disappear suddenly into the ground, only to reemerge later in their course or to drain into the Adriatic as submarine springs. Broad shallow valleys, or *polje,* usually provide the only areas suitable for cultivation.

Caves, Lakes, & Waterfalls

Some of the caves and sinkholes in Croatia are exceptionally deep. Lukina Jama (see p. 180) on northern Velebit is among the ten deepest sinkholes in the world, reaching down 4,567 feet (1,392 m) into the depths of the mountain. Nearby Patkov Gust contains a single vertical drop of just over 1,814 feet (553 m), the second largest in the world.

Contained within the Dalmatian hinterland, the lakes and waterfalls of Plitvice Lakes (see pp. 228–229) constitute one of the most remarkable landscapes in Croatia, their travertine barriers formed by the precipitation of calcium carbonate onto

mosses and algae over a period of several thousand years.

Slavonia, in contrast, is an extensive plain, broken only by a single range of hills, roughly at its center (Papuk). The confluence of the Drava and the Danube is marked by extensive wetlands (Kopački Rit; see pp. 114–115), which together with those on the Sava (Lonjsko Polje; see p. 105), provide a vital habitat for wading birds and a vital stop on the winter migration route of many species. Slavonia is extremely fertile, though some areas of this otherwise agriculturally rich landscape still lie fallow, awaiting mine clearance following the Homeland War.

The Dinaric Alps contain several national parks and nature parks, and constitute the finest hiking area in Croatia.

Croatia's weather variations generally reflect its geographic regions—a Mediterranean climate on the coast and islands, and a more extreme climate on the continent. The coast experiences hot, dry summers, with daytime temperatures averaging around 86°F (30°C), though frequently climbing quite a bit higher. Winters are relatively mild on the coast, though this is when much of the rainfall occurs. Inland temperatures reach up to 80°F (27°C) in the summer, though during the winter the temperatures are much lower than on the coast, usually around freezing during the day or a few degrees lower. In the mountains, winter temperatures can plummet to minus 11°F (−24°C), though around half that is more common. Snowfall is also heavy during the winter in inland Croatia and in the mountains, where it can lie for several months. A powerful northeast wind,

Hiking Through Croatia

Croatia has some great areas for hiking, from easy strolls on the islands to demanding mountain treks. Trails are usually well marked, and there is a good network of mountain huts, which provide places to stay. Detailed local hiking maps are available (smand.hr, gss.hr). Camping out in the wilderness is prohibited in national parks and many other areas (including along the coast). The best area for longer hikes is undoubtedly the Velebit range (see pp. 180–183), where forest trails give way to numerous spectacular limestone formations and rocky mountaintops.

Decent footwear is a must for the rocky trails here, as are warm clothes and wet-weather gear; no matter how balmy it may be on the coast, the weather is generally more changeable in the hills. Potable water is limited, and surface streams almost nonexistent, so you will also need to carry a full day's water supply. The best time of year for hiking is the late spring or fall; the midsummer months can be a little too hot for comfortable walks, especially along the coast. For more information on hiking in Croatia, see hps.hr. For mountain rescue, see gss.hr.

the *bura,* often blows over the mountains onto the Adriatic and can reach gale force. The southerly *jugo* wind is much milder, though it often brings clouds to the coast and mountains. The *maestral* is a brisk sea breeze.

Wild Mammals

Croatia's diverse range of habitats plays host to a wide variety of wildlife and plants. All three of the big European carnivores are present in Croatia: brown bear, gray wolf, and Eurasian lynx. However, numbers are very low and sightings extremely rare, particularly for the lynx. Bears are still hunted legally–if they can be found–and although wolves are protected, half the recorded deaths of wolves are from illegal shooting. Mammal species you are more likely to encounter include red and roe deer, chamois, mouflon (a wild cousin of the domestic sheep), pine marten, and edible dormouse.

Birds, Reptiles, & Amphibians

About 370 species of birds have been seen in Croatia. Many are rare, but there are good opportunities for bird-watching in every region. Griffon vultures nest on the sea cliffs of Cres, and white storks nest in large numbers in the Lonjsko Polje wetland and elsewhere. On the coast and islands you have a chance of seeing

EXPERIENCE: Watching Croatia's Wildlife

There are plenty of places for spotting wildlife in Croatia. Among the best spots for bird-watching are Kopački Rit and Lonjsko Polje, two wetland habitats in Slavonia. The latter area is particularly noted for its huge population of storks. Other important wetland areas for bird-life include Vrana Lake near Šibenik and Crna Mokra near Jastrebarsko. Krka National Park and Velebit are also good areas for spotting birds of prey.

The griffon vulture, once more wide-spread in Croatia, now only nests on the crags near Beli on the island of Cres. A falconry center near Šibenik, **Sokolarski Centar Dubrava** *(sokolarskicentar.com),* is the place to get up close to a range of birds of prey.

For Croatia's three elusive large carnivores—the brown bear, gray wolf, and Eurasian lynx—the remote areas of Korski Kotar and Velebit are your best bet, though sightings are extremely rare. You will also find brown bears at the

sanctuary for orphaned cubs at Kuterevo in Northern Velebit *(kuterevo-medvjedi .org).* Dolphins are regularly sighted off the coast and islands. The **Blue World Institute of Marine Research and Conservation** *(blue-world.org)* runs scientific, educational, and conservation projects from the islands of Lošinj and Vis. The Kamenjak Peninsula in Istria and the twin gorges of Paklenica in Southern Velebit are excellent areas for butterflies.

You can significantly increase your chances of spotting wildlife by joining a specialist tour, such as those operated by **ProBirder** *(probirder.com),* which will give you the benefit of local knowledge and expertise. For further information on the brown bear, wolf, and lynx, see the **LIFE Project for the Conservation and Management of Wolves in Croatia** *(life-vuk.hr).* Finally, for further information on protected areas within the country, see the **State Institute for Nature Protection** *(dzzp.hr).*

Croatia's national animal—the pine marten—searches for food in the winter snow.

great and pygmy cormorants, gray and purple herons, black stork, spoonbill, and Eleanora's falcon. Once inland, look for rock partridge, short-toed eagle, eagle owl, alpine swift, woodlark, red-backed shrike, ortolan bunting, and many more.

Croatia's rocky karst landscape provides an ideal habitat for reptiles, including the highly venomous nose-horned viper, called *poskok* in Croatian and easily recognized by the soft horn at the end of its snout. Other reptiles include the nonvenomous Balkan whip snake, the large Balkan green lizard, and Hermann's tortoise. Amphibians include the magnificent fire salamander and, in the watery pools of Krka National Park and a few other places, the olm, an unusual blind subterranean newtlike amphibian that lives only in the cave waters of southeast Europe.

Other Flora & Fauna

Croatia has numerous moths and butterflies (more than 180 species have been recorded), including the scarce swallowtail, southern swallowtail, great banded grayling, common glider, Dalmatian ringlet, southern small white, and holly blue.

Dominant trees in the mountain forest are beech and Aleppo pine, with much of the other vegetation made up of dense, hardy scrub or maquis, with holm oak predominating and dwarf mountain pine clinging tenaciously to rocky, windswept peaks. Croatia has a number of endemic flowers, including *Degenia velebitica* and *Dianthus velebiticus,* which as their specific names suggest are found only in the Velebit range. ■

Food & Drink

Most people think of char-grilled fish and squid when conjuring images of Croatian cuisine, and while it is true that there is certainly a lot of this delicious food available, there is a lot more to the Croatian table than just seafood, including some delicious regional dishes.

Croatia has some truly wonderful food and wine, and eating out here, whether in a top-rated restaurant or a simple pizzeria, really is a pleasure. Its distinctive cuisine (or cuisines, since there is quite a bit of regional variation; see sidebar p. 52) is infused with the delicate Mediterranean and Italian flavors on the coast and in Istria, with sturdier influences from Austria and Hungary in the northern provinces. Croatian cuisine understandably shares several dishes with its eastern neighbors Serbia and Bosnia, but for the most part the food available remains very much its own.

Fresh seafood served in a Rovenska restaurant on the island of Losinj

Fish Dishes

Some of the more commonly found fish on menus on the coast are gray mullet (*cipal*), red mullet (*arbun*), hake (*oslić*), bream (*orada*), John Dory (*kovač*), mackerel (*skuša* or *lokarda*), and eel (*jegulja*). If you eat in someone's home and the fish is caught locally, a whole host of local species that may be rather unfamiliar are possibilities. You will also find octopus (*hobotnica*) on the menu, as well as squid (*lignje*), mussels (*dagnje*), and oysters (*kamenice*). Inland, freshwater fish include trout (*pastrva*) and carp (*šaran*).

Fish is usually lightly boiled (*kuhano*), grilled (*na žaru*), fried (*prženo*), or baked (*pečeno*), and often served topped with a mixture of freshly chopped parsley, crushed garlic, and olive oil. A traditional and particularly delicious way of preparing fish and meat in Croatia is *ispod peke* (literally, "under the peka"), in which the food is placed under a domed cast iron lid and roasted in a wood fire. Octopus cooked in this way is mouth-wateringly good, though it just as often makes an appearance as a salad (*salata od hobotnice*) with potato, onion, and olive oil. Another favorite way of preparing shellfish (*školjke*), and in

> The best lamb, many consider, is from the island of Pag, where the animals graze on a diet rich in aromatic herbs.

particular lobster tails and large shrimp (both known as *škampi*), is as a *buzara,* simmered in an enormous pot with garlic, olive oil, and white wine and guaranteed to make a complete mess of your clothes. Fried squid (often referred to on English-language menus using the Italian word "calamari") is very popular and best when caught fresh, though you might also want to try them stuffed and roasted in the oven (*punjene lignje*). In Slavonia, carp caught from the rivers is prepared as a vast stew with spicy peppers (*fiš paprikaš*).

Meat Dishes

Croats are great meat-eaters. Lamb (*janjetina*) is a perennial favorite across Croatia, traditionally roasted on a spit with generous amounts of rosemary and garlic, or cooked ispod peke. The best lamb, many consider, is from the island of Pag, where the animals graze on a diet rich in aromatic herbs. Such grasses are rare in this otherwise arid landscape. The herbs are said to contribute much to the meat's flavor, as are the salty breezes that blow across the area.

Wild game is popular, particularly in the

mountainous Gorski Kotar and other high-
land areas, including wild boar *(divlja svinja),*
which makes an excellent stew, and venison
(srnetina). Frogs' legs and snails are also
served in some areas of Gorski Kotar. Amaz-
ingly, bear makes an appearance in some
mountain restaurants, despite its great rarity
in the wild, let alone the unsuitability of bear
flesh for human consumption.

Fruits & Vegetables

Two delicious baked vegetable dishes
are *zeljanica* (phyllo pastry with spinach,
cottage cheese, and sour cream) and
bučnica (with marrow or squash). Fruits
and vegetables tend to be seasonal
and grown locally, with the traditional
accompaniment to seafood dishes being
boiled potatoes *(krumpir)* with Swiss
chard *(blitva).* Sometimes the blitva is
substituted with cabbage *(kupus),* which
also makes a nice combination, and naturally the perennial French fries *(pomfrit)*
are always available. There are plenty of
mushrooms *(gljive),* from porcini to bole-
tus *(vrganj* in Croatian), and in season you
will find them piled high on market stalls.

   With the popularity of fish and meat,
vegetarians may find they have a bit of a
hard time in Croatia. However, there is usually something available for all tastes. If
you cannot find anything vegetarian on the menu, just ask the staff, *"Imate li nešto bez
mesa?"* ("Do you have something without meat?")

Enjoying Regional Specialties

Croatia has some wonderful regional
food and cuisine, ranging from local
cheeses to elaborate entrées. A Dalmatian specialty that does not involve seafood is *pašticada,* a fantastically rich dish
made with marinated beef or veal
cooked with dried plums, and often
served with homemade gnocchi and
Parmesan cheese. *Paški sir* from the island
of Pag is arguably the country's most
famous cheese (see p. 178), while Ston

near Dubrovnik is well known for its
oysters. The inland region of Slavonia has
some hearty local dishes, including *fiš
paprikaš* (a spicy carp and pepper stew),
sarma (stuffed cabbage leaves), and *kulen*
(the excellent dried local sausage), which
is delicious with *kajmak* (clotted cream).
Away from the coast, inland Istria is well
known for its excellent truffles, or *tartufi,*
which also tend to be cheaper than the
equivalent in Italy or France.

Croatia is renowned for its superb ice cream.

Desserts & Drinks

Cakes and desserts come in all shapes and sizes, from whisper-light *kiflice* to the creamy *Jelačić kocke,* and the distinctive *makovnjača* and *orahovnjača* (filled with poppy seeds and walnuts respectively), and there is plenty of very good ice cream (*sladoled*) both on the coast and inland.

Coffee (*kava*) is something of a national pastime—after all, with all that sunshine and cafés spilling out into the open on lovely medieval town squares, what better to do with your free time? The standard coffee is espresso, almost always excellent and served with a glass of water, as it should be. What an espresso is called depends a bit on where you are in Croatia. On the coast and islands (with stronger Italian links), it is usually called an espresso, while in the rest of the country it is *kava* or *obična kava* (an "ordinary coffee"). A coffee with milk is *kava s mlijekom,* a macchiato is a *makiato,* and a cappuccino is a *kapučino.* You can ask for small and large coffee. If you prefer tea (*čaj*), you usually have a choice, including various flavors of herbal tea (*voćni čaj*).

EXPERIENCE: Taste Fine Croatian Wines

With its steep, rocky hillsides and plenty of sunshine, Croatia produces plenty of wine, some of it very good. Quality is indicated by three main categories: *vrhunsko vino* (the highest quality, literally meaning "top wine"), *kvalitetno vino* (standard quality), and *stolno vino* (table wine), with the price usually (though not always) being another fairly good indicator.

In recent years, a number of boutique wines and vineyards have emerged, some excellent, though in some cases expensive when compared to what you can buy for a similar price in the United States or Western Europe. The best red wines *(crno vino)* tend to be from the **Dingač region** of the Pelješac Peninsula (see p. 259), which produces intense, fruit-driven wines from the Plavac Mali grape. There are also some very good reds from **Ivan Dolac** on the island of Hvar and from the Teran grape in Istria. ("Teran Ré," made by **Roxanich,** is one to try.)

For white wines *(bjelo vino),* look out for those made with the Traminac grape in Slavonia, such as **Iločki Podrum** in Ilok (see p. 119), and in particular the excellent **Malvazija** grape from Istria (try a Malvazija produced by **Benvenuti, Franc Arman, Kozlovii,** or **Trapan** if you can; see vinistra.com). Some of the Croatian islands also produce good white wines, such as **Žlahtina** from Krk and **Grk** from Korčula.

If purchasing some of the better wines, avoid buying them in general supermarkets if possible; these are likely to have been sitting on the top shelf, upright and in the heat, for far too long. Instead seek out a decent wine merchant or boutique, which you should be able to find easily in any of Croatia's larger cities, such as **Bornstein** *(bornstein.hr)* in Zagreb. You can also buy from the vineyard in most cases, and at open-air markets. Homemade wine is advertised by the roadside, some of which can be very good and remarkably cheap.

There are a number of **wine roads** in Croatia, including Plešivica (see pp. 96–97), Ilok *(turizamilok.hr),* and several in Istria.

There is plenty of fruit juice available *(voćni sok,* or more usually just *sok),* including blueberry juice *(sok od borovnice),* apple juice *(sok od jabuke),* and orange juice *(sok od naranče).* If you want mineral water, ask for *mineralna voda,* either *gazirana* (sparkling) or *negazirana* (still).

Local beers *(pivo)* include the widely available Karlovačko (brewed in Karlovac) and Ožujsko (brewed in Zagreb), as well as Tomislav (a dark beer from Zagreb) and the less common though excellent Velebitsko Pivo (brewed in Gospić, behind the Velebit mountains). Some consider the beers from the Ličanka microbrewery in Donje Pazarište to be very tasty.

Wine is available in nearly all food outlets (see sidebar this page). Another drink you may well encounter on your travels in Croatia is *rakija,* a fiery local spirit that comes in a number of guises: *Loza* made with grapes is similar to Italian grappa, *travarica* is made with herbs, *šljivovica* is made with plums, and *medovača* is made with honey. A decent homemade *(domaće)* rakija can be very good indeed, while other drinks offered are quite the opposite. Finding out is all part of the Croatian experience, but you should always drink responsibly and never drive. The legal blood-alcohol limit for drivers in Croatia is 0.05 percent.

Food Culture

Food, in particular home cooking, is an important part of Croatian life. The frozen dinner has not caught on here yet, though there are plenty of fast-food outlets. If you require a cheap meal, pizza is widely available and is usually excellent, with a thin, crispy base and plenty of toppings to choose from. Pasta is also served fairly widely. For many Croatians, lunch is the main meal of the day, beginning with soup *(juha)* and followed by either fish or meat as a main course *(glavno jela)* served with vegetables and a salad. Dinner is a lighter meal.

Tips on Tipping

In recent years, tipping has become more commonplace in Croatian restaurants, especially in cities and larger towns. Although not expected, it is always appreciated in restaurants and cafés where service has been good. Tip according to the quality of service you receive; something between 5 and 10 percent is plenty. Taxi drivers don't expect a tip, but, of course, a tip is always appreciated.

The traditional Christmas dinner in Croatia is *puretina* (turkey) with *mlinci* (flat dried noodles, rather like giant tagliatelle, cooked in the bird's own juices), while *bakalar* (salt cod stew) is traditionally eaten on Christmas Eve. ■

Barrels of locally produced wines and spirits for sale at Makarska

The capital of Croatia and the country's most vibrant city, with a beautifully preserved historic center

Zagreb

History and modernity mix in Zagreb's center.

Zagreb

With a population of a little under 800,000, the Croatian capital is a vibrant place with beautiful architecture, leafy parks and squares, an outstanding range of museums, and a beautifully preserved old town. Though all too many visitors head straight for the coast, no trip to Croatia is complete without at least some time spent here.

The day's business is put on hold during a coffee break at one of Zagreb's teeming cafés.

Zagreb sits below the flanks of Medvednica, a broad forested mountain north of the Sava River. The city's original form—the two medieval settlements of Gradec (now Gornji Grad; "upper town") and Kaptol, divided by a stream—is still clearly discernible, though the stream has now become Tkalčićeva, a delightful café-lined thoroughfare.

Gornji Grad is centered around beautiful St. Mark's Square, with its distinctive church surrounded by government buildings and narrow, winding streets. Kaptol is the site of Zagreb's 13th-century cathedral, with its neo-Gothic facade and twin spires, and close by is the city's largest outdoor market, Dolac.

Below Gornji Grad and Kaptol is Donji Grad ("lower town"), centered on Jelačić Square, the elegant, pedestrianized nodal point of modern Zagreb. South from Jelačić Square stretches the so-called Green Horseshoe—a series of green squares that were laid out following an earthquake in 1880. On the south bank of the Sava River, Novi Zagreb (New Zagreb) is a modern suburb that has developed since World War II.

For a city of its size, Zagreb has an exceptional number of museums and art galleries, some of them outstanding—in particular the Meštrović Atelier, the Ethnographic Museum, and the Modern Gallery—and some wonderful outdoor sculpture. There are great places to catch an opera or concert, as well as a thriving underground music scene and busy jazz clubs. The pretty streets of the town center are scattered with chic boutique shops, excellent restaurants, and endless cafés that spill out onto pavements and squares. Beyond the city center, you will find the atmospheric Mirogoj Cemetery and more green spaces, such as Maksimir and Jarun, while Medvednica itself is covered by a network of easy hiking trails.

Zagreb has some excellent festivals—standouts include Animafest *(animafest.hr)* and Cest is d'Best *(cestisdbest.com)*, both in June.

Driving in central Zagreb can be confusing as traffic is directed around pedestrianized precincts, many of which contain the sights on most visitors' lists. Parking is very difficult, so you are advised to stick to walking and public transportation. Most sights are best toured on foot anyway, which will allow you to discover the gems that will make your visit more of a personal journey. If you become foot weary, the city has a network of trams that is an adventure in itself (see sidebar p. 75). ∎

NOT TO BE MISSED:

The bustle of Gornji Grad, Zagreb's old town 60–67

The Church of St. Mark, with its colorful tiled roof 60

Checking out the sculptures at the Meštrović Atelier and other sites throughout the city 61–62

Riding the funicular at dusk to get a great view of the city 63

Searching for tasty treats at the Dolac open-air market 68–69

Joining the evening throng on Jelačić Square 70–71

Taking a stroll in Maksimir and Jarun, two leafy parks 83–84

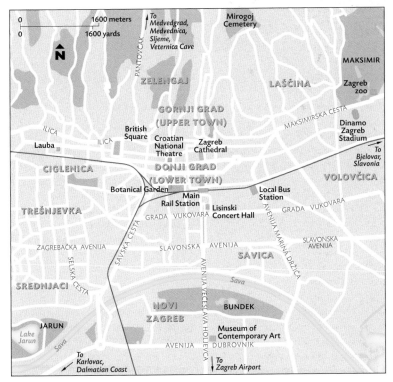

The Historic Center

In the 19th century, Zagreb underwent an enormously ambitious program of urban renewal following a devastating earthquake in 1880. The agricultural land south of the old city became Donji Grad, the lower town, built around an elegant string of parks and gardens that still form a "green horseshoe" through the city. The historic centers of Kaptol and Gradec were refashioned into Gornji Grad, the upper town.

The roof of the Church of St. Mark is one of the most iconic sights in Zagreb, and the whole of Croatia.

Gornji Grad

At the heart of Gornji Grad stands **St. Mark's Square** (Markov Trg), a large cobbled open space around the **Church of St. Mark** (Sv. Marko). Originally dating from the 13th century, the church was much rebuilt over subsequent centuries. Most of what you see today dates from the 14th and 15th centuries, although the church's distinctive baroque bell tower was a 17th-century addition. All of this was restored by renowned architect and town planner Herman Bollé (see sidebar p. 83) following the 1880 earthquake.

The church's tiled roof, revealed in 2009 after years of restoration, was added in the 19th century and features the coats of arms of Croatia and Zagreb (see sidebar opposite). The south door, also newly restored, has a beautiful set of late 14th- and early 15th-century sculptures of Christ, the Virgin Mary, and the Apostles created by Czech craftsmen from Prague. The interior features paintings by Jozo Kljaković (1889–1969) and a powerful "Crucifixion" by the sculptor Ivan Meštrović (see sidebar p. 62), who remodeled the 19th-century church features during the 1930s.

Around St. Mark's Square:

St. Mark's Square was a market in the 15th century, and the St. Mark's Fair held here annually was one of the key events in city life. The imposing buildings surrounding the square include the Croatian **Parliament** (Sabor), on the east side of the square, which was built in 1908.

On the west side is the former **Ban's Palace,** built in 1800. The palace was hit by a Serbian rocket in 1991 while the Croatian president and prime minister were both inside, though neither was injured. On the square's south side emerges a sculpture of a head said to be that of Matija Gubec, the leader of a failed peasant uprising in 1573, who was brought here by the Austrian rulers and executed by having a red-hot crown placed upon his head!

Just north of St. Mark's Square is the **Meštrović Atelier,** former home and studio of the great sculptor and now converted into an outstanding museum. An enormous wooden door leads off the street into a stone courtyard dotted with

INSIDER TIP:

At dusk, follow the lamplighters through the Upper Town as the gas streetlights are lit by hand. Sometimes they might even pose for photographs.

—CAROLINE HICKEY
National Geographic Travel Books editor

sculptures. The house itself is beautifully kept and preserves much of the original furniture alongside the artist's work, from drawings and working models— including a diminutive Grgur Ninski (more familiar in its monumental version behind Diocletian's Palace in Split; see sidebar p. 176)—to finished pieces.

The studio has been converted into a light and airy sculpture gallery, with a range of works such as "Mother and Child" (1942), "Moses" (1918), and "Woman Beside the Sea" (1926). More works in the garden include "History of the Croats" (1932).

Zagreb
- ⓜ Map pp. 59 & 65

Visitor Information
- ✉ Trg Bana J. Jelačića 11
- ☎ 014 814 051
- zagreb-touristinfo.hr

Zagreb County Tourist Office
- ✉ Preradovieva Ulica 42
- ☎ 014 873 665
- tzzz.hr

Church of St. Mark
- ⓜ Map p. 65
- ✉ Markov Trg Gornji Grad
- ⓢ donation

Meštrović Atelier
- ⓜ Map p. 65
- ✉ Mletaka 8, Gornji Grad
- ☎ 014 851 123
- ⓒ Closed Mon.
- ⓢ $
- mdc.hr/mestrovic /atelijer/index-en .htm

Flags & Symbols

The roof of the Church of St. Mark in Gornji Grad is decorated with several coats of arms, which may become familiar during your travels around Croatia. The shield on the left is a composite of the red-and-white checkerboard (*šahovnica*) that forms the basis of the Croatian flag. Next to the shield are the coats of arms of Dalmatia (the heads of three lions or leopards) and Slavonia (a *kuna*, or pine marten, running between the Sava and Drava Rivers). You will see elements of all these on the Croatian flag, together with the coats of arms of Istria (a golden, red-horned goat), the former Republic of Dubrovnik (two red stripes), and the oldest known Croatian coat of arms (the morning star over a silver moon). A turreted castle on the right of the roof is similar to the coat of arms of Zagreb.

Ivan Meštrović & Sculptures in Zagreb

Zagreb has a particularly impressive array of outdoor sculpture. With the notable exceptions of King Tomislav and Ban Josip Jelačić, most of the subjects are drawn from Croatia's great literary figures. As you wander around town, you will see works by many of Croatia's preeminent sculptors of the 19th and 20th centuries, including Ivan Kožarić, Ivan Rendić, Stjepan Gračan, Miro Vuco, and Marija Ujević Galetović. By far the greatest presence, however, is that of Ivan Meštrović (1883–1962), whose work can be found throughout Zagreb, from the "Well of Life" outside the Croatian National Theatre to his depiction of Bishop Josip Juraj Strossmayer on Strossmayer Square. His former house and studio in Gornji Grad, now the

Meštrović Atelier (see p. 61), is one of Zagreb's finest museums.

Best known to many visitors for his sculpture of Grgur Ninski in Split, Meštrović was born in Slavonia and raised in Dalmatia. He became an apprentice stonemason in Split before studying in Vienna and going on to live in Paris and Rome. He moved to Zagreb in 1920, and in 1947, he moved to the United States, 20 years after his monumental "The Bowman and the Spearman" was unveiled in Chicago. He taught at Syracuse University in New York and was the first artist to give a one-man exhibition at the Metropolitan Museum of Art in New York City. He is buried in Otavica near Drniš, inland from the Dalmatian coast.

Natural History Museum

- ▲ Map p. 65
- ✉ Demetrova 1, Gornji Grad
- ☎ 014 851 700
- ◷ Closed Mon.
- $ $

hpm.hr

Zagreb City Museum

- ▲ Map p. 65
- ✉ Opatička 20, 1000
- ☎ 014 851 361
- ◷ Closed Mon.

mgz.hr

Museum of Naïve Art

- ▲ Map p. 65
- ✉ Sv. Čirila i Metoda 3, Gornji Grad
- ☎ 014 851 911
- ◷ Closed Mon.

hmnu.org

Beyond the Meštrović Atelier, Demetrova leads left to the **Natural History Museum** (Hrvatski Prirodoslovni Muzej), with extensive collections of fossils, rocks and minerals, and specimens from the botanical and zoological worlds. Back to the right is the **Zagreb City Museum** (Muzej Grada Zagreba), housed in a 17th-century former Convent of St. Clare. It has fascinating and informative displays on the history of Zagreb from prehistory to the present day, including fragments of stonework from the original cathedral before it was damaged in the 1880 earthquake.

Past the City Museum is the so-called **Priest's Tower** (Popov Toranj), originally a 13th-century defensive tower in Kaptol (see pp. 74–75), which now houses an astronomical observatory. The street south of here is called

Opatička (Nun's Street) after the former convent.

South of St. Mark's Square:

The **Museum of Naïve Art** (Muzej Naivne Umjetnosti), just downhill from St. Mark's, has a wonderful collection of more than 1,600 works. Most of the pieces are by Croatian artists and from the school of painting that developed at Hlebine (in northern Slavonia) in the 1930s, under such local, self-taught artists as Ivan Generalić (1914–1992). The museum was founded in 1952 as the Peasant Art Gallery, making it one of the oldest museums of naïve art in the world.

Just south of the museum is the Greek Orthodox **Church of St. Cyril and Methodius.** *(Most of the time it is closed.)*

Opposite is Zagreb's most unconventional museum, the

excellent **Museum of Broken Relationships** (*Ćirilometodska 2, tel 014 851 021, brokenships.com/en, $*)— where various people describe, in their own words and through donated objects, the demise of a failed relationship. At turns hilarious and heartbreaking, it is quite unlike any other museum collection you are likely to find anywhere.

Other Squares: On the left, to the south of the church, you will find **Catherine's Square** (Katarinin Trg), at the far end of which is the **Church of St. Catherine** (Sv. Katarina), one of the finest baroque churches in the whole of Croatia. Built by the Jesuits in the 17th century on the site of an older Dominican church, the Church of St. Catherine has an impressive altarpiece and exquisite stucco work inside.

Next to St. Catherine's is **Jesuit Square** (Jezuitski Trg). The building along the eastern side of the square was once a Jesuit monastery. Part of it became Zagreb's first high school, or *gimnazija*, which is still in use today.

The building also houses the **Klović Palace Gallery** (Galerija Klovićevi Dvori), an art gallery for temporary exhibitions. Serbian sculptor Simeon Roksandić (1874–1973) created the attractive fountain on the opposite side of the square.

Walk down beside the church to the large open terrace, which provides fine views over the rooftops to the Church of St. Mary (see p. 68), Zagreb's Cathedral (see pp. 69–70), and beyond. Descending to the south of here

brings you around onto another tree-lined terrace with the sculpture of Matoš (see p. 67).

Around the Old Walls:

At the top of the **funicular,** installed in 1889, stands the **Lotrščak Tower,** part of the old town's original 13th-century fortifications. The tower once rung a bell every evening to announce the closing of the city gates, but ever since 1877, a (continued on p. 67)

Klović Palace Gallery
- Map p. 65
- ✉ Jezuitski Trg 4, Gornji Grad
- ☎ 014 851 926
- 🕐 Closed Mon.
- $ $

galerijaklovic.hr

Lotrščak Tower
- Map p. 65
- ✉ Kaptol 31
- 🕐 Closed Mon. & Nov.–April
- $ $

A funicular railway connects Gornji Grad to the city below.

Zagreb Walking Tour

Central Zagreb is entirely accessible on foot. This walking tour could be completed in a single day, but there is more than enough to warrant spreading your tour over a longer time. Use the city's elegant streetcar and bus network to join the route wherever you choose.

The bustling cafés of Tkalčićeva belie the fact that the street was once a babbling stream.

Begin at the equestrian sculpture of Ban Josip Jelačić (see sidebar p. 67) at the center of **Jelačić Square ①.** Walk to the northwest corner of the square, then turn right (north) onto Radićeva. Turn left into a narrow alley, Strossmayer Promenade (Strossmayerovo Šetalište), which ascends diagonally across the ramparts of **Gornji Grad.** At the top, you will find **Lotrščak Tower** (see p. 63) and the upper station of the **funicular** (see p. 63).

Upper Town

Before proceeding, turn right along the level, tree-lined terrace to find the **statue of Antun Gustav Matoš** (1873–1914), one of Croatia's best loved poets, seated on a bench. A little farther on the left, a terrace gives views out over the cathedral. Left

NOT TO BE MISSED:

Monuments of St. Mark's Square • Cafés on Tkalčićeva • Botanical Garden

(west) from the terrace brings you past the **Church of St. Catherine** and **Jesuit Square** (see p. 63). Turn right, passing the **Museum of Broken Relationships ②** (see p. 63) on the right and the Greek Orthodox **Church of St. Cyril and Methodius** (see p. 62) and **Museum of Naïve Art** (see p. 62) on the left. Continue on to cobbled **St. Mark's Square ③** (see p. 61), the heart of Zagreb's old town. At the center of the square is

the **Church of St. Mark** (see p. 60), with
its distinctive, tiled roof. Originally built in
the 13th century, much of it is more recent
reconstruction, but it's a lovely building,
with a large cross by Ivan Meštrović inside.
On the right (east) side of the square is the
Croatian **Parliament** (Sabor), and on the left
(west) side is the former **Ban's Palace** (once
the home of Ban Josip Jelačić, which today
houses the offices of the president).

Walk north from the square. On the right
is the excellent **Meštrović Atelier** ❹ (see
p. 61), former home of Croatia's greatest sculptor. Turn right onto Demetrova to find the
Zagreb City Museum (see p. 62), housed in

the former Convent of St. Clare. Walk south
on Opatička before turning left and descending
through **Stone Gate** (Kamenita Vrata; see
p. 67) to the top of Radićeva.

Market & Cathedral

Turn right and descend Radićeva, then turn
left onto Krvavi Most, crossing the café-filled

🗺	See also area map p. 59
▶	Jelačić Square
🕐	2.5 hours
⟷	3.5 miles (6 km)
▶	Jelačić Square

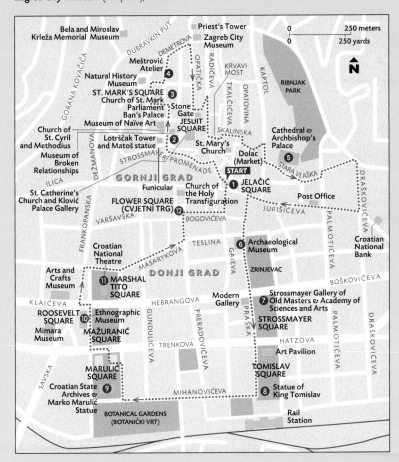

Tkalčićeva to arrive at the back of **Dolac** (see p. 68), Zagreb's open market. Cross to the far left corner of the market to emerge in front of Zagreb's **Cathedral ❺** (see pp. 69–70), its neo-Gothic facade and twin spires the work of Herman Bollé.

Turn right and go down to **Stara Vlaška** (see p. 72), with charming old shops and apartments and a **statue of Croatian poet August Šenoa** (1838–1881), who leans rather nonchalantly against a pillar inscribed with his verse. Turn right onto Draškovićeva then right onto Jurišićeva, passing in front of the main **Post Office** (see p. 73) to return to Jelačić Square.

Green Horseshoe

Walk south along Praška to reach **Zrinjevac** (full name, Trg Nikole Šubića Zrinskog), a green open square that marks the start of Zagreb's swath of grassy public squares dotted with museums and galleries. Note the meteorological station at the top (north) edge of the square, then continue south to arrive at the **Archaeological Museum** (see p. 73) **❻** on your right.

Continue to the southern end of the square, where, at the far side of Josipa Ruđera

Boškovićeva, you will arrive at the **Academy of Sciences and Arts ❼** (see p. 77) inside the airy atrium where you can see the original Baška Tablet, one of the most important documents in Croatia (see sidebar p. 164). The building also contains the **Strossmayer Gallery of Old Masters,** which has a collection of works by European masters from the 14th to the 19th century. Behind the building, on **Strossmayer Square** (Strossmayerov Trg), there is a fine **statue of Bishop Josip Juraj Strossmayer** (1815–1905; see sidebar p. 111).

Southwest on the next square is the **Modern Gallery** (see p. 77). Beyond the gallery, over Trenkova, is the **Art Pavilion** (see p. 77) on Tomislav Square. At the far (southern) end of the square is the equestrian **statue of King Tomislav ❽**, Croatia's first medieval king (see sidebar p. 77). South of Tomislav Square is the **railroad station** (Glavni Kolodvor; see p. 78). Turn right onto Mihanovićeva and walk a couple of blocks west to reach the **Botanical Garden** (Botanički Vrt; see p. 78) on your left.

At the far (west) end of the gardens, turn right past the **Croatian State Archives ❾** (see p. 78), in an art nouveau building sprouting huge owls from the corners of its roof. On its north side is a **sculpture of Renaissance writer Marko Marulić** (1450–1524). North of this is **Mažuranić Square** (Trg Mažuranića), on the left side of which is the **Ethnographic Museum ❿** (see p. 79) and, beyond, **Marshal Tito Square** (Trg Maršala Tita). From the southwest corner of the square, on Frankopanska, is the **Arts and Crafts Museum** (see p. 80), and past this, on Roosevelt Square, the **Mimara Museum** (see pp. 80–81). At the center of Marshal Tito Square is the **Croatian National Theatre ⓫** (see pp. 79–80).

Turn right onto Masarykova then left onto the pedestrianized **Flower Square ⓬** (Cvjetni Trg; see p. 81), packed with cafés. Proceed right along Bogovićeva past the sculpture **"Landed Sun"** (see p. 81). Then head left past the Hotel Dubrovnik and slowly make your way back to Jelačić Square.

Passersby pause for prayer at the Sanctuary of the Unburned Icon in the Stone Gate.

Ban Josip Jelačić: Croatia's Honored Officer & Viceroy

In 1848, Croatia agreed to help quell a Hungarian uprising against Austria in return for greater autonomy from Austria and the introduction of Croatian as the official language instead of Hungarian. Ban Josip Jelačić (1801–1859), a Croatian officer in the Austrian army and the Ban (Viceroy) of Croatia from 1848 to 1859, was dispatched into Hungary at the head of a large army to quell the unrest. Unfortunately for the Croats, once the uprising had been crushed, Austria, instead of rewarding them, introduced a period of even greater repression than before, with German becoming the official language in Croatian schools and the Croatian flag banned. Nevertheless, Jelačić is still depicted on the 20 kuna banknote.

cannon has been fired every day at noon, audible far across the city. You can climb the tower for good city views. Next to the funicular's upper station is a **terrace** that gives a good view out over the lower town.

On a seated bench a short way along on the left there is a well-known **sculpture of Antun Gustav Matoš** by Ivan Kožarić. Matoš (1873–1914), a Croatian poet, was particularly fond of this spot, writing of it, "there is a bench, from which Zagreb is most beautiful in its autumnal days."

Flights of steps and a sloping path (Strossmayer Promenade) lead down from here toward Jelačić Square. The broad, leafy promenade here on either side of Lotrščak Tower leads around the edge of the old town.

Stone Gate: To the east of St. Mark's Square is the Stone Gate (Kamenita Vrata), the only survivor of the old town's four original city gates, dating from the 13th century. The reason for its survival is an altarpiece icon of the Virgin Mary, discovered in a room above the gate following a fire in 1731, miraculously unscathed. It is still here behind an outstanding 18th-century wrought-iron grille, a pilgrimage site drawing the city's faithful to prayer. The interior of the gate, into which a small altar was later incorporated, is covered with votive plaques, and small candles burn in the dim interior.

There are also stories attached to the Stone Gate associating it with witches. Many of those accused of being witches were burned on St. Mark's Square during the 17th and 18th centuries. These events were immortalized by Croatian novelist Marijia Jurić Zagorka (1876–1957), who wrote a hugely popular cycle of novels entitled *The Witch of Grič*, and whose statue you will find on Tkalčićeva.

Near the Stone Gate you will find a small **pharmacy,** which has been in operation since 1355. Beyond the Stone Gate there is a statue of St. George vanquishing a dragon. The statue stands at the top of Radićeva, which leads down to Jelačić Square.

Kaptol

Toward the lower part of Radićeva, a street on the left

marks the site of a particularly bloody conflict between Gradec and Kaptol in 1396, after which this area is still named. **Krvavi Most** means "bloody bridge." There is no bridge here now, but the adjacent **Tkalčićeva,** now a pedestrian street lined with cafés and small boutiques, originally marked the course of the stream (called Medveščak) that divided the two settlements of Gradec and Kaptol and also powered a number of water mills along its course. Due to the occasional floods it caused in the lower town, however, the course of the stream was diverted in the 1930s and the old streambed filled in. The water now flows farther east, mostly through underground channels.

Across Tkalčićeva from Krvavi Most, Skalinska climbs to the back of the Dolac market (see sidebar opposite). Near the bottom of Radićeva on the right, before Jelačić Square, is the entrance to Strossmayer Promenade (Strossmayerovo Šetalište), which leads back up to Lotrščak Tower.

Occupying a large terrace behind Jelačić Square, **Dolac,** Zagreb's main open market, is a wonderfully colorful, bustling place. The site of the medieval settlement of Dolac was cleared to make way for the market in 1925. Just west of the market, on a narrow lane leading onto Tkalčićeva, is the **Church of St. Mary,** originally from the 13th century. But what survives now is mostly an 18th-century reconstruction.

A stallholder sells her flowers at the Dolac market in Zagreb's central district.

EXPERIENCE: Go Picnic Shopping on Dolac

Zagreb has several open markets, but the largest and busiest by far is Dolac, behind Jelačić Square. Dolac is a great place to buy supplies for a picnic or bus journey.

Start with the stalls on the **upper terrace,** where you can buy some fresh fruits and vegetables. Choose for yourself from the mountains of peppers, plums, ripe tomatoes, and other produce. Preserved foods, such as dried figs *(suho smokve),* olives *(masline),* and olive oil *(masline ulje)* from the coast are in this part of the market, too. The sizable **fish market** *(ribarnica)* in the back corner offers plenty of fresh local fish and shellfish.

Then head downstairs into the **covered area,** where stalls sell fresh and dried meat along with pickled foods on one half, and cheese and dairy produce on the other. You will find *Paški sir* here, from the island of Pag, plus all sorts of other varieties of cheeses, as well as *pršut* (Dalmatian prosciutto) and *kulen* (a Slavonian sausage). Be on the lookout for fresh corn bread among the other loaves on sale here, too.

Despite common misconceptions, haggling over prices and striking bargains are not appropriate here any more than they would be in your local supermarket.

Cathedral: East from Dolac, at the top of the street rising from the northeastern corner of Jelačić Square, is Zagreb's imposing Cathedral, its twin spires a distinctive landmark that can be seen from far across the city. Erected in the 11th century to honor the Assumption of the Virgin Mary, the original structure was destroyed in the 13th century and rebuilt in several stages, with a new west front added in the 14th and 15th centuries. New vaulting in the 17th century fixed damage by fire.

Following the earthquake of 1880—which felled the 17th-century neo-Renaissance bell tower—the Cathedral underwent extensive restoration under the direction of Herman Bollé (see sidebar p. 83), who gave the facade a complete face-lift and added the neo-Gothic spires. At the same time, a large round tower in front of the cathedral was removed. Recently, the spires have been encased in scaffolding for many years while they undergo thorough cleaning and repair.

Inside you will find 16th-century wooden choir stalls, a triptych (religious images on three panels around the altar) by Albrecht Dürer from 1495, and memorials to Petar Zrinski and Fran Krsto Frankopan, the two noblemen who were executed following a failed revolt against Austria in 1664 (and who are pictured on the 5 kuna banknote). There is also an enormous organ dating from 1855 and, on the back of the west wall, a large inscription in Glagolitic script from 1941.

Also inside is the **tomb of Cardinal Alojzije Stepinac** (1898–1960), Archbishop of Zagreb from 1937, which includes a sculpture by Ivan Meštrović. A controversial figure, Stepinac initially failed to speak out against the atrocities of the Nezavisna Država Hrvatska, or NDH, the puppet fascist government ruling

Buying a Zagreb Card

If you're spending some time in Zagreb and plan on visiting a lot of museums, consider purchasing a Zagreb Card (*zagrebcard.fivestars.hr*). The card is available online and from numerous hotels and other outlets across the city, and entitles the holder to significant discounts in museums (up to 50 percent), on theater tickets, free transport on ZET trams and buses within the central city zone, and a small (10 percent) discount in some restaurants. Note that some of the discounts are dependent on paying for goods or tickets in cash. There are two versions of the card available, valid for a period of 24 hours (*$$*) or 72 hours (*$$$*) from whatever start time and date you choose.

Croatia on behalf of the Nazis during World War II. Although later more critical of the brutal regime, the churchman spent five years sentenced to hard labor following the war and after that was confined to his home village of Krašić near Jastrebarsko,

INSIDER TIP:

For the best cafés and boutique shops, head off Jelačić Square along Tkalčićeva; on the opposite side of Ilica the streets around the Flower Square also have great cafés.

—HRVOJE PRCIC
*National Geographic
Croatia Editor in Chief*

southwest of the capital. Nevertheless, Stepinac was made a cardinal by Pope Pius XII in 1953.

The Cathedral stands at the center of what was once the medieval settlement of Kaptol, archrival of Gradec (which it actually predates) and the seat of a bishop from 1094. It is surrounded on three sides by fortified ecclesiastical buildings, the massive round towers from the 16th century.

Adjacent to the Cathedral is the fortified 18th-century **Archbishop's Palace** (*closed to the public*), which contains the Chapel of St. Stephen (Sv. Stjepan), with traces of frescoes from the 14th century. The rich collection of the **Archbishop's Treasury** includes an 11th-century cloak of King Ladislaus of Hungary.

In the square in front of the Cathedral is a **fountain** (also the work of Herman Bollé) surmounted by a tall column with a sculpture of the Virgin Mary by Anton Dominik Fernkorn (1813–1878), better known for his statue of Ban Josip Jelačić on Jelačić Square.

Donji Grad

Handsome **Jelačić Square** (Trg Bana Jelačića), now the central focus of modern Zagreb, was actually a busy market for many years (called Harmica until 1854) until the market moved to Dolac on the terrace behind it in the 1920s. The square was in a sorry state of neglect by the middle of the 20th century—even being used as a parking lot at one point—and owes its present appearance to a competition held to redesign the square in 1979. Following that, the buildings surrounding it were restored and the whole area pedestrianized.

At its center, the equestrian **statue of Ban Josip Jelačić** (see sidebar p. 67) by Austrian sculptor Anton Dominik Fernkorn, dates from 1866. The statue originally faced the other way, sword drawn defiantly toward the north (specifically toward Hungary). It was removed under Tito's Yugoslavia, when the square was renamed Republic Square and Jelačić was considered to have been a collaborator with Austria-Hungary. When it was reinstalled in 1991, the statue was repositioned to face the south, toward Knin, the embattled Dalmatian town occupied by the Serbs at the time.

Along Ilica: Stretching west from Jelačić Square is Ilica, which runs past the attractive **British Square** (Britanski Trg), site of a small vegetable and antiques market, toward the suburbs of western Zagreb, and the great new modern art space, **Lauba.** North of British Square is the lovely wooded area of **Zelengaj,** while running north from behind the buildings just northwest of the junction between Ilica and Frankopanska is leafy **Tuškanac.** Near the bottom of Tuškanac there is a **statue of Miroslav Krleža** (1893–1981), considered by many to be the greatest Croatian writer of the 20th century.

Lauba
- **A** Map p. 59
- ✉ Baruna Filipovića 23a
- ☎ 01 6302 115
- $ $
- **lauba.hr**

Traditional dresses on display at the International Folklore Festival held in Zagreb every July

Bela and Miroslav Krleža Memorial Museum

🅰 Map p. 65
✉ Krlezin Gvozd 23
☎ 014 834 922
🕐 Closed Wed.–Mon.
💲 $

mgz.hr

Croatian Visual Arts Center

✉ Trg Zrtava Fasizma bb
☎ 014 611 818
💲 $

hdlu.hr

Krleža's former home, the Villa Rein, is just across the road, and is now open as the beautifully preserved **Bela and Miroslav Krleža Memorial Museum,** complete with period furniture and Krleža's library. The house is one part of the Zagreb City Museum (see p. 62). At the top end of Tuškanac, in a park on the edge of Zelengaj, is another wonderful **statue of Vladimir Nazor** (1876–1949), Croatian poet, politician, and Partisan soldier, pacing beside the trees in a cloak.

East of Jelačić Square: On the far side of Palmotićeva, is **Stara Vlaška,** which, in the late 18th century, was the site of an orphanage and printing press that published works in "Illyrian"—that is, Croatian as opposed to German or Hungarian, the two languages that were imposed at the time. It is now the home of an atmospheric string of old shops and houses. Both the orphanage and printing press, by the way, were established with funds from

Maksimiljan Vrhovac, Bishop of Zagreb in the 1790s, who also established the large public park called Maksimir (see pp. 83–84).

On the near corner of Stara Vlaška is a **sculpture of August Šenoa** (1838–1881), a Croatian poet who was born on this street and served as local magistrate and later senator in Zagreb, a position he held at the time of the great earthquake of 1880. Šenoa leans against a pillar, on which is inscribed one of his poems about the city.

A few blocks southeast of here, on **Square of the Victims of Fascism** (Trg Žrtava Fašizma), is the **Croatian Visual Arts Center** (Dom Hrvatskih Likovnih Umjetnika). Built in the 1930s, this large, round building designed by Ivan Meštrović holds temporary exhibitions. The building became a mosque under Tito's Yugoslavia, complete with minarets, and following the Homeland War is said to have been considered by President Tuđman as a possible site for his own mausoleum.

Back toward Jelačić Square, on the corner of Draškovićeva and

City of Museums & Galleries

Zagreb has many truly outstanding museums and galleries. Among those institutions that you should not miss during your stay in the city are the beautifully kept **Meštrović Atelier** (see p. 61) in Gornji Grad, essential viewing whether you are a Meštrović fan or not; the **Archaeological Museum** (see pp. 73 & 76) on Praška, which contains the original Vučedol Dove (see p. 117); the **Ethnographic Museum** (see p. 79),

for its fine collections of traditional folk costume and lace; the **Modern Gallery** (see p. 77), with an unrivaled collection of Croatian art from the 19th and 20th centuries; and the **Museum of Broken Relationships** (see p. 63), with its emotive collection of words, and objects, telling the stories of demised relationships.

An invaluable reference source is the website of Croatian Virtual Museums (mdc.hr).

Račkoga, is the impressive building of the **Croatian National Bank,** and on Jurišićeva is Zagreb's elegant main **Post Office,** built in 1902–1904 by Greiner and Varoing on two stories, with an additional story added later.

Green Horseshoe

Turning south from Jelačić Square onto Praška brings you to the corner of **Zrinjevac Square** (known alternately as Zrinjevac, Zrinski Trg, and Trg Nikole Šubića Zrinskog), the beginning of Zagreb's so-called Green Horseshoe (Zeleni Potkov)—a series of open, mani-cured green squares and parks running through the center of the city. Conceived by civil engi-neer Milan Lenući (1849–1924) following the earthquake of 1880, these parks and squares incorporated a number of elegant buildings, including the Academy of Sciences and Arts (see p. 77) and the Croa-tian National Theatre (see pp. 79–80). The "horseshoe" runs south from Zrinjevac to the main railroad station, then west through the Botanical Gar-den, and north to Marshal Tito Square, and still constitutes an almost uninterrupted swath of green in the heart of Zagreb.

On the right hand side of Zrinjevac, walking south, is Zagreb's **Archaeological Museum,** which has a fascinating collection ranging from the pre-historic to the medieval periods, including inscriptions from the ancient Greek colonies on the Adriatic coast, jewelry, pottery, an

Statue of August Šenoa, on Stara Vlaška

extensive coin collection, and a collection of ancient pharmaceu-tical instruments.

Among the most important holdings of the Archaeological Museum are the bronze head of a young woman from Salona (which may be a portrait of the Roman empress Plautilla), the extraordinary Apoxyomenos statue (discovered off the coast of Lošinj), and a ninth-century inscription mentioning the Croatian prince Branimir. It also includes the **Vučedol Dove** (Vučedolska Golubica), discovered near Vukovar, the finest artifact to
(continued on p. 76)

Archaeological Museum
- Map p. 65
- Zrinski Trg 19
- 014 873 000
- Closed Mon.
- $

amz.hr

A Tale of Two Cities

Zagreb was once two towns, Gradec and Kaptol. The two were uneasy neighbors for centuries, divided only by a stream called Medveščak. In the 1930s, as the Zagreb of today was being developed, this crucial divide was diverted and filled in to become just another street (Tkalčićeva). As the two settlements merged into today's Gornji Grad, the city continued to expand into the fields below.

Golden angels stand before the Archbishop's Palace in Kaptol.

The medieval settlement of Kaptol, which once surrounded and stretched north from the Cathedral, is the oldest district in Zagreb. The first written record of the town comes from the 11th century and tells us that King Ladislaus of Hungary made the town the seat of a bishop in 1094.

A relative newcomer, nearby Gradec developed into a fortified town, as much in defense against Kaptol as any other enemy. In 1242, Gradec was given the status of a free city by the Hungarian king Bela IV, and today, it remains a cohesive district making up the bulk of the 19th-century upper town. Kaptol, on the other hand, has been reduced to an indistinct area around the Cathedral.

Trading Centers

Both settlements were strategic strongholds, located at the meeting points of several trade routes. The Medveščak provided water for both and powered several mills along its course, where the grain harvested in the fields below the two settlements was ground into flour.

The most important events in the lives of the inhabitants of Gradec and Kaptol were two large annual fairs, each lasting two weeks. Gradec gained permission from Hungary to hold a fair around St. Mark's Day in its main square, St. Mark's Square, in 1256, while Kaptol was later granted permission to hold its own fair, known as Kraljevo.

The uneasy rivalry between the two settlements, mainly over trade, descended into bloodshed on more than one occasion, most notably in 1396, when the two clashed near the Medveščak stream—a spot still marked by a street leading off Tkalčićeva, called Bloody Bridge (Krvavi Most). In later centuries, however, when the *ban* (noble ruler) moved his residence from Kaptol to Gradec for safety, this rivalry gradually decreased, as did the political importance of the Kaptol, though it remained the main religious focus of the two.

Historic Remains

Unlike Gradec, Kaptol was not initially fortified, and as a result, much of it (including the Cathedral) was destroyed by a Mongol raid in the mid-13th century. It was granted permission to build a set of mighty fortifications in the 15th century as protection against the advancing Ottomans. These were largely torn down in the 19th century. There was once a city gate between Jelačić Square and the Cathedral, but only traces remain between the Franciscan Church on Kaptol and Tkalčićeva.

The original, wedge-shaped form of Gradec is still easy to discern because it remains defined by the low hillside spur on which it was built. The boundaries of Kaptol are less easy to appreciate. The road heading north from the Cathedral, still called Kaptol, would once have been the site of the various residences of medieval canons, although nothing of these survives with the exception of the Franciscan Church. The adjacent settlement of Dolac was demolished in the 1920s to make way for the city's open market (see p. 68). Some of the buildings on Opatovina, however, which runs parallel to Kaptol from behind the market, preserve something of their 18th-century grandeur; a number of them were once owned by canons. The Franciscan Church, a short way up Kaptol from the Cathedral on the left, was built in the 13th century, though the present building dates from the 17th century, with 19th-century restoration once again by Herman Bollé (see sidebar p. 83).

The lower town was built over former agricultural land from the 18th century onward. With the ambitious urban planning in the 1880s, the focus of the city gradually moved south. The former cattle market of Harmica later becoming Jelačić Square, and more recently, the suburb of Novi Zagreb (New Zagreb) was built on the far side of the Sava.

EXPERIENCE: Ride the Rails

Zagreb's **streetcars** (*tramvaj*) are an easy way to travel around the lower town and to the city's more distant attractions. In addition, spending a few minutes riding the rails is a great chance to become a Zagreber for a short while. You will find clear route maps at all stops.

Tickets ($) can be bought from the driver or from newspaper kiosks. A rechargeable electronic ticket (*vrijednosna karta*) is also available from kiosks. In order to be valid, tickets must be stamped in—or electronic tickets touched against—one of the small ticket machines on board. Once stamped, tickets are valid for a period of 90 minutes for traveling in the same direction and can be used on multiple routes, both on trams and on local buses within the central district. A **Zagreb Card** (see sidebar p. 70) gives free travel on trams and buses within Zagreb.

Several generations of streetcars operate in the capital, from older, angular models to newer, sleeker machines. Zagreb's streetcar and local (blue) bus network (as well as the funicular) is managed by the state transportation company ZET (*zet.hr/english.aspx*).

A statue of King Tomislav graces the square of the same name.

have survived from the Vučedol culture (see pp. 116–117). The museum is housed in the former Vranyczány-Hafner Palace, designed by F. Kondrat in neo-Renaissance style and completed in 1879.

The Archaeological Museum originally formed part of the National Museum—the oldest museum in Zagreb—which was founded in 1846 and housed in a palace in Gornji Grad along with what would become the collection of the Natural History Museum (see p. 62). The Archaeological Museum became a separate entity in 1939 and moved to its present location in 1945.

Behind the museum there is a small café in the garden, surrounded by ancient sarcophagi and chunks of antique masonry. At the north end of Zrinjevac is a small meteorological station, donated by a local doctor in 1884, and farther south a large fountain designed by the city's dominant artist, Herman Bollé.

South to the Railway Station:

South of Zrinjevac is **Strossmayer Square** (Trg J.J. Strossmayera), at the northern end of which is the palatial, neo-Renaissance **Academy of Sciences and Arts,** completed in 1880. On display inside the light and spacious atrium is the original **Baška Tablet,** one of the most important historical documents in Croatia. The tablet records the donation of a piece of land by the Croatian king Zvonimir in the 11th century on the island of Krk (see sidebar p. 164).

Upstairs, the building houses the **Strossmayer Gallery of Old Masters,** which presents the work of European painters from the 14th through the 19th century, including pieces by the likes of Fra Angelico and Peter Brueghel the Younger, as well as a number of Croatian artists.

Strossmayer Square and Hebrangova, the **Modern Gallery** (Moderna Galerija) contains an unrivaled collection of works by Croatian artists from the 19th and 20th centuries. Some of the names of the artists here may be more familiar—Vlaho Bukovac, Ivan Meštrović, Frano Kršinić—others less so, but it is a remarkable and thoroughly engaging collection whatever your knowledge of Croatian art. The collection is housed in a late 19th-century neo-baroque palace, the former home of Baron Lujo Vranyczány. The palace was restored in the 1990s and two floors converted into a bright and spacious gallery.

South of Strossmayer Square is **Tomislav Square** (Tomislavov

Academy of Sciences and Arts
- 🗺 Map p. 65
- ✉ Trg Nikole Šubića Zrinskog 11
- ☎ 014 895 111
- 🕐 Closed Mon.
- 💲 $

info.hazu.hr

Strossmayer Gallery of Old Masters
- 🗺 Map p. 65
- ✉ Zrinskog 11
- ☎ 014 895 117
- 🕐 Closed Mon.
- 💲 $

info.hazu.hr/the_strossmayer_gallery_of_old_masters

King Tomislav's Statue

The statue of King Tomislav that stands in front of Zagreb's main railroad station was planned in the years after World War I, following Croatia's emancipation from Austrian rule (under which such a project would have been unthinkable). The statue was to have been built to coincide with the 1,000th anniversary of Tomislav's coronation in 925.

Due to political oscillations and insufficient funds, the statue wasn't completed until 1933. It took an additional 14 years before it was installed on its plinth in 1947. By then the sculptor, Robert Frangeš-Mihanović, had died and the Kingdom of Serbs, Croats, and Slovenes under which that statue had been conceived had become Tito's Yugoslavia.

Josip Juraj Strossmayer, the erstwhile Bishop of Đakovo (see sidebar p. 111), was instrumental in establishing the Academy of Sciences and Arts, and many of the works in the Strossmayer Gallery are pieces from his own collection. A fine statue of the bishop, by Ivan Meštrović, stands behind the academy, a fitting memorial to his work.

Located on the corner of

Trg), with the secessionist-style **Art Pavilion** at the near end, built as an exhibition pavilion for the Hungarian Millennium Exhibition in Budapest in 1896 and transported back to Zagreb two years later. At the far (southern) end of Tomislav Square is the immense equestrian **statue of King Tomislav,** Croatia's first medieval king (see sidebar this page) and the first thing that you

Modern Gallery
- 🗺 Map p. 65
- ✉ Andrija Hebrangova 1
- ☎ 016 041 040
- 🕐 Closed Mon.
- 💲 $$

moderna-galerija.hr

**Lisinski
Concert Hall**

🅰 Map p. 59

✉ Trg Stjepana
   Radića 4

☎ 016 121 111

💲 Performances:
   $–$$$$$

lisinski.hr

Botanical Garden

🅰 Map p. 65

✉ Marulićev Trg 9a

☎ 014 898 060

🕐 Closed Dec.–
   March

hirc.botanic.hr/vrt
/english/start.htm

**Croatian State
Archives**

🅰 Map p. 65

✉ Marulićev Trg 21

☎ 014 829 000

🕐 Closed Sat.–Sun.

💲 $

arhiv.hr

will see upon emerging from the railroad station.

South of Tomislav Square is the **main railroad station** (Glavni Kolodvor). Although the railway arrived in Zagreb in 1862, this neoclassical building was completed in 1892. It was designed by Hungarian architect Ferenc Pfaff, who also was responsible for numerous stations in Hungary as well as those in Rijeka and Osijek, Croatia. Zagreb's Glavni Kolodvor was one of the stops on the *Orient Express* route between Paris and Istanbul.

On the far (southern) side of the station (you can cross to the far side of the railroad tracks via the underground mall) is the

INSIDER TIP:

The Green Horseshoe is a series of parks and gardens in the shape of a *U*. Enjoy the green spaces, but take insect repellent: The squares and the lake provide a breeding ground for some of Croatia's 20 species of mosquitoes.

—CAROLINE HICKEY
*National Geographic
Travel Books editor*

Lisinski Concert Hall, Zagreb's premier classical concert venue, built in 1973 and named after Croatian composer Vatroslav Lisinski (1819–1854), who wrote the first Croatian opera in 1846.

More Green Spaces: West of the railroad station, on Mihanovićeva, is Zagreb's **Botanical Garden** (Botanički Vrt). It was laid out in 1889, under the direction of Antun Heinz of the University of Zagreb, like an English landscape garden—complete with meandering paths, lily ponds, glasshouses, and an exhibition pavilion. Most interesting are the three rock gardens with endemic species of Croatian flora, grouped as karst, Mediterranean, and sub-Mediterranean species.

Across the road from the Botanical Garden is **Marulić Square** (Marulićev Trg). Named after a 15th-century Renaissance writer from Split, the square marks the beginning of the western side of the Green Horseshoe.

At the near (southern) end of the square are the **Croatian State Archives** (Hrvatski Državni Arhiv), housed in what is probably the finest art nouveau building in Croatia. Built between 1911 and 1913 by local architect Rudolf Lubyinski (1873–1935), it is a wonderful construction (one of the first in Zagreb to use concrete), sprouting huge owls carrying globes from the corners of its roof. At the entrance are four sculptural reliefs representing the four "collegiate sciences"—philosophy, medicine, law, and theology—by Robert Frangeš-Mihanović, while the sumptuous interior has a large painting by Vlaho Bukovac—along with art nouveau chandeliers, wall mosaics, and stained-glass windows. The building housed the National and University Library

Ivan Meštrović's sculpture "Well of Life" stands in front of the Croatian National Theatre.

until 1995, when it moved to its new premises south of the main railroad station, toward the Sava River. On the north side of the building there is a **sculpture of Marko Marulić** (1450–1524).

Artistic Haunts: North of Marulić Square is **Mažuranić Square** (Trg Mažuranića), named after Croatian poet, linguist, and politician Ivan Mažuranić (1814–1890). A great reformer, Mažuranić was Ban of Croatia from 1873 to 1880 and is depicted on the modern 100 kuna note.

On the west side of Mažuranić Square is Zagreb's excellent **Ethnographic Museum** (Etnografski Muzej), housed in a large palace dating from 1904 that was formerly the Trade and Crafts Museum. The museum has an outstanding collection of Croatian folk costumes from the late 19th and early 20th centuries, highly varied and from all over Croatia, together with collections of lace (*čipka)*, including pieces from the famous lacemaking traditions of the island of Pag, Lepoglava in Hrvatsko Zagorje, and Dubrovnik. Also on display are traditional jewelry, musical instruments, and exhibits on agriculture and viticulture, as well as some non-Croatian material.

Beyond Mažuranić Square is Marshal Tito Square, at the center of which is the **Croatian National Theatre** (Hrvatsko Narodno Kazelište, or HNK for short), surrounded by colorful and well-maintained flower beds. Completed in 1895, the large neo-baroque building is the work of the Viennese architects

Ethnographic Museum
- Map p. 65
- Trg Mažuranića 14
- 014 826 220
- Closed Mon.
- $

emz.hr

Croatian National Theatre
- Map p. 65
- Trg Maršala Tita 15
- 014 888 418
- Performances: $–$$$$$

hnk.hr

Arts and Crafts Museum

- Map p. 65
- Trg Maršala Tita 10
- 014 882 111
- Closed Mon.
- $$

muo.hr

Mimara Museum

- Map p. 65
- Rooseveltov Trg 5
- 014 828 100
- Closed Mon.
- $$

mimara.hr

Hermann Helmer and Ferdinand Fellner, who together designed numerous theaters across Europe, including the Konzerthaus and the Burgtheater in Vienna and the Opera and Ballet Theater in Odessa, as well as the National Theatre in Rijeka. It was renovated in the 1960s. If you get the chance, it is well worth catching a performance of opera, drama, or ballet here during your stay in Zagreb (see sidebar this page).

In front of the theater you will find Ivan Meštrović's sculpture **"Well of Life"** (1905), dating from the period when the sculptor was exhibiting with the Vienna Secessionist Group. Just across Masarykova is a copy of one of Meštrović's most famous works, his **"Mother of the Croats"** (1932)—a powerful female figure sitting cross-legged, supporting a large stone tablet inscribed in Glagolitic—which sits outside Zagreb's Faculty of Law.

On the west side of the square is the palatial **Arts and Crafts Museum** (Muzej za Umjetnost i Obrt). Built by Herman Bollé

between 1888 and 1892, the building initially housed both a museum and a school of arts and crafts. It has served only as a museum since 1999. On display are ceramics, glass, furniture, clocks, religious art, and textiles, drawn from a huge collection of some 160,000 objects that illustrate the development of arts and crafts from the medieval period to the 20th century.

East From Tito Square

Just over from the southwest corner of Marshal Tito Square on **Roosevelt Square** (Rooseveltov Trg), is another sculpture of **St. George and the Dragon**—much more animated than the one by the Stone Gate (see p. 67). Also on the square and this time by Anton Dominik Fernkorn is the huge **Mimara Museum** (Muzej Mimara). Built in 1895 as a school, it was converted into a museum in 1986, displacing 4,500 students—it now houses the vast collection of Croatian art collector Ante Topić Mimara. The museum has

---

EXPERIENCE: Catch a Show

While in Zagreb, catch a concert, opera, or ballet at the **Croatian National Theatre** located on Marshal Tito Square. The stage is well trod as dramatists, musicians, and dancers alternate shows almost nightly to share the stage. Consider taking advantage of the ticket price—relatively cheap compared to the United States ($$–$$$$)—and the conveniently revolving schedule, to see more than one performance.

Check the theater's online schedule for Sunday morning "performances with coffee" that combine cake and coffee with an hour of chamber music. Another good place to catch a performance is the **Lisinski Concert Hall** (lisinski.hr), south of the railroad station. Stop at **Kazališke Kavana** on Marshal Tito Square for pre-performance drinks where Zagreb's early 20th-century poets, such as Antun Gustav Matoš and Tin Ujević, once held court.

1,500 objects on display, ranging from Persian rugs and ancient glassware to works by European masters such as Velásquez, Raphael, and Goya.

On the northeast corner of Marshal Tito Square there's a nice café, Kazališke Kavana, once a favorite haunt of Zagreb's literary elite. East from Marshal Tito Square along Masarykova, at the corner of Preradovićeva, is a Meštrović **statue of Nikola Tesla** (see sidebar p. 233). The Croatian electrical engineer's achievements laid the foundation for the way our modern electricity grids work. Turning right here will bring you to the small café in the garden at the back of the Archaeological Museum.

Left from here is **Flower Square** (Cvjetni Trg), a large, café-filled square, one of the nicest in Zagreb and very difficult to walk through without stopping for at least a coffee. At the far (north) side of the square is a **statue of Petar Preradović** (1818–1872), Croatian Romantic poet and officer in the Austrian military, by the important Croatian sculptor Ivan Rendić, and behind this stands the Orthodox **Church of the Holy Transfiguration.**

On the left (west) side of the square is the **Europa Cinema,** one of the best places in Zagreb to catch a movie. Just off one side of the square, on Varšavska, there is a **statue of Tin Ujević** (1891–1955), the much loved Croatian poet whose Bohemian lifestyle resulted in him being expelled from Belgrade on one occasion, and who regularly frequented the

INSIDER TIP:

Zagreb is the best place in Croatia to see street art (check out the wall along Branimirova, east of the railway station), and there are large international projects held annually.

—KENNY LING
*National Geographic contributor
& mapmaker*

Kazališke Kavana on the corner of Marshal Tito Square.

On the right is Bogovićeva, yet another pedestrian street lined with cafés, shops, and ice-cream parlors and with the sculpture **"Landed Sun,"** another work by Ivan Kožarić (b. 1921), whose better-known figure of Antun Gustav Matoš (1873–1914) sits on the edge of Gornji Grad. Kožarić's "Landed Sun" actually sits at the center of a series of sculptures of the planets of the solar system, installed by artist Davor Preis in recent years. All are located at the correct scale and distance in relation to a "Sun" in Bogovićeva, and therefore scattered at unlikely points through Zagreb's suburbs. Side streets leading off Flower Square and Bogovićeva often have stalls selling various arts and crafts, and are a good place to hunt for souvenirs. At the far end of Bogovićeva, Gajeva leads back past the Hotel Dubrovnik onto Jelačić Square. ∎

Beyond the Historic Center

While most that is interesting about Zagreb is contained within the area between Gornji Grad, Kaptol, and the main railroad station, there are a number of things to see outside the city center, from large green parks and Zagreb's newest art gallery to the beautiful historic cemetery at Mirogoj.

Exploring the huge Maksimir park in western Zagreb is a favorite day out for the city's families.

Mirogoj Cemetery

Mirogoj Cemetery *(Mirogoj 10, tel 014 696 700),* just a few stops on the bus from Kaptol (number 106), is one of the most atmospheric places in Zagreb and easily holds its own against better-known "cities of the dead" such as Recoletta in Buenos Aires. Laid out on the former estate of Ljudevit Gaj (leader of the Illyrian Movement) following his death in 1872, at a time when most of the graveyards in the city itself were full, the cemetery was designed by Herman Bollé (whose hand is all over Zagreb; see sidebar opposite). The first burial took place in 1876.

The cemetery is laid out in four quarters (Catholic, Orthodox, Jewish, and Protestant), though there is no fixed boundary between these areas. A network of broad, leafy avenues crisscrosses the cemetery, and lovely arcades, capped with distinctive domes, hug the high ivy-clad walls.

Many of Croatia's literary figures are buried at Mirogoj, including Tin Ujević, Miroslav Krleža, and Antun Gustav Matoš, along with prominent politicians, from Stjepan Radić (leader of the Croatian Peasant party, who was shot dead in the parliament in Belgrade in 1928) to Franjo Tuđman (Croatia's wartime president from 1990 until his death in 1999).

The cemetery also features a large number of sculptures by some of Croatia's finest sculptors, including works by Ivan Meštrović (the Rittig family tomb); Robert Frangeš-Mihanović, who created the sculpture of King Tomislav in front of the city's main railroad station; Ivan Rendić; and Antun Augustinčić, who is also responsible for the figure of Moses in the Jewish quarter.

Maksimir

As well as the string of green parks through its center and the nearby slopes of Medvednica (see p. 85), Zagreb has a number of other large parks just beyond the historic center. East of Jelačić Square, opposite the Dinamo soccer stadium, is Maksimir—781 acres (316 ha) of parkland only a few tram

INSIDER TIP:

You should check out the Museum of Contemporary Art in Novi Zagreb [see p. 84]. Upon finishing the museum tour, you can leave in an unusual way—via a large curving slide.

—IVOR KARAVANIC
National Geographic grantee

stops from the city center. The park was established by (and is named after) Maksimiljan Vrhovac, Bishop of Zagreb from 1787 to 1827, who, in the late 18th century, donated a large area of his estate to be turned into public parkland.

Although the initial plan was to create a park laid out in classical French style, it later developed along much less formal lines under Vrhovac's successor, Juraj Haulik, with meandering promenades and carriageways, artificial

Maksimir
- Map p. 59
- Maksimirski Perivoj bb
- 012 320 460
- Streetcars 11 & 12

park-maksimir .hr

Herman Bollé: Rebuilding Zagreb

The huge rebuilding project that followed the great earthquake of 1880 is particularly linked with Milan Lenući (1849–1924), the civil engineer who designed the Green Horseshoe, and Austrian architect Herman Bollé (1845–1926), who rebuilt numerous structures. Between them, they constitute the most prominent architectural legacy in Zagreb today.

Best known for his neo-Gothic restoration of the Cathedral, Bollé also designed the Arts and Crafts Museum

(see p. 80) and the cemetery at Mirogoj (see pp. 82–83). He added numerous touches throughout the city, from the Church of St. Mark to the fountain on Zrinjevac, and worked on projects elsewhere in Croatia, such as the cathedral in Križevci and the Church of the Virgin Mary in Marija Bistrice.

Bollé stayed in Croatia until his death. There is a bust of him near the entrance to Mirogoj Cemetery, while the road in front is named Hermanna Bolléa.

Zagreb Zoo
- Map p. 59
- Maksimirski Perivoj bb
- ☎ 012 302 198
- $$

zgzoo.com

Museum of Contemporary Art
- Map p. 59
- Avenija Dubrovnik 17
- ☎ 016 052 700
- Closed Mon.
- $$

msu.hr

lakes, a raised viewpoint (Vidiko-vac), and dense areas of forest.

Maksimir is also where you will find the **Zagreb Zoo.** Established in 1925, it now has more than 2,000 animals from some 275 species. Most of them are kept in open areas rather than cages, and the zoo is set on several islands in an artificial lake. The zoo partici-pates in the European Endangered Species Program, aiming to breed rare animals in zoos before reintro-ducing them to the wild.

Novi Zagreb

Museum of Contempo-rary Art: Established in 1954, Zagreb's Museum of Contem-porary Art (Muzej Suvremene Umjetnosti) was, until recently, housed in the Kulmer Palace—

a building it had long ago outgrown—in Gornji Grad. In 2009, however, the museum finally moved into its new prem-ises south of the Sava River, near the new shopping mall.

The museum has a collection of modern and contemporary works by a broad spectrum of international and Croatian artists in all mediums, including photog-raphy, film, and television.

Jarun: In the southwest part of the city is the equally popular Jarun *(streetcar 17 from Jelačić Square),* an artificial lake cre-ated for the Universiade (World University Games) in 1987 with beaches, running and cycling paths, and some nightclubs around the edge of the lakes.

Medvednica Nature Park offers spectacular views of Medvedgrad fortress and Zagreb.

Medvednica & Medvedgrad

Medvednica, the broad forested mountain rising above the northern edge of Zagreb that now makes up **Medvednica Nature Park,** is covered with clearly marked hiking trails and is a favorite escape for locals on weekends (see sidebar this page). The mountain's name derives from *medvjed,* meaning "bear," although any bears that

INSIDER TIP:

The Sljeme region is ideal for hiking, mountain biking, and skiing in winter. If you are in the area in January, check out the world-class Snow Queen Trophy slalom race on the mountain.

—IVOR KARAVANIC
National Geographic grantee

were once here were hunted out of existence many years ago. A road leads to the summit for those not up to the very easy walk, and a cable car runs from near the Mihaljevac streetcar station, although this station has been closed for major repairs and upgrading since 2009.

There is also a scattering of mountain huts, and one large hotel near the summit, which serve up hearty food to local hikers, and the upper slopes turn into a popular ski run in winter. On fine days, you can cross Medvednica to **Marija**

EXPERIENCE:
Hike on Medvednica

The summit of Sljeme, at 3,389 feet (1,033 m) the highest point on Medvednica, can be rather busy with a restaurant, cable car station, parking lot, and the nearby Tomislav Dom hotel. For a more authentic slice of Medvednica, why not walk 30 minutes west of Tomislav Dom to the **PD Graficar** mountain hut? The hut offers excellent lunches *(closed Mon.).* This is the place to sample some rich bean stew *(grah)* while sitting outside on the grassy terrace with members from the local hiking fraternity. There is an old mine not far from the hut, **Zrinski Mine,** where various ores were extracted during the medieval period. It has recently been restored and opened to the public on weekends *(pp-medvednica.hr, $).*

Bistrica (see p. 95), home to a pilgrimage site lined with sculptures by prominent Croatian artists.

On a spur of the southern slopes of Medvednica are the ruins of a medieval fortress, **Medvedgrad,** built in the 13th century, then long abandoned until partly restored in the 1990s. In front of the fortress is the Altar of the Homeland, a memorial to those who died in the Homeland War. It is made of blocks of stone from different parts of Croatia—somewhat controversially, in view of its expense—which was erected here in 1994, when the conflict was still unresolved.

Archaeological finds in the **Veternica Cave** on the western flanks of Medvednica indicate that it was inhabited by Neanderthal man as much as 40,000 years ago. ∎

**Medvednica
Nature Park**

🗺 Map p. 59
✉ Bliznec bb
☎ 014 586 317

**pp-medvednica
.hr**

A delightful medley of baroque towns, hearty meals, and imposing castles

Northern Croatia

Fine wines are one of the many attractions of northern Croatia.

Northern Croatia

Comprising the areas to the north, west, and south of Zagreb, northern Croatia abounds with historical finds stretching back thousands of years to the Neolithic period. The area's towns show off some outstanding baroque buildings, many home to museums and galleries, while in the countryside, which is now known for its vineyards, several impressive castles nestle among the hills.

The Stari Grad ("old fortress") dominates Varaždin, the largest town in northern Croatia.

In the second half of the 18th century, the well-preserved baroque city of Varaždin, in the far north, served as the capital of the country. Today the city is known for the Špancirfest, a huge annual arts festival. Beyond Varaždin, toward the Hungarian border, is the county of Međimurje and its capital Čakovec. Almost never visited by foreign tourists, this region is well known by Croats as the home of the mighty Zrinski family, who attempted to create an independent Croatia free from the Holy Roman Empire in the 17th century.

Southwest from Varaždin, Krapina-Zagorje County is scattered with spectacular castles. Best known among these are Veliki Tabor and Trakošćan, though there are many more. Most of the castles were fortified during the 16th century, when Austrian rulers attempted to use this part of Croatia as a final western frontier against the Ottoman Empire, which had begun to expand west from Turkey.

The history of Krapina is much older. In fact, some of the earliest Neolithic relics in Europe were found here. Nearby, in the village of Kumrovec, the birthplace of postwar president Josip Broz Tito (see sidebar p. 94) has been preserved as an ethnographic museum.

South of Kumrovec in Klanjec, the Antun Augustinčić Gallery showcases the work of one of Croatia's greatest 20th-century sculptors. And just north of Medvednica, a 15th-century wooden sculpture of the Madonna and Child attracts around 600,000 visitors a year to Marija Bistrica, making this small town one of Croatia's important pilgrimage sites.

West from Zagreb, the lovely little town of Samobor—a favorite getaway from the capital—offers the opportunity to hike in the local Samobor Hills (Samoborsko Gorje) or to enjoy some coffee and local cakes in the picturesque town square. South from here, the Plešivica Wine Road, leading up from the town of Jastrebarsko to the edge of the Samobor Hills, winds through quiet countryside and vineyards, many of which offer wine tastings.

South of Samobor and Jastrebarsko, just off the highway to Rijeka, is Karlovac. Bypassed by most visitors as they whiz by, Karlovac still bears the elements of a perfectly designed and fortified Renaissance citadel at its center, with another impressive castle just outside town. ∎

NOT TO BE MISSED:

A stroll through the baroque heart of Varaždin   90–91

Enjoying live music and street art during Varaždin's Špancirfest   91

A visit to the popular and imposing Trakošćan Castle   93

Exploring one of the earliest sites of prehistoric man in Europe   94

Kumrovec, the birthplace of Josip Broz Tito   94–95

Handmade crafts from a pilgrimage to Marija Bistrica   95

Traveling through vineyards along the Plešivica Wine Road   96–97

Sampling creamy *kremšnite* on Samobor's town square   99

North of Zagreb

Northern Croatia has elegant baroque architecture, some fascinating historic sites, and a string of sturdy castles. Yet with one or two exceptions, the region sees many fewer foreign visitors than most other parts of the country.

Locals stop for a chat in a street in Varaždin.

Varaždin

🅰 89 B3

Visitor Information

✉ Varaždin County Tourist Office, Uska ulica 4

☎ 042 210 096

turizam-vzz.hr

✉ Varaždin City Tourist Association, Ivana Padovca 3

☎ 042 210 987

tourism-varazdin.hr

Varaždin

Located only 50 miles (80 km) north of Zagreb, and roughly half that distance from the Hungarian border, Varaždin is a 90-minute train ride or 2.5-hour bus journey from Zagreb. Originally given the Germanic name of Garestin, the town is first mentioned in a document dated 1181 and issued by King Bela III of Hungary. In 1209, Varaždin was made a royal free city—the first place in Croatia to be granted this status by Hungarian rulers.

The castle at the center of town underwent major reconstruction during the mid-16th century, when it was fortified

by Italian architect Domenico dell'Allio (who also built the fortress in Graz, Austria). At the time, much of this part of Croatia was being fortified as a bulwark against the Ottoman advance westward through the Balkans.

Varaždin grew increasingly affluent in the following century and was briefly the capital of Croatia between 1756 and 1776. However, following a devastating fire in 1776, the capital returned to Zagreb.

Central District: Often described as the "Croatian Vienna," Varaždin has a beautifully preserved baroque center, with some wonderful architecture and plenty of pedestrianized streets.

The historic heart of the city is still the old fortress, or **Stari Grad,** which stands on the northern side of the city center. All sturdy white walls and bastions, its moats and defensive earthworks have been converted into luxurious gardens. The complex has been restored and well maintained, and since 1925, it has housed the **Town Museum** (Gradski Muzej Varaždin).

To the southeast side of the museum, the Franciscan **Church of St. John the Baptist** dates from 1650, on the site of an earlier church and monastery

INSIDER TIP:

Tito, president of the former Yugoslavia, was born north of Zagreb. A visit to his childhood home—now a museum [see pp. 94–95]—is a must for those wanting to understand the history of modern Croatia.

—GRACE FIELDER
National Geographic contributor

destroyed by fire. The nearby **Cathedral,** which also dates from the mid-17th century, but with numerous subsequent renovations, contains a flamboyant gilt altarpiece. The 18th-century **Church of St. Nicholas** (Sv. Nikola) is attached to an earlier, Gothic bell tower. Saint Nicholas is the city's patron saint.

Opposite the St. Nicholas church is the city's **Croatian National Theatre,** another grand building on the southwest side of a large park. The theater holds music and drama performances throughout the year, but one of the most popular events is the theater's Festival of Baroque Music in September.

Varaždin also hosts another major festival, the ten-day Špancirfest (*spancirfest.com*) in late August, which includes music and dance performances, as well as comedy and street theater. The Špancirfest draws a huge number of visitors from across Croatia, so if you are planning to stay in Varaždin at this

time of year, you should book in advance.

Also in the central district, the **Herzer Palace** houses the **World of Insects Museum.** The museum has a fascinating collection of several thousand specimens of butterfly, bug, beetle, and other insects. The majority of specimens were collected by local school teacher and entomologist Franjo Koščec, who donated his collection to the city in 1959, with more specimens added later by his daughter, Ružica.

An art gallery in the late 17th-century **Sermage Palace** boasts a collection of paintings, mostly by Croatian masters. Varaždin's beautiful **cemetery** is just a ten-minute walk west from the center.

Around Varaždin: Some 9.5 miles (15 km) southeast of Varaždin, you'll find **Varaždinske Toplice.** This was the Roman town of Aquae Iasae and is the site of a thermal spring, now a specialized medical spa center of the same name (*minerva.hr*).

Just north of Varaždin, wedged between the Drava and the Hungarian border, is the small Croatian county of Međimurje. The regional capital, **Čakovec,** has a 16th-century castle, once home to the Zrinski family—local nobles who once kept several forts in this region. Zrinski Castle now houses the interesting **Museum of Međimurje.** The wide-ranging collection includes Neolithic and Roman finds from the area, together with decorative arts, an ethnographic collection, and displays relating to the Zrinski family.

(continued on p. 94)

Town Museum
- ✉ Strossmayerovo Šetalište 7, Varaždin
- ☎ 042 658 773 or 042 658 754
- 🕐 Closed Mon.
- 💲 $
- **www.gmv.hr**

Croatian National Theatre
- ✉ Augusta Cesarca 1, Varaždin
- ☎ 042 214 688
- 💲 Performances: $–$$$$$
- **hnkvz.hr**

Herzer Palace
- ✉ Franjevački Trg 6, Varaždin
- ☎ 042 658 760
- 🕐 Closed Mon.
- **gmv.hr**

Sermage Palace
- ✉ Miljenko Stančić Trg 3, Varaždin
- ☎ 042 214 172
- 🕐 Closed Mon.
- **gmv.hr**

Čakovec
- 🔺 89 B3
- **Visitor Information**
- ✉ Međimurje County Tourist Office, Ruđera Boškovića 2
- ☎ 040 390 191
- **tzm.hr**

Museum of Međimurje
- ✉ Trg Republike 5, Čakovec
- ☎ 040 313 499
- 🕐 Closed Mon.
- 💲 $
- **muzej-medjimurja.hr**

Castles in Northern Croatia

A series of spectacular castles (*dvorac* in Croatian) stretches across northern Croatia. Many of these were built—or more often, rebuilt and refortified—in the 16th century, when this region formed a defensive line of fortresses, manned by Croatian noble families, that protected western Europe against the Ottomans.

The limestone Trakošćan Castle stands above a man-made lake created in the 19th century.

Though most of the castles obtained their present forms around the 16th or 17th century, many of the northern ones date from much earlier. Some were small forts built in the 13th century, while others, sitting atop mounds built up over millennia of human habitation, date back to prehistoric times. Most castles preserve their 16th-century utilitarian design, but some have been renovated over successive centuries, their earlier forms and styles masked by neoclassical or neo-Gothic face-lifts.

The names associated with Croatia's northern castles more than any other are those of the Zrinski and Frankopan families, both important Croatian noble families that produced a number of *bans*—Croatian rulers (see pp. 26–27)—some of whom were also major poets. Following the Peace of Vasvár treaty in 1644 (see sidebar p. 29), Austria handed over large areas of Croatian and Hungarian land to the Ottomans, land that the Croats had been fighting to defend against the Ottomans in Austria's name. In response, Petar Zrinski and Fran Krsto Frankopan—who were also brothers-in-law through Petar's marriage to the latter's sister Katarina—attempted to lead a revolt against Austria but were betrayed. They were executed in Vienna in 1671.

Myths & Legends

All good castles have legends attached to them. Maruševec is said to be named after a woman of Czech origin who once lived there, and a peasant girl is purported to have been bricked into the walls of Veliki Tabor after falling for the ban's son.

Not all of the region's castles are open to the public. Public transportation operates to some of them, but by no means all. If you really want to explore as much of what the area has to offer in a single day, you are better off renting a car (see Travelwise p. 275).

Drašković Family Homes

About 25 miles (40 km) southwest of Varaždin and 50 miles (80 km) north of Zagreb, **Trakošćan Castle** *(map 89 B3, tel 042 796 281, trakoscan.hr, $$)* is one of the most visited places in northern Croatia. Built in the 13th century, it came into the possession of the Drašković family in 1584 and remained in their ownership until 1944. Whatever form the castle was in the 16th century, we know from an inscription that the family added the round tower in 1592. By the 19th century, however, the place had been largely abandoned. The family was living in their other castle at Klenovnik. However, between 1840 and 1862 the Draškovićs transformed Trakošćan into a grand country mansion, giving it the eclectic, neo-Gothic look seen today. Inside, you will find an arms and armor collection, plenty of period furniture, and portraits by Juliana Drašković (1847–1901). Buses run between Varaždin and Trakošćan.

Not too far from Trakošćan, around 6 miles (10 km) outside Lepoglava, is **Klenovnik,** Croatia's largest castle. Built in the 1800s, it was home to the Drašković family until they moved back into Trakošćan and sold Klenovnik to pay for the renovations. The castle is now a sanitorium and has extensive parkland.

Five-Sided Fortress

Veliki Tabor *(map 89 A3, Košnički Hum 1, Desinić, tel 049 374 970, veliki-tabor.hr, $),* perched on a 1,093-foot (333 m) hill near Miljana, was built in the 12th century. It took the form of an irregular pentagon, with semicircular bastions added in the 16th century and further additions in the 19th century. Veliki Tabor recently enjoyed extensive renovations, and is now open to the public once again.

The interior of Trakošćan Castle is decked out with memorabilia of the Drašković family.

Other Attractions

Kalnik, another castle originally built in the 13th century, lies around 15 miles (25 km) southeast of Varaždin. Though now largely in ruins, it occupies a spectacular ridge-top position, from which there are extensive views across the surrounding area, including Medvednica Mountain to the southwest. Marked hiking trails lead up to the top.

Bežanec Castle *(map 89 A3, Valentinovo 55, Pregrada, tel 049 376 800, hotel-dvorac-bezanec .hr),* some 7.5 miles (12 km) east of Veliki Tabor, is a 17th-century castle restored in a more neoclassical style. It has been beautifully renovated and is now a hotel. Visits by appointment only.

Zrinski Castle in Čakovec was built in the 16th century and now houses the **Museum of Međimurje** (see p. 91)—where you can see an exhibit on the Zrinski family. The collection includes a letter written by Petar Zrinski to his wife Katarina the day before his execution for treason. **Feštetić Castle,** 2 miles (3 km) outside Čakovec in the village of Pribislavec, has been converted into a school.

Other castles and fortified manors in the area include **Miljana Castle** (west of Veliki Tabor), **Maruševec** (west of Varaždin), **Lovrečina** (south of Križevci), and of course the mighty **Stari Grad** in Varaždin (see p. 90).

Krakina

⬛ 89 A3

Visitor Information

✉ Magitratska 11

☎ 049 371 330

tzg-krapina.hr

Neanderthal Museum

✉ Šetalište V. Sluge bb, Krapina

☎ 049 371 491

🕐 Closed Mon.

💲 $$

tzg-krapina.hr/en/museum_of_early_man

INSIDER TIP:

When in Marija Bistrica, buy some local souvenirs—the town is famous for its traditional, handmade wooden toys and its gingerbread craft, both inscribed on the UNESCO List of Intangible Cultural Heritage.

—HRVOJE PRCIC

National Geographic Croatia Editor in Chief

East of Čakovec is the village of **Donji Kraljevac,** birthplace of philosopher Rudolf Steiner, who inspired the worldwide Waldorf school system. The house in which Steiner was born can be visited by prior arrangement (contact the Medimurje County Tourist Office).

Northwest of Čakovec and close to the Hungarian border is the überluxurious **Sveti Martin**

Spa Resort *(spa-sport.hr),* the largest spa resort in Croatia, with a nine-hole golf course.

Krapina

In 1899, archaeologist Dragutin Gorjanović-Kramberger discovered a rich **Neolithic site** on Hušnjak Hill, in the town of Krapina. The finds from the settlement, which dates back 130,000 years, included more than 800 fossil remains from some 75 Neanderthal skeletons, together with tools and weapons. Most of the artifacts are now in Zagreb's Natural History Museum (see p. 62).

The **Neanderthal Museum** is a new, state-of-the-art museum dedicated to the site in Krapina. As well as learning about Neanderthals and their environment through interactive multimedia displays you can visit the caves themselves on nearby Hušnjak Hill.

Kumrovec

The otherwise unassuming little town of Kumrovec holds a rather

---

Josip Broz Tito: The Partisan & the Party Man

Josip Broz Tito, leader of the Partisan movement fighting the Axis powers during World War II, served as president of the newly formed Yugoslavia from 1946 to 1980. He was born in the village of Kumrovec on May 25, 1892, of mixed Croatian and Slovenian ancestry.

During World War I, Tito served in the Austro-Hungarian army. Captured by the Russians, he fought for the Bolsheviks during Russia's revolutionary period. Returning home in 1920, Tito became a central figure in Croatia's Communist Party. Imprisoned then expelled for party activities, he went back to Russia then returned to become Secretary General of the Communist Party of Yugoslavia in 1937.

After World War II, Tito established the Federal People's Republic of Yugoslavia. He broke with Stalin in 1948 and followed a policy of nonalignment, garnering strong support from the West. He died on May 4, 1980, and his state funeral was attended by an astonishing array of rulers, royalty, and heads of state.

Exhibition on family life in a cave in Krapina's Neanderthal Museum

lofty position in the history of the former Yugoslavia since it was the birthplace of **Josip Broz Tito** (see sidebar opposite). Founded in 1953, the town's open-air **Staro Selo Museum** now comprises some 25 carefully restored houses (including the house in which Tito was born) and some traditional barns.

A few miles southeast of Kumrovec, in the small town of Klanjec, is the **Antun Augustinčić Gallery.** One of the preeminent Croatian sculptors of the 20th century, Augustinčić was born in Klanjec in 1900 and donated many of his works to the gallery. His "Peace" sculpture stands outside the United Nations building in New York.

Marija Bistrica

Standing on the northern flanks of Medvednica Mountain, the small town of Marija Bistrica is home to the **Church of the Virgin Mary,** Croatia's most important pilgrimage site. The church, built on various earlier structures, dates from the late 19th century and is the work of Austrian architect Herman Bollé—who also designed the facade of Zagreb Cathedral (see pp. 69–70). About 600,000 visitors journey here every year to see a small statue of the Madonna and Child, carved in dark black wood, the work of an unknown local sculptor of the 15th century.

Behind the church, you will find the **stations of the cross,** a trail marked by the work of several prominent Croatian sculptors. People often hike over Medvednica from Zagreb, descending along the stations of the cross to reach the church at Marija Bistrica, particularly on Assumption Day—August 15. ∎

Kumrovec
◪ 89 A3

Staro Selo Museum
✉ Kumrovec bb, Kumrovec
☎ 049 225 830
💲 $

mhz.hr

Antun Augustinčić Gallery
✉ Trg Antuna Mihanovića 10, Klanjec
☎ 049 550 093
🕐 Closed Mon. (Oct.–March)
💲 $

mhz.hr

Marija Bistrica
◪ 89 B2
Visitor Information
✉ Zagrebačka bb
☎ 049 468 380
info-marija-bistrica .hr

Plešivica Wine Road

This tour travels through the countryside, villages, and vineyards located between Jastrebarsko and Samobor. The first half of the route covered here is known as the Plešivica Wine Road (Plešivića Vinska Cesta). The tour then leaves the wineries behind and continues northeast through Rude to Samobor.

An antique wooden wine press at one of the Plešivica vineyards

NOT TO BE MISSED:

Wines from local vineyards
• Picturesque Samobor Hills
• Local cream pudding

As well as the beautiful scenery and historic buildings along the way, one of the attractions of this walking or cycling route is tasting the wines produced in situ at the vineyards located along the wine road outside of Jastrebarsko. *(If you want to add some wine tasting to your itinerary, it is best that you phone in advance.)* Several of the vineyards also offer food and overnight accommodation for those wishing to take their time.

The route could also easily be enjoyed as a scenic drive. However, the designated driver will not be able to taste any wines; the blood-alcohol limit for drivers in Croatia is 0.05 percent.

Begin by heading north from the center of **Jastrebarsko ❶** on the road toward Zagreb. Turn left at the small church of **Sveti Duha** onto the Plešivica Wine Road, where you arrive in the village of **Donja Reka,** home of **Tomac** *(Donja Reka 5, tel 016 282 617, tomac.hr),* the first of the wineries offering tastings. Continue north through Gornja Reka, turning right (to the east) at Vranov Dol and continuing through

Prilipje ❷, and the vineyards of **Zdravko Režek** *(Zdihovačka 83, tel 016 293 066).* Then, continue on to the **Church of St. George** (Sv. Juraj) in **Plešivica ❸,** which dates from the 16th century.

To follow the wine road, head southeast to the excellent and very popular **Ivančić Restaurant** *(Plešivica 45, tel 016 293 303, restoran-ivancic.hr),* which makes a great place to stop for lunch, then the wineries of **Jagunić** *(Plešivica 25, tel 016 293 094, jagunic.com)* and **Krešimir Režek** *(Plešivica 39, tel 016 294 836, rezek.hr)* ❹, a particularly friendly place that also has rooms available if you want to turn this into a two-day excursion. Nearby you will also find **Damir Režek** *(Plešivica 39 A, tel 016 294 800, vina-dragorezek.hr).*

Heading back into Plešivica, take the right (northern) branch of the road, passing the 17th-century baroque **Church of St. Francis Xavier** (Sv. Franje Ksaverskog), before turning left (west) back into Plešivica.

North Beyond Plešivica

From Plešivica, continue north through Jurjevčani and Prekrižje Pleš—where you will find the final vineyard, **Kurtalj** *(Plešivica 59, tel 016 293 145)*—to reach the village of **Rude ❺,** with its 17th-century **Church of St. Barbara** (Sv. Barbara), built by the local miners. (The village is also famous for *Rudarska greblica,* a savory "miner's cake" of cheese, spinach, and nuts.) Continue along the valley, with the low Samobor Hills rising on your left, finally arriving in **Samobor** ❻. You can take a rest in the baroque town square and enjoy a slice of *kremšnite*, the tasty local cake (see sidebar p. 99).

If you choose to return to Jastrebarsko, you can vary your return route by heading back to Vranov Dol, then continuing west to arrive in **Prodin Dol.** As a slight detour, turn left (south) here onto an unpaved road that will bring you to the welcoming vineyard and restaurant of **Klet Jana** (*Prodin Dol bb, tel 016 287 372, jana .hr*) ❼. Then continue west through Prodin

Dol and Ivančići and **Gorica Svetojanska** ❽ (also known as Sveta Jana; saint-day festivities are held on July 26). Turn south to Belčići, before going southeast through Srednjak and Črnilovec, and left (east) back to Jastrebarsko.

Detailed cycling maps are available free from the Zagreb County Tourist Board office (*Preradovićeva Ulica 42, Zagreb, tel 014 873 665, tzzz.hr*). The Samobor Tourist Board (*Trg Kralja Tomislava 5, Samobor, tel 013 360 044, tz-samobor .hr*) will provide further information. Maps are also available online at the Croatian Pedala website (*pedala.hr*). Further vineyards are listed at *plesivica.com/vinska-cesta.*

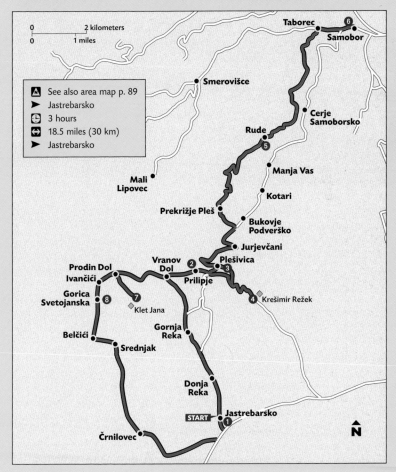

Southwest of Zagreb

Traveling west or southwest from Zagreb brings you to the rolling green hills along the Slovenian border, with more baroque architecture and many pleasant vineyards.

Liqueurs and local delicacies on sale in Samobor town center

Samobor

 89 A2

Visitor Information

✉ Trg Kralja
Tomislava 5

☎ 013 360 044

tz-samobor.hr

Samobor Museum

✉ Livadiieva 7,
Samobor

☎ 013 361 014

🕐 Closed Mon.

Marton Museum

✉ Jurjevska 7,
Samobor

🕐 Closed Mon.–Fri.

💲 $

muzej-marton.hr

Samobor

A deservedly popular getaway from Zagreb on weekends, Samobor lies on the edge of the rolling Žumberak Hills less than 12 miles (20 km) west of Zagreb. Buses leave Zagreb regularly from Cernomerec *(at the end of tram routes 2, 6, & 11)* to make the short trip between the Croatian capital and this charming little town.

Famous for its tasty *kremšnite* (see sidebar opposite), Samobor boasts a well-preserved baroque center set around an elongated square (Trg Kralja Tomislava), and nearby there is a park with

picnic tables and a small stream. A fine early baroque church, **St. Anastasia** (completed in 1675), stands near the square, and the **Samobor Museum** is located on the edge of the park. A short walk south from the main square brings you to the **Marton Museum,** which contains a range of objects from the collection of Croatian art collector Veljko Marton, one of the highlights being its holdings of European porcelain.

The sparse ruins of Samobor's 13th-century castle, or **Stari Grad** (meaning "old town"), which was inhabited up until the end of the 18th century, stand on a forested spur on the western edge of town. The castle can be reached by following a trail from the central park. *(Be warned, the route is becoming rather precarious in places; be wary of falling stones.)*

The surrounding hills, known as Samoborsko Gorje are part of **Žumberak-Samobor Highlands Nature Park** and are crisscrossed by numerous, easy hiking trails. The town also has its own festival, the **Salami Festival,** held in late March or early April each year.

Jastrebarsko

Though far removed from the regular tourist trail these days, Jastrebarsko was once a fairly important regional center. It was granted the status of a free city by Hungary's King Bela IV in 1257 and remained an important fortress during the medieval period. Vladko Maček (1879–1964), leader of the Croatian Peasant Party, was born in Jastrebarsko, and Cardinal Stepinac (1898–1960), Archbishop of Zagreb, was born in the nearby village of Brezarić.

Located about 21 miles (35 km) southwest of Zagreb, Jastrebarsko these days serves mainly as the gateway to the **Plešivica Wine Road** (see pp. 96–97).

Karlovac

Today, Karlovac is best known among Croats for **Karlovačko Pivo,** one of the country's most popular beers, which is brewed in the town. However, Karlovac began its existence as a near perfectly designed fortified Renaissance citadel—a

---

EXPERIENCE:
Indulge in *Kremšnite*

This wonderfully rich and creamy cake, consisting of a thick layer of custard cream sandwiched between two layers of crispy pastry—is a specialty of Samobor and you will have plenty of opportunities to sample around the town. **Gradska Slasti-čarnica** and **U Prolazu,** both on the main square, are good places to try this tasty local desert.

---

six-pointed star sprouting sturdy bastions at every corner. It is surrounded by moats and earthworks, with a neat gridwork of streets inside. Little more than ruins remain, although the citadel's original outline is still clearly discernible amid the town's modern street layout.

The citadel was built in the 1580s to guard the confluence of four rivers–the Kupa, Korana, Dobra, and Mrežnica—on the main trade route between Zagreb and the port city of Rijeka. Although Ottoman forces attacked Karlovac several times, the mighty citadel never fell.

On the main square (Trg Bana Jelačića) you will find a **plague column** dating from 1671–when the disease killed half the city–and the 17th-century **Franciscan Monastery and Church of the Holy Trinity.** The **Town Museum** *(Strossmayerov Trg 7, tel 047 615 980, gmk.hr, $)* occupies the early 17th-century **Frankopan Palace,** one of the oldest buildings in Karlovac. Just outside town is **Dubovac Castle,** dating from the 13th century. ∎

Žumberak-Samobor Highlands Nature Park

✉ Slani Dol 1, Samobor

☎ 013 327 660

$ $

park-zumberak.hr

Jastrebarsko

△ 89 A2

Visitor Information

✉ Vladka Mačeka 1

☎ 016 272 940

jastrebarsko.hr

Karlovac

△ 89 A1

Visitor Information

✉ Ulica Petra Zrinskog 3

☎ 047 615 115

karlovac-touristinfo.hr

One of the most hospitable regions of Croatia, with striking architecture, beautiful wetlands, and ancient history

Slavonia

The distinctive redbrick exterior of the Cathedral of St. Peter, Đakovo

Slavonia

The eastern province of Slavonia (Slavonija) sees far fewer tourists than the Adriatic coast, yet it is a fascinating region with a long and rich history. Despite deep scars from the recent war, it boasts outstanding architecture, hearty regional cuisine and local wines, and several major festivals that combine to make this a remarkably rewarding place to visit.

The history of Slavonia dates back to the third millennium B.C., when the Vučedol culture flourished in the east of the region. This civilization centered along the Danube River near the modern town of Vukovar, and the most famous artifact from the site (the so-called Vučedol Dove) can be seen in Zagreb's Archaeological Museum (see pp. 73 & 76).

Illyrian and Celtic tribes lived in Slavonia in the first millennium B.C., before the Romans established full control over the area, after which the region became Roman Pannonia. It was the Romans who first planted grape vines in the area around Ilok, which is still celebrated for its white wines—these days there is a popular wine route around Ilok.

The Ottomans controlled Slavonia during the 16th and 17th centuries. Later, the region became part of the Austro-Hungarian Empire, and in the 18th century a number of Slavonian cities were fortified as part of a strategic military frontier. You can still see many of these forts today, most impressively at Sisak and in the fortified old town at Osijek. The region was fought over most recently in the Homeland War (see pp. 34–35), with the battles and massacres in Vukovar coming to symbolize the horrors of that conflict.

Geographical Features

Slavonia's boundaries are defined by three great rivers—the Drava in the north, running along the border with Hungary; the Sava in the south, defining the border with Bosnia and Herzegovina; and the Danube (known locally as the Dunav) in the east, along the border with Serbia. Within these boundaries, Slavonia is almost uniformly flat, in particular the eastern half. The plain is broken only by the forested slopes of Papuk—which has some excellent hiking trails, not to mention several ruined castles and some bizarre rock formations—and a few other hills surrounding the town of Požega.

The extensive wetlands around the Sava River, and at the confluence of the Drava and the Danube, are the sites of two outstanding nature reserves, Lonjsko Polje and Kopački Rit, both of which are inscribed on the Ramsar List of Wetlands of International Importance. Lonjsko Polje is currently being considered for status as a UNESCO World Heritage site. Both parks are important stopping points on the migration routes of numerous species of birds and are excellent

---

NOT TO BE MISSED:

Storks and other birdlife in Lonjsko Polje Nature Park 105–109

Marveling at Đakovo's striking redbrick cathedral 111

A stroll through beautifully preserved Osijek 112–114

Sampling *fiš paprikaš*, the region's hearty fish stew 113

Exploring the extensive wetlands of Kopački Rit 114–115

Area of map detail

places for bird-watching. Lonjsko Polje (and in particular the village of Čigoč) is famous for its large population of storks, which arrive in spring, and is an area where you will also find several distinctive breeds of local livestock— Turopolje pigs, Posavina horses, and Podolian cattle. Farther east, the city of Đakovo is famous for its Lipizzaner horses, which have been bred here since the 16th century.

Regional Culture

Osijek, Đakovo, and Vukovar have some fascinating architecture, from the baroque to the neo-Gothic. Osijek and Đakovo in particular are famous for their outstanding

redbrick church and cathedral, respectively, and the fortified baroque core of Osijek (called Tvrđa) is one of the best preserved in Croatia.

Along the banks of the Sava, the rural villages in Lonjsko Polje preserve a traditional wooden architectural style that is unique in Croatia, with many of the buildings dating back more than 200 years. There are several major festivals in the area, including Croatia's largest folk dance festival in Slavonski Brod and an embroidery festival in Đakovo.

A large part of the baroque center of Vukovar has been rebuilt since the Homeland War, but some buildings (such as the old water tower) have been deliberately left in their ruined state. Stretching away on the edge of town, the city's vast war cemetery contains the largest mass grave created in Europe since the end of World War II. A moving memorial to yet another dark chapter in Croatia's history is in Jasenovac, a Nazi concentration camp operated during World War II. ∎

Western Slavonia

Traveling east from Zagreb into Slavonia brings you to the wetlands of Lonjsko Polje—with its wonderful birdlife, local livestock breeds, and distinctive rural architecture—and to the forested hills of Papuk, a nature reserve dotted with ruined castles.

A wild herd of sturdy Posavina horses trudge through the winter snows of Lonjsko Polje.

Sisak

🅰 103 A1

Visitor Information

✉ Rimska bb

☎ 044 522 655

sisakturist.com

City Museum, Sisak

✉ Kralja Tomislava 10

☎ 044 811 811

🕐 Closed Mon.

💲 $

Sisak

Southeast of Zagreb, and occupying the strategically important site at the meeting point of the Sava and Kupa Rivers, is the town of Sisak—which, perhaps not surprisingly, is an important river port. Sisak began its life as the Illyrian and Celtic town of Segesta. After it was conquered by Octavian (later to become the Roman emperor Augustus) in 35 B.C., the Romans went on to build their own town here, called Siscia.

Sisak's main claim to fame is as the site of the Battle of Sisak in 1593. Although outnumbered two to one by the invading Ottoman forces, the Croat army successfully brought the westward expansion of Ottoman control to a halt for a few decades.

Modern Sisak is largely dominated by industry, with an oil refinery on the southern edge of town. However, you can still visit the well-preserved, triangular **fort** (built between 1544 and 1550) that stands on the narrow neck of greenery just above the confluence of the two rivers. A few modest Roman ruins also remain on Jelačić Square. The **City Museum, Sisak** (Gradski Muzej Sisak) has a large collection of coins together with ethnographic and Roman finds, and those who stroll along **Sisak Walk** (Sisačka Setnica) may recognize the familiar statue of lauded Croatian poet Antun Gustav Matoš (see p. 81) seated on a bench. This is a copy of the better known version in Zagreb's Gornji Grad district.

Lonjsko Polje Nature Park

Farther southeast from Sisak, along the north bank of the Sava River, is Lonjsko Polje Nature Park, a beautifully lush landscape of watery meadows crisscrossed by streams and scattered with picturesque villages. An important stop on the migration routes of several species of wading birds, the park is one of the best places in Europe to see storks. These large birds nest on the roofs of village houses and barns, often on wooden nesting platforms erected by local people. Most of the birds are white storks, but you can also see the less common black stork, not to mention spoonbills and several other species of waders and wildfowl.

The main entry points to the nature park are the small villages of **Čigoč** and **Krapje.** The former has been proclaimed a "European Stork Village" by virtue of the sheer number of birds that nest there. There is an information center in both villages.

INSIDER TIP:

Take a guided tour along the Tena's Trail in Lonjsko Polje Nature Park and you'll appreciate the breadth of biological diversity in the area.

—MARLENA SERVISS
National Geographic contributor

Lonjsko Polje Nature Park covers a total protected area of more than 190 square miles (492 sq km). However, there are areas around **Jasenovac** (see pp. 108–109) that are suspected of still having land mines from the Homeland War. As a result, you should not wander off the well-trodden paths in these areas.

(continued on p. 108)

**Lonjsko Polje
Nature Park**

🗺 103 A1

✉ Krapje 16, Krapje

☎ 044 672 080

✉ Čigoč 26, Čigoč

☎ 044 715 115

💲 $

pp-lonjsko-polje.hr

EXPERIENCE: Experience Local Living

Village tourism *(seoski turizam)* is gradually increasing in popularity in several different regions of Croatia. The **Lonjsko Polje** region is one of the areas enjoying early success. Rather than staying in conventional hotels or taking private rooms, visitors have the opportunity to stay in a traditional village house, eat home-cooked food—often including plenty of regional specialties—and experience a genuine slice of life in rural Croatia. Two excellent choices to sample this for yourself in Lonjsko Polje—whether you are basing yourself in one place, or cruising through the area by car or bicycle—are **Usti Lonja,** in the village of Lonja, and **Tradicije Čigoč** (see Travelwise p. 285), in Čigoč.

Bike Tour of Lonjsko Polje

The almost flat terrain of the Lonjsko Polje wetland, combined with the relatively low volume of traffic, make it a perfect area for cycling. This route follows along the Sava River from Sisak to Jasenovac, passing though picturesque villages, with plenty of opportunities for seeing storks and other wading birds, and experiencing the area's fascinating cultural heritage. Despite the minimal traffic, you will still need to keep an eye out for speeding cars on the narrow, winding roads.

Storks find a home in Čigoč village.

NOT TO BE MISSED:

Traditional wooden houses in Čigoč • Local breeds of livestock near Preloščica • Delicious local cuisine

in the village of **Toplovac**. From here, the road turns south again, then veers sharply left alongside an oxbow lake and continues on through the village of **Preloščica.**

Along the Sava

From Preloščica the going becomes more straightforward. Simply follow the road as it meanders along the north bank of the Sava, noting the occasional detour around an oxbow lake. Keep an eye out for local breeds of livestock (see p. 108) grazing in the lush pastures beside the river. And, of course, look out for storks, which you will find nesting on rooftops—perhaps nowhere more so than in the village of **Čigoč ❶**, which lies some 15 miles (25 km) from Sisak. Also note the traditional wooden architecture in these villages (especially noticeable in Čigoč and Krapje) and the way the narrow houses and plots of land radiate away from the river itself. Some of the houses are more than 200 years old.

While in Čigoč, be sure to take the time to visit **Lonjsko Polje Nature Park** (see pp. 105–109). The route between Čigoč and Krapje is the more attractive and interesting section of the ride, so allow yourself plenty of time to explore this area—or simply start out

Head east out of **Sisak** from the City Museum, Sisak (see pp. 104–105). Follow Kralja Tomislava, crossing the Sava River and continuing along this road, which from here is renamed Galdovačka. Turn right onto Poljska then left onto Savska, before turning right again at the junction, then left to arrive

from Čigoč, Lonja, or Krapje if you are arriving by car.

As you pass through **Kratečko,** you should be on the lookout for the small ferry, which provides the only way to cross the river along this stretch of the Sava. Around 25 miles (40 km) from Sisak you arrive at the village of **Lonja 2**, also blessed with the distinctive wooden architecture, which (along with Čigoč) makes a good place to stop for the night. From Lonja, continue through the villages of Trebež, Plesmo, and **Krapje 3** to reach **Jasenovac** (see pp. 108–109), just over 40 miles (65 km) from Sisak.

Beyond Jasenovac

It is possible to extend the route at this point, for example north from either Krapje or Trebež, over the wetlands of Lonjsko Polje. Then follow the unpaved roads to **Lipovljani** on the far side of the highway. However this and other areas off the main road are subject to extensive flooding after heavy rain and may be impassable.

The area southeast from Jasenovac, towards the farming village of **Mlaka,** was hit hard by the Homeland War, so be wary of buried land mines away from roads in this area.

Organized Bike Rides & Village Festivals

For those travelers who do not feel like finding their own way around the area, a sociable and fun option is to join one of the organized bike rides in June (from Sisak to Čigoč) or September (from Krapje to the towns of Novska and Lipovljani, both north of the park). The tours, which coincide with festivals in Čigoč and Krapje, respectively (see sidebar p. 109), are popular, with plenty of local customers coming down on the train from Zagreb to Sisak. Details can be obtained from the nature park offices in Čigoč and Krapje.

From Jasenovac you can head north to Novska to catch the train back to Zagreb.

The Lonjsko Polje Nature Park office produces a good map, with details of bike routes and other visitor information about the area. The map is available at the information centers in Čigoč and Krapje.

Jasenovac

103 A1

Traditional wooden architecture: In addition to the birdlife and landscape, the park is known for its wonderful traditional wooden architecture, in particular in the village of Krapje, where some of the wooden houses are more than 200 years old. A few of these iconic buildings are working

restaurants and rent out rooms to travelers (see sidebar p. 105).

In the rural setting of Lonjsko Polje, you will also find several distinctive local breeds of livestock: Posavina horses, Turopolje pigs, and Podolian cattle. These animals are still grazed in communal herds, providing a window into a way of life now lost in most other parts of Croatia. Beware, the pastures often flood in spring and autumn, making it harder to visit some of the areas farther away from the main roads.

Getting to the Park: On weekdays, three or four buses a day ply the route from Sisak to the villages of Lonjsko Polje. Only one bus runs on Saturday, and there are no services on Sunday. If you're driving or cycling, there are no bridges over the Sava in this area. You will need to cross the river by the small ferry at Kratečko.

Jasenovac

Toward the southeast end of Lonjsko Polje, on the border with Bosnia and Herzegovina, you will come across the town of Jasenovac, which gained historical notoriety as the site of Croatia's most notorious concentration camp during World War II. The camp (one of several in the country) was established by the Ustaša (Croatian nationalist movement, see p. 32), after that organization had been installed by Berlin as a puppet fascist government following the Nazi invasion of Yugoslavia.

The ruins of Ružica Grad, or Rose City, near Orahovica, the largest preserved fortified city in Slavonia

Local Celebrations

Čigoč holds a small festival (European Stork Village Day) on the last Saturday in June every year, and Krapje has its own event (European Heritage Days) in September. Also worth a visit is the horse show in the village of **Sunja,** south of the Sava River and a little way outside the boundary of Lonjsko Polje Nature Park. This event, held in July, is a showcase for the local Posavina breed. During any of these occasions, you will need to book accommodations, which are already limited, well in advance.

No one knows exactly how many people were murdered at the Jasenovac camp between 1941 and 1945. Estimates range from around 60,000 to 700,000—primarily Serbs, Romanies (Gypsies), and Jews, but also many Croatian dissidents and other enemies of the Ustaša regime.

In contrast to concentration camps elsewhere throughout Europe, which have been preserved, Jasenovac was almost completely destroyed in the years following the war. Today's visitors to the **Jasenovac Memorial Site** on the edge of town encounter rolling fields and silent, leafy woods that once marked the position of the cells, barracks, and mass graves of the camp. Here you will find a large flower-shaped memorial to those who died, designed by Bogdan Bogdanović in 1966, and the **Memorial Museum,** which opened in 1968. Inside the park in the center of Jasenovac itself, you will come across another memorial, entitled "The Dead Open the Eyes of the Living," by Stanko Jančić.

Papuk Nature Park

Set in the midst of the otherwise almost pancake-flat land, Papuk's lushly forested slopes soar some 2,950 feet (900 m) above the Slavonian Plain. The nature park can be explored from the north or south, from the small towns of **Orahovica** and **Velika,** respectively, and it is bisected by a winding, hilly road.

Dotted across its leafy ridges is a series of nine ruined medieval fortresses, the most impressive being **Ružica Grad,** near Orahovica. The fortress is first mentioned in the 14th century, and its extensive ruins make an impressive sight. There is an easy trail up through the forest to Ružica Grad from Orahovica Lake. Allow about 25 minutes each way for the walk, and beware of falling stones when exploring the ruins. ∎

INSIDER TIP:

Check out the hexagonal rock columns at Rupnica in a valley near the southern entrance to Papuk Nature Park. They look man-made but are entirely natural.

—TOM JACKSON
National Geographic contributor

Jasenovac Memorial Site
✉ Braće Radić 147
☎ 044 672 319
🕑 Closed Mon.
jusp-jasenovac.hr

Papuk Nature Park
🅰 103 B1
✉ Stjepana Radića 46, Velika
☎ 034 313 030
💲 $
pp-papuk.hr

Eastern Slavonia

Between the striking cities of Đakovo, Osijek, and Vukovar, and the wetlands of Kopački Rit, eastern Slavonia holds a special place in Croatian hearts. It has long been at the frontier of the country, often fought over, and hard won once more only a few years ago.

The sun sets over the Drava River running through Osijek.

Slavonski Brod

🅰 103 B1

Visitor Information

✉ Trg Pobjede 28/I

☎ 035 447 721

✉ Brodsko-Posavska County Tourist Board, Petra Krešimira IV/2

☎ 035 408 393

tzgsb.hr

Slavonski Brod

Traveling east from Lonjsko Polje on the main road inevitably takes you past Slavonski Brod. A major transport hub, Slavonski Brod also harbors the remains of a star-shaped Austro-Hungarian fort built in the 18th century (located before the turnoff to Đakovo.) Anyone passing through the town in June may want to experience the Brodsko Kolo, Croatia's premier folkdance festival, which has been held annually for more than 40 years and has a huge attendance.

Đakovo

Đakovo, like much of the surrounding area of Slavonia, has a long history of human habitation. The town is first mentioned in written documents in the 13th century, at which time it became a bishopric. Following a spell under the rule of the Ottomans

INSIDER TIP:

Do not miss the excellent Brodsko Kolo if you're near Slavonski Brod in June, with unforgettable, colorful folk dancing performances in the sprawling ruins of the old fortress.

—HRVOJE PRCIC
National Geographic Croatia
Editor in Chief

from 1536 to 1690, the town became the center of the Đakovačko-Srijemska Bishopric in 1773, covering a large area of Slavonia.

Without a doubt, Đakovo's star attraction is the **Cathedral of Sts. Peter and Paul** (Katedrala Sv. Petra i Pavla)—a magnificent redbrick edifice that towers over the surrounding countryside. When seen at a distance, its twin spires protrude above seemingly

endless fields of sunflowers. Pope John XXIII once described the neo-Romanesque construction as the "most beautiful church between Venice and Istanbul."

It is actually Đakovo's third cathedral, replacing a more modest, late 17th-century structure. It was commissioned by Bishop Josip Juraj Strossmayer (see sidebar this page) and built between 1866 and 1882 by Viennese architects Karlo Rösner and Frederic Schmidt. The twin spires reach an impressive 275 feet (84 m), and a high dome rises from the center of the church. Frescoes decorate the walls of the vast interior, and the ceiling is painted with gold stars set on a blue background. Strossmayer's tomb lies in the crypt.

The **Church of All Saints** (Crkva Svi Sveti) was once the town's main mosque (Ibrahim Pasha Mosque) when the area was under Ottoman control, but it was converted into a baroque church during the 19th century.

The 18th-century **Bishop's Palace** still serves as the offices of

Đakovo

🅜 103 C1

Visitor Information

✉ Kralja Tomislava 3

☎ 031 812 319

tzdjakovo.eu

Brodsko Kolo

Visitor Information

✉ Radnicki trg 5, Slavonski Brod

☎ 035 445 801

fa-broda.hr

Bishop Josip Juraj Strossmayer

Bishop Josip Juraj Strossmayer (1815–1905), one of the most important and influential figures in the Croatian church and politics of the 19th century, was born in 1815 in Osijek and later studied in Budapest and Vienna. He was made Bishop of Đakovo in 1849, a position he held until his death in 1905, and was also leader of the Croatian People's Party from 1860.

Strossmayer's name is associated with numerous public and charitable works, including the establishment of schools, and he played a key role in founding the

Academy of Sciences and Arts in Zagreb. He commissioned Đakovo's cathedral.

Strossmayer pushed for Croatian schoolchildren to be taught in their native language. He was also a strong advocate of unity between Croats and Serbs, as well as other south Slavic peoples, albeit within the framework of the Austro-Hungarian monarchy, which ruled Croatia, Serbia, and Slovenia at that time. In this respect, Strossmayer's view contrasted sharply with those of Ante Starčević (see p. 32).

Strossmayer Museum
- ✉ Botića 2, Đakova
- ☎ 031 813 698

Museum of Đakovo
- ✉ Anta Starčevića 34, Đakova
- ☎ 031 813 254
- 🕐 Closed weekends
- 💲 $

muzej-djakovstine.hr

Lipizzaner Stable
- ✉ Augusta Šenoe 45, Đakova
- ☎ 031 813 286

ergela-djakovo.hr

the Đakovačko-Srijemska Bishopric. On the north side of the cathedral, you will find the **Strossmayer Museum,** with letters and other items associated with the local hero. More broadly appealing, however, will be the **Museum of Đakovo** (Muzej Đakovštine), the town museum, which has archaeological and ethnographic collections, as well as exhibits relating to the history of the town itself. The collection was housed in the Bishop's Palace for a number of years during Tito's communist Yugoslavia, but was shifted to new premises when the palace was returned to the clergy in the 1990s.

Đakovo is also famous for its Lipizzaner horses, which have been bred here since 1506 (though horses have been bred in the Balkans for much longer). A **Lipizzaner stable** (Državna Ergela Lipicanaca Đakovo) lies on the edge of town, about a 15-minute walk from the cathedral.

If you are here in early July, you won't want to miss the **Đakovo Embroidery Festival** (Đakovački Vezovi), which features traditional embroidery, concerts and parades, folk costumes, and a chance to see displays by Lipizzaner horses.

Osijek
Sitting on the banks of the Drava River, Osijek is one of the most attractive cities in Slavonia, with outstanding architecture, interesting museums and galleries, trams, luxury accommodations, and plenty to see in the surrounding area. It is a five-hour train ride or four-hour bus ride from Zagreb.

The Drava River attracts water-sports enthusiasts.

The Roman settlement here, called Mursa, was raised to the status of a colony under the emperor Hadrian. The town was under Ottoman rule, then it was taken by Austro-Hungary at the end of the 17th century. It was the Austro-Hungarians who built the heavily fortified citadel district Tvrđa. What is now the modern center of Osijek, Gornji Grad ("upper town"), developed as a separate town to Donji Grad, or Lower Town, farther down the Drava. The three settlements merged in the late 18th century.

Tvrđa: The **citadel** in Osijek featured a central square (Trg Sv. Trojstva), surrounded by a neat gridwork of cobbled streets, and grand architecture, enclosed within a formidable star-shaped set of fortifications. While most of the defensive walls have been demolished and the moats filled in, the central core of the citadel remains intact and constitutes one of the finest ensembles of baroque architecture anywhere in Croatia.

A plague column stands in the piazza, and on either side of the square you'll find the **Museum of Slavonia** (Muzej Slavonije) and Osijek's new **Archaeological Museum** (Arheološki Muzej), containing material from the Roman period as well as a Celtic helmet.

The buildings on the north side of the square once housed the Austro-Hungarian military command. A section of the original wall remains on the northeastern side of Tvrđa, which is

Fiš Paprikaš Stew

A specialty of eastern Slavonia, *fiš paprikaš* is a wonderfully rich and hearty stew. It is often fairly spicy, made with freshwater fish (mainly carp, *šaren* in Croatian) and lashings of paprika pepper. The dish is equally popular over the border in Serbia's Vojvodina region and in Hungary. There are annual fiš-cooking festivals and competitions across the region, including in Kutina and Slavonski Brod. Mind the bones!

best appreciated from the nearby bridge over the Drava.

One of the old **city gates** (the Vodena Vrata, or Water Gate) still leads out onto the banks of the Drava. On the west side of Tvrđa is the **Church of St. Michael** (Sv. Mihovil), with its distinctive twin onion domes, and the Franciscan **Church of the Holy Cross** is to the northeast. Both date from the mid-1700s and were built on the sites of former mosques.

Gornji Grad: The most impressive building in Osijek is undoubtedly the **Church of Sts. Peter and Paul** (Sv. Petra i Pavla) in Gornji Grad—a rather magnificent neo-Gothic construction, sprouting flying buttresses from its redbrick flanks. Often called the "cathedral" on account of its scale—the 295-foot (90 m) tiered spire is the second tallest in Croatia—after

Osijek
🗺 103 C1
Visitor Information
✉ Županijska 2
☎ 031 203 755
tzosijek.hr

Museum of Slavonia
✉ Trg Sv Trojstva 6, Osijek
☎ 031 250 730
🕐 Closed Mon.
💲 $
mso.hr

Osijek Archaeological Museum
✉ Trg Sv Trojstva 2, Osijek
☎ 031 250 730
🕐 Closed Mon.
💲 $
mso.hr

Gallery of Fine Arts, Osijek

✉ Europska Avenija 9, Osijek

☎ 031 251 280

🕐 Closed Mon.

💲 $

gluo.hr

Kopački Rit Nature Park

🅰 103 C2

✉ Titov Dvorac 1, Lug

☎ 031 285 370

💲 $, $$$ (includes standard boat trip and visit to Tikveš Castle)

kopacki-rit.hr

Zagreb's cathedral. It was another commission from Bishop Strossmayer (see sidebar p. 111) in 1894. Croatian artist Mirko Rački created the frescoes that decorate the spacious interior.

The adjacent square, **Trg Ante Starčevića,** was named after Croatian politician and writer Ante Starčević (1823–1896) and boasts a large statue of him. Often called the father of Croatia (Otac Hrvatska, as on the statue), Starčević founded the Party of Rights in 1861 and fiercely rejected any possible unity with Serbs. The cafés surrounding the square make a great place for coffee.

The **Gallery of Fine Arts, Osijek** (Galerija Likovnih Umjetnosti Osijek) has an excellent collection of paintings, prints, and sculpture by Croatian artists from the 18th through 20th centuries. The district also has several

interesting buildings from the early 20th century, particularly the 1912 **Urania Cinema** with its curved facade.

The food in Osijek is excellent, with plenty of local regional dishes to try, from opulent fish stew (*fiš paprikaš*; see sidebar p. 113) to game dishes and a dried sausage (*kulen*) something like a large and particularly tasty salami. Try some kulen with the local thick soured cream, *kajmak*. Osiječko is the eponymous local beer brewed in the town since 1687—the oldest brewery in Croatia.

Osijek makes a great base for exploring the surrounding area, with the wetlands of Kopački Rit Nature Park, and the nearby towns of Đakovo and Vukovar, all within easy striking distance and easily visited as day trips.

Kopački Rit Nature Park

Located within the enormous floodplain at the confluence of the Drava and the Danube, these unique wetlands include lakes, channels, and extensive reed beds, as well as areas of forest. The whole area is subject to flooding, starting in the spring and lasting through midsummer.

The area supports an exceptional number of wildfowl and wading birds; almost 300 species have been recorded here, more than 140 of them permanent residents or regular visitors. Species include the gray and purple herons, great white egret, white and black storks, white-tailed eagle, and an enormous colony of cormorants—the largest in Croatia. During the winter months, vast flocks of wildfowl stop here on

---

EXPERIENCE:
Watch Birds & Wildlife in Kopački Rit

Keen bird-watchers and wildlife enthusiasts will want to see more of the park than is possible on the standard boat trip. Join one of the special bird-watching tours available through the visitor center. The tours are accompanied by an experienced guide and last six hours. They include a visit, in small boats, to the Special Ornithological Reserve or, if the water level is not high enough, a hike through the forest. The tours take a maximum of 15 people, so booking in advance is essential. You will see the largest numbers of species in spring (April to June) and fall (August to October).

Egrets are common residents of Kopački Rit Nature Park.

their long winter migrations south.

The area is also popular for fishing (for which you need a license from the visitor center), and the now abandoned **Tikveš Castle** complex, located within the boundary of the park, was a favorite hunting lodge of Tito.

Getting to Kopački Rit:

Tours and day trips to Kopački Rit operate from Osijek, or you can reach the area by road by heading northeast from Osijek via Bilje. There are regular buses between Osijek and Bilje, from where it is roughly a 1.8-mile (3 km) walk along the road to the visitor center and information office at Kopačevo. Once in the nature park, you can enjoy a boat trip to the edge of the ornithological reserve—the best way to see some of the birdlife there and, effectively,

the only way to see more than the peripheral areas of the park.

Kopački Rit Nature Park operates a species adoption program, with proceeds from donations used to further support conservation work in the area. Further details are available at the visitor center or on the website.

Since Kopački Rit lies on the border with Serbia, it suffered damage during the Homeland War, and many parts are still blighted by land mines. You will pass several warning signs to this effect even as you cruise along channels on boat trips.

Vukovar

The once beautiful baroque town of Vukovar on the banks of the Danube River remains the most haunting symbol in Croatia of the Homeland War. Besieged *(continued on p. 118)*

Vukovar
🗺 103 C1
Visitor Information
✉ J.J. Strossmayer 15
☎ 032 442 889
turizamvukovar.hr

Vučedol Culture

The Vučedol culture flourished in eastern Slavonia, along the western banks of the Danube River and surrounding areas, between 3000 and 2200 B.C. The culture is named after the archaeological site of Vučedol (Wolf's Valley), some 3 miles (5 km) outside modern Vukovar, and artifacts from the site are now found in Zagreb's Archaeological Museum and in Vukovar's Town Museum.

A bronze ax head from the Vučedol culture

The Vučedol people lived by fishing, hunting, and farming, and their settlements took the form of compact villages or tells (hill settlements). Most of what we know about the culture comes from the Croatian valley, but archaeologists think that this was a hub of a larger civilization that spread north into the Pannonian Plain, across the Danube into modern-day Hungary. The Vučedol people were likely to be descended from immigrants arriving from farther east. Archaeological evidence suggests that they had established trading links with the Mycenaean civilization in southern Greece.

The Vučedol Site

The dwellings in the Vučedol Valley were of a rectangular or slightly rounded shape. They were partly sunk into the ground, with a floor of baked clay and a circular hearth. The roofs were a simple covering of branches.

Although hunting and gathering much of their food, the Vučedol also kept domesticated livestock, and it appears they used simple wagons possibly hauled by oxen.

Damaged during the Homeland War, Vučedol itself is a fairly large site, covering an area of some 7 acres (2.8 hectares), and may have possibly had some form of defensive walls. Excavations show it to have had a large, rectangular structure at its center, surrounded by ditches. During the Neolithic Period (Late Stone Age), the site appears to have been settled previously by the earlier Starčevo culture. Some estimates have placed the population of Vučedol at 3,000 inhabitants.

Copper Tools

An Indo-European people, the Vučedol culture had learned the art of copper making, and more important, they used a new method of casting, utilizing two-part clay molds that could be reused. Among the objects made using this method was a characteristic ax head, which flares at the bottom while the top of the blade is flat.

Increased demand for copper saw the culture spread over an increasingly large area of central and southeastern Europe, including parts of modern Austria, Hungary, the Czech Republic, and Bosnia and Herzegovina. It is only in the central, rectangular area of the Vučedol site (now known as Gradac) that evidence of copper making and molds have been found.

The prehistoric craftsmen also created some beautiful pottery—cups, bowls, and other vessels—and are associated in particular with biconical vessels (shaped like two cones joined together), sometimes with handles. They also produced ritual vessels, as well as small "models" and animal figurines.

Ceramics

The most celebrated artifact from the period is the so-called Vučedol Dove (Vučedolska Golubica), a three-legged pottery figurine of a bird (probably actually a male partridge), which would have been used as a ritual vessel. Approximately 7.5 inches (19 cm) high, it has a crest at the back of its head and incised linear decoration across its wings and breast, together with what appear to be stylized double ax heads around its neck. The decoration is filled with a pale paste, made from crushed shells mixed with resin. Found at Vučedol in 1938, the original is on display in Zagreb's Archaeological Museum (see pp. 73 & 76), though there is a copy in the Vukovar Town Museum (see p. 118). The Vučedol Dove holds an iconic status in Croatia. It appears on the reverse of the 20 kuna note, and copies of it can be found in souvenir shops across the country.

Also of great interest is a pottery vessel found beneath the

Vučedol Dove

INSIDER TIP:

If you get a chance to see any Vučedol relics in Vukovar, or perhaps in Zagreb, bear in mind that the people who made them were contemporaries of the ancient Egyptians.

—BARBARA JACKSON
National Geographic contributor

Hotel Slavonia in modern Vinkovci. Known as the Vučedol Orion, the vessel is an astrological calendar based on the movements of the constellations. The decoration is divided into four bands of distinct boxes, each containing a symbol representing an individual constellation as it would have appeared at twilight above the horizon. Together the four bands clearly illustrate the passing of the seasons. By this means, the Vučedol people were able to ascertain the beginning of each year, though today we do not know how many days constituted their "year." The Vučedol Orion probably dates from before 2600 B.C., and it is thought to be the oldest European calendar. It followed the same system as the ancient Sumerian and Egyptian calendars but was calibrated for northern latitudes.

New Museum

A new museum is currently under construction in the Vučedol Valley. It is an ambitious and architecturally stylish project, spread over several floors. Built directly into the hillside, with only its broad glass windows exposed, it blends in well with the natural topography of the site. The new museum is expected to be completed by 2018.

Franciscan Monastery

✉ Samostanska 5, Vukovar

☎ 032 441 381

Vukovar Town Museum in Exile

✉ Županijska 2, Vukovar

☎ 032 441 270

💲 $

and almost razed to the ground in 1991, it was once described by Croatian president Stipe Mesić as "Croatia's Stalingrad." Two thousand Croat defenders and civilians died during the siege of Vukovar (see sidebar opposite), and the town was only transferred back to Croatian authorities in 1998.

In the years since the war, Vukovar has been slowly rebuilt, and a number of its beautiful baroque buildings lovingly restored, including much of the **town center** (along Dr. Franje Tuđmana) and the **Franciscan monastery.** Nevertheless, numerous poignant reminders of the

INSIDER TIP:

You cannot visit buildings damaged by the Croatian Homeland War, such as Elz Castle, because they are being restored. But the unrepaired water tower still looms above the city as a reminder.

—IVOR KARAVANIC
National Geographic grantee

war still exist, perhaps none more prominent than the old **water tower,** originally built in 1913 and now deliberately left unrepaired, riddled with bullet holes and scarred by shrapnel.

Elz Castle, which dates from the 18th century, was badly damaged during the war and is

currently closed while it undergoes reconstruction. It used to house the Town Museum, but most of the collection was looted or destroyed during the war, though some items have since been recovered and have been subsequently transferred to the Mimara Museum in Zagreb (see pp. 80–81).

At the end of 1992, while Vukovar was still in Serbian hands, a new museum collection was founded. The **Vukovar Town Museum in Exile** consists of works donated by Croatian and foreign artists. Eventually this collection will be incorporated into the town museum and displayed in Elz Castle once it is restored. Until then the artworks are displayed in the former house of Croatia's first Nobel Prize winner, Lavoslav Ružička—who was born in Vukovar in 1887 and won the Nobel Prize in chemistry in 1939.

War Memorials: Vukovar's **War Cemetery** is located about 2 miles (3.5 km) outside town, on the road leading to Ilok. The site includes one of the largest mass graves created in Europe since World War II. Many of the cemetery's 938 anonymous white crosses are marked with Hravtski Branitelj—meaning "defender of Croatia"–for the untrained and ill-equipped civilian fighters who battled against the Serbian armored divisions.

There are numerous other memorials to the war, including a **bust of Siniša Glavašević,** a Croatian radio journalist, by Croatian sculptor Mladen Mikulin,

Siege of Vukovar

In September 1991, while the world's media attention was focused almost exclusively on the siege of Dubrovnik, Yugoslav People's Army (JNA) forces and Serbian militia surrounded and laid siege to Vukovar. For the next two months, the town was pounded relentlessly by artillery; residents took refuge in cellars, while defenders—vastly outnumbered and outgunned—fought fiercely in the streets above. When the town finally fell on November 18, many of the surviving inhabitants took refuge in the hospital. The next morning, ahead of an agreed evacuation by the Red Cross, over 200 of them (including one woman and local journalist Siniša Glavašević) were loaded onto buses and taken to Ovčara, just outside town—where they were slaughtered mercilessly and buried in mass graves.

in the atrium of the offices of **Radio Vukovar** (Hrvatski Radio Vukovar). Glavašević was among those killed following the siege of Vukovar, having chosen to stay on and broadcast from the town after most others had left.

Just outside Vukovar on the banks of the Danube River is the archaeological site of **Vučedol** (see pp. 116–117).

Ilok

Some 22 miles (35 km) southeast of Vukovar on the banks of the Danube, within a small finger of Croatian territory that juts out into Serbia, is the town of Ilok.

The citadel or **old town** (Stari Grad), set on a long narrow hill and surrounded by sturdy walls, is well worth visiting if you are in this far-flung corner of Croatia. At the center of the old town is **Odescalchi Castle,** built for the local ruler in the 15th century but often renovated and rebuilt since. The castle (along with its estates) was given by Hungary to the family of Pope Innocent XI (born at Odescalchi) during the 17th century and remained in the hands of their descendants until 1945. Parts of the castle now house the **Town Museum,** opened in 2010, as well as an upscale hotel and restaurant.

The town's **Franciscan friary** was founded in the 14th century, and you can still visit the **Church of St. John of Capistrano** (Crkva Sv. Ivan Kapestran), who died in Ilok. It has been renovated a number of times over the centuries, with Herman Bollé (who designed the facade of Zagreb's cathedral and numerous other buildings in Croatia) adding some neo-Gothic touches in the 19th century.

This has been a wine-growing region since Roman times, and the surrounding **vineyards** produce some good wine. Vines damaged or destroyed during the Homeland War have subsequently been replaced.

Traminac is a common local grape. Although originally from the southern Tyrol in Austria, it does well in the local climate and its white wines are worth sampling. There is also a local wine route, the **Ilok Wine Road** (turizamilok.hr), and the **old wine cellars** beneath the castle are very much in use and can be visited by arrangement. ∎

Radio Vukovar

- ✉ Dr. Franje Tuđmana 13, Vukovar
- ☎ 032 450 470

Ilok

- ▲ 103 C1

Visitor Information
- ✉ Trg Nikole Iločkog 2
- ☎ 032 590 020

turizamilok.hr

Old Wine Cellars

- ✉ Stari Podrumi, Šetalište O.M. Barbarića 4, Ilok
- ☎ 032 590 088

ilocki-podrumi.hr

A distinctive peninsula filled with Roman ruins, Byzantine mosaics, and medieval hill towns

Istria

A quiet backstreet offers an escape from modernity in the fishing port of Rovinj.

Istria

Istria (Istra) is a wedge-shaped landmass that projects out into the Adriatic Sea near the border with Slovenia. The charming peninsula still maintains its distinct regional identity as it provides both sunny beach resorts and picturesque hill towns.

The sun sets over the quiet harbor at Rovinj, on the eastern coast of the Istrian Peninsula.

NOT TO BE MISSED:

Istria takes its name from the Histri, an Illyrian tribe that inhabited the region before the Roman conquest. Over the centuries, Romans, Ostrogoths, Croats, and Venetians all played their parts in a sometimes turbulent history. By the second half of the 19th century, the east coast of Istria had become a fashionable destination for the Austro-Hungarian elite.

Behind this stretch of coastline rise the steep-sided Učka and Ćićarija Mountains, covered by a network of hiking trails. On the west coast, the cities of Poreč and Pula boast two of the most celebrated architectural monuments anywhere in Croatia. The Euphrasian Basilica in Poreč contains outstanding Byzantine mosaics and is a UNESCO World Heritage site, while Pula's Roman amphitheater remains one of the largest and best preserved in the world.

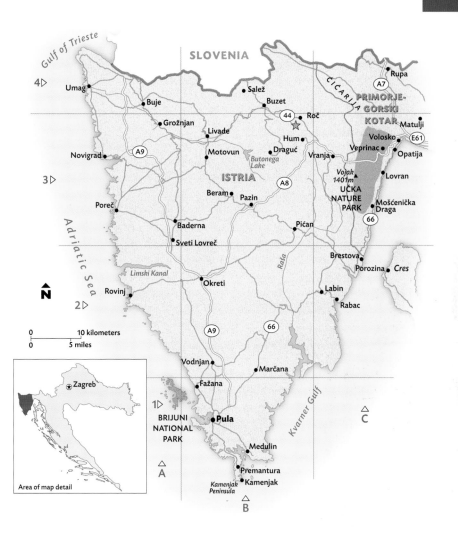

Between the two cities lies the attractive town of Rovinj, with its narrow atmospheric streets and seductive offshore islands. The dramatic Limski Kanal makes a 6-mile (10 km) gash through the coastline, while offshore from Pula, the Brijuni Islands are a national park. The Istrian interior is a different world, a rolling landscape dotted with picturesque medieval hill towns, with outstanding frescoes from the Istrian school of painters.

Istria has a strong reputation for its cuisine, which many consider one of the finest in Croatia. The region is a rich source of white and black truffles, and these luxurious foods feature prominently on many of the local menus. There is also plenty of wild asparagus in season. In addition, Istria produces some of Croatia's finest *pršut* (prosciutto) and olive oils, as well as some exceptional wines.

Finally, Istria is an extremely popular tourist destination and receives more foreign visitors than any other region in Croatia. Visitors should book accommodations well in advance, particularly during the summer months. ■

Pula & Coastal Istria

Pula is home to some of the finest Roman ruins anywhere in Croatia—including one of the largest Roman amphitheaters in the world—not to mention some wonderful restaurants, with popular beaches nearby. The town also hosts Croatia's largest film festival.

Pula's town square, near the restored Temple of Augustus, is a good place to relax over a coffee.

Istrian Tourist Board

✉ Pionirska 1, Poreč

☎ 052 452 797

istra.hr

Pula

🅰 123 B1

Visitor Information

✉ Forum 3

☎ 052 219 197

pulainfo.hr

Pula

An important Roman colony from the first century B.C., Pula boasts some of the finest **Roman ruins** (see pp. 126–127) anywhere. It was plundered by the Goths in the fifth century A.D., and later sacked repeatedly by the Venetians and Genoese in the 14th century.

By the 17th century, plague and malaria had decimated the population, leaving only 300 inhabitants. Pula was converted into a major port by Austria in the 19th century, but following Istria's transfer to Italian rule after World War I, the city once more lost its importance. Nevertheless, the port was bombed by both the Germans and the Allies during World War II.

Modern Pula is a thriving city drawing many tourists. The airport is located just north of town, with a shuttle bus running into the city center. The city is a five-hour bus ride from Zagreb and 11 hours from Split. A ferry between Pula and Venice runs in summer. There are a number of larger hotel complexes on the Verudela Peninsula, a bus ride to the south.

The city's main attraction, its huge **amphitheater,** lies just north of the old city on what was once the Roman road Via Flavia, now called Flavijevska Ulica.

Old Town: South of the amphitheater, on Carrarina, are the city's
two surviving Roman gates, the
Twin Gate and the **Hercules
Gate**—all that remains of the
Roman defenses. Beyond the
gates is the Roman **Arch of the
Sergii.** A plaque near the arch
marks the site of the old Berlitz
school, where James Joyce was an
English teacher a century ago.

The Twin Gate marks the
entrance to the **Archaeological
Museum of Istria** (Arheolski
Muzej Istre), which has collections of prehistoric and classical
pottery, stone, glass, weapons,
and jewelry, objects from the
medieval period, and Christian
floor mosaics.

INSIDER TIP:

Have coffee at the Uliks
(Ulysses) café beside
the statue of James
Joyce, who wrote some
of *A Portrait of the Artist
as a Young Man* in Pula.

—JUSTIN KAVANAGH
*National Geographic
Travel Books editor*

The **Cathedral of St. Mary**
was originally built in the sixth
century, possibly on the foundations of a Roman temple. Following damage by Venetian and
Genoese raids on the city, it was
almost completely rebuilt during
the 15th and 16th centuries, but
it still preserves most of its Byzantine plan.

The interior contains many
elements reused from the earlier
building, as well as from other
buildings of Pula's past, including
Roman and Byzantine columns,
and a lintel dated A.D. 857 embed-
ded in the south wall. The altar is
actually a 3rd-century sarcophagus
that, according to legend, contains
the relics of the 11th-century King
Solomon of Hungary.

The adjacent **bell tower** dates
from the 17th century and contains material from the amphitheater, including some of its seats.

Farther along Kandlerova Ulica,
on the corner of the Roman
forum, stands the beautifully
preserved **Temple of Augustus,**
which these days houses a sculpture collection. Walk around to
the back of the adjacent 13th-
century **Town Hall** to see the
shape of the now lost **Temple of
Diana** in its back wall.

East along Flaciusova Ulica
from the Temple of Augustus, the
tiny Byzantine **Chapel of Mary
Formosa** (Sv. Marija Formosa)
dates from the sixth century and
constitutes the last surviving frag-
ment of an enormous Byzantine
basilica. There are a few surviving
mosaics and frescoes, though
most are now displayed in the
Archaeological Museum.

Just around the corner, in a
courtyard, however, is an outstanding **Roman floor mosaic,** depicting
the punishment of Dirce (by tying
her to the horns of an enraged bull)
by the sons of Antiope, a scene
from Greek mythology. Part of a
Roman villa, the floor, probably dating from the third century A.D., was
found under ruined houses after a
World War II bombing raid.

(continued on p. 128)

**Archaeological
Museum of Istria**

✉ Carrarina Ulica 3
☎ 052 351 300
www.ami-pula.hr

**Cathedral of
St. Mary**

✉ Kandlerova Ulica
27

Roman Ruins in Pula

Legend has it that Pula was founded by the Colchians following their unsuccessful pursuit of Jason and the Argonauts (and their golden fleece) from the Black Sea. Be this as it may, Pula's history certainly goes back a long way, and there was an Illyrian settlement here from at least 500 B.C. The Romans arrived 400 years later.

The Arch of the Sergii leads into the old town of Pula.

Located a short way across the Adriatic Sea from the Roman motherland, Istria—and Pula in particular—preserves some of the finest examples of Roman architecture found anywhere. Pula's amphitheater rivals Rome's, and its temples and arched city gates have provided inspiration to great artists and architects through the ages.

Roman Pula, or to give it its full title, Colonia Julia Pollentia Herculanea, was probably founded by the first Roman emperor, Augustus (63 B.C.–A.D. 14), on the site of the Illyrian settlement. It rapidly grew into a flourishing commercial city, with an estimated population of some 30,000 people in its heyday. Its great wealth is clearly reflected in the quality of its surviving architectural monuments.

Stone Arena

Pula's star attraction is its magnificent and exceptionally well preserved Roman amphitheater, built from local limestone and known locally as the Arena. Located just outside the city walls on what was once the Via Flavia (the Roman road now leading to Poreč and Trieste, Italy), it was probably built in the early first century A.D., under Augustus, and was completed during the reign of Emperor Vespasian (r.69–79), which makes it a rough contemporary of Rome's Colosseum.

Slightly elliptical in form, and measuring some 433 feet long by 344 feet wide (132 m by 105 m), it is the sixth largest surviving Roman amphitheater in the world, with an estimated capacity of around 20,000 spectators. The remarkably intact outer walls, rising to a height of 105 feet (32 m), incorporate two tiers of arches surmounted by a third tier of rectangular apertures (the landward side, where the ground level is higher, has only two levels) and four stout towers. The towers served the dual purpose of giving access to the seats via a spiral stairwell and storing water from an aqueduct, which was then distributed around the arena by a series of channels.

The arena now holds major concerts and operas, and some screenings of the Pula Film Festival (see p. 129), usually seating between 5,000 and 8,000 spectators. The underground passages, once used by gladiators on their way into mortal combat, now hold an exhibition of wine and olive oil production in Roman Istria.

Roman Pula also had a smaller, more intimate theater. You can still see the remains of it in the old town between the central hilltop fort and the Archaeological Museum of Istria near the Twin Gate (see p. 125).

Temples

Along with the arena, the **Temple of Augustus** ranks as one of Pula's top sights. Located on what was once the city's forum–main square and marketplace–the temple was built between 2 B.C. and A.D. 14, and dedicated to the goddess Roma and Emperor Augustus. The Temple of Augustus is an exceptionally beautiful building, tall and elegant, with slender proportions, Corinthian columns, and a finely decorated entablature. The building was actually completely destroyed in a bombing raid during World War II, but it has since been lovingly and almost faultlessly restored.

INSIDER TIP:

Visit the Pula Arena in the early morning to avoid crowds and take time to sit on the steps and listen to the reverberations of the sea's waves— the acoustics are incredible.

—IVOR KARAVANIC
National Geographic grantee

The **Temple of Diana,** which also stood on the Roman forum, was incorporated into the Town Hall during the 13th century, though part of it is still clearly visible in the back wall of the latter building.

Walled City

Roman Pula originally had 12 city gates, of which two survive: the **Twin Gate** (Porta Gemina), which dates from the second century A.D., and the **Hercules Gate,** which dates from the mid-first century B.C. and constitutes the earliest surviving structure from the city walls. On the arch of the latter are the vestiges of the figure of Hercules, the Roman mythological hero, and an inscription bearing the name of the two Roman officials entrusted with the task of founding a colony at Pula.

The now iconic **Arch of the Sergii,** built against what would once have been another city gate (Porta Aurea), dates from the first century A.D. and was commissioned by the noble Sergi family as a memorial. Richly decorated on its western side and flanked by Corinthian columns, the Arch of the Sergii was drawn over the centuries by a succession of artists and architects, including Michelangelo, Palladio, and 18th-century neoclassical architect Robert Adam.

The city walls were pulled down in the 19th century, though you will see some fragments that have survived.

Kamenjak

⛰ 123 B1

Visitor Information

✉ Selo 120, Premantura

kamenjak.hr

Brijuni National Park

⛰ 123 A1

✉ Fažana

☎ 052 525 888

💲 $$$$$

brijuni.hr

Rovinj

⛰ 123 A2

Visitor Information

✉ Pina Budičina 12

☎ 052 811 566

tzgrovinj.hr

Medulin

⛰ 123 B1

Visitor Information

✉ Centar 223

☎ 052 577 145

medulinriviera.info

Church of St. Euphemia

✉ Zagrebačka 9, Rovinj

Uphill from the mosaic is the **Church and Monastery of St. Francis** (Sv. Franjo), built in the 14th century. Note the decorative western portal and the restored cloister. At the top of the hill is the Venetian **fort,** built in the 17th century with stone pillaged from the Roman amphitheater.

Istrian Wine

Istria produces some of Croatia's best wine. Don't leave without trying wine from its signature grape, Malvazija (a fine white), and Teran (a robust red). Standout vineyards include Benvenuti, Dešković, Franc Arman, Kozlović, Roxanich, and Trapan (near Pula).

Kamenjak: South from the town of Pula, Istria reaches its southernmost point on the long Kamenjak Peninsula, home to remote beaches, dinosaur footprints, and rare orchids. There are beaches at **Medulin** to the northeast.

Brijuni Islands

The Brijuni Islands (or the Brionians) lie about 2 miles (3 km) off the Istrian mainland. They consist of 14 islands; the largest, **Veliki Brijun** (Large Brijun), is only 2 square miles (5.2 sq km). The islands, which are now designated **Brijuni National Park** (Brijuni Naciona-lni Park), have many Roman and Byzantine remains. By the late 19th century, they were largely overgrown and rife with malaria.

In 1893, Austrian businessman Paul Kupelwieser purchased the archipelago, cleared the scrub, eradicated malaria, and converted the islands into fashionable luxury health resorts, complete with fine hotels, a zoo, and even an ostrich farm!

Tito had his summer home on the islands from the late 1940s onward, entertaining many dignitaries and celebrities. He also imported tropical plants and animals, and the islands are still home to hundreds of deer, not to mention blue antelope, mountain zebras, and Somalian sheep.

The way to visit the islands is on one of the tours that depart from the port of **Fažana,** north of Pula, where the park's visitor center is located. You can also book a tour with agencies in Pula, Poreč, or Rovinj. The tours include boat travel to and from the islands, and a guided tour around Veliki Brijun.

Rovinj

The center of Rovinj occupies an idyllic, rocky promontory that projects into the Adriatic and was originally an island, until it was joined to the mainland in the 18th century. The isolation led to Rovinj's charming urban core—a maze of streets, with multistory houses.

Rovinj is first recorded in the eighth century, though there was an earlier settlement here. The town was under Venetian rule from the late 13th century, when it operated as a thriving trade port. The large **Church of St. Euphemia** (Sv. Eufemij), built between 1725

EXPERIENCE: Attend the Pula & Motovun Film Festivals

Croatia holds several annual film festivals, and Istria is home to two of its finest, one held among the Roman ruins of Pula on the coast and one inland in the picturesque medieval hill town of Motovun. Pula is Croatia's premier festival (and also its oldest), Motovun a comparatively recent addition to the festival calendar. You can catch screenings of international and Croatian movies at both festivals in July in venues that put any multiplex to shame.

Pula

Established in 1953, the two-week-long **Pula Film Festival** (tel 052 393 321, pulafilmfestival.hr, $) is one of the oldest film festivals in the world. It was the top film festival in the former Yugoslavia and is still an important national and international event. Movies are screened at a number of venues throughout town (tickets are free for these showings), including within the hilltop fort and, most spectacularly, in the amphitheater itself (there is a small charge here).

In case of rain, outdoor screenings are moved to the National Theatre. After screenings, head down to the town square (the old Roman forum), where plenty of cafés and restaurants spill out onto the sidewalk.

The festival attracts huge crowds, including an increasing number of international celebrities. In the past, stars in attendance at the festival have included the likes of Orson Welles, Sophia Loren, John Malkovich, Ben Kingsley, and Ralph Fiennes.

Motovun

The **Motovun Film Festival** (motovunfilmfestival.com) started in 1999 in response to the ongoing closure of many of the small movie theaters throughout Croatia, and it has rapidly attracted a cult following. The annual five-day festival showcases smaller, low-budget movies and world cinema. Some screenings take place outdoors in the main square of this small, otherwise sleepy hill town (see pp. 133 & 136). Other showings are, appropriately enough, in a renovated movie theater that had previously been closed down.

Both festivals take place in July; tickets are available in advance online as well as at the door. Plan ahead and make reservations early.

An evening screening in Pula's Roman amphitheater during the town's annual film festival

Rovinj Heritage Museum

✉ Trg Maršala Tita 11, Rovinj
☎ 052 816 720
$ $

muzej-rovinj.com

Poreč

📍 123 A3

Visitor Information

✉ Zagrebačka 9
☎ 052 451 293

to-porec.com

Porec Town Museum

✉ Dekuma Nska 9, Poreč
☎ 052 431 585
🕐 Closed Mon.
$ $

Labin

📍 123 C2

Visitor Information

✉ Aldo Negri 20
☎ 052 855 560

rabac-labin.com

and 1736 on the site of an earlier church, dominates the old town from the top of the hill. The facade was added during the 19th century, but inside the church is the 6th-century sarcophagus (modified in the 15th century) of St. Euphemia, patron saint of Rovinj, who was martyred near Constantinople at the beginning of the 4th century. There is a 14th-century relief of the saint by the side door and another statue of her atop the bell tower. The **bell tower,** some 200 feet (62 m) high, is earlier than the church and dates from 1677. It was designed in imitation of the better known (and much taller) bell tower of St. Mark's in Venice.

The old town is entered through the 17th-century **Balbi Arch,** built on the site of one of the original city gates. Three of Rovinj's original city gates survive around the southeast corner of the old town: **St. Benedict Gate, Portico,** and **Holy Cross Gate** (Vrata Sv. Križ). The **Rovinj Heritage Museum,** housed in a baroque mansion by the Holy Cross Gate, has archaeological and ethnographic collections as well as artworks by old masters.

Southeast of the old town, on Trg Lokva, is the **Chapel of the Holy Trinity** (Sv. Trojstvo), or Baptismal Font of the Holy Spirit. Originally the baptistery of a church, this heptagonal building in Romanesque style dates from the 13th century.

A number of small, scattered islands just offshore from Rovinj (the nearest of them is **Otok Katarina**) constitute a nature reserve. They can be reached by boat from the old town. South of Rovinj, the **Zlanti Rt** (Golden Point) peninsula and forest park has pebble beaches and some lovely woodland paths to explore.

Festivals in Rovinj include the **Bale** (first Saturday in August) and the **Žminj** (last Saturday in August), with lots of folk costumes on display and local dishes to sample. On September 16, a procession and festivities in the square in front of the Church of St. Euphemia mark the saint's death.

INSIDER TIP:

Take a boat tour from Rovinj or Poreč to the mussel-farming inlet of Limski Kanal [excursion -delfin.com]. You may even see dolphins in this nature reserve.

—HRVOJE PRCIC
*National Geographic Croatia
Editor in Chief*

Poreč

Roman Poreč—known as Parentium—was built on an older Illyrian settlement during the first century B.C. and still preserves something of its Roman form in two of its streets, **Dekumanska Ulica** and **Ulica Cardo Maximus**—the Roman roads Decumanus Maximus and Cardo Maximus. Its most celebrated monument, the Euphrasian Basilica, was built after the city had fallen under Byzantine rule in A.D. 539. The city later allied itself to Venice but, like Pula, was in a sorry state by the 17th century, after plague left as few as 100 inhabitants in the city.

Euphrasian Basilica: One of Croatia's outstanding monuments, the Euphrasian Basilica was built between 543 and 553 by order of Bishop Euphrasius. It is thought that the basilica was erected on the site of the Oratorium of Maurus, which held the remains of St. Maurus of Parentium, an early Christian bishop who was martyred in the fourth century. UNESCO declared the basilica a World Heritage site in 1997.

Entering the building brings you into an atrium with the octagonal **baptistery** on your left, the **Bishop's Palace** ($$) ahead, and the church itself on your right. On the side of the baptistery is a stone inscription taken from the tomb of St. Maurus. Inside the church, note the columns. Although taken from other classical buildings, they have carved capitals bearing the monogram of Bishop Euphrasius. The sixth-century mosaics are dazzling. The dome mosaic features St. Maurus and Bishop Euphrasius alongside the Virgin Mary and infant Christ.

Roman Remains: The western end of Trg Miraflor was once occupied by the Roman forum, and the remains of the **Temples of Jupiter and Mars** are still discernible. The altar from the Temple of Jupiter is now in the **Town Museum.**

Labin & Rabac

Halfway between Lovran and Pula are the medieval hill town of Labin and the resort of Rabac in the sheltered bay below.

Labin is first mentioned in A.D. 285 as the Roman settlement of Albona, though there was an earlier Bronze Age and subsequent Illyrian settlement here. The town is dotted with Venetian and baroque palaces, and the **town gate** survives along with various other parts of the late 16th-century **fortifications.** Labin was the birthplace of Matija Vlačić Ilirik (Matthias Flacius Illyricus, 1520–1575), a Lutheran reformer, and a **Memorial Collection** commemorates his life in the town. Lubin had a prominent mining industry until the 1970s, when the mines were closed: You can see displays related to this in the **Town Museum** (Narodni Muzej). ∎

Matija Vlačić Ilirik Memorial Collection

✉ Giusepinna Martinuzzi 7, Labin
☎ 052 852 477
🕐 Open on request
flacius.net

Labin Town Museum

✉ Ulica 1 Maja 6, Labin
☎ 052 852 477
💲 $

Rabac

🅰 123 C2

Detail of a mosaic in the Euphrasian Basilica, Poreč

Inland Istria

Inland Istria is a place quite unlike the nearby coast or, for that matter, anywhere in Croatia. Enter a world of medieval hill towns, hidden frescoes, and exquisite truffles.

Motovun's citadel, topped by a bell tower, has a commanding view over the Istrian countryside.

Pazin
🗺 123 B3
Visitor Information
✉ Franine i Jurine 14
☎ 052 622 460
tzpazin.hr

**Pazin Museum/
Ethnographic
Museum of Istria**
✉ Trg Istarskog
Razvoda 1
☎ 052 625 040
(Pazin Museum)
☎ 052 625 220
(Ethnographic
Museum)
🕐 Closed Mon.
💲 $$
emi.hr

Pazin

Because Pazin was established as the administrative capital of Istria following the end of World War II, it is inevitable that you will pass through Pazin when traveling in inland Istria, especially if you are using public transportation. Of course, the town's history goes back much further. It is first mentioned as Castrum Pisinum in a tenth-century document.

The town still sports a 16th-century **castle,** built on the remains of an earlier fortress. The castle houses the **Pazin Museum** and the **Ethnographic Museum of Istria** (Etnogratski Muzeij Istre), the latter featuring displays of folk costumes and handicrafts. The

Pazin Museum has a collection of local church bells from the 17th through the 19th century.

Other sights include the 13th-century **Church of St. Nicholas** (Eufrazijeva Ulica 22, tel 052 622 198, open 11 a.m.–1 p.m. in summer), rebuilt in the 15th and 18th centuries, which has fine 15th-century frescoes inside by an anonymous master from the Austrian Tyrol, as well as a presbytery with star-shaped vaulting. The town also has a vibrant **market** (Šetalište Pazinske gimnazije) on the first Tuesday of each month.

Pazin's castle sits on a cliff above a dramatic gorge, through which flows the Pazinčica River. About 330 feet (100 m) below the castle, the Pazinčica disappears into a sinkhole, known as the **Pazin Abyss** *(Pazinska Jama, pazinska-jama.com)*, in the limestone cliff, from where it flows underground. After heavy rains the enlarged river is unable to escape down into the sinkhole, and the gorge floods, creating a temporary lake, which has been known to stretch back over a mile.

An easy, well-marked **walking trail** starts from the Vršić Bridge (near the castle) and descends to the Pazinčica. *(Entering the cave without a guide is strictly forbidden.)* It has been suggested that the gorge in full flood was one of the inspirations for the Gate of Hell in Dante's *Inferno*.

INSIDER TIP:

For the best views of Motovun, grab your camera and head south on the road toward Karojba. As the road climbs uphill, there are great views back to Motovun over surrounding vineyards.

—CHRISTOPHER AUGER-DOMÍNGUEZ
National Geographic International Editions photographer

West From Pazin

Just 1,000 yards (1 km) outside the small village of **Beram**, 3 miles (5 km) west of Pazin, is the **Church of St. Mary of the Rocks** (Crvkva Sv. Marija na Skrilinah). Inside hides an outstanding cycle of 15th-century

frescoes by a certain Vincent of Kastav. The frescoes date to 1474 and include "Dance of the Dead." Remarkably well preserved, they were discovered beneath a layer of plaster in 1913. The church is normally locked, so arrange your visit either through the Pazin tourist office or the Tinjan Parochial Office, or by contacting the key holder in Beram *(Sonja Šestan, Beram 38, tel 052 622 903).*

In Beram village is the **Parochial Church of St. Martin** *(Zupna Crkva Sv. Martina, tel 052 622 903);* though rebuilt in the last century, this church has 15th-century frescoes hidden behind the main altar.

Continuing southwest from Beram is the medieval fortified town of **Sveti Lovreč**. Many of the fortifications date from the town's many centuries under Venetian rule; Sveti Lovreč was the seat of Venetian power in Istria. The **Basilica of St. Martin** (Bazilika Sv. Martina) has frescoes from the 11th century, while the **Church of St. Lawrence** (Sv. Lovreč), just outside the town, dates from the 8th century.

South from here in **Vodnjan,** the 18th-century **Church of St. Blaise** (Sv. Blaž) has the relics of various saints—including one of the oldest and best preserved mummies in Europe—and a bell tower that is the highest in Istria.

Motovun

Motovun is undoubtedly one of the most picturesque Istrian hill towns. Well fortified, the
(continued on p. 136)

Beram
🗺 123 B3

Church of St. Mary of the Rocks
✉ Half a mile (1 km) from Beram
☎ 052 626 016 (Tinjan Parochial Office)
💲 $ (donation)

Vodnjan
🗺 123 B2

Motovun
🗺 123 B3
Visitor Information
✉ Trg Andrea Antico 1
☎ 052 681 726
istria-motovun.com

Bike Istria's Hill Towns

Not all of inland Istria is accessible by public transportation, and if you want to visit the likes of Roč and Hum, you will either need to do a bit of walking, rent a car, or better still, visit them by bicycle. Istria has a vast amount of information available for cycling in the region through its excellent Istria-Bike service *(bike-istra.com)*. Be warned, though—getting up to some of the higher hill towns can be tough!

The medieval hill town of Draguć in Istria, used as a location in Croatian and international films

From **Buzet,** head southeast, passing Selca and Čiritež, before turning left up to the tiny hilltop settlement of **Roč ❶** (once the Roman settlement of Rotium). The tiny **Chapel of St. Roch** *(Sv. Roč)* has frescoes (paintings on the walls and ceiling) dating from the 14th and 15th centuries, and two more churches in town, **Sv. Antun** (14th century) and **Sv. Bartolomej** (restored during the 18th century), are also worth a look.

The road south from Roč to Hum, a distance of roughly 4.5 miles (7 km), is known as **Glagolitic Alley ❷,** and the route is marked with 11 sculptures or monuments relating to Glagolitic priests and the ancient Slavic Glagolitic alphabet scattered at intervals along the length of the road. The sculptures date from 1977 and begin with the Glagolitic letter "S" just outside Roč.

NOT TO BE MISSED:

Sculptures of Glagolitic Alley
• 12th-century frescoes at the Church of St. Jerome in Hum

Detour south to the tiny hilltop settlement of **Hum ❸**—regularly touted as the "smallest town in the world"—which consists of little more than a church, several houses, and a single *konoba* (restaurant). It is a lovely, quiet place, except when a tour bus arrives, at which point it fills up rapidly. The little **Church of St. Jerome** has some very fine 12th-century frescoes inside, including fragments of an Annunciation and the Life of Christ, along with various bits of Glagolitic graffiti dating back centuries (see pp. 26–27). There is also a 16th-century painting of St. Anthony.

You could return to Buzet by the same route, or turn left (west) at Brnobići, following unpaved roads and paths through **Kotle** 4 (also known as Kotli), once a milling village. Cross the Mirna River and turn south through Pašutići and Šengari to reach the paved road at Oslići. If you turn left (south) here, an additional 3 miles (5 km) brings you to the picturesque hill town of **Draguć** 5.

Draguć was once a center for silkworm cultivation, though it is now better known as a location for film and television productions. The main reason to come here, however, is its medieval frescoes. Near the entrance to the town is the **Church of St. Roch** *(Sv. Rok)*,

built during the early years of the 16th century as a votive offering to ward off the plague. Inside are a remarkable cycle of frescoes by Anton of Padova, who was also responsible for the 16th-century work at Hum and frescoes in Oprtalj. Dating from the 1520s and 1530s, the paintings feature the Adoration of the Magi, Baptism of Christ, and Temptation Into the Wilderness. Just outside town, the Romanesque **Chapel of St. Elisha** *(Sv. Elizej)* is older and contains fragmentary frescoes from the 13th century as well as a Roman stela for an altar.

Return to Oslići and continue northwest through Krušvari and Prodani, then turn right at Kožari and cycle though Marinci and Juričići and back into Buzet.

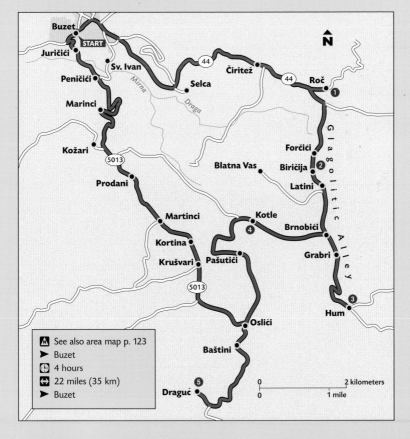

Grožnjan

🗺 123 A3

Visitor Information

✉ Umberta
    Gorjana 3

☎ 052 776 131

tz-groznjan.hr

restored Venetian walls provide a pleasant walk around the town, with spectacular views. The **Church of St. Stephen** (Sv. Stjepan) dates from the beginning of the 17th century and possibly follows designs by the great Italian architect Palladio (1508–1580). Its bell tower can be seen for miles.

Since 1999, Motovun has hosted an annual film festival in July (see p. 129). The town is associated with the story of the giant Veli Jože, by Croatian poet, writer, and politician Vladimir Nazor (1876–1949). And it was the birthplace of Italian racing stars Aldo and Mario Andretti in 1940, when this part of Croatia formed part of Mussolini's Italy.

Grožnjan

The town of Grožnjan (Italian Grisignana) sits perched on a cliff, northwest of Motovun and only 9 miles (15 km) from the sea. In response to the dwindling population in the 1960s, Grožnjan became something of an Istrian artists colony. Now it has a thriving atmosphere and numerous private galleries and studios open to visitors.

Notable buildings include the 14th-century **Church of Sts. Vito and Modesto,** renovated in the 18th century, with its tall bell tower. The **Church of Sts. Cosimo and Damian,** outside the town walls, was built in the mid-16th century and renovated in the 19th.

Festivals in Grožnjan include the **International Jazz Festival** in July and August, recently voted Europe's best boutique jazz festival, and **Extempore,** an art and music event held in September.

Buzet

Perched above the Mirna (meaning "peaceful") Valley, northeast of Motovun, is the town of Buzet. Like other hilltop

Truffle shops, selling oils and pastes, are a common sight across Istria.

settlements, Buzet has been inhabited since the Bronze Age.

Buzet's **Regional Museum** (Zavicajni Muzej Buzet), which occupies the 17th-century Bigatto Palace, has a modest collection of artifacts from the surrounding area. Farther afield is the ruined **Petrapilosa Castle,** 3.5 miles (6 km) to the west.

Buzet hosts many events and festivals, from its **Carnival in February** and paragliding contest in August to **grappa tasting** in October and the **Weekend of Truffles** on the first weekend in November. And if it is truffles you have come here to savor, the latter is not the only truffle-related event in Buzet. During the second weekend in September, an enormous omelet is prepared on Fontana Square, using 2,000 eggs and 22 pounds (10 kg) of truffles.

INSIDER TIP:

Truffle aficionados must stop at Zigante Tartufi [tel 052 663 340] in Buzet, the City of Truffles, to sample the region's renowned black truffles.

—MARLENA SERVISS
National Geographic contributor

Just northwest of Buzet, near the village of **Salež,** is a rare example of a **pillar of shame,** carved from stone in the shape of a human figure. It is thought that offenders were once bound to this and subjected to public torment.

Truffle Treasures

Truffles are fungi that grow underground and are found with the aid of specially trained dogs. The season for collecting white truffles—the largest, most intensely flavored variety—lasts between September and December, though black truffles are collected year-round. The largest white truffle found to that time was discovered in Istria in 1999 near the village of Livade. It was nicknamed Millennium and weighed 2.89 pounds (1,310 g).

Roč & Hum

Southeast of Buzet are the small villages of Roč and Hum, both important centers of learning in the Middle Ages.

In Roč, the **Church of St. Roch** (*Sv. Rok*) has frescoes dating from the 14th and 15th centuries, whereas the little **Church of St. Jerome** in Hum has 12th-century frescoes, along with various bits of graffiti in the Glagolitic (ancient Slavic) alphabet (see pp. 26–27) dating back at least 500 years. The road between the towns is known as **Glagolitic Alley** (see p. 134).

There is no public transportation to either Roč or Hum, but both are near stations on the railway line (Stanica Roč and Ročko Polje, respectively) for those who like a walk. The road from Roč to Hum passes through attractive scenery. Alternatively, both are in easy biking distance of Buzet. ∎

Buzet

⛰ 123 B4

Visitor Information

✉ Trg Fontana 7/1

☎ 052 662 343

tz-buzet.hr

Buzet Regional Museum

✉ Bigatto Palace, Buzet

☎ 052 662 792

🕐 Closed Mon.–Fri.; open Sat.–Sun. by appt. only

💲 $

Roč & Hum

⛰ 123 B3

Church of St. Roch

Visitor Information

✉ Buzet Tourist Office, Šet. Vladimira Gortana 9, Buzet

☎ 052 662 343

tz-buzet.hr

Church of St. Jerome

✉ Hum Kbr 11, Hum

From the Romanesque bell towers of Rab to the snow-dusted
peaks of Gorski Kotar, a region that rarely disappoints

Kvarner Gulf
& Islands

The cathedral towers over the beach area in Novi Vinodolski.

Kvarner Gulf & Islands

The Kvarner Gulf is a triangle of the Adriatic Sea with Istria to the west and the northern tip of Dalmatia nudging up from the southeast. Most visitors to the region focus on the charming islands that riddle the gulf, but on the coast the port city of Rijeka offers a slice of cosmopolitan life and the Opatija Riviera a taste of 19th-century grandeur, while a rugged landscape inland awaits the more intrepid traveler.

At the head of the Kvarner Gulf is Rijeka, Croatia's busiest port and home to its most spectacular carnival, one of the biggest in Europe. Following World War I, when much of the region became part of Italy, Rijeka was a divided city shared by Italy and the kingdom of Yugoslavia. West of Rijeka, the Opatija Riviera became an extremely fashionable tourist destination in the 19th century, and it is home to some of Croatia's most highly rated restaurants.

Traveling southeast along the coast from Rijeka brings you to the popular vacation spots of Crikvenica and Novi Vinodolski, and the town of Senj, once the stronghold of the Uskoks, near legendary pirates and scourge of both Ottoman and Venetian shipping. Their stout castle still stands above the town.

Inland from these towns is Gorski Kotar, the broad, rugged swath of mountains that forms the northernmost part of the Dinaric Alps, including Risnjak National Park and the wild limestone formations of Bijele and Samarske cliffs (stijene). The forested slopes and rocky hollows are home to a broad range of wildlife and plants, including Eurasian lynx as well as endangered brown bears and gray wolves.

Kvarner Gulf Islands

The two largest islands in the Kvarner Gulf are Cres (which is separated from neighboring Lošinj by a narrow channel) and Krk. Also here is the beautiful island of Rab. The sea cliffs at Beli on Cres provide a last stronghold in Croatia for the griffon vulture. Krk and Rab have two of Croatia's most popular beaches: Paradise Beach (Rajska Plaža), on Rab's Lopar Peninsula, and Vela Plaža at Baška, on Krk. Both islands were also centers of Glagolitic learning. The Baška Tablet, bearing one of the earliest Croatian inscriptions in the Glagolitic script, was discovered just outside Baška.

Cres town (the capital of the island of the same name) is a lovely place to while away a few days, and Rab has a wonderfully preserved historic center, its quintessential skyline pierced by four Romanesque bell towers.

In general, the islands of the Kvarner Gulf tend to be less crowded than those along the central Dalmatian coast. (Cres has a population of just over 3,000, while neighboring Krk has almost 18,000 residents.)

NOT TO BE MISSED:

Carnival in Rijeka, one of Europe's biggest parties **143**

Strolling around the opulent Opatija Riviera **146–149**

Spending a night in the mountains of Risnjak National Park **150–153**

Hiking through the Devil's Pass near Skrad **151**

Lubenice, Cres's beautiful cliff-top village **156**

Spotting griffon vultures at Beli on the island of Cres **156 & 157**

Exploring the atmospheric town of Rab **159–161**

The channels between these islands were once a key to Adriatic shipping, upon which the fortunes of neighboring cities (such as tiny Osor on Cres) waxed and waned. In more recent times, Goli Otok (meaning "naked island"), near Rab, was once the site of a notorious maximum security prison, something of a Croatian Alcatraz.

The Kvarner Gulf and its islands have been inhabited since Neolithic times, and proof lies in the traces of Illyrian hill forts in the area dating back to before Roman times. The Frankopans, a prominent noble family, long played a key role in the region's fortunes, and many of

their castles are dotted around the coast and islands. In the 18th century, Kvarner became an Austrian possession, resulting in the rapid growth of tourism, making the islands the destination of choice for the region's elite. ∎

● Zagreb

Area of map detail

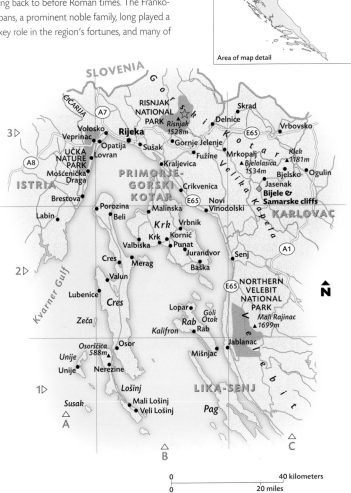

Rijeka

Rijeka, Croatia's main cargo port, sits at the head of the Kvarner Gulf, backed by the great arc of mountains that form the Gorski Kotar range. Comparatively few foreign visitors stop in Rijeka, though as a major ferry port it sees plenty of people pass through on their way to the islands or Dalmatia. This is rather a shame, since it is an attractive city with plenty of grand architecture.

The famous clock tower keeps time for people in the cafés on Rijeka's Korzo thoroughfare.

Kvarner Gulf

141

Visitor Information

✉ N Tesle 2, Opatija

☎ 051 272 988

kvarner.hr

Rijeka

Like many other towns and cities in the region, Rijeka was once an Illyrian and then a Roman settlement. Unlike much of the rest of the coast, however, it never came under the thumb of Venice.

The Habsburgs ruled Rijeka from the 15th to the 18th century, then the city fell under Hungarian control. Following World War I, Italian poet Gabriele D'Annunzio arrived and set up his own short-lived kingdom here. Later, Rijeka (known as Fiume by Italians)

INSIDER TIP:

If you happen to be in the area around Carnival time, make sure to visit Rijeka. It is the largest party in Croatia.

—IVOR KARAVANIC
National Geographic grantee

became part of the Kingdom of Italy, with the border running down the Rječina River, until the end of World War II. During this period the eastern suburb of Sušak (across the river border in then Yugoslavia) thrived as a busy shipyard.

Rijeka's main pedestrian artery is **Korzo,** an attractive, café-filled street surrounded by grand architecture. The old town lies inland (north) of this, roughly the area between Korzo, Museum Square (Muzejski Trg), and Jelačić Square (Jelačićev Trg). The area south of Korzo is all land reclaimed from the sea. An earthquake struck the city in 1750, so what you see of Rijeka today dates largely from the 18th century onward.

Old Town: Within the old town are the 17th-century Church of St. Vitus (these days a cathedral) and the 18th-century **Church of the Blessed Virgin,** built on the site of an earlier church. The latter has a freestanding **bell tower,** which leans considerably. There is also a first-century **Roman arch,** roughly at the center of the old town.

The old **clock tower** on Korzo dates from the 15th century, though it was later renovated in its current baroque style. At the northeast corner of the old town you will find the **Maritime and History Museum**—which has maritime, archaeological, and ethnographic displays—and the **Town Museum,** in a large 19th-century mansion, formerly the governor's palace.

Away From the Old Town: North of the old town there is a small park, **Park Vladimir Nazora,** where the **State Archives** are located in a suitably grand villa once owned by the brother of the Austrian emperor Franz Joseph I. Down on the **Riva** (waterfront) is the imposing building of the **Jadrolinija ferry** *(jadrolinija.hr),* which

Rijeka
- 141 B3
Visitor Information
- Korzo 14
- ☎ 051 335 882
tz-rijeka.hr

Church of St. Vitus
- Gravica 11

Church of the Blessed Virgin
- Trg Vele Crikve

Maritime & History Museum
- Muzejski Trg 1
- ☎ 051 213 578
- 🕐 Closed Sun.–Mon.
- 💲 $
ppmhp.hr

Rijeka Town Museum
- Muzejski Trg
- ☎ 051 336 711
- 💲 $ (Mon. free)
muzej-rijeka.hr

EXPERIENCE: Enjoy the Rijeka Carnival

The **Rijeka Carnival** *(ri-karneval.com.hr),* is held just before Lent each year. Take in as many of the events as suit your style. On Saturday, kick off the celebrations with the **Children's Carnival Parade.** But if you can make just one festivity, it should be the colorful culmination event, the **International Carnival Parade**—a huge (and hugely entertaining) event with up to 10,000 participants from up to 100 carnival groups. This is followed by the **burning of the Pust.** Satirically representing a government official, the Pust is paraded through the streets, publicly read its sins, and then taken from the harbor and burned at sea.

Crikvenica

◪ 141 B3

Visitor Information

✉ Trg Stjepana
Radića 1C

☎ 051 241 051

rivieracrikvenica.com

Novi Vinodolski

◪ 141 B2

Visitor Information

✉ Kralja Tomislava
6

☎ 051 791 171

tz-novi-vinodolski.hr

Cathedral of Sts. Philip and Jacob

☎ 051 244 205

Senj

◪ 141 C2

Visitor Information

✉ Stara Cesta br. 2

☎ 053 881 068

tz-senj.hr

connects the mainland with the islands, Split, and Dubrovnik.

To the northwest of the center is the suburb of **Trsat,** once the site of an Illyrian hill fort. A long flight of steps, called Trsatske Stube, leads up from Tito Square. The 13th-century **castle** here was once a stronghold of the Frankopans. It was bought in 1826 by Marshal Laval Nugent of Austria, who set about restoring it in its current ornate 19th-century style. The nearby **Sanctuary of Our Lady of Trsat,** where wood from the Virgin Mary's house in Nazareth is said to have rested on its journey to Loreto, is a major pilgrimage site.

Crikvenica & Novi Vinodolski

Southeast of Rijeka on the main coastal highway are the towns of Crikvenica and Novi Vinodolski, both of which are popular with local tourists. Juraj Julije Klović (also known as Julius Clovius, 1498–1578), Croatia's most

celebrated painter of miniatures and one of the greatest of the Italian High Renaissance, was born near Crikvenica.

In Novi Vinodolski, the 18th-century **Cathedral of Sts. Philip and Jacob** has carved wooden stalls from the 17th century, and there are also remains of a Frankopan castle. In addition, one of the oldest complete historic documents in Croatia, the Vinodol Statute (Vinodolski Zakon), was signed in Novi Vinodolski in 1288. The original is now in the National and University Library in Zagreb. The town's carnival—**Mesopust** as it is known locally—includes the Novljansko Kalo, a colorful folk dance that is performed over three days in late February.

Senj

Approximately 37 miles (60 km) southeast of Rijeka, Senj (not to be confused with Sinj, farther south) has a long and interesting history, and was for a long time one of the most important

The Uskoks of Senj

With the Ottomans advancing through the Balkans during the 16th century, displaced locals instigated a guerrilla war against the invaders. These Uskoks (Uskoci in Croatian, meaning "to jump in") were initially based at the fortress of Klis, near modern Split. When Klis finally fell to the Ottomans, many of them moved north to the port of Senj—where they settled with the blessing of the Austrian authorities, whose policy it was to establish a frontier of mercenaries across the Croatian and Bosnian hinterland as a bulwark against the Ottomans.

In Senj, the Uskoks turned to piracy, using small, fast boats to launch their notorious raids on Venetian as well as Ottoman shipping. (Austria, as Venice's trading rival, turned a blind eye.) Some Uskoks even served at the Battle of Lepanto (1571), at which the Ottoman fleet was spectacularly defeated. The raiders eventually provoked open war between Venice and Austria. However, one of the conditions of the eventual 1617 peace treaty was the end of the Uskoks. The leaders were executed, and the rest were exiled far inland.

INSIDER TIP:

Croatians pronounce the letter *j* as the *y* in yellow. Remember this when talking about a visit to Senj, Sinj, or Lošinj.

—TOM JACKSON
National Geographic contributor

ports on the northern Adriatic. The city was probably founded in the fifth century B.C. by a Celtic tribe, the Senones, and later became the Roman port of Senia. In contrast to much of the rest of the coast, it never submitted to Venice, though in the 16th century, the city passed to Austria. Around this time, Senj became the center of the Uskoks (see sidebar opposite). Following the disbanding of the Uskoks in 1617, the city went into a gradual decline, and it was badly bombed by the Allies in World War II.

Senj's cultural importance is exemplified by the fact that it had the earliest known Glagolitic printing press in Croatia, dating from 1493. It was also the birthplace of a large number of Croatian writers, including Vjenceslav Novak (1859–1905) and Milan Ogrizević (1877–1923).

Old Town: The 11th-century **Cathedral** at the center of the old quarter of Senj was remodeled in the 18th century. By chance, bombing during World War II revealed parts of the original facade. The late 14th-century **sarcophagus** of Ivan de Cardinalibus, Bishop of Senj, is inside. The oldest quarter of the town, **Gorica,** lies north of the Cathedral, enclosed by a section of the old city walls. Senj also has a number of Renaissance palaces.

The **Town Museum** has a good collection of material, ranging from archaeological fragments to flora and fauna from the nearby Velebit mountains. Part of a plate from Senj's famous 500-year-old printing press is also preserved here. Just beyond the southwestern edge of the old town (marked by another fortress tower) is **Senj Writers' Park** (Park Senjskih Knijizvenikal), with sculptures of the town's clutch of literary figures.

Above the Town: Above Senj Writers' Park on Trbušnjak Hill is the imposing **Nehaj Tower,** a 16th-century fortress built by one of the town's most famous sea captains, Ivan Lenković. With massive corner towers and 60-foot-high (18 m) crenellated walls, the fortress has more than 100 loopholes to rain down firepower on would-be attackers, and in its heyday housed 11 heavy cannon.

The fortress incorporates various bits of masonry from other buildings, including an inscription from a 13th-century monastery that is still visible in the walls of the ground floor.

The castle holds musical performances during the summer and commands exceptional views over the surrounding area. ■

Senj Cathedral
- ✉ Trg Cimiter, Senj

Senj Town Museum
- ✉ Milana Ogrizovića 5, Senj
- ☎ 053 881 141
- 🕐 Closed Sat.–Sun. Sept.–June
- 💲 $

Nehaj Tower
- ✉ Nehajeva bb, Senj
- ☎ 053 885 277
- 🕐 Closed Nov.–April
- 💲 $

tz-senj.hr/en /nehaj-tower

Opatija Riviera

The east coast of the Istrian Peninsula stretches down from the Austro-Hungarian resort of Opatija, backed by the steep Učka and Ćićarija Mountains. In the 19th century, the area became a haven for tourists from Austria seeking time by the sea. Tourism was aided by the completion of the railroad from Budapest to Rijeka in the late 1800s.

A view of a quiet bay on the Opatija Riviera from the forested hills above

Opatija

⛰ 141 B3

Visitor Information

✉ Vladimira Nazora 3

☎ 051 271 710

opatija-tourism.hr

Villa Angiolina

✉ Angiolina 1, Opatija

☎ 051 603 636

🕐 Closed Mon.

opatija-tourism.hr

Opatija

A Benedictine abbey (*abbazia* means "abbey" in Italian), built here in the 15th century, gave Opatija its name. The town was a quiet little place until the mid-19th century, when Iginio Scarpa, a wealthy Rijeka businessman, built the **Villa Angiolina,** after which Opatija was transformed into a fashionable health resort for Austrian high society. Tempered from the summer heat by the Učka Mountains, Opatija was immensely popular, drawing everyone from composer Gustav Mahler to author Vladimir Nabokov. Even Emperor Franz Joseph purchased a villa in nearby Volosko for his mistress.

Opatija has maintained something of its late 19th-century imperial air, making it a pleasant place to wander. The large Villa Angiolina still stands, amid its elaborately tended and exotic **gardens (Park Angiolina,** notable in particular for its camellias), and now houses the **Museum of Tourism** (Hrvatski Muzej Turizma), which documents the rise of tourism in Opatija and Croatia as a whole.

Nearby you will find the 19th century **Swiss House,** with various displays outlining the history of Opatija, the **Juraj Šporer Arts Pavilion** (Umjetnicki Paviljon "Juraj Matija Šporer"), and a large open-air theater.

The **Church of St. Jacob** (Sv. Jakov), on the waterfront, is the only part of the original Benedictine abbey to have survived, though later renovations have made its original form almost unrecognizable. It does, however, contain a copy of the famous "Pietà" by the great Croatian sculptor Ivan Meštrović (see sidebar p. 62). The **Church of Our Lady of the Annunciation,** built in neo-Romanesque style with a prominent green dome, dates from 1906.

One of the most beloved and recognizable symbols of Opatija is the "**Maiden With Seagull**" (see p. 149), a sculpture by Zvonko Car erected in 1956 on the waterfront on a promontory by the Juraj Šporer Arts Pavilion, replacing an earlier sculpture of the Madonna del Mare. There are several other interesting sculptures to look out for in Opatija, including one of Croatian author Miroslav Krleža (by Marija Ujević Galetović) and an old boatman (the work of Tatjana Kostanjević), both on the seaside promenade. Also on the waterfront, you'll find the **Hotel Jadran,** the oldest in Opatija, which was opened in 1884, complete with a beautiful crystal ballroom. Opatija remains a hugely popular resort in the summer, even now, a century after its heyday.

The Opatija Riviera waterfront promenade, or **Lungomare,** runs some 7.5 miles (12 km) from Volosko in the north to Lovran in the south. It makes for a lovely, easy walk, often shaded with trees, meandering around coves and passing small swimming spots, children's playgrounds, and grand architecture. It is the perfect way to fully appreciate the joys of the Opatija Riviera.

Church of St. Jacob
✉ Park Sv. Jakova 2

Volosko
Ⓜ 123 C3 & 139 B3

EXPERIENCE: Try a Culinary Tour or Workshop

If you want to learn more about the local cuisine, you can join one of the culinary workshops arranged by **Croatia Culinary Tours** (croatiaculinarytours.com), a Zagreb-based agency that also runs culinary tours of Kvarner and other areas throughout Croatia. As well as teaching cooking techniques for local dishes, workshops incorporate visits to local food markets and local cultural sights.

If you're traveling through Lovran in the spring or the summer, you certainly won't want to miss the local Asparagus and Cherry Festivals (held in April and June, respectively—see p. 149).

Volosko

Just north of Opatija is the attractive little fishing port of Volosko, which, before Opatija rocketed to fame as a tourist resort in the 19th century, was actually the district's main administrative center. It is now famous as one of the most highly rated gourmet enclaves in Croatia, with such top-notch restaurants as Plavi Podrum

Lovran

⚠ 141 A3

Visitor Information

✉ Šetalište Maršala Tita 63

☎ 051 291 740

tz-lovran.hr

Church of St. George

$ Free tours: Mon., Weds., & Fri., 7 p.m.–9:30 p.m., July–Aug.

(see Travelwise p. 294) clustered around the waterfront, and steps spilling down through arched passageways from the streets above.

Lovran

About 3.5 miles (6 km) south of Opatija is the pretty coastal town of Lovran, named after the laurel trees *(lovor)* that you will find growing in profusion on the surrounding slopes, along with chestnut, cherry, and other trees and an abundance of flowers. Lovran has been a popular resort since the late 19th century.

Some traces of the town's medieval fortifications remain, namely the **City Tower** and **Stubica,** one of the old city gates. Built in the 14th century and renovated in the 15th, the **Church of St. George** (Sv. Juraj) features a star-shaped vault modeled on the Church of St. Nicholas in Pazin

INSIDER TIP:

The "Maiden With Seagull" statue (on Opatija's waterfront) makes a fabulous photo on a clear, moonlit night—and it's even more dramatic on a stormy night.

—CHRISTOPHER AUGER-DOMÍNGUEZ
National Geographic International Editions photographer

(see p. 132) and frescoes from 1479 by two local artists, which include scenes from the life of Christ, the Last Judgment, and the Legend of St. George, the patron saint of Lovran. The **Church of the Fraternity of John the Baptist** (Crkva bratovština Sv. Ivana Krstiteglia), dating from the 14th century

---

EXPERIENCE: Take a Hike on Učka

While a road will take you all the way to the summit of Učka, it is much more rewarding to hike up the mountain from the small village of **Lovran** on the coast. The route involves around 4,500 feet (1,400 m) of ascent, starting from almost sea level, but the hike is fairly easy. The clearly marked trail passes through forest and the occasional meadow, to eventually reach the summit of Učka (a peak known as **Vojak**), with its large telecommunications tower and extensive views in all directions. Allow about four and a half hours for the climb, plus three hours for the descent. Make sure you carry a decent map as well as plenty of water

and suitable warm and waterproof clothing. A restaurant called Dopolavoro *(dopolavoro.hr)* is a 30-minute walk down the road on the far side of the summit. Bus service runs from Rijeka to the nearby mountain lodge (Poklon Dom) on Sundays.

For a more gentle hike, there's an easy, low-level path through the woods, known as the **Carmen Sylva Forest Path.** This 3-mile (5 km) forest promenade on Učka starts in Potok (Vrutki) and continues to Vela Fortica (Varljeni). Alternatively, you could follow the **Lungomare** (coastal promenade) stretching between Volosko, Opatija, and Lovran.

"Maiden With Seagull" on Opatija's Lungomare (waterfront) is known locally as the "Nymph."

and built on the foundations of an earlier church, also contains the last remaining fragments of a similar fresco cycle.

Lovran holds several popular annual food festivals *(tz-lovran.hr /english/calendar.html).* The **Asparagus Festival** runs for two weeks in April, culminating in an "Asparagus Feast" featuring a giant omelet. In June, the **Cherry Festival** celebrates the local cherry (called *brtosinska* by locals), and once again culminates in the preparation of an enormous dish, this time a giant strudel.

Lovran's longest running festival, however, is the **Marunada,** or Chestnut Festival, which has been held each year since 1973 and features a vast array of desserts and other dishes made with the local sweet chestnuts (*maruni* in the local tongue).

Regular buses pass through Lovran from Opatija and Rijeka.

South of Lovran the coast road continues to **Mošćenička Draga,** another pretty spot on this stretch of coastline, and the beautifully preserved little medieval village of **Brseč.**

Učka & Ćićarija

Rising steeply and dramatically above the coast on your right as you travel south are the forested mountains of Učka (4,596 feet/1,401 m) and Ćićarija, with a scattering of villages and some well-marked hiking trails on their slopes in **Učka Nature Park** (see sidebar opposite). The park has a dazzling variety of wildflowers, as well as brown bears and golden eagles, together with numerous other species of birds and animals. Caves in this area have been excavated and show traces of habitation as early as 12,000 B.C. The Učka tunnel cuts through the mountain between the coast and inland Istria, passing through the pleasing mountain village of **Veprinac.** The village is named for the wild boar *(vepar)* hunted in the surrounding mountains. The mountains also contribute to the Opatija Riviera's moderate climate—one of the reasons it gained popularity as a 19th-century health resort in the first place. ∎

Mošćenička Draga
🅰 141 A3
Visitor Information
✉ Aleja Slatina bb
☎ 051 739 166
tz-moscenicka.hr

Učka Nature Park
🅰 141 A3
✉ Liganj 42, Lovran
☎ 051 293 753
pp-ucka.hr

Gorski Kotar

The great arc of mountains that is Gorski Kotar stretches down from the Slovenian border to a point inland from Senj. There it merges into the even longer Velebit range (see pp. 180–181). More heavily forested than most of Croatia's southerly ranges, these mountains are the refuge of numerous unusual and rare species. Many of the region's remote villages are little touched by the advent of modern tourism.

Wild garlic (Allium ursinum) carpets the forest floor.

Delnice

🅰 141 B3

Visitor Information

✉ Lujzinska Cesta 47

☎ 051 812 156

tz-delnice.hr

Excellent for hiking, Gorski Kotar includes Risnjak National Park in the north and the wild limestone formations of the Bijele and Samarske cliffs farther south, an area that is known collectively as Velika Kapela. The mountains here are very cold during the winter months, with temperatures sometimes dropping as low as minus 11°F (-24°C).

Delnice

The gateway to Gorski Kotar is the mountain town of Delnice, strategically located on the railroad between Zagreb and Rijeka. Delnice was a center of Partisan resistance during World War II, and if you travel beyond the nearby village of **Mrkopalj,** on the unpaved road to the Bjelolasica and Samarske cliffs, you will pass 24 lonely stone slabs planted in a meadow. The stones commemorate two dozen Partisan fighters who froze to death in the area.

Risnjak National Park

Risnjak National Park covers an area of 25 square miles (64 sq km) in the north of Gorski Kotar. The peaks of **Risnjak** (5,013 feet/1,528 m) and **Snježnik** (4,938 feet/ 1,505 m) dominate the park, which is particularly beautiful and endowed with well-marked hiking trails and a scattering of mountain huts. Detailed local hiking maps are readily available.

The area is home to a small population of brown bears, gray wolves, and Eurasian lynx (see sidebar p. 153), though your chances of seeing these animals are extremely unlikely. You are more likely to spot red deer, roe deer, and chamois. The main access point to the park is just outside the village of **Crni Lug,** around 7.5 miles (12 km) from Delnice. Several trails radiate from the information center there. An alternative way in is from the village of **Gornje Jelenje,** from where it is a shorter walk up to Risnjak peak.

INSIDER TIP:

Local legend has it that witches gather on the summit of the great mountain Klek. The annual Witches' Festival in June in the nearby town of Ogulin is well worth a visit.

—BARBARA JACKSON
National Geographic contributor

Caves, Peaks, & Gorges

South of the Zagreb-Rijeka motorway lies the attractive mountain town of **Fužine,** which makes a pleasant stop if driving through Gorski Kotar. Just outside Fužine is the impressive **Vrelo Cave** and its 984-foot-long (300 m) interior festooned with stalactites and stalagmites. The cave—which was discovered accidentally in the 1950s—is sometimes flooded after heavy rain.

Food in this part of Croatia often makes use of local game—and frogs' legs—and there is a homemade cheese called *skripavac.*

The town of **Skrad,** northeast of Delnice toward the Slovenian

border, has a spectacular narrow gorge—in places just 7 feet (2 m) wide—appropriately known as **Vražji Prolaz** (Devil's Pass), which makes it worth a detour.

Ogulin: Lying on the eastern edge of Gorski Kotar, Ogulin is about 22 miles (35 km) southwest of Karlovac, on the Dobra River, and on the railroad to Zagreb and Rijeka.

Ogulin was the birthplace of Ivana Brlić-Mažuranić (1874–1938), Croatia's greatest writer of children's stories and fairy tales. She was nominated for the Nobel Prize in literature four times. There is an excellent new interpretation center about her work, **Ivanina Kuća Bajke** (Ivana's Fairytale House), with interactive displays and explanations in English. Kids in particular will love it. Ogulin celebrates its annual **Fairytale Festival** in June, with creative workshops, puppet shows, and storytelling.

Ogulin's imposing 16th-century castle is perched on the edge of **Đula's Abyss**—a steep gorge into which, according to local legend, a noblewoman (the eponymous Đula) threw herself when her love was slain in battle. The castle now houses the **Ogulin County Museum** *(tel 047 522 502, $).*

People also come to Ogulin to climb the mountain of **Klek** (3,878 feet/1,181 m). The north face has long lured local climbers. A mountain hut close to the summit is open on weekends throughout the summer. An easy trail (6 miles/9.5 km; 3.5 hours) leads out from the railway station. ∎

Risnjak National Park
🄰 141 B3
Visitor Information
✉ Bijela Vodica 48, Crni Lug
☎ 051 836 133
💲 $$
risnjak.hr

Fužine
🄰 141 B3
Visitor Information
✉ Sveti Križ 2
☎ 051 835 163
tz-fuzine.hr

Vrelo Cave
☎ 051 835 163
🕐 Closed Sat.–Sun. Oct.–May
💲 $

Skrad
🄰 141 C3
Visitor Information
✉ Goranska bb
☎ 051 810 316
tz-skrad.hr

Ogulin
🄰 141 C3
Visitor Information
✉ Aleksandra Kolić Puškarić
☎ 047 532 278
tz-grada-ogulina.hr

Ivanina Kuća Bajke
✉ Trg Hrvatskih Rodoljuba 2, Ogulin
☎ 047 525 398
💲 $
ivaninakucabajke.hr

Hiking in Risnjak National Park

The area around Risnjak and Snježnik, part of Risnjak National Park, is one of the best areas for hiking in Gorski Kotar (mountain district). A labyrinth of well-marked hiking trails crisscrosses the area, and the mountain hut below the summit of Risnjak makes a perfect base for exploring this part of the park.

Risnjak has hiking trails and climbing routes to suit all abilities.

NOT TO BE MISSED:

Views from Risnjak and Snježnik
• Lush mountains of beech forests
• The Horvatova Staza trail • Park's animals and rare flowers • A night in a mountain hut

Take one of the local buses from Delnice to the village of **Crni Lug,** for the start of the walk. From here continue on foot a short distance to the national park office at **Bijela Vodica ①**. Purchase park entry tickets and maps here, or later from one of the huts (*$$*). From park headquarters, proceed west through the forest, following a section of the circular trail called **Leska,** with a series of information boards (mostly in Croatian), then climb gradually around three hours along the stone-covered path to reach Medveđa Vrata, where the trail converges with another from Gornje Jelenje.

From here continue northwest an additional 30 minutes to the mountain hut, **PD Risnjak ②** (also known as Schlosserov Dom; *tel 051 836 133, open May–Nov, $$$$*), which sits perched on a saddle below the peak of the same name and makes a great place to stop for the night. During the winter, a small, unstaffed section of the hut remains open as a shelter.

From PD Risnjak, follow the trail, which climbs steeply through hardy dwarf mountain pine bushes up to the limestone crags at the summit of **Risnjak ③** (5,013 feet/1,528 m; 30 minutes). There you are rewarded by spectacular views out over the undulating green peaks of Gorski Kotar to the nearest part of the Adriatic Sea, the Kvarner Gulf.

After returning to the hut, descend west and bear left to a forest road, following signs to Snježnik and Platak, before ascending again to the rocky peak of **Snježnik** ❹ (4,938 feet/ 1,505 m; 2.5 hours from PD Risnjak). Return to PD Risnjak by the same route, or vary your return by heading northeast to the road at **Lazac,** then southeast toward PD Risnjak for a second night at the hut.

To vary your return to Bijela Vodica, descend east from the cabin, following a series of switchbacks, on a trail known as **Horvatova Staza,** named for the Croatian botanist Ivo Horvat. Pass the sinkhole known as **Vučja Jama,** then after crossing the forest road, bear right to arrive back in Bijela Vodica in about four hours. If you need to stay a night in Crni Lug, contact the park office *(tel 051 836 133),* where a few rooms are available. *(Camping in the park is strictly prohibited.)*

The best time of year for hiking in Risnjak is between June and September, when temperatures are warm, though cooler than on some of the mountains farther south. Winter hiking is also possible, though you must come suitably equipped for deep snowfields and freezing temperatures.

If you plan to explore the area further, make sure you pick up one of the detailed hiking maps of the area published by SMAND—"Sheet 14, Gorski Kotar IV" covers

Eurasian Lynx

Risnjak is named for the Eurasian lynx (*ris* in Croatian), which, after being hunted to the verge of extinction in the Balkans, has gradually been reintroduced into Croatia and Slovenia. The lynx is a magnificent animal, standing about 30 inches (75 cm) at the shoulder, with large paws and distinctive, tufted ears. Your chances of seeing one in the wild, however, are extremely slim; there are thought to be only 40 to 60 individuals in the whole of Croatia.

the whole area of this walk. You can purchase a copy (*$$*) at the park office in Bijela Vodica or from bookshops in Zagreb. There are numerous other trails in Risnjak and the surrounding area, with scope for trekking over several days.

🄼 See also area map p. 141
► Crni Lug
↔ 19 miles (30.5 km)
🕒 3 days
► Bijela Vodica

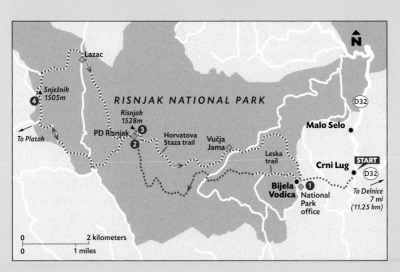

The Islands

Though perhaps less familiar to foreign visitors than some of the islands farther south in Dalmatia, the islands of the Kvarner Gulf are nevertheless some of the loveliest in the Croatian archipelago. With a fantastically rich cultural heritage and some truly gorgeous architecture, they are equally good as a leisure destination and boast some of the best beaches anywhere in Croatia.

At night, the central square of Rab town fills with alfresco diners.

Cres

141 B1–B3

Visitor Information

✉ Cons 10,
Cres town

☎ 051 571 535

tzg-cres.hr

Cres

The long, slender island of Cres is the second largest island in the Adriatic after Krk, and almost touches the neighboring island of Lošinj to the south, to which it is linked by a short road bridge. The highest point on Cres is **Gorice** (2,126 feet/ 648 m) in the north, which overlooks the steep cliffs on the island's eastern coast. The western coast, where most of the towns are, slopes more gently.

Cres has been inhabited since the Neolithic period, and the Illyrian Liburnians built a number of hill forts here. Of the two main settlements on the island in its early history, Osor (Apsoros, later Ossero) rather than Cres town (Crpesa) was the more important. Sacked by Attila the Hun in the fifth century, Osor grew in importance under Byzantium.

The island then became part of Tomislav's medieval kingdom of Croatia in 928, but it later sought

Venetian protection from pirates. Osor gradually lost its importance to Cres, which became the Venetian capital of the island in 1459. The islands formed part of the Kingdom of Italy in the 1920s and 1930s.

Cres Town: Situated on a natural harbor, Cres is the largest town on the island of Cres. Although you won't find a lot to see in the town itself, it is a lovely place to while away a few days. It is also well placed if you plan to take any day trips to Valun, Lubenice, Osor, Beli, and even across to Lošinj while you are in the region.

The **Church of Our Lady of the Snow** (Sv. Majka Božja Snježna) has a Renaissance doorway and a remarkable 15th-century carved wooden Pietà fresco inside. The tower dates from the 18th century. Other notable buildings include the **Church of St. Isodore** (Sv. Sidar), built in the 12th century; the 15th-century **Palača Petris,** which now houses the **Town Museum** *(Ribarska 7, tel 051 571 127);* a 15th-century loggia (covered gallery); and on the south side of town, a 14th-century **Franciscan monastery.**

Three of the old town gates survive: the **Bragadina Gate** (note the Lion of St. Mark), the **Marcela Gate,** and **Sv. Mikulo Gate,** along with a section of the old Venetian town walls (near the Bragadina Gate), and a tower located in the north of town.

Cres's ferries operate between Porozina (in the north of the island) and Brestova on the Istrian

coast, and Merag (on the east coast, near Cres town) and Valbiska on Krk. This is the route to Rijeka's airport (on Krk island) and the toll bridge to the mainland. There are also ferries to Zadar and Pula during the summer *(jadrolinija.hr/en/sailing-schedule).*

Valun: The quiet village of Valun lies in a deep bay in the south of Cres. It is celebrated as the site where the Valun Tablet was found. This 11th-century stone tablet (actually a tombstone), inscribed with

INSIDER TIP:

For a real taste of nature, explore the eco-trails that wind around Beli. The seven trails lead you through forests, abandoned villages, marshes, meadows, and labyrinths of stone.

—ALISON INCE
National Geographic contributor

both Glagolitic and Latin scripts, is one of the earliest Glagolitic inscriptions in Croatia and is now built into the wall of the **Church of St. Mark** *(A. Tentora 16, tel 051 571 255).*

Very few buses run to Valun—fewer than one a day—though you can walk from the junction on the Cres–Lošinj road, or even around the coast from Cres town. If driving, the last section of road

Cres Town

🔺 141 B2

Valun

🔺 141 B2

Lubenice
141 B2

Beli
141 B3

Osor
141 B2

Lošinj
141 B1

Visitor Information

✉ Riva Lošinjskih Kapetana 29, Mali Lošinj

☎ 051 231 884

tz-malilosinj.hr

down to the village is open only to pedestrians.

Lubenice: The tiny village of Lubenice sits perched spectacularly on a cliff on the western coast of Cres island, 2.5 miles (4 km) along the winding road past Valun. It is a lovely spot, all narrow cobbled streets and diminutive churches, and a path leads down to the sheltered bay below, with a good beach for swimming. North along the peninsula, beyond Lubenice, in an area called **Ekopark Pernat,** various trails lead to more remote villages.

Beli: In the north, perched near the wall of cliffs that make up this part of the island's east coast, is the village of Beli. The village is attractive enough, but an additional incentive to come here is to see the griffon vultures that nest on the cliffs nearby (see page opposite). There is also a network of hiking trails in the area.

Many visitors reach Beli by bus from Cres town (there are two a day). For the more energetic, there are marked trails from Porozina, or it is a 90-minute walk from Križić on the Cres–Porozina road.

Osor: IIn its heyday, Osor was the capital of the two islands of Cres and Lošinj, with a population topping 20,000 even during the Roman period. Its position on the narrow strait between the two islands—the main shipping route between Dalmatia and the northern Adriatic until

INSIDER TIP:

If you take an island boat tour to see the cliffside vulture nests at Beli, don't make too much noise. The birds may try to fly away, and the unfledged chicks might fall into the water and drown.

—LARRY PORGES
National Geographic Travel Books editor

the 15th century—gave the city great strategic importance. In decline since those days, Osor is now only a small village with a tiny population. It has the feel of an open-air museum. Traces of its former glory include the 15th-century **Cathedral,** a **bishop's palace,** and a **Town Hall** with a loggia. The latter now contains the **Town Museum** *(tel 051 233 892, $),* with various Roman and Illyrian finds from across the island. The **Town Square** has sculptures by Ivan Meštrović and others, alongside architectural fragments from the town's long history. Music is performed here in the summer.

Lošinj

The history of Lošinj follows that of Cres fairly closely, and it was only with the decline of Osor that it began to develop a separate identity, culminating in its importance as a major shipbuilding center during the 18th and 19th centuries under Austria-Hungary. Lošinj

EXPERIENCE: See Kvarner's Vultures & Dolphins

The Croatian islands can be a great place to see wildlife. The dramatic sea cliffs at Beli, on the island of Cres, are home to the magnificent griffon vulture. On boat trips run from Beli, you will see the birds soaring through the skies, and dolphins in the waters of the Croatian Adriatic. The Blue World Institute on the neighboring island of Lošinj runs an education center and initiated the Cres-Lošinj Marine Protected Area for the dolphins.

Griffon Vultures of Cres

These amazing birds of prey, which feed exclusively on carrion, boast an imposing wingspan of up to 9 feet (2.75 m). Heavyweights of the avian world, they weigh in at around 31 pounds (14 kg). Once fairly widespread throughout Croatia, they nested on the island of Rab and among the crags of Paklenica National Park, among other places. Sadly, the last birds in Paklenica were poisoned some years ago, and Beli is now the only place in Croatia where these creatures still nest.

It is thought that the number of nesting pairs is around 85, though these are threatened by a lack of carrion: A decrease in sheep farming has led to a dearth in sheep carcasses. Another problem is posed by tourist boats that come in too close to the cliffs, sometimes scaring young birds, which are still unable to fly and fall into the sea and drown.

The best way to arrange to see the birds is to contact the **Pansion Tramuntana** (beli-tramontana.com) in Beli, which has been at the forefront of promoting local sustainable tourism in the area for years.

A rare griffon vulture on the lookout for prey

Adriatic Dolphins

The Cres-Lošinj Marine Protected Area, the first dolphin sanctuary in the entire Mediterranean, is the brainchild of the **Blue World Institute of Marine Research and Conservation** (tel 051 604 666, blue-world.org, $). The scheme is one of several scientific, educational, and conservation projects that the organization runs from the islands of Lošinj and Vis. It opened the **Marine Education Centre** at Veli Lošinj in 2003, hosting educational workshops and lectures for different age groups.

The Blue World Institute carries out research on the ecology, genetics, acoustics, and habitats of bottlenose dolphins and other cetacean species of the Adriatic. It also runs an "adopt a dolphin" program and operates a turtle rescue center.

The annual Dolphin Day has a variety of activities for children (in several languages), including treasure hunts, arts and crafts workshops, and a storytelling workshop, all designed to encourage awareness of the marine environment and to promote conservation of the oceans among children.

Nezerine

 141 B1

**Franciscan
Monastery**

✉ Franjevacki
Samostan,
Nerezine

☎ 051 237 123

tz-malilosinj.hr

**Mali Lošinj
& Veli Lošinj**

 141 B1

Visitor Information

✉ Riva Lošinjskih
Kapetana 29

☎ 051 231 547

tz-malilosinj.hr

**Lošinj Aromatic
Garden**

✉ Bukovica 6

miomirisni-vrt.hr

**Church of St.
Antun**

✉ Trg Sv. Antun,
Veli Lošinj

☎ 051 237 123

eventually lost its importance to Rijeka and Trieste.

Though smaller than Cres, Lošinj attracts a disproportionately larger number of visitors than its neighbor. **Nerezine,** an old settlement (it is mentioned in the 14th century), is the first tourist destination, just 2.5 miles (4 km) south of the bridge to Osor on Cres. The **Franciscan monastery** there dates from the early 16th century.

Rising above Nerezine is the slender peak of **Osorščica** (1,929 feet/588 m), which can be approached by clear hiking trails from both Nerezine and the narrow strait opposite Osor. On the lower of the mountain's two peaks is the small **Chapel of St. Michael.**

Mali Lošinj & Veli Lošinj:

Despite its name (*mali* means "small"), Mali Lošinj is actually larger than Veli Lošinj (*veliki* means "large"), although in the past it was the other way around, as the names imply. Ferries and catamarans run from Mali Lošinj to Zadar. Buses arriving from Cres stop in Mali Lošinj before heading south to Veli Lošinj. It is also possible to walk between the two towns in less than an hour, an easy route following a pleasant coastal promenade.

Mali Lošinj has a scenic waterfront clustered with cafés and souvenir shops. On the edge of town, the fragrant **Lošinj Aromatic Garden,** where medicinal herbs are grown, can be visited. **Ćikat,** the lovely forested area to the south of town, has plenty of good hotels, 19th-century villas, and some great spots for swimming. The handsome **Church of St. Antun** in Veli Lošinj dates from the 18th century and has a number of paintings from the

Luxury yachts mingle with fishing boats and water taxis in the harbor at Mali Lošinj.

Venetian school in its interior.

On the other side of the harbor are the **Blue World Institute** (see p. 157) and the well-fortified *kula* (tower), built by Venice in 1455 as a defense against the Uskoks (see sidebar p. 144). The kula now houses the **Town Museum** *(Kaštel bb, tel 051 236 594, closed Mon., $).*

Rab

The island of Rab was inhabited by the Illyrian Liburnians, and later by the Romans, who knew it as Felix Arba. (*Felix* means "lucky"; even then Rab had its admirers.) The island is mentioned by both Pliny the Elder and Ptolemy. Rab passed from Roman to Byzantine possession, then following a brief period as part of the medieval kingdom of Croatia under King Tomislav, it came under the alternate control of Venice and Hungary. In 1409, however, the island was sold to Venice, along with much of the rest of the coast, by Ladislas of Naples (r. 1390–1414), the king of Hungary. Venetian rule was followed by successive periods under Austria and the French Emperor Napoleon. Both Italy and Germany occupied the island during World War II.

A long range of stony hills (called Kamenjak) on the eastern side of Rab shelters the western part of the island from the *bura* (the northeast wind), giving it a mild climate and a surprisingly green and fertile landscape. The east coast of the island provides excellent views across the **Velebit Channel** (Velebitski Kanal) to the Velebit range (see pp. 180–181).

Rab Town: One of the most attractive towns on the Adriatic, Rab Town has an old quarter that occupies a long, slender peninsula, sprouting four bell towers and giving the impression that it has changed very little in centuries. The earliest part of the town, called **Kaldenac,** is toward the southern tip of the peninsula and forms a warren of narrow, traffic-free streets and alleyways. The more northern

Susak & Unije

A string of small islands lies offshore from Lošinj. Two of the most attractive are Susak and Unije. The former is unusual for the Adriatic, being composed of sand and loess. Wines have long been produced in its fertile soil. Unije was settled by the Romans, but these days it is a quiet place with one town and no cars. Boat trips run to the islands from Mali Lošinj, and a catamaran connects them to Rijeka.

part of the old town, called **Varoš,** dates from a slightly later period, mostly from the 14th through the 17th century. West from Varoš are the large, **landscaped gardens** of Komrčar, laid out in the 19th century, while the modern town, **Gradska Luka,** spreads out around the north side of the harbor.

Kaldenac: The old town's main entrance is on **St. Christopher's**

Rab

⛰ 141 B2

Visitor Information

✉ Trg Municipium Arba 8, Rab town

☎ 051 724 064

tzg-rab.hr

Square (Trg Sv. Kristofora), which leads onto **Srednja Ulica,** the main shopping street, which runs down toward Kaldenac. Walking along Srednja Ulica, you'll pass the well-preserved **Palača Dominis,** an imposing palace with Gothic windows and a carved Renaissance portal, above which you can still see the family crest. Farther along is a **loggia,** which dates to 1509.

INSIDER TIP:

For the quintessential view of Rab, with all four of its graceful bell towers, walk up to the old town's fortifications near St. Christopher's Church.

—CHRISTOPHER AUGER-
DOMÍNGUEZ
*National Geographic
International Editions photographer*

The most impressive building in Rab is the Romanesque **Cathedral of St. Mary,** near the end of the peninsula. You enter the building, which dates from 1177, through a late 15th-century doorway, above which is a Pietà fresco dating from 1514. Inside are choir stalls carved from walnut dating from 1445 and a hexagonal ciborium, which includes three very early columns (perhaps from the ninth century) with beautiful carving. Though still called a cathedral, it has been a church since 1828. The cathedral's museum includes a silver reliquary, purported to contain the head of St. Christopher, the patron saint of travelers.

Opposite (and separate from) the cathedral is the beautiful 13th-century Romanesque **bell tower,** one of the finest of its kind in Croatia. It rises some 92 feet (28 m) over several stories, each story pierced by an increasing number of apertures, from one at the bottom to five at the top, bathing the tower's interior with light. In an interesting turn of fate, 19th-century English architect T. G. Jackson modeled the upper portion of the cathedral bell tower in Zadar (which had been left unfinished since the 15th century) on Rab's cathedral bell tower. You can climb the stairs inside the bell tower for fine views of the town.

Just beyond the cathedral, at the very tip of the peninsula, is the **Franciscan Church and Nunnery of St. Anthony,** originally built in the 14th century. Next to this complex is a small park with a statue of San Marino, a 14th-century Bishop of Rab. Marino was made a saint after he was deemed responsible for the miraculous breaking of a Norman siege of the town in 1358.

Heading north from the cathedral, along Ivana Rabljanina, brings you to the 11th-century **Benedictine Church and Monastery of St. Andrew,** where you will find Rab's oldest bell tower, a comparatively small Romanesque structure dating from 1181. The church was largely renovated in the 16th century. The polyptych (painted panels) by 15th-century Venetian painter Bartolomeo Vivarini is actually a copy, with the original now part of the collection at the Boston Museum of Fine Arts.

Varoš: Heading into Varoš, beyond St. Andrew's, is **Freedom Square** (Trg Slobode), where a single tree (a holm oak) planted in 1921 commemorates the liberation of the town from Italian occupation after World War I. Two palaces face onto the square, and another bell tower once stood near here, named for St. Stephen.

Continuing onto Gornja Ulica from Freedom Square, you arrive at the baroque **Church of St. Justine,** built in the 16th century, its bell tower capped by a distinctive, bulbous spire. The adjacent monastery was pulled down in the 19th century. Farther along Gornja Ulica is the small **Church of the Holy Cross** (Sv. Križ), built on the site of an earlier church, with its late 18th-century stuccoed ceiling.

Just after the Church of the Holy Cross you come to the ruins of the **Church and Monastery of St. John,** probably built in the 11th century on the site of an even earlier fifth-century church. Mosaics and an early stone reliquary found here are now in the **Bishop's Palace.** The Romanesque bell tower provides great views back across Kaldenac and the town's three other bell towers.

A little farther still you will find **St. Christopher's Church** (which now houses a collection of stone monuments from around town) and part of the old town **fortifications,** from where you have fine views of all four bell towers.

On the far (northern) side of the Komrčar gardens are the small **Church of St. Francis** and ruins of the adjacent **Franciscan monastery,** pulled down in the 19th century and replaced with a cemetery. The church dates from 1490, and its floor has an interesting array of carved tombstones of prominent local figures. Note, for example, the tombstone of a shipbuilder, decorated with the various tools of his trade.

Bay of St. Euphemija: Northwest from Rab town is the Bay of St. Euphemija, at the far end of which is the attractive **Franciscan Monastery of St. Euphemija,** built in 1446. Beyond this is the huge forested **Kalifron Peninsula,** covered by a network of hiking and

Franciscan Monastery of St. Euphemija

✉ Kamporska Draga, Rab

Rab Medieval Crossbow Tournament

If you're in Rab town on July 27 (St. Christopher's Day), don't miss the Medieval Crossbow Tournament, which takes place on St. Christopher's Square (Christopher is the town's patron saint). Dating back to the 14th century, the tournament commemorates the successful defense of the city against a siege in 1358 and is one of only two such tournaments in the world using the large, heavy medieval crossbow. The colorful tournament was revived by the Rab Crossbowmen's Association in 1995 and is also held on May 9, June 25, and August 15.

Memorial Cemetery

✉ Kamporska Draga, Rab

Lopar

🛆 141 B2–B3

Visitor Information

✉ Lopar bb

☎ 051 775 508

lopar.com

Krk

🛆 141 B2–B3

Visitor Information

✉ Trg Sv. Kvirina 1, Krk town

☎ 051 221 359

krk.hr

Krk Town

🛆 141 B2

Visitor Information

✉ Vela Placa 1

☎ 051 221 414

tz-krk.hr

Cathedral

✉ Ulica Antuna Mahnica, Krk town

biking trails. North of Kalifron is **Memorial Cemetery,** built on the site of an Italian World War II concentration camp. The island's most famous beaches are near **Lopar.**

Rab's main **ferry terminals** are at Lopar, in the north of the island, which has services to Krk. Ferries also run from Mišnjak in the south to the mainland.

INSIDER TIP:

For the best hiking on the Croatian islands, head for the network of well-marked trails around Baška [see pp. 164–165]. They range from easy to demanding, with breathtaking views.

—IVANA JOVIĆ ABRAHAM
Croatian translator

Krk

The largest island in the Croatian Adriatic, Krk covers an area of just over 158 square miles (410 sq km). Named Cyractica by the Greek philosopher Strabo, called Vecla during the later Byzantine era, and then Veglia by Venetian rulers, Krk had also been settled by the Romans. (Julius Caesar is thought to have had a base on Krk.) The island's later history was for many years associated with the Frankopan family, who effectively ruled the island as feudal lords under a nominal Venetian suzerainty until 1480, when Venice placed the island under its own direct rule. Krk was another important center of Glagolitic learning, and a bastion of the Glagolitic liturgy until well into the 19th century.

Connected to the mainland by a mile-long (1.6 km) toll bridge since 1980, and with Rijeka's airport actually on the island itself, it is also enormously popular for diving and ruins, so book accommodation in advance. Ferries run from Valbiska to the island of Cres.

Krk Old Town: Although the modern town of Krk (Roman Curicum) is large and steadily growing, the old town itself is actually fairly small and quite well preserved.

The Romanesque **cathedral** was built in the late 12th century on the site of a 5th-century church and some Roman baths. The interior has arches supported by reused Roman columns, as well as columns from the earlier church, though the capitals were carved specifically for the cathedral. One of the columns, an anomaly, has a beautifully carved Romanesque capital with two birds eating a fish, an early Christian symbol for the Eucharist. There is also a 17th-century carved wooden pulpit and, in the floor, a 14th-century memorial to the founder, Bishop John. The early 15th-century Chapel of St. Vitus (off the north aisle) is dedicated to the ruling Frankopan family, whose coat of arms is clearly visible among the elaborate vaulting. Mosaics from the former Roman baths have been found below the floor of one of the other side chapels.

A scuba diver explores one of several old wrecks in the waters around the island of Krk.

Across the vaulted passage from the cathedral is the unusual 11th-century **Church of St. Quirinus** (Sv. Kvirina, the patron saint of Krk), which was built on two levels. On the lower level, piers support heavily ribbed vaulting. On the upper level, which you can access from the bell tower, arcades are supported by plain columns. Also unusual is the building's north–south orientation, instead of the more conventional east–west. Used as a wine cellar for many years, the lower story was restored in the 1960s.

The **bell tower,** shared by the cathedral and St. Quirinus, is one of the town's most recognizable landmarks. The 16th-century structure is capped by a rather incongruous superstructure and a bulbous, onion-shaped dome supports an angel, added in the 18th century.

To the east of the cathedral is the square known as **Kamplin,** where you can explore a large section of the old town's **fortifications,** the earliest part of which is the squarish tower dated to 1191. You will also find a well-preserved section of the **town walls** standing to the west of the cathedral, between Obala Hrvatske Mornarice and Vela Placa.

Near Vela Placa, there was another **Roman bath,** and you can see some well-preserved mosaics here from the first century A.D. depicting the god Triton surrounded by dolphins and other sea creatures. On the opposite (northern) side of the old town, on **Trg Krckih Glagoljaša,** is the 12th-century Romanesque **Church of Our Lady of Health**

Church of Our Lady of Health

✉ Trg Krckih Glagoljasa, Krk town

Church of St. Francis

✉ Trg Krckih Glagoljasa 2, Krk town

Punat

⛰ 141 B2

Visitor Information

✉ Pod Topol 2

☎ 051 854 860

tzpunat.hr

Baška

⛰ 141 B2

Visitor Information

✉ Kralja Zvonimira 114

☎ 051 856 817

tz-baska.hr

(Majka Božje od Zdravlja). Like the cathedral, it has reused capitals in the interior, one of which is carved with an eagle attacking a lizard. The building was much restored in the 18th century.

Nearby, the 14th-century **Church of St. Francis** (Sv. Franjo) has corbels (supports) carved in the shape of human heads in one of the chapels and 19th-century Viennese stained-glass windows. Among the tombstones on the floor is a memorial to the captain of a ship at the Battle of Lepanto, in which the mighty Ottoman fleet was destroyed in 1571.

Buses run from Krk town to Rijeka, stopping at several other points in between before continuing to Punat and Baška to the southeast. There are also regular ferries between Baška and Lopar (on Rab) and Merag (on Cres).

East to Punat: Heading east from Krk town toward Kornić and Punat, along the large, sheltered inlet on Krk island's south coast, stands the church of **St. Donat** (Sv. Dunat)—a tiny pre-Romanesque building, badly damaged, but with the remains

of a Byzantine-style dome. The village of **Punat** lies farther around the far side of the bay, southeast of Krk town.

In the middle of the bay, opposite Punat, is the partially forested island of **Košljun,** with a 16th-century **Franciscan Monastery** *(tel 051 854 017, kosljun.hr),* built on the remains of an earlier Benedictine structure. The museum has an ethnographic collection, including local folk costumes, and the monastery also boasts a huge library of rare books and manuscripts. Water taxis to the islands depart from the waterfront in Punat; you can also get a boat directly from Krk.

South to Baška: The town of **Baška,** at the southern end of Krk, is the island's most popular resort and the site where one of Croatia's greatest cultural treasures was discovered. Inhabited by the Illyrian Iapodes people and then the Romans, the town (or at least Castelum Besca, the castle on this site) is first mentioned in 1232.

Baška's main attraction for many visitors is its long pebble beach (often described

---

Baška Tablet & Glagolitic Script

The Baška Tablet (Baščanska Ploča) is a slab of white limestone, some 7 feet (2 m) wide with a border of vine leaves along its upper edge, bearing one of the earliest inscriptions in the Croatian language written in the Glagolitic script. It was found in 1851, in the floor of the small Church of St. Lucy (Sv. Lucija) in Jurandvor, near Baška, by Petar Dorčić, the local priest.

Dating from the late 11th century, the 13-line inscription clearly documents a donation of land to the Church and Monastery of St. Lucy by Croatian king Zvonimir (r. 1075–1089). The version on display in the church is actually a copy; the original, which took many years to decipher, is now in the atrium of the Academy of Sciences and Arts building in Zagreb (see p. 77).

misleadingly as sandy), the 1.1-mile-long (1.8 km) **Vela Plaža.** Vela Plaža can become fairly crowded, but there are other beaches nearby.

Above the town, the **Church of St. John the Baptist** (built in the 11th century but restored last in the 19th) contains the oldest church bell in the area, dating from 1431. Among the paintings in the 18th-century **Church of the Holy Trinity** is a Holy Trinity by Venetian artist Palma the Younger (1548–1628). The church also contains a small but interesting **Folk Museum.**

Just inland from Baška is the village of **Jurandvor,** noteworthy for little apart from the small **Church of St. Lucy** (Sv. Lucija), famous as the site where the 107-word **Baška Tablet** (see sidebar opposite) was discovered. The church dates to the 11th century and was at one time

attached to a Benedictine abbey.

Vrbnik: The town of Vrbnik overlooks the mainland from the east coast of Krk, with good views of the Velika Kapela (Great Chapel) Mountains. Part of Gorski Kotar, this range includes the Klek peak (see p. 151). Turning to the south, you can see Sjeverni (Northern) Velebit, the beginning of Croatia's greatest mountain range (see pp. 180–181).

Vrbnik's 15th-century **Church of St. Mary** has a bell tower dating from the early 16th century, which, like the cathedral in Krk, has an incongruous, bulbous spire added at a later date. The **Dinko Vitezi Library** has a collection of rare manuscripts, including one of only two copies of Johann David Kochler's Atlas (1612), and several illuminated Glagolitic missals from the 15th century. ■

Folk Museum

✉ Ulica Kralja Zvonimira 28, Baška

Vrbnik

🅰 141 B2

Visitor Information

✉ Placa Vrbničkog Statuta 4

☎ 051 857 479

vrbnik.hr

The Romanesque church of St. Lucy, Jurandvor, where the Baška Tablet was discovered

Evocative islands and Croatia's finest mountain range, as well as some of the best medieval towns in the country

Northern Dalmatia

Sea kayaking at sunset near an island in northern Dalmatia

Northern Dalmatia

Stretching south from Kvarner Gulf, northern Dalmatia includes one of Croatia's most important historic centers, the city of Zadar, as well as national parks covering both mountains and islands. The region also has world-famous architecture, not least the cathedral in Šibenik.

Northern Dalmatia holds a key position in Croatian history. From the 9th through the 11th century, the kings of medieval Croatia had their seat in the cities of Zadar, Nin, and Biograd na Moru. Before and after this period, the historical fortunes of northern Dalmatia mirror those of much of the rest of the Adriatic coast. Settled by Illyrians, Greeks, and Romans, the region has Roman remains in several places, including Zadar and Burnam, near the Krka River. Later, the area fell under the control of Venice, Austria, and, for a spell, the Kingdom of Italy.

The largest city in northern Dalmatia,

Zadar has a beautiful historic center with some fascinating architecture, most especially the distinctive Church of St. Donatus. And with far fewer visitors than Split farther south, it is simply a wonderfully relaxed place to wander. Beyond the city's stone-paved, café-lined streets, churches, and fragmentary Roman ruins lies a broad waterfront promenade, where the ingenious Sea Organ blows watery notes with the softly lapping waves of the Adriatic. Zadar was sacked during the Fourth Crusade, and soon after by the Mongols—something to bear in mind when standing under its massive defensive walls. German and Italian occupation during World War II was accompanied by heavy Allied bombing, and the city and surrounding region suffered heavily during the war in the 1990s. The nearby town of Nin, now a small and sleepy place, has a tiny but quite wonderful ninth-century church.

In the town of Šibenik, to the south of Zadar, the magnificent cathedral is another UNESCO World Heritage site and one of the finest Renaissance buildings in Croatia. Made entirely of stone, the building (and particularly its barrel vaulting) is an astounding feat of engineering.

Velebit Mountains & the Offshore Islands

This stretch of the Dalmatian coast is backed by the Velebit mountain range—the most extensive and impressive range in Croatia, home to brown bears, spectacular karst scenery, and some of the finest hiking opportunities to be found anywhere

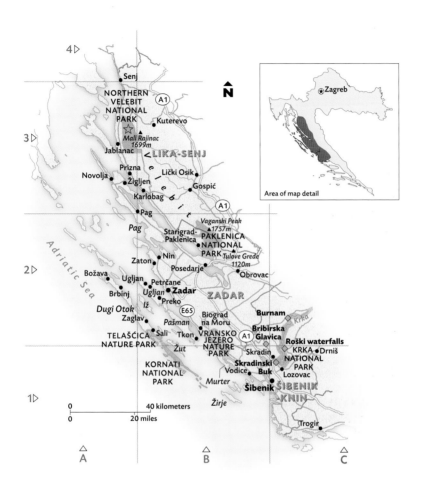

4▷

Senj

NORTHERN
VELEBIT (A1)
NATIONAL
PARK •Kuterevo

3▷ ☆
Mali Rajinac
1699m
Jablanac ◁LIKA-SENJ

Prizna e •Lički Osik
Novolja •Žigljen
•Gospić
Karlobag

•Pag

Pag *Vaganski Peak*
▲1757m
Starigrad- PAKLENICA
Paklenica •NATIONAL
PARK *Tulove Grede*
Zaton •Nin *1120m*
Posedarje
2▷ •Obrovac
Božava
Ugljan •Petrčane
Brbinj Ugljan •Zadar ZADAR
Iž •Preko
Dugi Otok (E65) Biograd Burnam
Zaglav na Moru
Pašman Bribirska
TELAŠĆICA •Sali Tkon VRANSKO (A1) Glavica
NATURE PARK JEZERO Roški waterfalls
Žut NATURE ◇ KRKA •Drniš
PARK Skradin KRKA
KORNATI Skradinski◇ NATIONAL
NATIONAL Vodice• Buk PARK
PARK Murter Lozovac
Šibenik ŠIBENIK
1▷ *Žirje* -KNIN

0 40 kilometers
0 20 miles •Trogir

△ △ △
A B C

↑N

Zagreb

Area of map detail

in Croatia. Velebit forms part of the Dinaric Alps, beginning in the Gorski Kotar region farther north (see pp. 150–151) and continuing south all the way to Montenegro. Velebit includes two national parks, the beautiful Northern (Sjeverni) Velebit and, farther south, Paklenica with its dramatic twin gorges. The gorge and waterfalls of the Krka River north of Šibenik constitute another national park, where the river tumbles down travertine steps. Between Zadar and Šibenik lies Vrana Lake, an important wetland area and Croatia's largest freshwater lake.

Offshore from Velebit is the long, slender island of Pag, a harsh, desiccated landscape famous for its firm cheese (*Paški sir*), salt pans (which have been here since Roman times), and exquisitely intricate handmade lace. The center of Pag is a beautifully preserved medieval town, while nearby Novalja becomes the clubbing capital of Croatia during the summer. Farther south, Zadar is surrounded by the densely populated Ugljan and Pašman islands, and farther offshore lies the Kornati archipelago, a place of remote, high sea cliffs, rugged bays, and crystal clear waters. ∎

Zadar & Around

Though it sees slightly fewer foreign visitors than central Dalmatia, northern Dalmatia still holds many wonderful sights for travelers wishing to leave the tourist hubs. Beyond the laid-back bustle of historic Zadar, visitors can find some of the most spectacular scenery anywhere in Croatia, from the rocky heights of the Velebit mountain range to the maze of rugged coves and bays of the Kornati archipelago.

Life runs at walking pace in Zadar's old town.

Zadar

🅰 169 B2

Visitor Information

✉ Zadar County
    Tourist Board,
    Ilije Smiljanića 5

☎ 023 212 222

visitzadar.net

Zadar's History

The most important city in northern Dalmatia, Zadar has a long and fascinating history. The city occupies a peninsula on the edge of the Ravni Kotari region, with a sheltered natural harbor behind. Zadar's old town contains a wealth of architectural monuments. In spite of this, the city sees a fraction of the number of visitors in Split or Dubrovnik, and it is a favorite "discovery" of more wide-ranging visitors.

A stronghold of the Illyrian Liburnians from around the ninth century B.C. The first recorded mention of Zadar is in the fourth century B.C. as the Greek city of Idassa. It became Roman Jadera in 59 B.C. and was the main city in Byzantine Dalmatia from A.D. 752 before becoming part of Hungary in the early 12th century.

Following this period, Zadar alternately belonged to Venice and Hungary. While in the hands of Hungary, the city was sacked, at Venetian instigation, during the infamous Fourth Crusade of 1202. Not long after, Zadar was struck again by the Mongol hordes sweeping in from Asia. Finally, the city was sold to Venice in 1409, along with much of the rest of the coast. It was the main Venetian city in Dalmatia until it passed to Austria in 1797. It then became part of the Kingdom of Italy following World War I, and was the center of Italian operations on the coast during World War II. As a result, Zadar was heavily bombed by the Allies, until it become part of Tito's Yugoslavia.

INSIDER TIP:

Zadar is one of the most attractive, and least busy, historic cities on the Dalmatian coast. Don't miss the ingenious Sea Organ or sampling a delicious ice cream in the old town.

—HRVOJE PRCIC
*National Geographic Croatia
Editor in Chief*

Zadar and the surrounding area suffered heavily during the Homeland War, and photographs from this time show its streets filled with antitank mines. Today, Zadar is gradually gaining popularity as a tourist destination, drawing history enthusiasts along with a younger crowd arriving for the Garden Festival *(thegardenfestival .eu)*, an enormous music festival held in July in the nearby village of Petrčane.

Zadar's most famous son is arguably Petar Zoranić, the great Renaissance writer who was born here in 1508. (Some may see Croatian soccer star Luka Modrić, born in a village nearby, as an equally eligible candidate.) Fifteenth-century sculptor Juraj Dalmatinac, responsible for the outstanding cathedral in Šibenik, was also born in Zadar.

The Old Town & Beyond

Most of the sights worth seeing in Zadar are found in the Old Town. Entering through the gate in the old town's stout defensive **walls** from the footbridge over the marina (Luka Jazine) brings you to pleasant, café-filled **People's Square** (Narodni Trg), an unbeatable spot to sit and watch the world go by over a cup of coffee, before or after exploring the town. The **Loggia**, on the southeast side of the square, dates from the 16th century and now houses various exhibitions.

Across the square stands the **Town Hall,** built by the Italians in the 1930s. The **clock tower** dates from the late 18th century. On the northern corner of the square you will find the tiny, 11th-century **Church of St. Lawrence** (Sv. Lovro), with Roman and pre-Romanesque capitals on its columns. The large, bustling open-air **market** in the mornings, just to the north of People's Square, is easily reached from the side street on the right as you head to the square from the walls.

Cathedral of St. Anastasia:

Široka Ulica, usually referred to by locals as Kalalarga, leads off People's Square to the right (northwest). This is Zadar's main, pedestrianized thoroughfare. Follow it past the ruins of the Roman forum (see p. 172) to the **Cathedral of St. Anastasia** (Sv. Stošija), Dalmatia's largest Romanesque cathedral.

Built in the 13th century on the foundations of an earlier building—a cathedral is mentioned on the site as early as the 10th century—and rededicated in 1285, the cathedral was damaged when the Crusaders sacked Zadar in 1202. The building was also badly

Cathedral of St. Anastasia

✉ Trg Svete Stošije

damaged by Allied bombing during World War II, along with more than half of the old town. Despite this, the cathedral has been beautifully restored.

The upper portion of the facade has two circular **wheel windows** placed one above the other, as well as rows of **blind arcades** (one of which continues along the north wall), giving it an appearance similar to the cathedral in Pisa, Italy. The three entrance portals have beautiful **carvings,** including a Virgin and Child flanked by St. Anastasia and St. Chrysogonus above the main portal and, to either side, four lesser saints, which appear to be from an earlier date.

The cathedral interior includes a ninth-century **sarcophagus** containing the relics of St. Anastasia (the patron saint of widows), 15th-century **stalls** in the choir, and a 14th-century **ciborium** (ornate canopy over the altar) that is higher than the one in St. Mark's in Venice. Among the **columns** are some of Roman origin at the east end, and some with spiral fluting and pre-Romanesque capitals near the west door.

The lower section of the **bell tower** (actually around the corner on the forum) dates from the 15th century. The upper portion of the tower, however, was not built until the late 19th century, following a design by English architect T. G. Jackson, who modeled it on the famous bell tower that stands on the island of Rab (see p. 160).

Roman District: The Roman **forum** (the town square and marketplace of a Roman city) runs roughly east–west from just behind the cathedral, parallel with Kalalarga and originally measuring 311 feet (95 m) long by 147 feet (45 m) wide. Little now remains of the Roman buildings apart from a single **column;** look for the griffon at the top and the small plaque near its base, both dating from the ninth century, when the column was probably used as a pillory for petty criminals.

The forum remains a suitably atmospheric place, littered with pieces of columns and cracked sarcophagi. A large **temple** once stood at the far (western) end.

On the right (north side) as you enter the forum from Kalalarga is the **Church of**

EXPERIENCE:
View Zadar's Sunset

Alfred Hitchcock, one of Hollywood's iconic directors, declared that the sunset from Zadar's waterfront was better than any he had seen during his years in California. These days the favored spot for sunset-watching is the **"Greetings to the Sun"** installation on the waterfront, which flickers and pulses with its own emotive light show. A sunset shows on many an evening, of course, but in July you can join thousands of local people who switch off the city's electric lights and gather with candles at dusk to watch the celebrated sunset in the clear skies of high summer. Another of Hitchcock's fond memories of Zadar was the local cherry brandy, an exquisitely sweet (but also strong) liqueur called maraschino.

St. Donatus (Sv. Donat), a tall (88 feet/27 m), circular construction that must be counted as one of the most striking buildings in Dalmatia. Work began on the church (originally called the Church of the Holy Trinity) in the 9th century, perhaps under the direction of the local Bishop Donat, soon to be canonized and with whose name the church has been associated since around the 15th century. Built into the sturdy walls are numerous fragments of earlier buildings, including pillars and even the altars from two long-gone Roman temples near the main entrance.

In later centuries, the Austrians used the church as an ammunition store, and following this it housed a lapidary collection—the stonework you now see scattered around the forum itself. Today it is a venue for evening concerts during the summer months.

Opposite the church, on the corner of Kalalarga, is Zadar's celebrated **Archaeological Museum** (Arheološki Muzej). Founded in 1832, the museum houses an outstanding collection dating from the Late Stone Age (around 10,000 B.C.) to the medieval period, including two beautifully carved stone friezes from the 11th-century **Church of St. Dominica** (Sv. Nedelja), which is no longer standing, and artifacts from the nearby town of Nin (see pp. 176–177). The museum also puts on temporary exhibitions at the church.

South of the Archaeological Museum is the 11th-century **Church of St. Mary** (Sv. Marija),

Locally produced laces are on sale in Zadar's Roman forum outside the Church of St. Mary.

which once formed part of a Benedictine nunnery founded by a noblewoman from Zadar named Čika. The church facade and doorway date from the 16th century. Next door to the church, the former nunnery now houses Zadar's **Museum of Church Art,** containing a wealth of reliquaries in gold and silver from Zadar and the surrounding region, along with various manuscripts, sculpture, and embroidery. The elegant Romanesque **bell tower** dates

Archaeological Museum

✉ Trg Opatice Cike 1

☎ 023 250 516

💲 $

amzd.hr

Museum of Church Art

✉ Trg Opatice Cike 1

☎ 023 250 496

🕐 Closed Sun.

from 1205, making it one of the oldest surviving bell towers of this size in Dalmatia, with only minor restoration work from the 1400s.

The Waterfront: South of the forum you will find **Obala Kralja Petra Krešimira IV,** the town's balmy *riva*–waterfront promenade–perfect for a late afternoon stroll after a delicious seafood lunch. Toward the northwestern end you will find Zadar's **Sea Organ** (Morske Orgulje). Completed in 2005, this curious stepped construction is a great spot in which to sit in the sun and watch the boat traffic, and it will provide its own sound track to the scene! Beneath the marble steps are several pipes of varying widths

and angles. The motion of the water up and down inside the pipes pushes on the air farther up, creating harmonious hums with a tempo set by the motion of the waves. Farther along at the end of the peninsula is another recent art installation, **"Greeting to the Sun,"** a large circle composed of some 300 lights topped with colored glass, all powered by solar panels.

Also toward the northwestern end of the waterfront is the **Franciscan monastery,** purportedly founded by St. Francis of Assisi himself. Although originally built in the 13th century in early Gothic style, the monastery that the visitor sees today dates mostly from restorations made in the 18th century.

Relaxing at the Sea Organ on Zadar's waterfront

Medieval Monuments:

Heading north from the Franciscan monastery on Božidara Petranovića brings you to **Three Wells Square** (Trg Tri Bunari). Just north of the square is the old **Chain Gate** (Lančana Vrata), from which a massive defensive chain was strung across the harbor in the medieval period, and the 18th-century **Arsenal,** these days a place of shops and concerts. Turn right (east) from here to find the remains of a Roman **Triumphal Arch,** which gives access to the marina.

Turning right (south) from here brings you to the **Church of St. Chrysogonus** (Sv. Krševan, one of the city's patron saints). The church, which once formed part of an early tenth-century Benedictine monastery (one of the earliest anywhere in Croatia), was consecrated in its present form in 1175. The plain western facade contrasts strongly with the elaborately decorated south wall, with its shallow arcades and spiral columns, and the central apse with its semicircular colonnade. The Romanesque frescoes of the interior have been restored. The tower, of which only the lower portion was completed, dates from the 16th century.

East of People's Square, Kalalarga becomes Ulica E. Kotromanić, leading onto Simeon Square (Trg Šime Bundića), the site of the 17th-century **Church of St. Simeon** (Sv. Šimun), renovated from an earlier building. Inside is the impressive **silver sarcophagus** of St. Simeon,

INSIDER TIP:

As darkness falls, head to the far end of Zadar's seaside promenade. The "Greeting to the Sun" art installation will be waking up, creating a swirling colored light show for passing strollers.

—TOM JACKSON
National Geographic contributor

dating from 1377–1380 and commissioned by local nobles at the request of the ruling family of Croatia-Hungary. The sarcophagus is the work of a Milanese goldsmith, Francesco di Antonio da Sesto, together with local craftsmen, including Andrija Markov of Zagreb. Its elaborate decorative panels include scenes such as the discovery of the body of St. Simeon and the boat that is said to have brought the saint's body to Zadar in the 13th century, as well as figures from the Croatian-Hungarian royal families. For example, Queen Elizabeth of Bosnia, wife of King Ludovik of Hungary, is shown handing a casket to St. Simeon on the reverse side.

Turning right (south) from St. Simeon's takes you across another square, **Five Wells Square** (Trg Pet Bunara), named after the five ornamental wellheads that once supplied the town with drinking water, during times of siege, from a large cistern below. On the other side of the square is the

Museum of Ancient Glass

✉ Poljana Zemaljskog Odbora 1, Zadar

☎ 023 363 831

🕐 Closed Sun.

💲 $$

mas-zadar.hr

Nin

🅰 169 B2

Visitor Information

✉ Trg Braće Radić 3

☎ 023 265 247

nin.hr

imposing 15th-century **Land Gate** (Kopnena Vrata). To the south of the gate you will find a little harbor known as **Foša,** and to the east, set in a park, is the 16th-century **fortress** (Fortea).

Around the Marina: The footbridge over the marina leads to the modern suburb of **Borik,** where several of Zadar's hotels and private accommodations are to be found. Agencies and kiosks on the marina sell tickets for excursions by boat to **Kornati National Park** (see p. 187), **Krka National Park** (see pp. 190–191), and elsewhere. Just west of the footbridge, outside the old walls, Zadar's new **Museum of Ancient Glass** (Muzej Antičkog Stakla) is located in the renovated 19th-century Cosmacendi Palace and boasts an extensive

a little over 5 miles (9 km) from town, to which it is connected by shuttle buses.

Nin

Though it may be hard to imagine now, the tiny town of Nin (the Roman name was Aenona), 9 miles (15 km) northwest of Zadar, was once the seat of Croatian kings during the ninth century. In the 11th century, it was the seat of the great Croatian bishop Grgur Ninski (see sidebar this page). The town maintained its importance under Hungarian rule, but it sought Venetian protection in the 14th century. Partly abandoned in the 16th century in the face of possible Turkish invasion, the town was deliberately burned down in 1646 and never recovered its former glory.

Nin stands on an island (originally a peninsula) in an artificial

Grgur Ninski & the Language of the Liturgy

An 11th-century Croatian bishop, Grgur Ninski (Gregory of Nin) came to prominence in 1059 at the Council of Salona, where he championed the Glagolitic (Croatian) liturgy. This was at a time when the Catholic Mass was held in Latin and therefore not understood by the

majority of the Croatian population. A well-known statue of the bishop in powerful, wizard-like pose was created by Croatian sculptor Ivan Meštrović, and it exists in three versions—one standing behind Diocletian's Palace in Split, another in Varaždin, and one in Nin.

collection of Roman glassware from the surrounding region.

Zadar is easily reached by bus; there are regular services to Zagreb, Split, Šibenik, and most other major towns in Croatia. Ferries sail to the islands of Ugljan, Dugi Otok, and Lošinj, and across to Ancona in Italy. The airport is

lake, surrounded by salt flats, and is entered by a narrow stone bridge. The most interesting building is the **Church of the Holy Cross** (Sv. Križ), a small building of cruciform plan built in the ninth century, which served as the town's first cathedral. It has now been lovingly restored. An

Traditional folk costumes are worn on Assumption Day (Velika Gospa), in Pag.

inscription above the door records that the church was built at the order of a local Croatian *župan,* or feudal lord, Godežav. A **statue of Grgur Ninski** stands outside.

Just outside Nin, on a small hill topped by a lone tree, is the tiny 11th-century **Church of St. Nicholas** (Sv. Nikola), with trefoil plan and octagonal tower. Familiar to Croatians, this location often appears in historical television dramas and movies.

Buses stop at Nin en route between Zadar and Zaton.

Pag

The long slender shape of Pag, the fifth largest island on the Croatian Adriatic, parallels the coast, divided from the Velebit range by a narrow channel, called the Velebitski Kanal. The island has a particularly indented coastline—161 miles (260 km) long but only around 37 miles (60 km) wide—and is largely barren in appearance, a landscape of dry stone walls, where hardy-looking sheep graze on sage and other wild herbs. Its highest point rises to only 1,145 feet (349 m). Of course, Pag once had much more vegetation than it does today, but like the surrounding islands, most of its trees were felled to supply wood for the Venetian fleet, and subsequent overgrazing has led to an almost complete loss of its topsoil.

Though Pag technically qualifies as part of the Kvarner region, it is connected by a bridge (Paški Most) in the south to the Dalmatian mainland near Zadar. The island is perhaps best known for its lace (*čipka*) and local cheese

Pag
🗺 169 A3–B2

Pag Town

⚠ 169 B3

Visitor Information

✉ Od Špitala 2

☎ 023 611 286

pag-tourism.hr

INSIDER TIP:

The sheep's cheese from the island of Pag is rightly famous for its sharp tang and clean flavor. Enjoy it in the town of Pag itself, on a bench in the square with fresh bread and perhaps a glass of the local wine.

—ANDREW MOORE
National Geographic grantee

(Paški sir), and its distinctive salt beds, which have been part of the landscape since Roman times.

Paški sir is a hard, salty cheese made from Pag sheep's milk and rubbed with olive oil and ash before being left to mature. Some say the diet of the island's sheep, which graze on the wild herbs (sage, in particular) of this otherwise largely barren landscape, contributes to its distinctive flavor. One of the best known cheeses in Croatia, Paški sir is frequently served as an entrée along with *pršut* (local air-dried ham) in restaurants across the country. It is a stiff cheese. If a slice bends when held in the middle, it may be an inferior variety.

Roman settlements on the island of Pag included Cissa (modern **Caska**) and Novalia **(Novalja),** as well as the old town of Pagus just to the south of the modern town of Pag. Cissa was the main center under the Romans. Novalja predominated

under the medieval kingdom of Croatia, before the island was divided administratively between rule from Rab in the north and Nin (and subsequently Zadar) in the south by the Croatian king Krešimir IV in 1071. This division was maintained, off and on, over the following centuries with spells under Venice and Hungary. In 1409, the island was sold to Venice. It passed to Austria in 1797 and suffered Italian occupation during World War I and Italian and German occupation during World War II, before becoming part of Yugoslavia and modern Croatia.

Pag Town: The new town of Pag is a misnomer considering its first streets were laid out in 1443, following plans by architect Juraj Dalmatinac, the man responsible for the second stage of construction of Šibenik's magnificent cathedral (see p. 189). Pag remains a good example of Renaissance town planning. It sits around the head of a bay, on the neck of a narrow channel leading to the salt pans (an area called Solana, from *sol,* meaning "salt"), on which its income was based before the advent of tourism.

At the center of a neat gridwork of streets is **Krešimir IV Square** (Trg Kralja Krešimira IV), where you will find the **Church of the Assumption of the Virgin Mary** (constructed between 1443 and 1488), the work of local architects from Zadar. Flanking the single entrance portal and rosette window are four unfinished sculptures in Gothic style; the Virgin Mary and archangel Gabriel stand on either side of the window. Above the portal is a relief of the Virgin Mary sheltering the townspeople of Pag, their 15th-century local costumes (including distinctive headdresses) still recognizable. The facade is based on that of the Church of the Dormition of the Virgin in old Pag, which still survives, in parts, along the west shore of the lagoon south of Pag.

The interior of the church has Gothic-Renaissance columns with beautifully carved capitals, including acanthus leaves and animals. Look for the dolphins near the back of the church.

Also on the main square, the 15th-century **Duke's Palace** has some nice carving (including a 15th-century coat of arms) and an ornate wellhead in the courtyard. Next door is the incomplete **Bishop's Palace.** Pag's **Lace Museum** has displays of the

intricate local lace for which the island is famous (see sidebar this page). The museum also holds a lacemaking school.

North of the square is the **Skrivanat Tower,** a surviving part of the 15th-century fortifications, which originally had nine towers and four gates, and nearby you will find a **Benedictine monastery.** Northeast of the square, at the intersection with Ulica Jurja Dalmatinca, is the small Renaissance **Church of St. George** (Sv. Juraj). Across the other side of the channel at Prosika are several old **salt storage houses,** some dating from the 17th century.

Pag's **Carnival** takes place every February and then again in July. The town's **Lace Festival,** which began here in 2010, is now an annual event.

Novalja: Around 13 miles (22 km) north of Pag, the town of Novalja is a hugely popular

Lace Museum
✉ Kralja Zvonimira, Pag
🕐 Closed Oct.–May

Novalja
🅰 169 A3
Visitor Information
✉ Trg Briščić 1
☎ 023 661 404
visitnovalja.hr

The Lace of Pag

Paška čipka is a traditional type of handsewn lace from the town of Pag. You can still see women, dressed all in black, engaged in lacemaking work (or *teg,* as it is known) or selling their lace items around the old town. The work is extremely intricate, and traditionally the Pag lacemakers work without any formal patterns, following instead designs passed down from mothers and grandmothers, which are further embellished in their own style. Pag lace has been highly prized for many years, having been ordered by Carmen Sylva, the queen of Romania, and the Austrian emperor Franz Ferdinand.

A lacemaking school was reopened in 1995, in the same building that also houses the Lace Museum and that once housed Pag's original lacemaking school at the turn of the 19th century. The pieces of lace on sale are usually small but nevertheless require a considerable amount of time and skill to make, so do not expect the genuine article to come particularly cheap. Along with lacemaking traditions on the island of Hvar to the south and at Lepoglava near Varaždin, Pag lace was inscribed on the UNESCO List of Intangible Cultural Heritage in 2009.

Northern Velebit National Park

- 169 A3
- Krasno 96, Krasno
- 053 665 380
- $$–$$$

np-sjeverni-velebit.hr

Paklenica National Park

- 169 B2
- Dr. Franje Tuđmana 14a, Starigrad-Paklenica
- 023 369 155
- $$–$$$

paklenica.hr

destination with numerous hotels and clubs.

Pag has a regular bus service from Zadar (over the island's bridge) and Rijeka. The Rijeka bus arrives by the ferry between Prizna on the mainland and the terminal at Žigljen on the island. There is also a catamaran service from Novalja to Rijeka (via Rab).

INSIDER TIP:

You'll often find an all-night party at the long expanse of pebbles on Zrče Beach, just north of Novalja.

—JUSTIN KAVANAGH
National Geographic Travel Books editor

Velebit

Croatia's most extensive mountain range, Velebit stretches more than 70 miles (114 km). Its karst landscape runs from the southern parts of Velika Kapela to the north, in the Kvarner region, to the twin gorges of Velika and Mala Paklenica in the south, before petering out in the striking limestone formations of Tulove Grede.

The whole Velebit range (775 sq mi/200,000 ha) has been classified a UNESCO World Biosphere Reserve since 1977 and contains two national parks. **Northern (Sjeverni) Velebit** was established in 1999. **Paklenica,** to the south, has been a protected national park since 1949. Of the two parks, Paklenica sees far more foreign visitors than

Northern Velebit, although the latter park has the most striking wilderness areas.

While not quite the highest point in Croatia—that accolade goes to Dinara, near Knin (see pp. 233–234)—Velebit is arguably its most attractive mountain range, with areas of lush forest, stunning limestone formations (including the specially protected reserves of **Hajdučki** and **Rožanski cliffs,** or *kukovi*), plenty of wildlife and flowers (including several species that are endemic to the region), and excellent hiking trails.

There are plenty of peaks to climb, the highest being **Vaganski Peak** (5,764 feet/1,757 m), and some good rock-climbing routes in Paklenica. Brown bears live here (see sidebar p. 182), as well as gray wolves, red and roe deer, wild pigs, chamois, short-toed eagles, capercaillie, and various species of reptile, including the nose-horned viper (known locally as *poskok*), Europe's most venomous snake, although it is likely to attack only in self-defense.

The area's spectacular karst features have a complex underground drainage system, including some particularly deep sinkholes. **Lukina Jama** in Hajdučki cliffs reserve in Northern Velebit was discovered in 1992 by Ozren Lukic, a local caver. Lukic, a member of a special mountain division during the Homeland War, was killed by a sniper. The cave system named in his honor reaches depths of 3,280 feet (1,000 m). The nearby Patkov gust has a vertical drop of more than 1,640 feet (500 m), the second largest in the world. In the depths of one of these sinkholes, scientists discovered a species of leech that lives nowhere else.

VPP Hiking Route: Croatia's most extensive long-distance footpath, the **Velebitski Plani-narski Put** (or VPP for short), runs some 62 miles (100 km) along the spine of the range from the village of **Oltare** in the north to Paklenica National Park in the south. Its northern section, the wonderfully engineered **Premužičeva Trail,** is the finest walking trail in Croatia.

Walking the full length of the VPP requires commitment, as it takes 10 to 12 days to complete, during which you will have to carry a sleeping bag and most of your own food, though accommodations are provided by a series of staffed and unstaffed mountain huts and shelters (see pp. 182–183). You will also need to carry enough water for each day; springs are few and far between in the porous rocks of limestone country such as this.

Some of the southern parts of the route also come close to areas that still have land mines from the Homeland War, so take additional care in keeping to the correct route. Decent hiking maps and a good guidebook are essential.

Northern Velebit is best explored from the mountain hut **PD Zavižan,** which can be reached on foot from the villages of Gornja Klada (in 4.5 hours), Krasno, and Oltare (see pp. 182–183). Note, however, that public transportation to Krasno and

Paklenica National Park is a haven for rock climbers.

Oltare is limited. Cars arrive on a winding, mostly unpaved road. Parking near the hut is limited.

Paklenica is accessible from the town of **Starigrad-Paklenica.** At the entrance to the gorge of Velika Paklenica, is the gateway to the park, a national park office, and the start of the hiking trails. A road leads to the parking lot, and there is a large hut called **PD Paklenica,** around 2.5 hours away. ■

Hiking in Northern Velebit

This is a wonderful trek through some outstanding limestone scenery, with plenty of opportunities for spotting local wildlife and flora. Clearly marked hiking trails lead to well-placed mountain huts (PD Zavižan and Alan). Nevertheless, the area is surprisingly infrequently visited by nonresidents.

Day One

Northern (Sjeverni) Velebit National Park can be reached by any bus running along the coastal highway south of Senj. Get off at the village of **Gornja Klada** ❶, which is a few minutes' walk from the main road. Walk through Gornja Klada, and pick up the marked trail heading up the rocky hillside beyond. Ascend a series of switchbacks through forest to **PD Zavižan** ❷ *(tel 053 614 209 or 014 824 142, $$$)*, which you will find on the far side of a grassy slope. This leg of the hike takes 4.5 hours. Open year-round, the hut doubles as a weather station.

Day Two

After staying the first of two nights at PD Zavižan, head east from the hut, cross the road, and continue to a point where the path splits, with trails leading to the village of Krasno and another to the nearby peak Zavižanski Pivcevac. Take the trail to **Mali Rajinac** ❸ (5,574 feet/1,699 m; 2.5 hours). As the highest peak in the park, it provides excellent views. The prominent peak to the southwest is Gromovača, your goal for later. Return as far as the junction with the trail to

NOT TO BE MISSED:

Wild crags of Rožanski kukovi • Views from Mali Rajinac and Gromovača • Botanical Garden near Zavižan

Zavižanski Pivčevac (5,498 feet/1,676 m), then turn left to reach this peak. Descend on the far side, turning right on the road back to the Zavižan hut, passing a large cave that often has snow in it. Just before reaching the hut, turn left into the grassy dell to find Velebit's **Botanical Garden** ❹ (Botanicki Vrt), which was established in 1966.

Day Three

After a second night at the cabin, head south past the Botanical Garden, then turn right onto the path marked **Premužićeva Trail** *(staza)*; it was built in the 1930s under the direction of Ante Premužić, a local forestry engineer. After winding through the spectacular limestone formations of **Rožanski cliffs,** take the path (less than two hours from PD Zavižan) up to the peak of

Brown Bears

The brown bear *(Ursus arctos)* is found in small numbers in the mountain regions of Croatia, in particular Velebit and Gorski Kotar. Attacks on humans are extremely unusual, and your chances of actually seeing a brown bear in the wild are slim since they keep clear of people. Hunting bears is still legal in Croatia. Although some question the numbers, the annual quota is based on population figures supplied by hunters. A sanctuary for orphaned cubs at the village of Kuterevo *(tel 053 799 222, kuterevo-medvjedi.org)*, in Northern Velebit, runs volunteer programs.

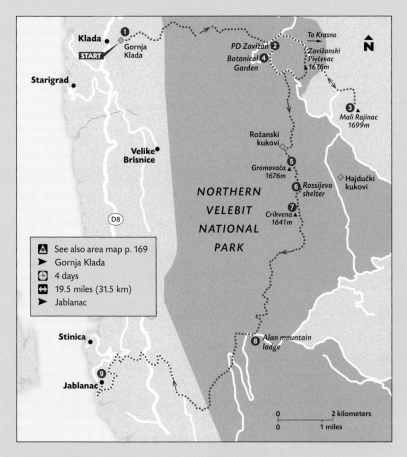

Klada ①
Gornja
Klada
START

Starigrad

To Krasno
PD Zavižan ②
Botanical ④
Garden
Zavižanski
Pivčevac
▲ 1676m

N

③ ▲
Mali Rajinac
1699m

Rožanski
kukovi

Velike ●
Brisnice

Gromovača ▲
1676m

⑤

⑥ Rossijevo
shelter

◇ Hajdučki
kukovi

⑦
Crikvena ▲
1641m

NORTHERN
VELEBIT
NATIONAL
PARK

(D8)

🅐 See also area map p. 169
► Gornja Klada
🕘 4 days
↔ 19.5 miles (31.5 km)
► Jablanac

Stinica

⑧ Alan mountain
lodge

⑨
Jablanac

0   2 kilometers
0   1 miles

Gromovača ⑤ (5,498 feet/1,676 m).

Continue on the Premužićeva Trail to **Rossi-jevo shelter** ⑥ (*sklonište;* about 2.5 hours from PD Zavižan), an unstaffed stone shelter that can sleep up to eight people *(the well water needs purifying)*. Beyond this, the Premužićeva Trail ascends to a pass below **Crikvena** ⑦ (5,383 feet/ 1,641 m), which you can scramble up to in a few minutes with the aid of some steel pegs, before descending into forest. Pass a trail on the left to Lubenovac, an open area between the **Hajdučki cliffs** and Rožanski cliffs reserves. After crossing open grassland, descend to the **Alan mountain lodge** ⑧ (*tel 01 467 4259 or 098 9218 587, $$$*) for your third night. Open in summer, this hut is a four-hour walk from PD Zavižan.

Day Four

From the Alan hut, follow the road to **Jablanac** ⑨ on the coast (3.5 hours). There is a small shelter here *(Planinarska kuća Miroslav Hirtz, tel 098 1743 755, open summer)*, at the head of a narrow inlet called **Zavratnica.** For accommodations and subsequent transportation, contact the Senj Tourist Office *(tel 053 881 068, tz-senj.hr)*.

Entry tickets are available from the hut in Gornja Kalada and cover 3- to 7-day stays *($$–$$$)*. Detailed maps are published by SMAND ("sheet 16, Sjeverni Velebit"; *smand.hr, $$*). Food is available at the Alan hut by prior arrangement. You will need a sleeping bag, and warm, wet-weather gear even in summer.

South of Zadar & the Islands

The region between Zadar and the country's second largest city, Split, in the south, is filled with ancient towns from the historic heyday of Croatia. These picturesque villages are sandwiched between rustic isles, water-sport playgrounds, and idyllic national parks.

A small fishing village on a remote island in Kornati National Park

Ugljan

🄰 169 B2

Visitor Information

✉ Šimuna Kožičića Benje 17, Ugljan town

☎ 023 288 011

ugljan.hr

The islands of Ugljan and Pašman lie only a few miles offshore from Zadar. They were joined to each other until the late 19th century, when a channel was dug between them (now spanned by a road bridge). Both islands are a popular getaway for residents of Zadar and Biograd na Moru, with a few decent beaches and some interesting monasteries.

Ugljan

On Ugljan, you will see a lot of olive trees. In fact, some consider the olive oil produced here to be the best in Croatia. With its proximity to Zadar, the island is also one of the most densely populated in the Adriatic.

At **Preko,** the largest town on Ugljan, the small 12th-century **Church of St. John** (Sv. Ivan) has part of a Roman frieze incorporated into the wall. A short hike (allow about an hour) from Preko, up an 860-foot (262 m) hill will take you to the ruined **Fortress of St. Michael** (Sv. Mihovil). Built by the Venetians in 1203 following their sack of Zadar during the Fourth Crusade, the fortress was restored during the 14th century. Among the ruins are the remains of a 10th-century church that was once part of a monastery. The views of the surrounding islands and Velebit mountains are spectacular.

Just offshore from Preko is the tiny and very photogenic island of **Galovac,** with a 15th-century Franciscan monastery, another stronghold of the Glagolitic priests. Taxi boats ply the straights between Preko and the island, which also has some good beaches.

The settlement of **Ugljan** itself has a 15th-century Franciscan monastery, with some lovely Romanesque capitals—carved with foliage, fish, and various heads—in the cloister.

Pašman

Near **Tkon,** the largest settlement on Pašman to the south, is the **Benedictine Monastery of St. Cosmas and St. Damian** (Sv. Kuzma i Damjan) on Čokovac hill. It was founded by monks from Biograd (now Biograd na Moru) after it was sacked by Venice in the 12th century. A great center of Glagolitic learning in its time, the monastery was used briefly as a headquarters by Allied intelligence services during World War II and is now the only functioning Benedictine monastery in Croatia. Regular ferries run between Zadar and Preko and between Biograd na Moru and Tkon.

Dugi Otok

Farther offshore from Ugljan and Pašman, beyond the small island of Iž, is Dugi Otok (Long Island), its western shore hemmed by steep cliffs. Since there is no source of fresh water on the island—it relies entirely on rainwater and drinking water

INSIDER TIP:

While in the Zadar region, explore Telašćica Nature Park on Dugi Otok. The large island is beautiful and the nature park has tall sea cliffs and an inland salt lake.

—MICHAEL CALDWELL
National Geographic grantee

shipped from the mainland—tap water is a fairly precious commodity, and wasting it is to be avoided. Although one road runs most of the entire length of the island *(there is only one gas station),* the best way to explore is by boat or, failing that, by bike or on foot, at least around Telašćica Bay.

Five-mile-long (8 km) **Telašćica Bay,** narrow and indented like the rest of the island, sits at the southern end of Dugi Otok. It is now a nature park and forms part of Kornati National Park (see p. 187). The long arms on either side of the bay and the fact that it faces south make it exceptionally sheltered, while the sea-facing cliffs on

Pašman

■ 169 B2

Visitor Information

✉ Pašman bb, Pašman town

☎ 023 260 155

pasman.hr

Dugi Otok

■ 169 A2–B2

Visitor Information

✉ Obala Perta Lorinija bb, Sali

☎ 023 377 094

dugiotok.hr

EXPERIENCE: Sail the Croatian Adriatic

The scope for exploring the Croatian Adriatic by boat is almost limitless, and traveling between the coves and inlets of the country's myriad islands by yacht is arguably one of the most pleasant ways of experiencing the area. Moreover, it allows you to visit the more remote parts of the archipelago—particularly the more distant islands—to which there is no access by ferry or land transport.

One of the greatest ways to explore the scattered islands of the **Kornati** archipelago—or any of the other islands on the Croatian Adriatic, for that matter—is by boat. Numerous agencies, both in and outside Croatia, specialize in nautical vacations here (see Travelwise p. 311). These range from simple one-day cruises with a traditional seafood picnic lunch to all-inclusive packages lasting one or two weeks, where customers are taught to sail.

You can also charter your own yacht and set sail into Croatia's wide blue yonder. The latter option obviously depends very much on your level of sailing experience, or that of the best sailor in your party. If you are lacking in the requisite skill level, you can simply hire a skipper. There is a wide range of boats available from which to choose.

Most marinas in Croatia are owned by the Croatian Association of Nautical Tourism, with almost half of these run by the **Adriatic Croatia International Club,** or ACI (*aci-club.hr*). In general, the marinas are in good order and well equipped with fuel and water, and they have plenty of access to food and other supplies.

Weather forecasts are issued (in both Croatian and English) by harbor offices (Rijeka on VHF 69, Pula on VHF 73, Split on VHF 67, and Dubrovnik on VHF 73) and by Radio Rijeka, Radio Split, and Radio Dubrovnik's VHF channels. Do not underestimate the strength of the northeast wind known as the *bura*, which can blow at gale force.

The standard reference guide for all those planning a nautical holiday in Croatia is *Adriatic Pilot* by T. and D. Thompson, published by Imray (*imray.com*).

Bear in mind that you can sail into some areas set aside as reserves, such as the crucial vulture sanctuary on Cres (see p. 157). Restraint is required to avoid overcrowding in these areas.

The Adriatic islands are fast becoming a sailor's paradise.

INSIDER TIP:

If you are in Sali in early August, make a point of joining the fun at the Saljski Užanci—a three-day festival that includes donkey racing.

—TOM JACKSON
National Geographic contributor

its western arm rise to 528 feet (161 m) at **Grpašćak.** Toward the tip of the southern arm is **Peace Lake** (Mir Jezero), which is very warm in the summer. The lake is connected to the sea by underground channels but has a raised saline content due to evaporation.

The main settlement on the island, **Sali,** is at the southern end of the island and reasonably close to Telašćica Bay. There are also a number of fairly ancient, ruined churches near Sali.

Ferries run from Zadar to Brbinj and Božava in the north of Dugi Otok and Sali and Zaglav in the south.

Kornati Islands

The Kornati Islands form the most wildly indented part of the Croatian archipelago, consisting of around 150 islands and islets (depending on who is counting them) scattered over an area of some 200 square miles (320 sq km). Although two of the islands, **Kornat** and **Žut,** are much larger than the others (Kornat is around 20 square miles/32.5 sq km),

the average size of the various islands is a mere 0.3 square mile (0.47 sq km).

A large part of the archipelago was declared **Kornati National Park** in 1980, covering an area of 137 square miles (220 sq km), containing some 89 islands, and including **Telašćica Nature Park** (Park Prirode Telašćica) at the southern end of neighboring Dugi Otok. Irish writer George Bernard Shaw was certainly impressed by the area when he traveled through the Adriatic in the early 20th century, writing that "On the final day of the Creation, God created the Kornati Islands from a blend of stars, tears and wind."

As well as exploring the remote cliffs and coves by boat—the only way to reach the national park in the first place—the area is excellent for scuba diving, and there are numerous easy hiking trails leading to cliff-top views.

Ticket prices are calculated per boat per day, depending on the length of the craft, and are much cheaper if bought before entering the park. A list of places where tickets can be purchased appears on the national park website. The visitor center is on the island of **Murter,** northwest of Šibenik. Connected to the mainland by a road bridge, Murter is a good place to arrange day trips to the islands or longer stays.

Biograd na Moru

Some 16 miles (27 km) south of Zadar, the town of Biograd na Moru (meaning "Biograd on sea") is a popular holiday destination. It was actually an

Kornati National Park
🗺 169 B1–B2
kornati.hr

Telašćica Nature Park
🗺 169 B2
Visitor Information
✉ Ulica Danijela Grbin bb, Sali
☎ 023 377 096
telascica.hr

Murter
🗺 169 B1
Visitor Information
✉ Rudina bb
☎ 022 434 995
tzo-murter.hr

Biograd na Moru
🗺 169 B2
Visitor Information
✉ Trg Hrvatskih Velikana 2
☎ 023 383 123
tzg-biograd.hr

Šibenik's Cathedral of St. Jacob is known for the ornate carvings inside and out.

Vransko Jezero Nature Park

⛰ 169 B2

✉ Kralja Petra Svacica 2, Biograd na Moru

☎ 023 383 181

vransko-jezero.hr

Šibenik

⛰ 169 C1

Visitor Information

✉ Fausta Vrančića 18

☎ 022 212 075

sibenik-tourism.hr

important city during the medieval period (then just called Biograd), a bishopric and a seat of the Croatian kings—not that you would know it now, however, since it was sacked beyond recognition by Venice in 1125 and then torched during the 17th century.

Vransko Jezero Nature Park

Roughly halfway between Zadar and Šibenik, just southeast of Biograd na Moru, is **Vrana Lake** (Vransko Jezero), Croatia's largest natural lake. Declared a nature park in 1999, the lake, which is actually below sea level, lies at the bottom of a long karst valley, close to and parallel with the coast. Its brackish waters and extensive reed beds are home to numerous species of bird. In fact, some 241 species have been recorded here, of which 102 actually nest in the park. Among the residents

is the largest nesting population of pygmy cormorants in Croatia, and the only nesting area on the Croatian coast of the purple heron and great white egret. There is a special ornithological reserve in the northwest corner of the lake, and a network of bike paths and walking trails.

Šibenik

Settled by Slavs around the small hill of St. Anna (Sv. Anna), Šibenik was first mentioned in 1066 in connection with an assembly called by Croatian king Krešimir IV. Refugees fled here from what is now Biograd na Moru after it was sacked by Venice in the 12th century. It became a bishopric in 1298, then came under the sway of Venice in the early 15th century.

The city suffered several attacks by the Ottomans and came under Austrian rule in 1797. World War I saw it occupied by the Italians, but it became part of the kingdom of Yugoslavia in 1921. A period of Italian and German occupation followed during World War II. After the war ended, the town became part of Tito's Yugoslavia and then modern Croatia.

Cathedral of St. Jacob:
Šibenik is a pleasant enough town in its own right, but it is worth coming here to see one building alone: the magnificent Cathedral of St. Jacob (Sv. Jakov), a masterpiece of Renaissance architecture and a UNESCO World Heritage site.

Built between 1431 and 1535 on the site of an earlier church, the cathedral is a curious fusion of Gothic and Renaissance styles. The building is the work of three successive architects. Francesco di Giacomo began the project, but was replaced in 1441 by Juraj Dalmatinac (also known as Giorgio Orsini), a sculptor from Zadar with whose name the cathedral is indelibly linked. Following the latter's death in 1475, Nikola Firentinac completed the facade and added the tall, octagonal dome.

Some restoration work took place in the 19th century. The building employs some highly original construction techniques and is made entirely from stones—including the barrel vaulting—all perfectly joined as if in a work of fine carpentry, without the use of any bricks.

The finely carved **west portal** (the work of Bonino da Milano) has figures of Christ and the Apostles, while the so-called **Lion Portal** (Lavlja Vrata) on the north wall contains Romanesque elements from the earlier church that once stood here. The capitals on the main door's columns have statues of Adam and Eve. The east wall is decorated with a wonderful frieze containing some 74 sculpted portrait heads, all highly realistic and each with individual facial expressions. There is also an inscription recording the laying of the foundations by Juraj Dalmatinac in 1443.

The interior has columns with stylized Corinthian capitals, together with a sculptural frieze of acanthus leaves blowing in the wind, and a 17th-century wooden pulpit. Juraj Dalmatinac's carved baptistery is reached from the south apse, with a domed roof supported on columns, above a marble font.

EXPERIENCE: Learn Falconry Near Šibenik

Sokolarski Center Dubrava (tel 091 50 676 10, sokolarskicentar.com, closed 1 p.m.– 4 p.m., $$–$$$$, larger groups should call in advance) is a falconry center about 5 miles (8 km) from Šibenik, near the village of Dubrava. The center runs one-day and five-day falconry courses. The longer option covers theory as well as practical disciplines, including coping (trimming a bird's beak and talons) and making equipment. There are regular 45-minute presentations on birds of prey and education programs. The center also has a small hospital where sick or injured birds are rehabilitated before being released back into the wild.

Town Museum

✉ Gradska Vrata 3, Šibenik

☎ 022 213 880

muzej-sibenik.hr

Krka National Park

Ⓜ 169 C1

Visitor Information

✉ Trg Ivana Palva II, Šibenik

☎ 022 201 777

💲 $$$

npkrka.hr

Skradin

Ⓜ 169 C1

Visitor Information

✉ Trg Male Gospe 3

☎ 022 771 329

skradin.hr

Next to the cathedral on **Trg Republike Hrvatske,** the town's main square, is the 15th-century **Bishop's Palace,** and on another side of the square there is a 16th-century **loggia** (restored after being bombed in World War II). The **Town Museum** is also on the square. At the far (east) end of the cathedral, you will find the small 15th-century **Church of St. Barbara.** Farther afield is the late 15th and early 16th-century **New Church** (Nova Crkva), with some good carving and a Pietà by Nikola Firentinac, and the late 14th-century **Church of the Assumption** (Uspenje Bogorodice), with its distinctive protruding bell cots. The latter was originally Benedictine, but in the 19th century became Serbian Orthodox and is said to stand on a site once occupied by the Knights Templar. Finally, a stroll up to the **fortress** on St. Anna's hill gives a good aerial view of the old town.

Traditional Dalmatian singing (*klapa*; see sidebar p. 206) is performed in Šibenik during the summer months, and church organ workshops are also run in August. The town makes a good base for visiting Krka National Park (see below) as well as Vransko Jezero Nature Park (see p. 188).

Getting to Šibenik is easy, with most buses traveling up or down the main coastal highway stopping in at the bus station, which is almost on the waterfront.

Krka National Park

The Krka River cuts a deep gorge on its way down from its source at the base of Dinara,

INSIDER TIP:

INSIDER TIP:

The monastery garden of St. Lawrence (Sv. Lovro) in Šibenik is a hidden marvel, with spectacular views. Look for it just off the lane that leads up to the St. Anna Castle. The café is a special treat.

—ANDREW MOORE
National Geographic grantee

near Knin (see pp. 233–234), descending over a series of spectacular waterfalls before flowing into the Adriatic Sea near Šibenik.

Covering more than 67 square miles (109 sq km), the area was declared a national park in 1985 and is one of the most popular parks in Croatia. The main entrance points are from **Skradin** and Lozovac. Boats from Skradin head upriver to the base of the waterfalls, from where the area can be explored on foot by an easy series of wooden boardwalks. From the parking lot at Lozovac, a shuttle bus runs down to the beginning of the boardwalks. In each case, transport to the beginning of the walkways is included in the price of the entrance ticket.

Like those in Plitvice Lakes National Park (see pp. 228–229), the cascade beds on the Krka are made of travertine, limestone deposits made over many thousands of years. The most impressive groups of falls are those at

Skradinski Buk, where the boat from Skradin drops you off, and **Roški waterfalls,** farther up the course of the river, where it plunges into Lake Visovac.

There is plenty of birdlife in the national park—some 221 species have been recorded here—and it is also a very good place to see dragonflies in the summer months. A most unusual amphibian, the olm, lives in the area. The olm is a blind, pink creature that lives its entire life in the dark waters of caves.

A Franciscan monastery stands on the island of **Visovac,** slightly farther upriver from Skradinski Buk, which can be visited by boat tour *(2 hours, $$$).* Boat trips from Skradinski Buk to Roški waterfalls are also available, including a short visit to Visovac and to the old 19th-century water mills in the area *(3.5 hours, $$$$).* In both cases, the price does not include the entrance to the park.

Tours also run to the Roman military camp at **Burnam** *($$),* built between the first century B.C. and the first century A.D. near a strategic fjord over the Krka. The site has an amphitheater and the remains of a praetorian building, which belonged to the crack troops under the direct command of the Roman emperor.

Some agencies organize boat trips to the national park starting from the center of Šibenik. Near Skradin is **Bribirska Glavica,** an Illyrian and Roman hilltop site with ruins from the Roman and medieval periods. You can see for 9 miles (15 km) at the top. ∎

Visitors enjoy a swim beneath a waterfall at Krka National Park.

Beautiful islands guarding this part of the coast, and the city of Split harboring an immense Roman palace

Central Dalmatia

The central Dalmatian islands, especially Hvar, are famous for lavender.

Central Dalmatia

Central Dalmatia has some outstanding historic sites, not least the waterfront palace of the Roman emperor Diocletian in the city of Split, which has been continuously inhabited for more than 1,700 years. The region also boasts exceptionally beautiful islands, great hiking trails, some vibrant towns, and an unrivaled clutch of UNESCO World Heritage sites.

Split, Croatia's second largest city, is a busy transportation hub and industrial center, with the unforgettable Roman palace of Diocletian at its heart. The palace (a World Heritage site) is an incredible living ruin, which has been continuously inhabited since the fourth century A.D. Wandering its maze of alleys, ruins, and underground chambers is one of the highlights of any visit to this part of the coast. Split also has some excellent museums. A park extending over the Marjan Peninsula provides a counterpoint to the bustling city below.

Just to the west of Split is Trogir, another

World Heritage site. The city's beautifully preserved historic center lies on an island just offshore and is connected to the mainland by a short bridge. Its cathedral is celebrated for its magnificent portal and Orsini Chapel. Inland from Split is the strategic old fortress of Klis. Southeast of Split, the rocky karst landscape of the Mosor and Biokovo mountain ranges (easily accessible from Split and Makarska, respectively) provide dramatic hiking opportunities, from day walks to extended treks.

The Islands

Offshore and south from Split are the enormously popular islands of Brač and Hvar. Brač is home to the most iconic beach in Croatia, Zlatni Rat—a slender cape of golden sand and pebbles that stretches off the coast near the town of Bol—as well as some fascinating historic sites, including the secluded monastery of Pustinja Blaca and a cave with strange, cultic carvings. Inland, Vidova Gora, the highest point on the island (on any Croatian island for that matter), makes a great hike from Bol, with spectacular views back down over Zlatni Rat.

Located just south of and parallel to Brač, the long, slender island of Hvar is a place of gorgeous old towns—in particular Hvar itself, yet another World Heritage site—and lavender-covered fields, with seemingly endless hours of sunshine, more than anywhere else on the Adriatic. It, too, has an excellent day walk, to Sveti Nikola, from where on a clear day you can see the Apennines in Italy. You will find some very fine wines on Hvar, including Zlatan Plavac, a red wine, and Bogdanjuša,

Area of map detail

a distinctive local white. Hvar is also, it must be said, extremely busy, though most of the action is concentrated in the western part of the island; head east, and you will see progressively fewer people.

Far out into the Adriatic is the more sedate and thoroughly idyllic island of Vis, with its small, quiet towns and villages and secluded coves, where you can swim in some of the clearest waters anywhere on the Adriatic. Vis was a headquarters for Tito's Partisans during World War II. A cave bearing his name can still be visited on the island and, as the naval headquarters of the former Yugoslavia, remained closed to foreigners until as recently as 1989.

Ancient to Modern Times

Settled from as far back as the fifth millennium B.C. in places, central Dalmatia was home to Greeks and Illyrians during the last few centuries before the time of Christ, before the area became a Roman stronghold in the first century B.C. Salona, the old Roman capital of Dalmatia, was sacked by barbarian hordes following the collapse of the Roman Empire. Its scattered, fragmentary ruins lie just outside Split. Later, the region variously came under the rule of Byzantium, Hungary, Venice, Austria, and Italy, with a short interlude as part of Napoleon's Illyrian Provinces, before becoming a part of Yugoslavia and finally the modern Republic of Croatia. ■

Split & Around

Central Dalmatia is one of the most popular areas of the Croatian coast, with unrivaled historical monuments in Split and Trogir and the nearby mountain hiking opportunities above the city. Split is the transportation hub of the Dalmatian coast, the terminus of the railway line from Zagreb, and the point from where numerous ferry routes fan out among the islands and beyond.

Split's pedestrianized Riva waterfront lights up at dusk.

Split

🗺 195 B2

Visitor Information

✉ Peristil bb

☎ 021 345 606

visitsplit.com

Split is the second largest city in Croatia, with a population of more than 200,000. It is by far the largest along the Dalmatian coast, with a busy ferry port and with a greater emphasis on manufacturing than elsewhere.

The city occupies a broad peninsula, jutting out from the mainland and terminating in the green hilltop park of Marjan. The old town and Diocletian's Palace lie on the south-facing side. The city's urban sprawl stretches north and east of here, while the northern shore of the peninsula and the area opposite its base are heavily industrialized. Recently a number of large hotel complexes have developed along the coast to the east of the old town. Opposite Marjan is the long, equally green arm of the island of Čiovo, with the two of them enclosing, pincer-like, a broad sheltered area stretching from the picturesque city of Trogir in the west to the ruins of Salona in the east.

Split's old town consists of the more or less rectangular

area of Diocletian's Palace—the labyrinthine alleys of which alternately give onto Roman ruins and Gothic palaces, bustling markets and sun-drenched squares—and an area west of this of roughly equal size.

Past Rulers

Modern Split, as opposed to ancient Salona, effectively came into being with the founding of Diocletian's Palace here in A.D. 295, and it was at that time known as Aspalathos. The population grew considerably in the seventh century, following the sacking of Salona by the Avars, when many of the inhabitants fled to Split.

A prosperous free city under the rule of Byzantium, Split became subject to Hungary in 1205, and then, in 1420, it fell under the protection of Venice. By that time the city had been renamed Spalato.

The loss of the nearby fortress of Klis (see sidebar p. 200) to the Ottomans in 1537 was a blow to the city's fortunes. In 1797, it fell under the control of Austria before becoming part of the kingdom of Yugoslavia following World War I. The city was occupied by the Italians during World War II, and bombed by the Allies as a result, before becoming part of Tito's Yugoslavia and the modern Republic of Croatia.

Palace District

In front of Diocletian's Palace is the long, café-filled **Riva.** This is all on land reclaimed from the sea; the palace wall was originally the waterfront. The Riva is a popular spot to sit and watch the world go by over a cup of coffee or an ice cream.

Dragging yourself away from all those ice-cream and cake shops, enter **Diocletian's Palace** (Dioklecijanova Palača) through the **South Gate.** Originally named Porta Aenea by the Roman builders, this gate once led straight to the sea. The gate leads you down into a vaulted underground hall, which has now become an **arts and crafts market.**

On either side of this area is the **Podrum,** an extensive system of vaulted underground chambers that mirrors the layout of the emperor's apartments that once

INSIDER TIP:

Go where the locals go for bargains. Spend some time cruising the open-air market next to Diocletian's Palace, which is always bustling with activity.

—GRACE FIELDER
National Geographic contributor

stood above. Inside the Podrum you will find everything from temporary exhibitions to enormous basilica-shaped halls and wooden beams from the original Roman construction. Various musical performances are sometimes held here, too. This fascinating, maze-like place is well worth visiting before or after your tour (continued on p. 200)

Diocletian's Palace

Diocletian's Palace in Split is an extraordinary place, a complex multilayered slice of history that is at once Roman ruin and Split's downtown with several thousand inhabitants. Continually inhabited for more than 1,700 years, Diocletian's Palace simply oozes atmosphere.

A shrine stands in the crypt of Split Cathedral in the heart of Diocletian's Palace.

Perhaps not surprisingly, Diocletian's Palace is a UNESCO World Heritage site, but more than that, it effectively remains a living, breathing ruin—at once thoroughly modern and thoroughly ancient—in a way very few places in the world can match.

Imperial Retirement Home

The Roman emperor Diocletian (r. 284–305) was born in nearby Salona. He divided the Roman Empire into two administrative spheres in the late third century A.D. After a few years of being ruled from central Turkey, the Eastern Roman Empire got a new capital at Byzantium, soon to become the great city of Constantinople (now Istanbul). Rome remained the capital of the Western Roman Empire. Diocletian then set about

constructing a suitably grand palace for himself near his hometown of Salona, now the suburb of Solin on the fringes of modern Split. Since the first century A.D., Salona had been the administrative capital of the Roman province of Dalmatia.

Diocletian abdicated due to ill health and retired to his waterfront palace. He died there of natural causes in 313, one of the few Roman emperors from this period to escape meeting a violent end.

Palace Design

Construction on the palace began in 295, using white limestone from the island of Brač, and was completed in 305. The complex is more or less rectangular in plan, measuring around 705 feet by 590 feet

(215 m by 180 m), slightly less along the opposite side, with walls rising some 92 feet (28 m) on the south (sea-facing) side, less on the higher ground of the north side. The walls are up to 6.5 feet (2 m) thick and originally included 16 towers, of which 3 corner towers remain. The palace was originally much closer to the waterfront, with the whole south wall meeting the sea.

Inside, the complex was arranged around two main arteries, the *decumanus* (now Krešimirova Street) running roughly east to west between the **Porta Argentea** (Srebrena Vrata, or Silver Gate) and the **Porta Ferrea** (Žetnjeza Vrata, or Iron Gate), and the *cardo* (now Dioklecijanova Street), which extends more or less south from the **Porta Aurea** (Zlatna Vrata, or Golden Gate). Originally the main entrance to the palace, the Porta Aurea in the north wall led to the Roman road to Salona. The imperial quarters of the palace lay to the south of the decumanus, while the area to the north of it was taken up by the military garrison and servants' quarters.

Roman Layout

At the center of the imperial quarters was the **peristyle,** an open courtyard surrounded by colonnades measuring roughly 115 feet by 43 feet (35 m by 13 m). To the west of this stood a Temple of Jupiter, now a baptistery. To the east of the peristyle is the octagonal **Mausoleum of Diocletian,** which—most ironically, bearing in mind the emperor's infamous persecution of early Christians during his lifetime—was converted into a cathedral in 652. The tall, Romanesque bell tower standing next to it was added in the 13th century, though much of it is now a late 19th-century restoration.

Beneath the palace complex is an extensive underground system of vaulted chambers (the **Podrum**). These were long filled with rubble and waste and have been excavated and restored only since the end of World War II. Over the years, particularly during the early

medieval period, the area west of the palace developed as a residential area of roughly equal size. The two areas now form an almost seamlessly unified district.

Rise of Split

Following the sack of Salona by the Avars in 614, the population took refuge in Split—and never left. People continued building dwellings within the palace complex using whatever material was at hand from newly plundered buildings. It is not so unusual for an apartment in the old town to have a piece of a Roman temple in the wall!

In 1757, Scottish architect Robert Adam visited Split. His drawings of the palace laid the foundations for the so-called Adam style and shaped neoclassical architecture from the streets of London and Edinburgh to the federal style in the United States.

The octagonal cathedral was once Diocletian's mausoleum.

Klis Fortress

Traveling around 5.5 miles (9 km) north from Split, heading toward the town of Sinj, will bring you to the ruined cliff-top fortress of Klis. Already a strategic site during Roman times, Klis was once the fiefdom of the ninth-century Croatian prince Trpimir. The fortress took its present shape during the 15th century. It was a stronghold of the Uskoks (see sidebar p. 144) before falling to the Ottomans in 1537. The Ottomans further fortified the place, until the Venetians ousted them in the 17th century. You can reach Klis on bus 34 or 36 from Split bus station.

Cathedral of St. Dominus

✉ Katedrala Svetog Duje

🕐 Closed midday

💲 $

Ethnographic Museum

✉ Iza Vestibula 4

☎ 021 344 164

🕐 Closed Mon.

💲 $

etnografski-muzej-split.hr

of the city above. At the end of the craft market, steps lead up to the **peristyle,** which once formed the heart of the palace.

Cathedral of St. Dominus:

Diocletian's octagonal mausoleum stands on the right as you enter the peristyle. It was converted into the Cathedral of St. Dominus (Sv. Duje) in 652 by the first Bishop of Split and is an atmospheric place with a hushed, much venerated interior. The church's magnificent carved wooden doors date from 1214 and are decorated with panels showing the life of Christ, divided by human and animal figures among vine leaves.

Inside, you can see the beautifully carved Romanesque **pulpit,** which, according to some, is the work of Radovan, whose masterpiece is the cathedral portal in Trogir (see p. 206). An **altar**—actually an early Christian sarcophagus—is dedicated to St. Dominus, who was martyred at Salona by Emperor Diocletian. Look up to see an elaborate sculptural **frieze** that includes what are thought to be portraits of Diocletian himself and his wife Prisca. In one of the niches on either side of the altar is a 15th-century work by the sculptor Juraj

Dalmatinac—of Šibenik's Cathedral of St. Jacob fame (see p. 189)—with a dramatic "Flagellation of Christ." More exquisite carving can be found in the **screens** from the stalls, dating from around 1200 and among the oldest in Dalmatia.

You will find a **treasury** on the second floor as well as a **crypt** beneath the nave. The tall, Romanesque **bell tower,** which stands next to the cathedral—clearly visible from outside the palace walls and one of the city's most familiar landmarks—was added during the 13th century onward, though much of what you see now is a 19th-century restoration. Guarding the entrance are two stone lions.

Imperial Quarters: Wandering south from the cathedral takes you up over the ruined apartments of the imperial quarters of the palace. The spacious **vestibule,** which once served as the entrance to the imperial quarters, would have originally been domed and filled with mosaics and sculptures. Adjacent to this is the city's **Ethnographic Museum.**

The peristyle is surrounded by Egyptian granite columns (some in local limestone) with Corinthian capitals, freestanding on one side while on the other incorporated into the surrounding houses.

On the opposite (west) side of the peristyle, down a narrow alleyway, is the former **Temple of Jupiter,** later converted into a **baptistery,** and now devoid of its original columns. The granite sphinx is one of a pair that once flanked Diocletian's mausoleum. The barrel-vaulted interior has a statue of St. John the Baptist—to whom the baptistery was dedicated—by Ivan Meštrović, an 11th-century baptismal font with pre-Romanesque carvings, and panels with elaborately carved flowers on the vaulted ceiling.

Silver & Golden Gates:

On the east side of the palace, just beyond the Srebrena Vrata, or **Silver Gate**—restored after bombing during World War II— is the 13th-century **Church**

of St. Dominic (Sv. Dominik). South of the church is a large open **market.** You might want to stock up on some fruits and vegetables here rather than on the islands, where they will naturally be more expensive.

Walk north from the peristyle along Dioklecijanova Street to the large, imposing Zlatna Vrata, or **Golden Gate,** originally the main entrance to the palace, which leads out through the north walls to a small park. The gate would once have been flanked by octagonal towers, of which traces remain, and statues would probably have stood in the niches above. Between the inner and outer gates was a rectangular vestibule. The gallery around the top was originally a guardhouse, through which visitors to the palace were admitted before being allowed to enter the palace proper. (Today, the structure is a

Locals buy vegetables from the market in the shadow of Diocletian's Palace.

One of several restored chapels on Marjan hill behind the city of Split

small church.) The **north walls,** when viewed from the exterior, though lower than the south walls along the Riva, give a much clearer impression of the original fortified nature of the palace.

Just beyond the Golden Gate is the best-known version of Ivan Meštrović's monumental sculpture of the Bishop of Nin, Grgur Ninski (see sidebar p. 176). This monument dates from 1927 and was unveiled in the city in 1929. The statue originally stood in the peristyle but was moved out of the palace by the Italians when they occupied the city during World War II. It was finally shifted to its present position in 1954. According to popular tradition, rubbing the bishop's big toe brings good luck—which is why this feature has been polished smooth by more than half a century of passing hands. Beyond the statue, a small park with benches provides a welcome spot for enjoying a quiet rest beyond the bustle of the palace interior.

The nearby **bell tower** once formed part of a larger Benedictine monastery, which burned down in the 19th century. All that survives is a small chapel that has a 15th-century carved altar by the great Juraj Dalmatinac.

From the Iron Gate

Heading west along Krešimirova Street from the peristyle, you will pass under the Žetnjeza Vrata, or **Iron Gate** (Porta Ferrea to the Romans). You are now technically leaving the palace—not that you would know it, so well are the different parts blended together. Soon you will reach the café-filled **Pjaca,** or **People's Square** (Narodni Trg). There's a medieval **clock tower** by the Iron Gate, not to mention a particularly tempting ice-cream shop in the vicinity.

On the north side of Pjaca is the 15th-century **Town Hall** (Vijećnica) with its distinctive, triple-arched Gothic facade, once the home of Split's ethnography museum. West of the square, at the edge of the old town by Marmont Street, there is a **fish market** (Ribarnica).

Heading south from Pjaca on Marulićeva Street brings you to **Renaissance Square** (Trg Preporoda), another extremely attractive square with a statue of Croatian Renaissance writer Marko Marulić by Ivan Meštrović, and the baroque **Milesi Palace.** A small café on the east side of the square has an old sarcophagus built into the wall.

On the south side of the square there is a 15th-century Venetian tower (Hrvojeva Kula), beyond which an entrance to the old town lets you out onto the Riva once more.

Marjan Park & Beyond

When you tire of the bustle of central Split, wander west from the waterfront in front of the palace, then up through the quiet residential streets of Veli Varoš to the hilltop park of Marjan. Marjan offers a welcome green and breezy refuge after the often oppressive heat of the city below, with several pleasant footpaths and a number of small restored chapels.

Most of the sites in Split are concentrated in and around the palace, but a few of the museums are a short walk outside. North of the palace is the **Archaeological Museum** (Arheološki Muzej), established in 1820, with collections spanning the prehistoric,

Archaeological Museum

- ✉ Zrinsko Frankopanska 25, Split
- ☎ 021 329 340
- 🕐 Closed Sun.
- 💲 $

mdc.hr/split -arheoloski/index .html

Salona

The ancient settlement of Salona was originally a stronghold of the Illyrian Delmatae, who left their name in the region—Dalmatia—despite being subdued by the Romans in the first century A.D. During the reign of Emperor Augustus, Salona developed into the chief city of Roman Illyria (later renamed Dalmatia), reaching its peak under Diocletian, when it had 60,000 inhabitants. Following the persecution of early Christians under Diocletian and the martyrdom of several who would later become saints—including St. Dominus, patron saint of Salona—their graves here developed into centers of worship and later became the sites of early Christian churches.

Salona suffered the usual barbarian depredations following the fall of the Roman Empire. It was occupied by the Ostrogoths under Theodoric, but the real blow came in 614, when the Avars sacked and almost completely destroyed the city. Most of its inhabitants fled to Diocletian's Palace in Split, never to return.

Salona lies under the modern suburb of Solin and can be reached via local bus (No. 1). Stones from the amphitheater and other buildings have been pillaged wholeheartedly over the centuries and carried off for use in other constructions, so there is little to see now. Most of the finds have been moved to the Archaeological Museum in Split.

Trogir's marina abuts the historic city center.

**Gallery of
Fine Arts**

✉ Lovretska 11 &
Kralja Tomislava
15, Split

☎ 021 350 112

🕐 Closed Mon.

💲 $

galum.hr

**Meštrović
Gallery &
Kaštelet-Crikvine**

✉ Šetalište Ivana
Meštrovića 46,
Split

☎ 021 340 800

🕐 Closed Mon.

💲 $$

mdc.hr/mestrovic
/galerija/index-en
.htm

Greco-Roman, early Christian, and medieval periods, as well as exhibitions about stone inscriptions, primarily from Salona (see sidebar p. 203), and marine archaeology. A couple of blocks east of the Archaeological Museum, Split's **Gallery of Fine Arts** (Galerija Umjetnosti) has a collection of paintings by Croatian masters from the 14th century onward.

Around a 15-minute walk west of the palace, below the green slopes of Marjan, you will find the **Meštrović Gallery,** which showcases some of the works of the great 20th-century Croatian sculptor in a suitably grand, palatial building. The building was actually designed by Meštrović himself, as a family home and atelier in Split, and was converted into a museum in 1952 following the artist's move to the United States.

A little farther on and across the other side of the road is **Kaštelet-Crikvine,** a 16th-century summer palace bought by Meštrović in 1939, with a chapel housing a striking series of carved walnut panels by the artist illustrating the life of Christ. Entry tickets for the gallery are valid here as well.

Just to the east of the Meštrović Gallery, the **Museum of Croatian Architectural Monuments** (Muzej Hrvatskih Arheoloških Spomenika) houses a wonderful collection spanning from the 7th to the 15th century. Its exhibits include architectural fragments, sculpture, inscriptions, screens, and sarcophagi, with a whole lot more besides.

There are plenty of annual festivals in Split, from the February Carnival to the mid-July to mid-August Split Summer Festival (Splitsko ljeto; *splitsko-ljeto .hr*), which has been going since 1954 and features drama, dance, exhibitions, and music at various venues throughout the city.

As Croatia's second largest city, Split is connected to most places in Croatia by bus, and there is a railway line to Zagreb (including high-speed services that cut the journey time down to 5.5 hours). Both the train and bus stations are located near the ferry terminal, just south of Diocletian's Palace (a five-minute walk along the quay). A few catamaran services (for example, to Bol and Jelsa) leave from the waterfront directly in front of the palace. Shuttle buses and taxis for Split's international airport—northwest of the city, between the towns of Kaštela and Trogir—leave from just next to the private jetty. Some local buses stop here, while others depart from the bus station along Domivinskog Rata, a short walk north of the palace.

Above the City

The long mountain ridge of **Mosor** stretches southeast from Split and offers some good hiking opportunities (hot in summer, but with breathtaking views). The trails start either from the villages of **Gornje Sitno** or **Kućine** (both accessible by local buses) or from **Grlo** near Klis.

Those after a day's walk are best starting fairly early to Gornje Sitno. Follow the trail markings up to the mountain hut (open weekends only), from where a steep path climbs up onto the ridge itself and leads to the tiny red shelter—with room for half a dozen people to stand or sit, and not much else. Allow five hours to return from Gornje Sitno, or extend the route farther along the ridge before descending.

Trogir

Some 15 miles (25 km) west of Split, the town of Trogir, a UNESCO World Heritage site since 1997, includes one of the most beautifully preserved historic town centers anywhere on the Adriatic. The old town is built on a small island, originally a peninsula, which was divided from the mainland by an artificial channel cut in the medieval period, spanned by a short stone bridge.

Founded by Greek colonists from Syracuse (in Sicily) in the third century B.C. and called Tragurion, Trogir became part of the Roman province of Dalmatia at the beginning of the first century A.D. The city's prominence waned with the rise of the Roman town of Salona down the coast (see sidebar p. 203). However, following the destruction of Salona by the Avars in the seventh century, Trogir's fortunes turned

INSIDER TIP:

Trogir, a walled city on its own island, is a compact microcosm of Croatian culture. Do what the locals do: Buy a gelato and walk the maze of streets to see and be seen.

—GRACE FIELDER
National Geographic contributor

upward once again. It fell under Byzantine suzerainty and later paid tribute to the medieval Croatian kings in the ninth century, but it was taken by Venice in 998 and then in the 12th century came under Hungarian rule. Following this, like so many towns along the coast, Trogir formed part of an ongoing tussle between Venice and Hungary.

Museum of Croatian Architectural Monuments
- Stjepana Gunjače bb, Split
- 021 323 901
- Closed Sun.
- $

mhas-split.hr

Trogir
- 195 B2

Visitor Information
- Trg Ivana Pavla II 1
- 021 881 412

tztrogir.hr

Cathedral of St. Lawrence

✉ Trg Ivana Pavla II, Trogir

🕐 Closed midday

💲 $

Trogir was sacked by Arab raiders in 1123 and by Venice in 1171. In 1242, King Bela IV of Hungary took refuge here during his flight from the Mongols, though the city was spared a further sacking when the Asian invaders were forced to return to their homeland on hearing of the death of their leader's father. The city was taken decisively by Venice in 1420, becoming the Venetian city of Traù until 1797, when it became part of Austria (with a short spell under Napoleon). Following World War I, Trogir became part of the kingdom of Yugoslavia, then of Tito's Yugoslavia after World War II, and finally part of modern Croatia.

Old Town: From the bridge to the mainland, enter Trogir's historic core through one of the old city gates, **Kopnata Vrata.** Look for the figure of the town's patron saint, St. John Ursini, above the gate. Then continue south into the old town a short way along narrow streets to reach the main **John Paul II Square** (Trg Ivana Pavla II).

The north side of the square is occupied by Trogir's star attraction, the 13th-century **Cathedral of St. Lawrence** (Sv. Lovro), with its magnificently carved **west portal**—one of the finest examples of Romanesque sculpture anywhere in Dalmatia. The portal is the work of a local master, Radovan, who signed his work with a Latin inscription above the door, along with the date 1240. The portal is flanked by two lions, above which stand the figures of Adam and Eve, and within these are pillars carved with an elaborate array of vine leaves, beasts, Apostles, and other figures, including rural and hunting scenes. The figures supporting the pillars appear to be Turks and Jews. Above the doors, a lunette is decorated with a Nativity scene.

Inside the cathedral, you will find a 13th-century ciborium over the altar, a 13th-century carved Romanesque pulpit, wooden stalls in Venetian Gothic style—and the truly spectacular **Ursini Chapel,** the work of Nikola Firentinac (1468–1497), a pupil of the great Italian Renaissance master Donatello. The

EXPERIENCE: Listen to *Klapa*, Dalmatian Songs

Klapa is the traditional, hauntingly beautiful style of Dalmatian a cappella song, sung without accompaniment by a small group of singers, often male though increasingly these days female, too. You can hear klapa performed at many places on the coast and islands during the summer, from the vestibule of Diocletian's Palace in Split to the medieval town of Korčula, where it forms a prelude to *Moreška* performances (see p. 263). If you are near the town of Omiš in July (see p. 208), however, you can catch part of its annual **Festival of Dalmatian Klapa** *(fdk.hr),* which features performances by klapa groups from all over Croatia in the town's central St. Michael Square (Trg Sv. Mikul).

walls are decorated with a series of torch-bearing cherubs emerging from partially open doors and niches containing statues of saints. Ursini, who died in 1111, was the first Bishop of Trogir and is one of the town's patron saints. A sarcophagus of his remains rests here, above the altar.

The **baptistery** is the work of Andrija Aleši from the 15th century. Both Nikola Firentinac and Andrija Aleši worked on another Renaissance masterpiece in Dalmatia, the Cathedral of St. Jacob in Šibenik (see p. 189). The cathedral's **bell tower,** built in several stages between the early 15th and late 16th century, shows a progression from Gothic (lower story) to Venetian Gothic (middle story) to the Renaissance (upper story).

Across the square from the cathedral are the two halves of the 15th-century **Čipiko Palace,** with large Gothic windows, once home to a local noble family and connected over the alleyway between them by an impressive stone arch.

On the south side of the square is the 15th-century **Loggia** and next to this, the old **clock tower,** both more work by Nikola Firentinac. Behind the Loggia is the small 11th-century **Church of St. Barbara** (Sv. Barbara). The southeast corner of the square is occupied by the large, 15th-century **Town Hall,** renovated in the 19th century, with the coat of arms of St. John Ursini over one of the side doors and many more in the courtyard.

Continuing south from the square brings you to the

INSIDER TIP:

Wherever you are in Croatia, try a local wine, perhaps a Vugava from Vis or Graševina from Ilok. Many traditional grape varieties still survive in Croatia.

—CAROLINE HICKEY
National Geographic Travel Books editor

15th-century **Church of St. Nicholas** (Sv. Nikola), built on the site of an earlier Romanesque church, and out onto Trogir's attractive waterfront, or **Riva.** Continuing west along the Riva, you arrive first at the 14th-century **Dominican Church,** with a carved Virgin and Child in the lunette above the door, and, farther along, at the stout **Kamerlengo Fortress,** built by the Venetians.

From the eastern end of the Riva, another bridge gives access to the town's more modern quarter on the island of **Čiovo,** which stretches east toward Marjan in Split, with a few quiet rocky beaches.

Intercity buses traveling north from Split along the main coastal highway stop at the entrance to Trogir—which is a real bottleneck for traffic—and local bus number 37 makes the trip between Split and Trogir roughly every half hour. Split's international airport is actually much closer to Trogir than it is to Split, so if arriving by air and planning to stay in Trogir, head straight there rather than into Split first.

Beach at the Makarska Riviera, with the mountains of Biokovo Nature Park in the background

Omiš
- 🅰 195 B2

Visitor Information
- ✉ Trg Kneza Miroslava bb
- ☎ 021 861 350

tz-omis.hr

Makarska
- 🅰 195 C2

Visitor Information
- ✉ Obala Kralja Tomislava 16
- ☎ 021 612 002

makarska-info.hr

Seashell Museum
- ✉ Franjevački Put 1, Makarska
- ☎ 021 611 256

South From Split

Omiš: Traveling south from Split takes you though the town of Omiš, at the mouth of the dramatic **Cetina Gorge**—where the Cetina River flows into the Adriatic—and overshadowed by the stark **Omiška Dinara** mountain. There's a road leading up the mountain, as well as a footpath—sometimes poorly marked—that climbs up from the town itself. In July, the town hosts an annual Festival of Dalmatian Klapa (see sidebar p. 206), which has been staged since 1996.

Makarska: Farther south from Omiš, below the spectacular Biokovo mountain range, is Makarska (Roman Murcurum),

which was taken by the Ottomans in 1499 and became their main port on the Adriatic for the next 150 years. The town was bombed during World War II and damaged by an earthquake in 1962.

Most people come here for the long, popular beach, right in front of town and part of the balmy **Makarska Riviera.** Set back from the waterfront at the eastern side of town, the main square has a statue of 18th-century Croatian writer Andrija Kačić Miošić by Ivan Rendić, a prominent 20th-century Croatian sculptor. The **Franciscan monastery,** dating from around 1400 with 17th-century reconstruction work, contains Makarska's **Seashell Museum** (Malakološki

Muzej), with a collection of shells from around the world assembled by one of the monks living here during the 1960s.

Intercity buses traveling south from Split on the main coastal highway pass through both Omiš and Makarska.

Biokovo Nature Park: Rising almost sheer from the coast behind Makarska is **Biokovo,** a rugged limestone range pitted with limestone dells and sinkholes, and including the second highest peak in Croatia, **St. Jure** (Sv. Jure; 5,781 feet/1,762 m). A winding mountain road leads up to the summit, which is crowned by an enormous radio and television antenna.

Chamois and rare mouflon sheep wander its rocky heights, and there are around 30 species of reptiles and amphibians. Biokovo, which was declared a nature park in 1981, is also home to a number of endemic plants.

Various travel agencies in Makarska run day trips up here for those who do not fancy the climb.

Crossing Through Bosnia

Just south of Metković, and perhaps rather unexpectedly, the Croatian coast is interrupted by a tiny sliver of Bosnia and Herzegovina at the town of Neum—an essential duty-free stop for many bus drivers. Though it is only 4 miles (7 km) wide, you will nevertheless need a passport. For most this will not be a problem, but for some nationals, it may require getting a Bosnian visa. (If you did not need a visa for Croatia, the chances are you will not need one for Bosnia either.)

If you are a citizen of a country that does require a visa for travel in Bosnia, and are planning only on crossing through at this point, you will probably find it easier to take the ferry from Ploče to Trpanj, on the Pelješac Peninsula, and continue your journey south from there, bypassing Bosnia. There are also plans afoot to build a new highway around the border over the ocean at this point, which would thus remain completely in Croatian territory. ■

Biokovo Nature Park

✉ Marineta, Mala Obala 16

☎ 021 616 924

🕐 Closed Nov.–March

biokovo.com

EXPERIENCE: Hike on Biokovo

Biokovo is a great place for hiking, and though it is short on mountain huts, there are plenty of good, clearly marked trails that whisk you up from sea level to its craggy limestone heights. One of the most straightforward routes starts from the town of Makarska, before climbing relentlessly to the summit of **Vošac** (4,675 feet/1,425 m)—quite a workout for the legs, but the views from the top are magnificent. Allow 3.5 hours for the climb,

slightly less for the descent, and take plenty of water; there is none available en route. For those who want to climb **St. Jure** as well, allow an additional three hours there and back from Vošac. Longer, overnight routes head northwest along the spine of the mountain, over the peak of **St. Elijah** (Sv. Ilija) and down to the villages of **Gornja Brela** or **Bast.** SMAND (*smand.hr*) publishes an excellent map ("sheet 32, Biokovo Park Prirode"; $$).

The Islands

Few tourists visit Dalmatia without making time to visit its islands. Split is the staging post for trips to fun-filled Brač and stylish Hvar, two of the hottest destinations in the whole of Croatia. Their once overlooked near neighbors, Šolta and Vis, are now becoming increasingly attractive destinations for those travelers wishing for the chance to see beautiful islands while avoiding some of the crowds.

Sailboarders take to the water off Zlatni Rat on the southern coast of Brač.

Brač
🔺 195 B1–B2

Brač

People have lived on Brač since the Neolithic period, including the Illyrians. Indeed, the name of the island may derive from the Illyrian word *brentos,* meaning "stag" or "deer." (The island's Greek name, Elaphos, also means "stag.")

Brač's main settlement was originally Škrip, though later the population moved farther inland to Nerežišća to avoid pirate raids. More recently, Supetar developed into the island's main hub.

Brač is the third largest island in the Croatian Adriatic, yet despite the island's relative size, it has never developed an enduring, major city—unlike the similar islands of Rab, Korčula, and Hvar. Until the advent of modern tourism, Brač had instead remained largely rural.

The great Croatian poet and politician Vladimir Nazor was born in a village just east of Supetar, and his best known work, "Pastir Loda" (translated as "Loda the Shepherd"), describes the island of his birth, rich in local customs and obscure, rustic dialect.

The southern half of the island rises quite high, with Vidova Gora reaching the highest point of any island in the Croatian Adriatic. The brilliant white limestone from its northern shore was used to build Diocletian's Palace in Split (see pp. 198–199) and Trogir's Cathedral of St. Lawrence (see p. 206), as well as for the columns of the White House in Washington, D.C.

Bol & Around: Despite the huge number of visitors, the pretty town of Bol is a largely unspoiled part of Brač's southern coast. The primary attraction for many here is **Zlatni Rat** ("golden cape"). This long spit of fine pebbles and sand protrudes from the forested coastline, a 15-minute walk west from Bol. The action of the currents between Brač and Hvar is continually changing its profile slightly. The word for "cape" in Croatian is *rt. Rat* in modern Croatian actually means "war," but the spelling here is a legacy of an old, local dialect. Zlatni Rat is a lovely place to swim, but it does get frenetic during the summer season, with Jet Skis racing around the surrounding waters. Those wanting greater solitude can wander along the coast to one of the other more secluded rocky coves in the area, often shaded by the low-hanging pine trees that grow here.

On the east side of Bol is a 15th-century **Dominican monastery** on a headland overlooking its own attractive little cove and beach.

Almost directly above Zlatni Rat is the 2,560-foot (780 m) peak of **Vidova Gora,** which can be reached by car from the northern side of the island, or by foot from Bol following an easy, clearly marked trail (allow four hours round-trip). It can get incredibly hot on the way up, however, since there is almost no shade—so take plenty of water and a sun hat. The view from the top is excellent, and there is a small *konoba* (café) serving food and refreshments.

West from Zlatni Rat, above the coast road, there is a cave, **Dragon's Cave** (Zmajeva Špilja; see sidebar p. 212) with some fascinating stone carvings, including a toothy dragon and various cultic devices. The cave was inhabited by Glagolitic priests in the 16th century. A faint trail leads up to

Bol
△ 195 B1
Visitor Information
✉ Porat bolskih pomoraca bb
☎ 021 635 638
bol.hr

EXPERIENCE:
Get Around by Ferry

Traveling by ferry in Croatia is without a doubt the nicest way to get about the coast and islands, and (at least for foot passengers) comparatively inexpensive. Ferry types range from large car and passenger vessels to smaller craft and speedy catamarans (foot passengers only). Most services are run by the state ferry company, **Jadrolinija** *(jadrolinija.hr),* though there are private companies operating, in particular the catamaran services and shorter routes. In general, private services are more expensive. Routes and schedules are fairly comprehensive, and you can get to most of the islands. For catamarans and smaller boats, tickets are in high demand. However, they are seldom put on sale earlier than a day in advance.

Supetar

🅰 195 B2

Visitor Information

✉ Porat 1

☎ 021 630 551

supetar.hr

the cave from the village of **Murvica** (where there is another nice konoba), though it is normally locked, so you will have to go as part of a tour or content yourself with looking in through the barred metal gate.

Farther west along the coast and on much higher and less accessible ground is the monastery of **Pustinja Blaca,** again founded by Glagolitic priests in the 16th century (see sidebar this page). To

the latter town was the administrative capital of the island. However, Supetar eventually superseded its inland neighbor and developed into the main town on Brač. As the closest point to Split, it exported the famous limestone from nearby quarries, and a few sandy beaches have made it popular with day-trippers.

Škrip is another town that once dominated the island but

Zmajeva Špilja & Pustinja Blaca

In the relatively inaccessible Poljica area, nestled behind Mosor (the great blade-like ridge stretching southeast from Split), a small semi-independent principality known as Poljička Kneževina developed in the 11th century. In the face of Ottoman attacks during the 16th

century, the people of Poljička, including their Glagolitic priests, moved to the island of Brač. The priests took up residence on the far, seaward slopes, where they settled at Zmajeva Špilja (Dragon's Cave) before founding the monastery of Pustinja Blaca.

get here from Bol, take one of the daily excursions by boat that drop you on the coast below the monastery. From there you can walk up following a clear trail. There is also an unpaved road from Nerežišća —which you can also reach by the road past Murvica—from the end of which you again have a clear path leading to the monastery. The last monk died here in 1963.

Bol is connected by fast catamaran services to Split on the mainland and Jelsa on the island of Hvar, and there is regular local bus service to Supetar.

Supetar & Beyond

Set attractively around its small harbor, Supetar began life as the port for Nerežišća when

has since waned in importance. It is less than 2 miles (3 km) inland from Splitska, just east of Supetar, and still has the remains of a massive Illyrian **defensive wall,** and the small **Church of the Holy Spirit** (Sv. Duh) dating from the 11th century, with a 14th-century bell cot. Here you will also find a castle dating from the 16th century and the **Museum of Brač.** A popular sandy beach is at **Lovrečina,** farther east.

Milna, briefly a Russian naval base during the Napoleonic Wars, is a small and increasingly popular settlement at the western end of the island, with some good beaches for swimming and an 18th-century stucco-encrusted **baroque church.**

Šolta

Many visitors to Brač ignore its small, westerly neighbor and head back to the mainland or are lured south by the genteel towns of Hvar. However, little Šolta is not without its merits. Emperor Diocletian recognized them when he chose to base his fishing fleet on the island in A.D. 295. Today, the fish still have an appeal, along with Šolta's other underwater life, because the clear waters around the island are some of the best places for snorkeling and scuba diving in this part of Dalmatia.

Šolta has been inhabited since prehistoric times and has passed between the regional powers several times over, like regions all along the Croatian coast. It has its fair share of ancient hill forts, classical ruins, and centuries-old churches, but nothing to compete with its rival islands. Like on Brač, the development of Šolta's settlements has been arrested at the level of a large village.

The biggest village is also the oldest on the island; **Grohote** is a warren of narrow alleys nestled on the main ridge at the center of the island. It lies at Šolta's main crossroads that connect Rogač on the north coast to the hill town of **Gornje Selo** in the east and the fishing village of **Maslinica** to the west. **Rogač** is the main port on the island, situated in a natural harbor; the daily ferry service from Split docks here.

A short way to the east of Rogač is **Nečujam,** the newest

Šolta

⛺ 195 B2

Visitor Information

✉ Trg Sv. Stjepana bb, Hvar town, Hvar

☎ 021 741 059

solta.hr

The quay at Supetar, a working fishing village in northern Brač

The streets and quaysides of Hvar town are filled with shops and stalls selling homemade jewelry, ornate lace, oils, liqueurs, and lavender bags filled from the island's own harvest.

Hvar

△ 195 B1–C1

village on the island and Šolta's main tourist resort. Large hotel developments, summer houses, and private apartments have grown up around the island's largest bay, complete with a sheltered sandy beach, a rare asset in this part of Dalmatia.

Šolta has its own school of naïve art., which was at its height in the 1980s and made famous by the works of Eugen Buktenica, Dinko Sule, and Marin Kalajzic. All of these artists hail from Grohote, which is often the subject of their paintings, along with other aspects of life on quiet Šolta.

Hvar

The long (42 miles/68 km), slender island of Hvar, divided from Brač by the powerful currents of the Hvar Channel, boasts more hours of sunshine than anywhere else in the

Adriatic and is considered by many Croatians the hippest destination on the coast—the ultimate blend of beautiful architecture, endless sun, and perennial chic. The fourth largest island on the Croatian Adriatic, its major cities and most of its population are concentrated at the broader western end of the island, while its narrow, extended "tail" remains sparsely populated.

A center of the Danilo culture during the early Neolithic period, the island was colonized by the Greeks in the fourth century B.C., initially at Pharos (the site of modern Stari Grad), which was founded around 385, and later at Dimos (today's Hvar town). It came under the powerful Illyrian kingdom of Scodra before being taken by Rome in 229 B.C. Later it was passed among Byzantium, medieval Croatia, Hungary, and Venice, and its capital moved from Stari Grad to Hvar town before becoming part of Venice in 1420.

From this time in particular, the town of Hvar became fantastically wealthy, as the main port for Venetian ships traveling through the Adriatic. The island suffered frequent Ottoman attacks in the 16th century and became part of Austria in 1797 (with short spells under Napoleon and then the British), before being occupied by the Italians during World War I. It then joined the kingdom of Yugoslavia in 1921 and Tito's Yugoslavia after World War II.

Hvar grows vast amounts of lavender, which you will find for sale all over the island in wonderfully scented little bags. It produces some good wines, in particular Zlatan Plavac, a hearty red from near Sveta Nedjelja.

The island has a long theatrical tradition. The theater in Hvar town, built in 1612, is one of the earliest to have opened to the general public in Europe. The island's fine literary history stretches back to the Renaissance, including poet Petar Hektorović, whose best known work is his bucolic "Ribanje i Ribarsko Prigovaranje" ("Fishing and Fishermen's Talk").

Catamarans and ferries stop at Hvar town and Stari Grad, respectively, on their way between Split and the islands of Korčula, Vis, and Lastovo (including the Rijeka Dubrovnik ferry, which calls in at Hvar). Jelsa is connected by catamaran to Bol on Brač and Split. Ferries also operate from Sućuraj at the eastern tip of the

INSIDER TIP:

To walk up to Hvar's castle, take the steps leading from the main square. As you pass beneath an ornate arch, look for a stone hare to your left to check that you are on the correct route.

—TOM JACKSON
National Geographic contributor

island to Drvenik on the mainland. Regular bus services connect Hvar town and Stari Grad with Vrboska and Jelsa.

Hvar Town: The town of Hvar is the undisputed favorite of Croatia's well-heeled and well-to-do. The old town center really is a lovely place, its beautiful main square leading onto the waterfront where elegant palaces sit below the steep-sided Španjola hill, encrusted with old fortifications. Much of the town had to be rebuilt after a devastating Ottoman attack in 1571, so what you see today is mostly from after that date, with a marked Venetian influence. Hvar can get extremely busy during peak season, and accommodations at this time are usually fully booked months in advance, so be sure to plan.

The main square, the **Square of St. Stephen** (Trg Sv. Stjepana), said to be the largest in Dalmatia, stretches inland from the small,

(continued on p. 218)

Hvar Town
◮ 195 B1
Visitor Information
✉ Trg Sv. Stjepana bb
☎ 021 741 059
tzhvar.hr

A Walk to Sveti Nikola

The nicest walk on Hvar gives spectacular views from the summit of Sveti Nikola (St. Nicholas)—on a good day all the way to the Apennines in Italy. The route climbs slowly from the village of Vrbanj, which lies on the bus route between Stari Grad, Vrboska, and Jelsa, and can be reached easily by public transportation.

Vineyards grow beneath Sveti Nikola's seaward cliffs.

NOT TO BE MISSED:

Spectacular views from the summit of Sveti Nikola
• Peaceful villages off the tourist trail

Vrbanj ❶ is a pretty little village just above the road between Stari Grad and Jelsa, surrounded by a landscape of dry stone walls and fig trees, and overlooking Stari Grad Plain (see p. 220). The bus drops passengers off near the village church, from where red-and-white trail markings lead you to the village square. Take the trail to the left from here—not right, which would lead you to the village of Dol. It brings you shortly to the village of **Svirče** and the road to Pitve.

Turn left on the road to the **Church of St. Mary Magdalene** (Sv. Magdalena) ❷, a striking building with domed roof and surrounded by palm and cypress trees. The church actually dates only from the early 20th century, though it is built on the site of an earlier building.

Retrace your steps along the road, but continue past Svirče, following signs to Sveti Nikola, before turning right off the main road and passing two small devotional shrines by the roadside. A marked path leaves the road, crossing it and rejoining it at several points as you climb slowly up the hillside. The trail passes a small chapel at one point, then rejoins the road before wandering between two low hills. Turn right beyond this, following an unpaved road with scattered houses on your right. Then take the clearly marked, walled footpath that leads off toward the high ground on your left. This brings you up onto the increasingly rocky ridge and the summit of **Sveti Nikola** ❸.

At 2,053 feet (626 m), Sveti Nikola is the highest point on Hvar, and the views are simply breathtaking. A long, broken ridge stretches off to the southeast, forming the spine of the island and continuing past Pitve and Jelsa, where the island narrows into its long, extended tail. (You can walk along several sections of the ridge, but paths are often hard to read.) The ground falls away steeply to the vineyards of Sveti Nedjelja to the south. The view to the south stretches to Korčula and the Pelješac Peninsula, with Lastovo and Vis visible. You should also be able to make out the tiny, distant island of Palagruža, and on a good day you can clearly see the Apennines in Italy.

The small **chapel** on the summit was originally built in the 15th century but has been struck by lightning and rebuilt more times than anyone cares to remember. Next to it is an enormous cross.

Descend by the same route back to Vrbanj, or take the unpaved road beyond Sveti Nikola and descend to the village of **Dol.** The rustic Konoba Kolumbić, a short way along this route, makes a great spot for lunch and produces its

own wine, and much of the unpaved road to Dol is through forest, which provides welcome shade on a hot afternoon. From Dol follow the paved road to Stari Grad.

You can also walk down from Sveti Nikola to the village of **Sveta Nedjelja** (see p. 221) on the south coast. However, be warned, getting to or from Sveta Nedjelja is tricky; a water taxi is your best bet. The road here passes through a tunnel under the mountains, so there is no shortcut back to Vrbanj.

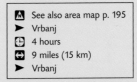

▲	See also area map p. 195
▶	Vrbanj
🕐	4 hours
↔	9 miles (15 km)
▶	Vrbanj

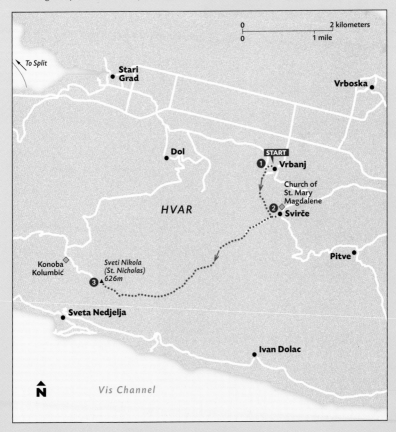

enclosed harbor called **Mandrać.** At the far end, if you are coming from the waterfront (or near end if arriving from the bus station) is the late 16th- and early 17th-century **Cathedral of St. Stephen** (Sv. Stjepan), built on the site of an earlier cathedral, probably founded in the 12th century. The elegant facade and adjacent bell tower are one of the most recognizable sites in Hvar.

In the streets above the north side of the square you will find

A picturesque cul-de-sac in Stari Grad, Hvar

the Venetian Gothic facade of the ruined **Hektorović Palace** and, higher still, the **Benedictine Nunnery.** Continue climbing slowly through a forest of pines and succulents along an easy switch-back trail to reach the 16th-century **Španjola Fortress.** The battlements and towers offer great views over the town and the nearby Pakleni Islands in the bay below, and a restaurant inside the old garrison building is open in the summer season. A castle has been located on this site since the rule of the Roman emperor Justinian in the sixth century A.D., and it has been variously added to and improved by the Venetians and Austrians. The dungeons have recently been opened to the public down a steep stone staircase. Down in the cells, you find yourself among the foundations and can see the strata of different building materials used over the years.

On the corner of the square by the waterfront is the large, 16th-century **Arsenal** (completely rebuilt after the Turkish raid), which has a large vaulted space forming a covered dock for galleys. The **theater** added above the Arsenal in 1612 has recently been renovated.

Turning left from the Arsenal along the café-filled **Riva** (water-front) brings you past the spot where ferries and catamarans arrive, above which narrow flights of steps lead up into the old residential quarter, **Burg.** Farther along the Riva, you turn a corner to arrive at the 15th-century **Franciscan monastery,** which houses a small museum and has a

Procession of the Cross

On Maundy Thursday (the last Thursday before Easter) at 10 p.m., in a tradition going back to the 17th century, a Procession of the Cross (Za Križen) leaves each of the villages of Jelsa, Pitve, Vrisnik, Svirče, Vrbanj, and Vrboska, visiting the other villages over the course of the next eight hours and 14 miles (22 km). The cross-bearer walks barefoot or in socks, with a procession of followers in the robes of religious brotherhoods, bearing candles and singing lamentations. The cross itself is covered with a black veil. The cross-bearer is supposed to run the last 330 feet (100 m) or so. Hvar's Procession of the Cross is inscribed on the UNESCO List of Intangible Cultural Heritage.

number of paintings, including an enormous 17th-century rendition of the Last Supper.

Just offshore from the tip of the peninsula south of Hvar, the pine-clad **Pakleni Islands** are the place to go for the best beaches in the area. Taxi boats make the trip out from the waterfront.

Around Hvar: The metaled seafront road continues from the monastery through another bay, where the less expensive apartments and hotels are located, as well as the town's soccer pitch. From here you leave the built-up town, although a ribbon of houses has grown up along the shore for the next mile or so, as a rugged shore plunges away from the roadside.

At the far end of the road, perhaps a 40-minute brisk walk from the center of Hvar, is a charming pebble beach in a quiet bay. From here the coast path turns to a rock trail and can be confusing in places. There are several small coves to be found here, and another 90 minutes along the coast takes you to the village of

Milna (also accessible by the taxi along the main road from Hvar).

Milna is a good place for lunch. You could picnic on a shaded headland or eat at the excellent Milina restaurant *(tel 021 745 023; closed in winter)* on the quay. Milna's cooks use olive oil produced in the groves above the town. An award-winning organic white wine, Bili Potok, is also made locally.

Stari Grad: Stari Grad sits at the head of a long harbor on the north of the island and, though busy, sees fewer visitors than Hvar town.

Without a doubt the most interesting place to visit in town is **Tvrdalj** *(tel 021 765 068, open May–Oct.)*, the fortified palace of Croatian Renaissance poet Petar Hektorović (1487–1572). Begun in 1520, it is a wonderful, almost mystical place, with a shady garden and, appropriately enough, a lovely cloistered stone fish pool; Hektorović's most famous work is entitled "Fishing and Fishermen's Talk." The pool is surrounded by various inscriptions from Hektorović's poetry on the walls and topped off by a stone dovecote.

Stari Grad
🗺 195 B1
Visitor Information
✉ Obala dr. Franje Tuđmana 1
☎ 021 765 763
stari-grad-faros .hr

The deep waters around Vis are home to a wealth of sea life.

Stari Grad Museum

✉ Ulaz Braće Biankini 2

☎ 021 766 324

🕒 Closed Oct.–April & Sun., May–Sept.

💲 $

stari-grad-museum.net

Vrboska

🗺 195 B1

Visitor Information

✉ Vrboska bb

☎ 021 774 137

vrboska.info

Nearby, the small 16th-century **Church of Sveti Rok,** built as the Hektorović family chapel, has traces of floor mosaics from an old Roman bath. Just around the corner, you will find the **Dominican monastery,** rebuilt in the 16th century (after more Ottoman raids), which contains the **Stari Grad Museum.** A short walk east from this, toward the bus station, you will find the small Romanesque **Church of St. John** (Sv. Ivan), which is thought to stand on the site of the island's earliest cathedral. There's also a museum in the **Biankini Palace.**

The car ferry to Hvar docks at Stari Grad. The ferry port is some distance west from the town center but is on the local bus route.

East From Stari Grad: To the east of Stari Grad stretches

the UNESCO World Heritage site known as the **Stari Grad Plain** (starogradsko-polje.net), a level agricultural area with a neat gridwork of dry stone walls (suhozid), which almost perfectly preserves the pattern of land use established by the Greeks some 2,400 years ago. To the south, beyond the villages of Dol and Vrbanj, the land rises steadily to the highest point on the island, **Sveti Nikola** (see pp. 216–217).

Vrboska, a fairly sleepy little fishing village largely given over to tourism, makes a good place to stay if you want a more low-key alternative to Hvar and Stari Grad, with rocky beaches along the headland and a pretty center at the head of a long cove. Southeast of Vrboska, at the point where the island narrows into its slender tail, is the small, attractive town of **Jelsa,** the departure point for the catamaran to Bol.

On the south coast of the island, nestled below vineyards and the slopes of Sveti Nikola, is the small town of **Sveta Nedjelja.** Zlatan Otok, the producer of the Zlatan Plavac wine *(zlatanotok.hr),* organizes wine tours here. Sveta Nedjelja can be reached by road from Jelsa, passing through a long tunnel under the mountains, although bus services in the region are infrequent.

Vis

The island of Vis is one of the more remote islands in the Croatian archipelago and sees far fewer visitors than its neighbors despite being easily accessible by catamaran from Split—and despite being a wonderful place to visit.

The Greeks founded their first colony on the Adriatic here in the fourth century B.C., at Issa, the modern town of Vis. Issa grew into a thriving town, and it was from here that further colonies

were established on the Adriatic, including Salona, which became the capital of Roman Dalmatia. Later the island was under Rome and then Byzantium. It fell to the Venetians in the 15th century (when it was administered from neighboring Hvar), then Austria, and Napoleonic France. Vis became an important naval base in the early 19th century under the British and was the location of the Battle of Lissa between Italy and Austria in 1866, the first sea action fought between ironclad battleships.

The island's strategic importance continued during World War II, when a system of caves in its mountainous center was used as a temporary headquarters by Marshal Tito's Partisans. The island was the site of a diplomatic meeting in 1944 between Tito; Randolph Churchill, the son of Britain's war prime minister, Winston Churchill; and English novelist Evelyn Waugh that helped to establish relations between the western Allies and the nominally communist Partisan force in the latter stages of the war.

Jelsa
195 B1

Visitor Information
✉ Riva bb
☎ 021 761 017
tzjelsa.hr

Vis
195 A1

Visitor Information
✉ Šetalište Stare Isse 5, Vis town
☎ 021 717 017
tz-vis.hr

EXPERIENCE: Explore Hvar by Bike

While buses run between Hvar town, Stari Grad, and Jelsa, you can easily explore this part of the island by bike. Heading west from Jelsa on the main road to Stari Grad will bring you past the villages of **Vrbanj** and **Dol,** below **Sveti Nikola** (see pp. 216–217), before continuing to **Stari Grad,** where you can visit the fortified home of Renaissance writer Petar Hektorović (see p. 219). Those wanting a longer ride can continue from Stari Grad to **Hvar.** Otherwise, return to Vrboska and Jelsa along the unpaved road passing across **Stari Grad Plain** (see p. 220), a rural landscape that has changed little since the Greeks were here 2,500 years ago. Rejoin the main road and head down into the fishing village of **Vrboska,** where you can stop at a café on the waterfront. Then continue following the narrow coast road that winds around the headland back into the town of **Jelsa.**

Town Museum

✉ Riva bb, Vis town

☎ 021 713 455

tz-vis.hr

Komiža

🅰 195 A1

Visitor Information

✉ Riva Sv. Miikule 2

☎ 021 713 455

tz-komiza.hr

There were still mines from World War II in some parts of the island until quite recently. In fact, as the naval headquarters of Yugoslavia, the town of Vis remained closed to foreign visitors until 1989, which perhaps explains why it still feels slightly removed from the tourist trail.

INSIDER TIP:

Stroll east along Vis town's waterfront to the Kut district, where a war cemetery contains the graves of British sailors lost during the Napoleonic Wars.

—BARBARA JACKSON
National Geographic contributor

The main towns on the island are Vis in the northeast and Komiža in the southwest, with a number of smaller settlements scattered in between, mainly along the island's southern coast. The island relies in large part on drinking water brought over from the mainland, so it is a fairly precious commodity not to be wasted. Vugova Viška is a good local white wine, and there is a particularly tasty local pie filled with anchovies and capers called *poga a*—similar to Italian calzone. Local buses travel regularly between Komiža and Vis.

Vis Town: The town of Vis is situated on a bay in the northeast of the island, with a lovely Riva stretching along the waterfront. The **Town Museum,**

part of Split's Archaeological Museum, has a good collection of finds from the island from the Neolithic period forward, including pottery, ancient jewelry, Roman floor mosaics, and a beautiful bronze head of the goddess Aphrodite dating from the fourth century B.C. There are various old palaces dotted around the town and a **Franciscan monastery** on the Prirovo peninsula (on the northern side of the bay), built on the site of a Roman amphitheater.

Up on the headland you will find the ruins of the **Wellington Fort,** one of a series of forts built by the British between 1811 and 1814. Another legacy of the British is cricket; a club was established here by Captain William Hoste, who had served under Lord Nelson. The club has recently been revived *(viscricket.com).*

Komiža: Komiža sits at the head of a broad bay with a scattering of elegant 16th- and 17th-century houses and good, uncrowded beaches. A 16th-century **Venetian tower** on the pretty waterfront houses the town's **Fishing Museum** *(tel 091 902 7031, vis-central.com/en /vodic/fishing-museum, $),* with exhibits that include a copy of the traditional local fishing boat *(gajeta Falkuša),* which has been used on the island for centuries.

Above the town is a partially fortified **Benedictine monastery and Church of St. Nicholas** (Sv. Nikola), often called Muster. The fortifications date to the 16th century. On December 6, the feast day of St. Nicholas, a wooden boat is burned in front of the church, an indication of the importance that fishing has always held within the community.

Beyond Vis & Komiža: Away from Vis and Komiža, the island is even more peaceful. **Milna** and **Rukavac,** two of the small settlements along the island's south coast—and located only some 5.5 miles (9 km) and 6 miles (10 km) respectively from Vis—are near **Srebrena** and **Zagla beaches,** among the nicest beaches on the island and certainly the most popular.

Hum, at 1,926 feet (587 m) the highest point on Vis, is in the east of the island near Komiža, and not far from here is **Titova Špilja,** the cave where Tito stayed at various times during World War II. There is a short, marked trail to the cave from a parking lot beyond the village of Podšpilje. Hum itself is crowned by radio antennas and is out of bounds, but nearby **Sveti Duh** is only a few feet lower and can also be reached by a hiking trail (starting farther up the road from Podšpilje) for panoramic views of the island.

A few years ago, a tourist stepped on a World War II land mine on this part of Vis. Although the area was subsequently swept for ordnance and declared safe; it is probably best to stay on the trail.

Biševo

Finally, a few miles offshore from Komiža is the islet of Biševo, location of the great attraction **Blue Cave** (Modra Špilja), an

A donkey helps with the grape harvest below the Church of St. Nicholas in Komiža.

idyllic natural wonder lit by sunlight reflected from the seafloor. It can get crowded with tourists, and the number of boats at the cave has been known to make it all a little less idyllic at peak time. Boat trips head out for the cave from Komiža and Vis, as long as the sea is not too rough. ∎

Milna
🅼 195 B2

Biševo
🅼 195 A1

Hidden away behind the Dinaric Alps, a region home to Croatia's greatest natural wonder and most spectacular festival

The Dalmatian Hinterland

A knight, or *alkari*, races toward a target during a centuries-old jousting tournament in Sinj.

The Dalmatian Hinterland

With the exception of one area, the Dalmatian hinterland is a part of Croatia hardly seen by foreign visitors. That exception is Plitvice Lakes (Plitvička Jezera) National Park, without a doubt one of the most heavily promoted tourist destinations in Croatia, but no less captivating for all that.

The Dalmatian hinterland is fairly well hidden away from most of the rest of the country, divided from the more familiar towns of the Adriatic coast by the rugged mountain ranges that make up the Dinaric Alps in the west, and sandwiched against the Bosnian border in the east.

Plitvice Lakes National Park

Beautiful Plitvice Lakes National Park, another item on Croatia's list of UNESCO World Heritage sites, is the area that makes it on the must-do itineraries for foreign visitors, thousands of whom do day trips from the Dalmatian coast or from Zagreb. Creating a wonderful watery landscape, the park's travertine falls were created over many thousands of years as the calcium carbonate dissolved in the mineral-rich waters forming crystals on the mosses and algae growing at the surface. A network of hiking trails meanders around the lakes and through forest, boats and a shuttle "train" carry visitors to various points in the park, and wooded boardwalks make it easy to get right up close to the waterfalls themselves.

Not far from one of the entrances to the park, the village of Rastoke has a number of attractive old water mills—some of them still working—and plenty of gushing waterfalls at the point where the Sljunčica River flows into the Korana River. Between Plitvice Lakes and the Velebit mountains to the southwest lies the fertile Lika region, a rural area with a low population density—even lower since the Homeland War, at the end of which many ethnic Serbs left the newly formed nation of Croatia. Both the 19th-century Croatian politician Ante Starčević and the great electrical engineer Nikola Tesla were born here. The house where Tesla was born is located in the village of Smiljan, near Gospić, and has been turned into a small but informative museum.

Knin & Around

The ancient city of Knin sits some 87 miles (140 km) south of Plitvice on the railway line between Zagreb and Split, its brooding fortress overlooking the city from a hill. Dinara, at 6,007 feet (1,831 m), the highest mountain in Croatia, looms to the east of Knin, and the headwaters of the Cetina and Krka Rivers both rise near here before they go on to carve deep gorges on their way to the Adriatic Sea.

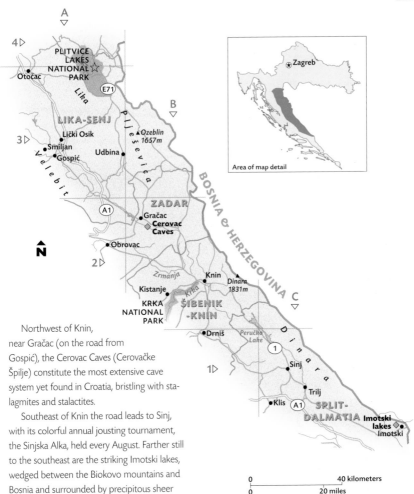

Northwest of Knin, near Gračac (on the road from Gospić), the Cerovac Caves (Cerovačke Špilje) constitute the most extensive cave system yet found in Croatia, bristling with stalagmites and stalactites.

Southeast of Knin the road leads to Sinj, with its colorful annual jousting tournament, the Sinjska Alka, held every August. Farther still to the southeast are the striking Imotski lakes, wedged between the Biokovo mountains and Bosnia and surrounded by precipitous sheer cliffs. Many families chose to leave Imotski and the surrounding area during the last century, preferring to settle in the more fertile region of Slavonia to the north.

Historically, the inland region of Dalmatia was certainly no backwater, as attested by the Roman ruins near the upper reaches of the Krka and by the fact that, during the 11th century, the city of Knin was a seat of the medieval kings of Croatia. Knin's position on the main Zagreb–Split railroad line means that the city maintains its strategic importance to the present day.

This area of Dalmatia also suffered heavily during the Homeland War. The first casualties were lost during an encounter in the unlikely location of a national park office. Despite its tranquillity, the park was a valuable source of income and prestige worth fighting for. Numerous Croats fled the area during the war, while Knin became the capital of the breakaway Serbian Republic of Krajina (Republika Srpska Krajina), which was retaken by Croatia in a massive military operation in August 1995. There are still land mines in some areas along the Bosnian border, around Knin and on the southeast slopes of the Velebit range. ■

Plitvice Lakes National Park

Croatia's most famous natural monument, Plitvice Lakes (Plitvička Jezera), is, despite the crowds of visitors, a truly wonderful place—all rushing water, emerald- and turquoise-colored lakes, moss-festooned crags, and sudden, almost unexpected pockets of silence.

A boat tour is the best way to see the spectacular features of Plitvice Lakes up close.

Plitvice Lakes National Park

🗺 227 A3–A4

Visitor Information

✉ Znanstveno Stručni Centar "Ivo Pevalek," Plitvička Jezera

☎ 053 751 015

np-plitvicka-jezera.hr

Plitvice Lakes is the oldest and largest of Croatia's national parks, having been established in 1949 and now covering an area of nearly 115 square miles (300 sq km). It was declared a UNESCO World Heritage site in 1979. The centerpiece of the park—and the only part most people actually see—is a series of 16 vividly colored lakes, flowing into each other over a spectacular series of travertine falls. The lakes descend roughly 425 feet (130 m) over about 5 miles (8 km), before flowing on as the **Korana River.** They are set amid lush vegetation and dense beech forest. The park is home to a variety of birds and animals, including black storks, brown bears, and rare Eurasian lynx.

A network of well-marked trails and wooden boardwalks makes access to the lakes and waterfalls very easy. Boats ferry visitors across some of the lakes, and a shuttle bus runs from one end of them to the other. The park does get extremely busy, seeing 4,000 visitors a day during the summer. Aim to start exploring the lakes as early as possible, before the park gets too crowded.

Rock Formations

Travertine (also known as tufa) is a porous sedimentary rock, formed through the precipitation of calcium carbonate from the area's lakes and rivers. The mineral also forms deposits on mosses, leading to their gradual petrification. Travertine grows vertically from the lake beds to form barriers and waterfalls, and horizontally from the lip of the waterfalls, extending in the direction of the water flow and leaving a cave beneath the falls.

The formation of travertine is an ongoing process. Four hundred years ago **Kozjak Lake** was actually two lakes, but continual deposits on the lake beds raised the water level, submerging the travertine barrier between the lakes. The old barrier is still visible beneath the surface.

Local legend has its own, more poetic version of the creation of the area. According to folklore, during a terrible drought locals prayed to the infamous Crna Kraljica, or Black Queen—and she replied by unleashing spectacular rainstorms that flooded the whole area and created the lakes.

INSIDER TIP:

Climb to the top of the stairs next to the 250-foot (76 m) Veliki Slap waterfall—you'll be rewarded with a breathtaking view of the falls and Plitvice Lakes National Park.

—JUSTIN KAVANAGH
*National Geographic
Travel Books editor*

Getting to the Park

Plitvice Lakes National Park lies on the E71, the main highway between Karlovac and Knin, about 93 miles (150 km) south of Zagreb. Buses run regularly from the main cities, but getting a bus *from* the park can sometimes be difficult, since they fill quickly. The shuttle buses and boats in the park itself run every 20 minutes or so.

There are two entrances *(ulazi)* to the park: near the parking lot (Ulaz 1) and near the **Hotel Jezero** (Ulaz 2). There are several large hotels around Ulaz 1. The nearest **camping ground** is at Korana, 5 miles (8 km) north of Ulaz 1. Camping in the park itself is prohibited. ∎

First Casualties of War

Despite its stunning scenery, there is a darker side to the history of Plitvice Lakes National Park. In 1991, Serbian militia occupied park headquarters, and the standoff, and shoot-out, with Croatian police that followed resulted in the first deaths of the Homeland War (see pp. 34–35). The park itself was spared the excesses of the conflict, though troops occupied the area's hotels, which were later used to house refugees and had to undergo renovation after the war.

Plitvice Lakes Walk

Naturally, the best way to explore Plitvice Lakes National Park is on foot. Walking on the main trails is straightforward. They are clear (mostly on wooden boardwalks), and you can easily get around most of the lakes in a day, though having two days to wander at a more leisurely pace will be even more rewarding.

Boardwalks take visitors through the heart of the watery world of Plitvice Lakes.

South End

Starting from **Hotel Jezero** ❶ *(located at Ulaz 2)*, follow the path down to the ticket office, then continue descending to the shore of **Kozjak Lake.** Here a boat will ferry you over to the other side of the lake. Once there, follow the clear, well-marked trail, mostly on wooden boardwalks, that meanders through a succession of small lakes, passing reed beds and travertine falls.

The mosses—mainly *Cratoneuron,* but also *Brium*—which, through a gradual process of petrification, form into rocky features, can be seen growing on the surface of travertine barriers and waterfalls. Beneath the water you will often see pale, ghost-like tree trunks and branches, which are

NOT TO BE MISSED:

Boat trip across Kozjak
Lake • Veliki Slap waterfall
• Korana River cascades

undergoing a similar process as calcium carbonate is deposited on them from the mineral-rich waters in the region. Those with an interest in botany should keep a watch for unusual plants; several species do not grow anywhere outside the national park. Continue as far as either **Galovac Lake** ❷ or **Okrugljak Lake** ❸ before ascending back to the road.

North End

Take the shuttle bus, which departs every 20 minutes or so, to **Milanovac 4**. Resume walking from the bus drop-off point, arriving at a spectacular viewpoint high above the lakes. Pause here to fully enjoy one of the classic views in the park.

Rather than continue along the high trail, turn right and descend the fairly steep steps leading down through an enormous hole in the rock. At the bottom, turn right and follow the boardwalks, which now lead you alongside a series of rushing **cascades.** After a short distance, you pass another boardwalk trail on your right (marked "parking"). Ignore this for the time being and keep straight ahead, passing **Sastavci** on your right, where one of the final lakes pours into the Korana River, then

descends dramatically to a pool at the base of **Veliki Slap 5** (literally, "big waterfall"), which tumbles 250 feet (76 m) down the cliff opposite.

Backtrack to the boardwalk marked "parking" and follow this across the lake, then ascend the trail on the far side, from where there are particularly good views back to Veliki Slap. At the top, turn right to reach the bus back to the ticket office near Hotel Jezero.

Depending on your time and level of fitness, there is plenty of scope for further exploration in the park, and you can buy a fairly detailed map ("Nacionalni Park Plitvicka Jezera Tourist Map," scale 1:50,000) from the ticket office or from shops at the entrances to the park and in hotels. Make sure you stay on the marked trails to avoid erosion and environmental damage.

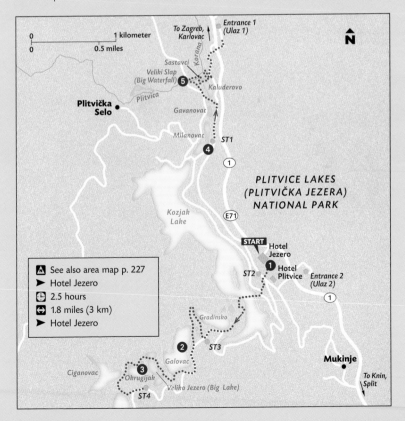

South of Plitvice Lakes

The Dalmatian hinterland southeast of Plitvice Lakes, tucked between a range of mountains running along the coast and the western border of Bosnia, sees very few foreign visitors. It is a completely different rugged landscape from the parched forest of the better-known, sunny coastline or the verdant green plain of Slavonia.

For centuries, the massive fortress at Knin controlled the land for miles around.

Gospić & Smiljan
🅰 227 A3
Visitor Information
✉ Bana I Karlovića 1, Gospic
☎ 053 560 752
tz-gospic.hr

Nikola Tesla Memorial Center
✉ Smiljan
☎ 053 746 530
🕒 Closed Mon.
💲 $
mcnikolatesla.hr

Lika

Lika, the sparsely populated and largely agricultural area of which Plitvice Lakes is a part, stretches southwest from the park, where it is bounded by the Velebit and Velika Kapela mountain ranges.

Just outside **Gospić**, the capital of Lika, is the village of **Smiljan**—a place that is largely unremarkable except for its association with Lika's most famous son, inventor and electrical engineer Nikola Tesla (see sidebar opposite). The

house of Tesla's birth still stands in the center of the village, near a statue of the man by Mile Blažević. It is open to the public as a museum, and forms part of the **Nikola Tesla Memorial Center**, opened in 2006.

The **Cerovac Caves** (Cerovačke Špilje), some of the most impressive caves in Croatia, sit beneath the southern foothills of the Velebit range near the town of **Gračac**, on the road between Gospić and Knin.

INSIDER TIP:

Make sure to visit the Cerovac Caves, situated in the southern part of the Velebit mountains, and enjoy the beautiful features, such as stalactites and stalagmites.

—IVOR KARAVANIC
National Geographic grantee

The cave system extends some 7,000 feet (2,150 m) under the hills and contains highlights such as the Well of Life, the Crystal Hall, and an eroded rock that is said to look like the head of Santa Claus.

Knin

Located about 87 miles (140 km) south of Plitvice Lakes on the E71 highway, and set amid a harsh, karst landscape, is the town of Knin. Knin lies in the shadow of Dinara—at 6,007 feet (1,831 m), the highest peak in Croatia—and though located far from the tourist trail, it is a town of considerable strategic and historical importance for the country.

Knin was the capital of the medieval kingdom of Croatia under King Zvonimir during the 11th century, and the railway line between Zagreb and Split—the vital link between the Croatian capital and the main Adriatic port—runs straight through it. For this reason, it was a key possession during the Homeland War, when it became the capital of the breakaway Republic of Serbian Krajina (Republika Srpska Krajina). At its height, this entity arced from Knin in the south, around the Bosnian border to western Slavonia. The republic was ruled by Milan Babić (1936–2006), a dentist from Knin who oversaw the removal of non-Serbs from the territory throughout the 1990s, a war crime for which he was later convicted. Knin and the rest of the Krajina were retaken by Croatian forces during the 1995 Operation Storm.

Cerovac Caves
✉ Cerovačke Pećine
☎ 023 689 920
pp-velebit.hr

Knin
🅜 227 B2
Visitor Information
✉ Dr. Franje Tudmana 24
☎ 022 664 822
tz-knin.hr

Nikola Tesla: Croatia's Brightest Scientist

Nikola Tesla (1856–1943) was a scientist, inventor, and electrical engineer born in Smiljan. The son of a Serbian Orthodox priest, he studied in Graz, Austria, and later lived and worked in Maribor (now in Slovenia), Budapest, and Paris before moving to the United States in 1884, and then becoming a citizen.

One of the greatest figures in the birth of modern commercial electricity, Tesla wrote numerous patents and is credited with the development of the AC (alternating current) motor and polyphase system, which laid the foundation for the modern AC electricity supply. Many also consider him to be the inventor of radio. Today, the strength of magnetic fields is measured in teslas (T).

Tesla's work is showcased in Zagreb's Technical Museum and in the Nikola Tesla Museum in Belgrade, Serbia. There is also a fine statue of him—in somewhat pensive mood—by Ivan Meštrović (see sidebar p. 62) in Zagreb.

Sinj

🗺 227 C1

Visitor Information

✉ 12 Put Petrovca

☎ 021 826 352

visitsinj.com

Knin's huge medieval **fortress,** which was much restored by Ottoman rulers during the 16th century and then by Venice during the 18th century, broods over the town from the neighboring hill of Sveti Spas. Now thankfully no more than a tourist attraction, the fortress offers fine views of the town.

The countryside surrounding Knin is rich in archaeological finds, including the Roman settlement of **Burnum** and the medieval Croatian site of **Biskupija.** Both the Krka and Cetina Rivers have their sources near Knin. However, you should be aware that much of the countryside around Knin is still heavily afflicted by hidden land mines from the Homeland War.

Wandering off the road in this part of Croatia should be avoided at all times.

Sinj

An additional 44 miles (70 km) south from Knin will bring you to the town of Sinj, perhaps best known for its colorful annual jousting tournament, the **Sinjska Alka** (see sidebar opposite), held in early August. This lively event evokes a considerable amount of local pride and draws huge crowds.

If you find yourself in Sinj at other times of the year, you can also visit the **Franciscan monastery,** where the town's most famous painting, the "Gospa Sinjska" ("Madonna of Sinj"),

The Topolskij Buk waterfall is the source of the Krka River near Knin.

INSIDER TIP:

If you are planning to watch the Sinjska Alka, check at the tourist office in Split to reserve a seat before heading inland. Even if a seat is not available, the unique event is still worth the trip.

—TOM JACKSON
National Geographic contributor

is kept on display. The work of an unknown 16th-century artist from Venice, the painting played a crucial role, according to popular belief, in Sinj's seemingly miraculous defeat of a numerically vastly superior Ottoman Turkish force in 1715.

Imotski

Hidden away behind the towering Biokovo mountain range and situated close to the border with Bosnia is the town of Imotski. The main reason most people come to Imotski is to see the town's two dramatic karst lakes, **Blue Lake** (Modro Jezero) and **Red Lake** (Crveno Jezero). Surrounded by high cliffs—785 feet (240 m) and almost sheer in places—the lakes were formed when the roof and sides of a huge sinkhole and underground cave network collapsed.

Blue Lake is a popular spot for swimming, with several easy, well-engineered trails originally built when the area was part of the Austro-Hungarian Empire in the 1900s. There is a small entrance fee to access the paths.

The water in Red Lake is thought to be about 980 feet (300 m) deep, which puts its bed at somewhere below sea level, though its precise depth is still unknown. The water level in Blue Lake varies depending on the time of year. It can be very high in spring, the result of snowmelt, but by late summer the bottom of the lake can dry out completely—at which point it becomes the favored local soccer pitch, complete with its own goalposts!

EXPERIENCE:
Attend Sinjska Alka

The Sinjska Alka *(tzsinj.hr, alka.hr)* is an annual contest held in Sinj, where jousters in traditional costume compete to spear a target using a lance from the back of a galloping horse. The target is called the *alka* and consists of a small metal ring with four compartments (the central one is the highest score) suspended above the track. Competitors are known as *alkari*. The event commemorates the local victory, despite overwhelming odds, over Ottoman forces in 1715. It begins on the first Sunday in August and lasts for three days.

Zvonimir Boban, one of Croatia's most famous soccer stars, is from Imotski. Boban played 51 times for Croatia and captained the Croatia team that finished in third place at the 1998 World Cup. Even if you do not follow the game, you can visit his bar (called Boban), which is a popular spot in Zagreb, and learn about his "kick heard around the world." ■

Imotski
🅰 227 C1
Visitor Information
✉ Jezeranska bb
☎ 021 842 221
tz-imotski.hr

Dubrovnik, a city of red roofs that wins the hearts of visitors, with the rocky Pelješac Peninsula and the quiet Gulf Islands

Southern Dalmatia

In Dubrovnik's old town, the dome of the cathedral rises high above the surrounding rooftops.

Southern Dalmatia

Southern Dalmatia includes the historic city of Dubrovnik—a UNESCO World Heritage site—and the slender Pelješac Peninsula, along with the islands of Korčula, Mljet, and Lastovo, and the Elaphite Islands closer to the coast. For three centuries, this area formed the Republic of Ragusa (the name by which Dubrovnik went until after World War I), until its dissolution under Napoleon.

Dubrovnik's marble-lined old town has many places to sit and watch the world go by.

Dubrovnik, described by Lord Byron, 18th-century English poet and adventurer, as the "pearl of the Adriatic," is one of the most beautiful places anywhere in Croatia—even after repeated visits. It is remarkable as much for its long maritime history and liberal system of government as for its exceptionally well-preserved fortifications. By the early 15th century, the city had abolished slavery (400 years ahead of the United States) and established its own public health service and one of the first orphanages in Europe. It also introduced one of Europe's earliest quarantine systems to protect itself from the plague. And it achieved all this without its own standing army, relying instead on careful diplomacy and wealth created through a vibrant maritime trade.

South of Dubrovnik is the small town of Cavtat, formerly the Greek colony of Epidaurus. After this Greek city had been sacked in the seventh century, the displaced population moved up the coast to found Ragusa, soon to be joined by Slav neighbors to form the kernel of today's city of Dubrovnik.

Beyond Cavtat is the border with Montenegro. On the other side of the frontier lies the gorgeous Bay of Kotor, tantalizingly close by.

Area of map detail

NOT TO BE MISSED:

A walk around the mighty walls of Dubrovnik's old town, one of the most beautiful and atmospheric places in Croatia 244–245

Sampling oysters cultivated off the shore of Mali Ston 257

A hike on Sveti Ilija to see some of the best views anywhere on the Dalmatian coast 258

A visit to the medieval town of Korčula, supposedly the birthplace of legendary Venetian traveler Marco Polo 262 & 264–265

Witnessing the *Moreška* sword dance performed on the island of Korčula 263

Exploring the saltwater lakes and virgin Mediterranean forests of Mljet National Park 269–270

To the northwest of Dubrovnik, the Pelješac Peninsula boasts yet more superb fortifications at the town of Ston, whose salt pans contributed much to Ragusa's wealth. Farther north on the peninsula, some of Croatia's finest red wines are produced in the Dingač region. At the base of the peninsula are a string of tiny islands known as the Elaphites.

Across a narrow strait from Pelješac, the medieval walled town of Korčula is one of the loveliest of any in the Adriatic. It is popularly believed to have been the original home of explorer Marco Polo, whose book of travels arguably went on to shape the history of western travel literature and certainly influenced western perceptions of eastern Asia for many centuries.

South of Korčula and Pelješac, the island of Mljet is one of Croatia's most popular national parks, noted for its lush forests and rather idyllic saltwater lakes. Farther still from the mainland, the island of Lastovo—about as far-flung as the main islands of the Croatian archipelago get—is home to an offshore nature reserve. The island has comparatively few visitors, despite the pre-Lent carnival that is one of the wildest in Croatia. ■

Dubrovnik

Dubrovnik, perhaps the best known city in Croatia, remains a quite unforgettable place, with a huge number of interesting sights crammed within its outstanding medieval city walls. The sheer wealth of sights and sounds in the city is enough to absorb the days of several vacations, yet there is plenty more to see in the region beyond the old town, such as the quarantine houses of Lazareti and the views from Mount Srđ.

The old town of Dubrovnik is protected by its world-famous walls.

Dubrovnik

🅰 239 C1

Visitor Information

✉ Brsalje 5

☎ 020 323 887

**experience
.dubrovnik.hr**

Dubrovnik's old town occupies a rocky headland, surrounded on all sides by massive and utterly impenetrable-looking walls. Within, the old town is divided along its central axis by Stradun—its broad, elegant main street—from which smaller streets and alleys radiate at right angles. Almost all of Dubrovnik's main sights—and there are a lot of them, from churches and monasteries to museums and palaces—lie within the confines of the old city walls, making it a remarkably easy place to navigate (there are no cars in the old town). The eastern side of the old town is occupied by the old port. To the east of the old town is the upscale suburb of Ploče, while to the west lie the suburbs of Lapad, Babin Kuk, and Gruž. Above the old town stands a prominent hill, Mount Srđ. Several scenes from the hit HBO TV series *Game of Thrones* were filmed in Dubrovnik and on nearby Lokrum island.

Dubrovnik's airport is at Čilipi, about 12.5 miles (20 km) south of town, and connected to the city by shuttle buses. Local buses leaving from outside Pile Gate connect the old town with the suburbs. The intercity bus station and main ferry port are located in Gruž. Ferries run to Split and Rijeka up the coast, as well as to Korčula town, Sobra on Mljet, and the Elaphite Islands (Šipan, Lopud, and Koločep). Ferries also run to Bari in Italy. Local ferries to Cavtat and Lokrum depart from the port by the old town. If you are here with your own car, parking anywhere near the old town can be a challenging and expensive business. Instead, use the parking lot at Gruž, then walk or take a bus or taxi from there. There is no rail connection to Dubrovnik.

City Walls

Dubrovnik's medieval city walls, among the best preserved in Europe and one of the defining features of the old town, are one of the most iconic landmarks anywhere in Croatia. Extending for some 1.25 miles (less than 2 km) in length, they rise to a height of 82 feet (25 m) in places and are up to 20 feet (6 m) thick. The walls are fortified by no fewer than 12 rectangular towers and 3 round ones, 2 corner towers, 5 bastions, and a large fortress.

A second, outer wall rises on the landward side, lower than the main wall but with an additional ten semicircular bastions, and originally with a moat between them and the main wall. Also, outside the main system of walls are two more fortresses, **St. Lawrence's Fortress** (Lovrijenac, on the headland west of Bokar Fortress) and the **Revelin Fortress,** by the Ploče Gate.

The walls were begun during the 8th century and had completely encircled the town by the 12th century. They were extended and enlarged from the 14th to the 17th century, partly in response to an increased threat from the Ottomans and Venice.

INSIDER TIP:

Your Dubrovnik City Walls ticket also entitles you to visit St. Lawrence's Fortress on the sea cliffs outside Pyle Gate. The fort has terrific harbor views without the crowds, but be warned: It is a climb to the entrance.

—CAROLINE HICKEY
National Geographic Travel Books editor

The largest of the fortresses, **St. John's Fortress** (Tvrđana Sv. Ivan) was built in several stages between 1346 and 1557. The construction of the walls and towers involved some of the leading architects of the day, including Michelozzo Michelozzi from Florence and Juraj Dalmatinac of Zadar. Major renovations were carried out following the Homeland War.

Touring the Walls: The main entrance up onto the walls is just inside the Pile Gate, but there are two other entrances, on Sv. Dominika (by the Dominican monastery) and on Kneža

Damjana Jude (by St. John's Fortress). The 15th-century **Pile Gate,** at the west end of the old town and the point through which most visitors enter the city, is reached by a wooden drawbridge and surmounted by a statue of St. Blaise (Sv. Vlaho), the city's patron saint and a figure with whom you will become increasingly familiar as you wander around the old town. Set in a niche inside the gate itself is a second St. Blaise, this one by Ivan Meštrović (see sidebar p. 62).

Stradun & Around

The Pile Gate leads onto Stradun (also known locally as Placa), a broad, straight thoroughfare between the Pile Gate and the Ploče Gate, widening slightly at its far end, its limestone paving slabs worn smooth over the centuries by passing feet. Stradun marks the ancient division between the area settled by the displaced former inhabitants of Cavtat, after their town had been sacked by the Avars (on the right, south of Stradun), and the area settled later by Slavs (the steep streets on the left, north of Stradun).

Stradun was originally a marshy area, becoming a street as the two communities gradually merged over the centuries, and was paved in the 15th century. Note the distinctive old **shop fronts,** with a door and window combined within a single arched frame,

Onofrio's Great Fountain was one of the few sources of clean water during the Homeland War.

Summer Festival

The annual Dubrovnik Summer Festival (*dubrovnik-festival.hr*), one of the largest in Croatia, has been going since 1950. The 45-day event takes place in July and August and features a superb program of performances (including music, opera, theater, and dance) by Croatian and international artists.

Much of the festival takes place within the old town, which turns into something of a living stage during this period. The festival kicks off with an opening ceremony in Luža Square (the old heart of the city), an event that typically continues as an all-night party enjoyed by locals and visitors alike.

allowing the closed lower portion to function as a shop counter (a feature known as *na koljeno*).

Just inside the Pile Gate on the right is a small square with the domed, 16-sided structure of **Onofrio's Great Fountain** on the right. Built in 1444 as a cistern for the city's drinking water, it has 16 waterspouts in the form of sculpted heads. In its more recent history, it provided one of the only sources of drinking water for the city when it came under bombardment and siege during the Homeland War. The immense fountain is named after the architect who designed it, Onofrio della Cava of Naples.

Behind the fountain, on the far side of the square, is the former **Convent of St. Claire** (Sv. Klara), built in the 13th century and dissolved by Napoleon in 1806, which housed an orphanage from the 15th century but these days has a restaurant in its well-restored cloister. Beyond this, along Garište, is the small 16th-century **Church of St. Roch** (Sv. Rok), built as a votive church against the frequent outbreaks of plague. On one of the exterior walls is carved the curious inscription, in Latin: "Peace be unto you, but remember that

you will die, you who are playing ball, 1597."

To the left of the Pile Gate is the small 16th-century **Church of Our Savior** (Sv. Spas), built in thanksgiving following the earthquake of 1520, the work of Petar Andrijić of Korčula. The facade with its wheel window hides a

INSIDER TIP:

Game of Thrones **fans should head for the Rector's Palace, the market square, and the island of Lokrum, just some of the spots in Dubrovnik where the TV show was filmed.**

—KENNY LING
*National Geographic contributor
& mapmaker*

Gothic interior, where concerts are sometimes held during the summer months.

Franciscan Church & Monastery: Just past the Church of Our Savior on the left, and entered through a late 15th-century carved portal, (continued on p. 246)

Franciscan Church & Monastery

⛰ Map p. 245

✉ Placa 2

💲 $$

Dubrovnik Walking Tour

With so much to see in Dubrovnik, any tour of the city is correspondingly long. This one falls easily into two parts that can be spread over two days or broken with a stop for lunch. In either case, walk around the city walls in the morning before it gets too hot, then head down Stradun for lunch before resuming the itinerary.

The vaulted loggia outside the Rector's Palace

Atop the Walls

Enter the old town through the **Pile Gate** ❶ (see p. 242), noting the first of many statues of the city's patron saint, St. Blaise. Then, after purchasing a ticket (*$$$*), follow the steps up to the left onto the city walls. After getting a good view of Stradun, turn left (south) and follow the walls toward **Bokar Fortress** (with views over the bay to St. Lawrence's Fortress) and on along the old town's seaward side. Notice the aqueduct here, part of Onofrio della Cava's system for supplying the city with water.

At the far (southeast) corner of the walls you reach the huge **St. John's Fortress** ❷ (see p. 241), from which a massive protective

NOT TO BE MISSED:

Walking the medieval walls
• The Cathedral Treasury, the resting place of St. Blaiset
• Lunching at Gundulić Square

chain once stretched across the old harbor. Toward the northeast corner of the walls, you have good views down on the Dominican monastery. Climb up past **St. James (Sv. Jakov) tower** ❸, which marked the eastern extremity of the walls until the 14th century. From here, along the northern section of the walls to the **Minčeta Fortress** ④ (the highest point on the walls), you have unrivaled views over the old town. The best views of the Franciscan monastery look down over the cloister from the following section of wall before the Pile Gate, where you will descend again.

Street Level

Stop to fill up water bottles at **Onofrio's Great Fountain** (see p. 243) and continue onto **Stradun**, stopping first at the **Franciscan Church & Monastery** ⑤ (see pp. 243 & 246) on the left, with its fine cloister. Continue ahead to **Luža Square** ⑥ (see pp. 246–247 & 250), the center of public life during the republic, where you will find the **Sponza Palace** and the **Church of St. Blaise.**

Turn right (south) onto Pod Dvorom, arriving first at the **Rector's Palace** ⑦ (see pp. 250–251), on the left followed by the **Cathedral of the Assumption of the Virgin** ⑧ (see pp. 251–252), with its treasury full of exquisite gold and silver filigree

reliquaries of St. Blaise. Turn right to **Gundulić Square** ⑨ (see pp. 252–253), an open market square that makes the perfect spot for lunch. Backtrack to Luža Square and follow the narrow lane up to the right onto Svetog Domenika, where you will find the **Dominican Church & Monastery** ⑩ (see pp. 254–255).

From the church, turn west along Prijeko (or walk back along Stradun) as far as Antuninska, where you arrive at **War Photo Limited** ⑪ (see p. 254), a gallery showcasing war photography from conflicts across the globe. Return to the Pile Gate along Stradun. Or, if you have time, leave the old town by the **Ploče Gate** and follow Put Frana Supila to the **Museum of Modern Art** (see sidebar p. 251).

🗺	See also area map p. 239
▶	Pile Gate
🕐	5 hours
↔	2.25 miles (3.5 km)
▶	Pile Gate

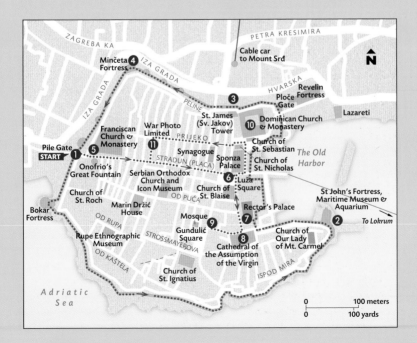

Priests prepare to celebrate a Mass on the steps of Dubrovnik's Cathedral.

with a Pietà (meaning "pity" and depicting Mary holding the body of Christ) flanked by St. Jerome and St. John the Baptist, is Dubrovnik's wonderful Franciscan Church and Monastery. Work on the church began in 1343, though it was badly damaged during the great earthquake of 1667 and had to be largely rebuilt. The renowned Croatian poet Ivan Gundulić, whose statue you will find in Gundulić Square (see pp. 252–253), is buried here.

The **cloister** of the monastery is outstanding and, unlike the church, survived the 1667 earthquake more or less intact. The work of Mihoje Brajkov of Bar (Montenegro), it features pairs of slender, octagonal columns with joint capitals, each of these carved individually with a different set of animals, birds, human heads, and fantastic beasts. It is said that one of the heads near the entrance is a self-portrait. Brajkov died here in 1348 of the plague, and the cloister was completed by Mijen Radimislić and Leonard Stjepanov of Florence, to whom the cross-vaulting is attributed.

The arcades surround a small **garden** with trees and a 15th-century wellhead, an oasis of shady peace and quiet when Dubrovnik gets just a bit too busy for its own good during peak season. The upper story of the cloister, not open to the public, also dates from after the 1667 earthquake. The **pharmacy**, established in 1317, is said to be the oldest surviving in Europe, and the small **museum** just off the cloister contains various old jars, manuscripts, pestles, and mortars from the 15th and 16th centuries. The **bell tower** dates from the 15th century, except for the top, which was replaced after an earthquake felled the original.

Luža Square

At the far end of Stradun is Luža Square, the center of public life at the time of the republic (see pp. 248–249). At the center of the square is **Orlando's Column,** with its early 15th-century sculpture of a sword-wielding Roland (of the epic poem *The Song of Roland*).

Public proclamations were read from the top. Roland's forearm (and an equivalent length marked at the base of the column) was the standard unit of measurement in old Ragusa.

The **clock tower** on the square, originally dating from the 15th century, was rebuilt in 1929. Its original mechanism—featuring two little green figures (called *Zelenci*) that strike the hour on the early 16th-century bell with their hammers—moved to the Sponza Palace. Also on the far side of the square is **Onofrio's Small Fountain** (named for the same Italian engineer), an octagonal basin with somewhat worn relief sculptures, dating from the mid-15th century.

On the left (northern) side of Luža is the elegant Renaissance-Gothic **Sponza Palace,** built in 1522 according to designs by architect Paskoje Milicevii. Two brothers from Korčula, Blaž and Petar Andrijić (who were responsible for the outstanding work on the facade of Korčula's Cathedral of St. Mark) played a leading role. The Sponza Palace served as the

INSIDER TIP:

After a morning in Stradun, try a lunch of glistening black risotto, *crni rizot*, colored with cuttlefish ink that will turn your tongue black, making for an amusing vacation photo.

—ALISON INCE
National Geographic contributor

city's customs house (though at times it has also served as the city mint, an arsenal, and a cistern). A Latin inscription on the wall (adjacent to where goods would have been weighed) reads: "As we weigh goods so will God weigh us." The building, which survived the 1667 earthquake, now houses a museum, including the original inner workings of the clock tower, and the **Museum of the Dubrovnik Defenders,** a moving place with photographs of all
(continued on p. 250)

Sponza Palace
- Map p. 245
- Općina Dubrovnik

Remembering the Siege of Dubrovnik

As you enter the old town through the Pile Gate, a small sign serves as a reminder of what happened here just two and a half decades ago. In October 1991, the JNA (Yugoslav People's Army) and Montenegrin militia positioned themselves around Dubrovnik, beginning a siege that would last until August the following year as the world watched. From positions on the hill above Dubrovnik, the attackers relentlessly shelled the UNESCO World Heritage site, hitting 70 percent of its houses in the process. The city has since been painstakingly repaired, but an appreciation of just how much was damaged can be gained from looking at the roof tiles as you are walking around the city walls: Almost all of them are new, replaced following the war. More than 100 civilians and a further 200 of the city's defenders lost their lives. They are commemorated in the Museum of the Dubrovnik Defenders in the Sponza Palace.

Republic of Ragusa

Dubrovnik was founded in the seventh century A.D. by refugees fleeing from the neighboring Greco-Roman colony of Cavtat (see sidebar opposite). The settlers named their city Ragusa, after the rocky promontory they chose for its location. Slavs then settled on the wooded hills opposite (*dubrava* in Croatian means "grove of trees"). The two settlements merged into one and maintained the name Ragusa until 1918, when it became Dubrovnik under the kingdom of Yugoslavia.

The sleepy ancient town of Cavtat gave rise to the mighty Republic of Ragusa.

The Ragusans showed themselves to be astute diplomats throughout their long history. In 1358, when the city passed to Hungary—having previously been forced to submit to Venice in the 13th century—it agreed to pay an annual tribute to the Hungarians, in return for which it was allowed almost complete autonomy. When Dalmatia was sold back to Venice in 1420, the city carefully maintained its links with Hungary, thus protecting itself against its Adriatic rival. By paying an annual tribute to the Ottomans as well (much increased in later years), the city received trading privileges throughout the extensive Ottoman territories. Through maritime trade and its control of overland trade from the coast, Ragusa became fantastically rich.

At the height of its powers during the 16th century, its territory stretched south to the Bay of Kotor (in modern Montenegro) and north to Neum (in modern Bosnia), and included the Pelješac Peninsula as well as the islands of Korčula, Mljet, Lastovo, and the Elaphites. It had a fleet of almost 200 ships, some of which formed part of the Spanish Armada against England in 1588.

Social Policy

Dubrovnik's list of public and social works is extraordinary within the context of medieval Europe. It had a public pharmacy in 1317, a public health service as early as 1432, one of the earliest orphanages in Europe, and a free refuge for the elderly, all by the 15th century. Slavery was abolished in 1416—centuries before its neighbors. It also had one of the earliest quarantine systems in Europe, established in the 14th century following the Black Death to avoid any future epidemics or plagues within the city, with a period of quarantine lasting 40 days. You can still find evidence of all this within the city. The pharmacy can still be visited near the cloisters of the Franciscan monastery, the refuge for the elderly continues to function as a retirement home, and the quarantine houses at Lazareti are now used as artists' studios.

System of Government

Although its strict social hierarchy prevented intermarriage between classes and thus maintained power among the nobles, Ragusa had an enlightened system of government. The city's governing body consisted of a Grand Council, on which all nobles took a seat from the age of 18; a Minor Council of 11 nobles, which wielded executive power; a Senate, which acted as a consultative body; and a Rector, or Kne. The Rector (a native Ragusan since 1358), who appointed the Minor Council but otherwise held no effective powers, served for a period of only one month to avoid any form of corruption and was not permitted to hold office again for at least two years.

In Decline

A massive earthquake in 1667 flattened most of the city. With the exception of the walls and a few other buildings (including, remarkably, the beautiful cloister of the Franciscan monastery), Ragusa had to be largely rebuilt. With the advent of new shipping routes outside the Adriatic, the republic's fortunes gradually declined, and in 1806, after a month-long siege by the Russians, the city of Ragusa was forced to invite Napoleon into the city as its "protector."

In 1808, the Republic of Ragusa was dissolved by Napoleon's Marshal Marmont, becoming part of France's Illyrian Provinces then part of Austria and just another region of the Dalmatian coast. During the Homeland War, the illustrious city and its lucrative tourism trade came under siege for ten months, sustaining a huge amount of damage from shelling (see sidebar p. 247).

Cavtat Today

The city of Cavtat (*tzcavtat-konavle.hr*), Greek Epidaurus, did not completely disappear after the seventh-century attack by Avar raiders. Cavtat remains a pleasant seaside town that can be reached by the number 10 bus from outside Pile Gate. There is also a ferry from Dubrovnik's old harbor, next to the old town.

Vlaho Buhovac (1855–1922), one of Croatia's best known painters, was born in Cavtat, and his former house is now a museum (**Kuia Bukovac**) with paintings from throughout his lifetime. There is also a late 15th-century **Franciscan monastery,** and the **Town Museum** is housed in the former Rector's Palace. In the leafy cemetery on the hill above Cavtat's harbor, you can find the impressive **Račić Family Mausoleum,** completed in 1923 by sculptor Ivan Meštrović.

Rector's Palace

⬛ Map p. 245

✉ Pred Dvorom 3

🕐 Closed Sun. in winter

those who lost their lives during the bitter siege of 1991–1992 (see sidebar p. 247). It is also home to the extensive **State Archives** of the Republic of Ragusa.

On the right (south) side of Luža is the baroque **Church of St. Blaise** (Sv. Vlaho), patron saint of Dubrovnik. Built in 1706–1714 on the site of an earlier building destroyed by fire, it is the work of Venetian architect Marino Gropelli, who modeled it on the Church of San Maurizio in Venice. Inside there is a 15th-century silver gilt statue of St. Blaise, which survived the fire that destroyed the older church. The saint holds a model of Dubrovnik as it looked in the late 1400s, before the

devastating earthquake in 1667. The early 18th-century painted organ loft is by Petar Matejević (1670–1726).

Rector's Palace

South of St. Blaise, across Pred Dvorom, is the Renaissance-Gothic Rector's Palace (Knežev Dvor), once the official seat of the figurehead of the Ragusan government. Built on the site of an earlier, more heavily fortified construction destroyed in an explosion, the "new" Rector's Palace was built by Onofrio della Cava, the man responsible for designing the city's public water supply, before this too was damaged in another explosion.

A casket is paraded on the feast of St. Blaise, Dubrovnik's patron saint.

Going Beyond the Old Town

Dubrovnik's **Museum of Modern Art,** just east of the old town in Ploče, has works by many of Croatia's greatest modern masters, including Ivan Meštrović, Vlaho Bukovac, and Frano Kršić, as well as a good collection of work by contemporary local artists. Built as a mansion for wealthy businessman Božo Banac in the 1930s, the building was converted into a museum in 1950.

Between here and the old town you will see renovated quarantine houses, or **Lazareti,** from the 17th century. North of the old town is 1,352-foot (412 m) **Mount Srd,** from which Dubrovnik was shelled during the siege. You can take a cable car to the top (*$$*), or walk up the steep path from Državna Cesta.

Further renovations were undertaken by Juraj Dalmatinac (of Šibenik cathedral fame; see p. 189) and Michelozzo Michelozzi, both of whom are linked with the city's fortifications.

The exterior consists of a beautiful loggia, with rib-vaulting springing from carved capitals. (Note the capital on the far right, which depicts Asclepius, the Greek god of healing.) The main entrance has yet another statue of St. Blaise and a lion-headed bronze door knocker. The inner **courtyard,** which sometimes holds concerts in the summer, is an arcade and has a statue of Miho Pracat (1528–1607), a wealthy 16th-century merchant from Lopud, who left a fortune to the republic on his death. The only statue of a private citizen erected by the republic, it dates from 1628.

On the first floor is the **Hall of the Great Council,** at the entrance of which an inscription in Latin admonishes councillors to forget their private affairs and concern themselves only with matters of business. The rooms on the upper floor now house a **museum** with period furniture and various paintings. Among the other buildings on the east side of Pred Dvorom is the former **town hall,** which now plays host to one of Dubrovnik's most famous cafés (Gradska Kavana).

Cathedral of the Assumption of the Virgin

Dubrovnik's cathedral was built between 1672 and 1713 on the site of an earlier Romanesque cathedral that is said to have been built with funds from the English king Richard the Lionheart (see sidebar p. 253) and then destroyed during the great earthquake. Designed by Andrea Buffalini of Urbino, the "new" cathedral is cruciform in plan, with a row of sculpted saints around the balustrade of the exterior. Inside there is also a large painting by Titian—or more likely, the school of Titian—above the unusual west-facing altar.

Held in a baroque chapel, the cathedral **treasury** (Riznica Katedrale) contains more than 130 relics dating from the 11th through the 19th century, including the head, arms, and leg of St. Blaise, brought from Byzantium in 1026 and contained in gold reliquaries made by local craftsmen during

Cathedral of the Assumption of the Virgin
- Map p. 245
- Držićeva Poljana
- $

Museum of Modern Art
- Put Frana Supila 23
- 020 426 590
- Closed Mon.

ugdubrovnik.hr

One of Dubrovnik's many mainland fortresses overlooks Lokrum Island.

Maritime Museum

Map p. 245

St. John's Fortress

020 323 904

Closed Mon.

$$

mdc.hr/dubrovnik /eng/pomorski /index.html

Aquarium

Map p. 245

Institute for Marine and Coastal Research, Kneža Damjana Jude 12

020 323 125

imp-du.com

the 11th and 12th centuries. The saint's head is held in a reliquary of gold and silver filigree work in the form of a Byzantine crown, decorated with 24 Byzantine enamel plaques dating from the 12th century. The treasury also contains a fragment of the True Cross, and a beautiful 16th-century ewer and basin wildly decorated with animals and foliage. The treasures are carried around the old town on the feast day of St. Blaise (February 3).

In past centuries during the republic's existence, access to the treasury was much more difficult, requiring special permission from the Grand Council, the Bishop, and the Treasurer, each of whom carried one of three separate keys required to open the door.

Pustjerna & Prijeko

Diagonally across from the cathedral, up in the streets that compose the area called Pustjerna and tucked below the city walls, is the small 17th-century **Church of Our Lady of Mt. Carmel** (Gospe od Karmena), with its three bells.

Within the massive St. John's Fortress are the **Maritime Museum,** spread over two floors and documenting the city's extraordinary maritime history, and the city's **Aquarium,** run by the university's Institute for Marine and Coastal Research.

Around the corner from the back of the cathedral, heading back toward Stradun, is the lovely old market square, **Gundulić Square,** surrounded

INSIDER TIP:

To get away from the afternoon heat and crowds, consider a short bus ride north to the botanical garden at Trsteno *[Potok 20, Trsteno, tel 020 751 019].*

—GRACE FIELDER
National Geographic contributor

by restaurants and cafés. In the morning there is a small low-key open **market** here, with stalls selling everything from fresh fruits and vegetables to local honey and olive oil to arts and crafts.

At the center of the square stands a **statue of Ivan Gundulić,** a Croatian poet who was born in Dubrovnik in 1589 and who appears on the reverse of the 50-kuna note. The statue was created by the great Croatian sculptor Ivan Rendić (1849–1932). Dating from 1892, it is decorated with scenes from Gundulić's best known work, the epic poem *Osman.* Note the **lion-headed fountain** on the corner of the square by the supermarket.

South of Gundulić Square, a long flight of steps (modeled on the Spanish Steps in Rome) leads up to the early 18th-century Jesuit **Church of St. Ignatius.** The church was designed by Italian artist, architect, and Jesuit brother Andrea Pozzo (1642–1709), who modeled it on the Gesù in Rome.

West from Gundulić Square on Od Puća, past Dubrovnik's small **mosque** *(džamija),* is the **Icon Museum.** Housed in a building once belonging to a local aristocratic family, the museum has an outstanding collection of icons from the 15th through the 19th century, from numerous different schools and including several by Croatian painter Vlaho Bukovac (1855–1922). The nearby **Serbian Orthodox Church** dates from the late 19th century. A little farther along Od Puča is the former house of 16th-century Renaissance playwright Marin Držić, now open as a small **museum.** South of here toward the city walls, the **Ethnographic Museum** is housed in a cavernous 16th-century granary.

Prijeko, a restaurant-filled street running parallel to Stradun through the higher part of

Icon Museum
✉ Od Puća 8
☎ 020 323 242
🕐 Closed Sat.–Sun.
💲 $

Marin Držić Home
✉ Široka 7
☎ 020 323 242
🕐 Closed Sun.
💲 $
muzej-marindrzic.eu

Marin Držić Theater
✉ Kovačka 1
☎ 020 321 088
kazaliste-dubrovnik.hr

Ethnographic Museum
✉ Od Rupa 3
☎ 020 412 545
🕐 Closed Sun.
mdc.hr/dubrovnik/eng/etnografski/index.html

Lokrum: A Leafy Retreat from the City

Only 15 minutes by boat from Dubrovnik's old harbor, the tiny island of Lokrum is a leafy nature reserve that provides the perfect counterpoint to the dizzying historical and architectural history of Dubrovnik. According to legend, the English king Richard the Lionheart was shipwrecked here during a storm in 1192, on his return from the Crusades. In thanks for his salvation, he pledged to build a church on the island, but nobles from Dubrovnik convinced him to give money to build a cathedral in Dubrovnik instead. Whether a true story or not, the island is a lovely place to spend an afternoon, wandering between rocky beaches, the old botanical garden, and the ruined French fort, which has great views back to Dubrovnik's old town.

Venturing Into Montenegro

Dubrovnik is only some 28 miles (45 km) from the Montenegrin border, where Kotor—a beautifully preserved old town on the bay of the same name and a UNESCO World Heritage site—can easily be reached as a day trip. Travel agencies in Dubrovnik run day trips over the border, and there is a bus in the morning from Dubrovnik, returning from Herceg Novi in the afternoon. Alternatively, take a taxi from the airport at Čilipi to Herceg Novi in Montenegro, from where you can continue by local bus around the enormously photogenic Bay of Kotor, passing Perast and the tiny islands of Sveti Djordje and Gospa od Škrplja. (If returning by taxi from Herceg Novi, not all drivers are willing to take you across the border into Croatia, so you may be stuck with having to take an additional taxi ride on the Croatian side at premium rates.) Citizens of the United States, Canada, and any EU countries do not need a visa to enter Montenegro.

War Photo Limited

- ▲ Map p. 245
- ✉ Antuninska 6
- ☎ 020 322 166
- 🕐 Closed Nov.– April; & Mon. May & Oct.

warphotoltd.com

Dominican Church & Monastery

- ▲ Map p. 245
- ✉ Sv. Dominika 4
- 💲 $$ (museum)

town to the north, is frankly best avoided around lunchtime when wait staff are busy.

On Antuninska, a narrow street leading up to Prijeko from Stradun, is the outstanding—and at times harrowing, heartbreaking, and deeply disturbing—**War Photo Limited**, established in 2003 by New Zealand–born war photographer Wade Goddard, who came here during the Homeland War. The gallery aims to show war free from any of the glamour. The collection includes images from conflict zones around the globe by some of the world's leading war photographers.

On Žudioska, a narrow street between the eastern ends of Stradun and Prijeko, is Dubrovnik's **synagogue,** the second oldest in Europe, which continued to function throughout World War II. At the far end of Prijeko is the small **Church of St. Nicholas** (Sv. Nikola), rebuilt in the 17th century but with some pre-Romanesque carvings in the interior.

INSIDER TIP:

The Jewish synagogue in Prijeko is not usually on the tour circuit, but it's worth a visit. There is also a mosque nearby. Dubrovnik has been multicultural for centuries.

—GRACE FIELDER
National Geographic contributor

Dominican Church & Monastery

Beyond the far end of Prijeko, on Sv. Dominika, is the Dominican Church and Monastery. The church, originally built in 1315, has been rebuilt and renovated several times since: after the 1667 earthquake and after being used as a stable during Napoleon's occupation of the city. The monastery has suffered similarly through the ages, but underwent recent restoration. This beautiful refurbishment unifies the past and promises a future. The cloisters still have the water troughs that were cut into their walls by Napoleon's troops for their horses.

Inside the sizable Gothic church is a huge 14th-century **Crucifixion** by Venetian painter Paolo Veneziano, together with several other artworks and a 15th-century **stone pulpit.** The beautiful **cloister,** the work of local masons following a design by Maso di Bartolomeo of Florence, surrounds a peaceful grove of citrus trees. The 16th-century well provided part of the city's water supply during the 1991 siege.

The church's Romanesque south door, with its flight of steps cascading down into the street below, is best appreciated from a section of the city walls. Adjacent to the south door is the former **Church of St. Sebastian** (Sv. Sebastijana), which was built during the 15th century and used as a prison by Napoleon.

Dominican Monastery Museum:
The interesting Dominican Monastery Museum (Muzej Dominikanskog Samostana) has a 16th-century altarpiece by Titian showing St. Blaise with Mary Magdalene and the archangel Raphael, and various works from the Dubrovnik school of the 15th and 16th centuries, including a restored triptych by Nikole Božidarević (1460–1517), which shows St. Blaise holding a model of the old town, and St. Dominic holding a model of the church and monastery. The monastery also houses an enormous **library,** containing 16,000 volumes. ■

A kitchen garden planted among the ramparts shows that Dubrovnik is very much a living city.

Pelješac Peninsula

The slender Pelješac Peninsula, some 40 miles (65 km) in length, stretches northwest from its narrow isthmus around the town of Ston until its rocky spine culminates in the peak of Sveti Ilija above Orebić near the seaward tip. The peninsula's long coast gives this region a similar appeal to the islands easily seen just across the sea, but it can be enjoyed for a few hours without having to catch a ferry—and without the crowds.

Cyclists take in the view of the narrow strait between Orebić and Korčula (top right).

**Pelješac
Peninsula**
🅰 239 A2, B1–B2
Visitor Information

visitpeljesac.hr

There were several Illyrian settlements on Pelješac, and the Greeks and Romans both built small towns here, followed by the Byzantines. Then the whole peninsula was part of the wealthy Republic of Ragusa (Dubrovnik) from 1333 to 1808. Later still, Napoleon began to construct a road along the peninsula, which was continued under the Austrian monarchy.

The peninsula is a fascinating area that sees comparatively few visitors. Here you will find extraordinary medieval fortifications, delicious oysters, and some excellent wines, not to mention some of the best windsurfing in Croatia and the elegant Renaissance mansions of wealthy Ragusan sea captains.

Pelješac has several ferry routes, from Orebić to Korčula,

from Trstenik to Mljet (summer only), and from Trpanj on the northern side of the peninsula to Ploče on the mainland.

Ston

Ston is actually two settlements: **Mali Ston** (Little Ston) to the north and **Veliki Ston** (Big Ston) to the south. The latter is often just known as Ston. The town sits at the slender base of the Pelješac Peninsula, at its narrowest point on a land bridge that connects the long mountainous peninsula to the mainland.

The most striking feature of the town is its massive set of **medieval walls** and fortifications, built between the 14th and early 16th century onward by the Republic of Ragusa. The walls, which completely sealed the peninsula off from the mainland, still constitute one of the most outstanding sets of fortifications anywhere in Croatia. The reason for building the walls can still be seen in the flats below the town— Veliki Ston's **salt pans,** which contributed enormously to the medieval republic's income and maritime trade.

Mali Ston is also famous for its oysters, considered by many to be the best in Croatia. Sampling a platter of these (and the local mussels, for that matter) is something of a requirement of any visit here. The oysters are cultivated on the shallow seabeds around Mali Ston. Ston has a Summer Festival in July and August with music and theater.

Veliki Ston is remarkably well preserved considering it was subjected to devastating Allied bombing raids during World War II and shelled by the Serbs during the Homeland War. The area was then struck by a massive earthquake in 1996, and it is amazing that anything is still standing at all, and perhaps gives an idea of just how solid those walls really are.

More than 3 miles (about 6 km) of walls still stand, including 20 of the original 40 or so towers and bastions and a number of fortresses, including **Koruna** in Mali Ston, **Kaštio** in Veliki Ston, and **Tvrđava Podzvizd** up on the high ground between the two settlements. Entry to the walls is from either side of Veliki Ston or from the fortress of Koruna at Mali Ston. Walking up to Tvrđava Podzvizd is rewarded with outstanding views out over the fortifications, the Pelješac Peninsula, and the distant island of Mljet.

The hill between the two towns was actually the site of the

Ston
⚑ 239 B1
Visitor Information
✉ Pelješki put 1
☎ 020 754 452
ston.hr

EXPERIENCE:
Gather Salt in Ston

Salt is gathered from Ston's extensive salt pans from July to September every year— one pool per day, all by hand. If you feel like getting your hands dirty (or at least salty), **Ston Salt** (tel 020 754 027, solana ston.hr) organizes salt-gathering camps in town. Workers receive free accommodation in private rooms, a "lunch" (actually served between 9 a.m. and 9:30 a.m.), and free access to the summer concerts and other performances in Ston, in exchange for working in the salt pans from 6 a.m. until around midday.

Orebić

△ 239 B2

Visitor Information

✉ Trg Mimbeli bb

☎ 020 713 718

tz-orebic.hr

Maritime Museum

✉ Trg Mimbeli bb, Orebić

☎ 020 713 009

🕐 Closed Oct.–May

original settlement here, before Ragusan funds built Mali and Veliki Ston. There is still a very early Romanesque church here, the small **Church of St. Michael** (Sv. Mihael), built around 1080 and containing some of the oldest preserved frescoes in Croatia.

Other buildings of interest in Veliki Ston include the 16th-century **Bishop's Palace** and the **Church of St. Nicholas** (Sv. Nikola). You will notice a number of relief sculptures of St. Blaise (Sv. Vlaho), the patron saint of Dubrovnik, on the architecture of both settlements.

Regular buses from the main Dubrovnik bus station stop at Ston on the way to Orebić, toward the end of the peninsula (before going on by small ferry to Korčula).

INSIDER TIP:

Dingač, a local red wine, is a must-try. It is considered to be one of the best vintages on the eastern Adriatic. But be warned: It should be consumed respectfully and in small quantities.

—IVOR KARAVANIC
National Geographic grantee

The two settlements are only a short distance apart. It is a pleasant 20-minute walk between the two.

Orebić

The coastal town of Orebić sits sheltered below the steep ramparts of **Sveti Ilija** (St. Elias) mountain. This small town's sheltered position gives it a relatively mild climate.

As the center of the peninsula's merchant fleet from the 16th century, Orebić has something of an air of faded grandeur and contains the former **mansions** of a number of wealthy local sea captains. The town's **Maritime Museum** documents a proud seafaring history over several centuries. Beyond the town center there is a 15th-century **Franciscan monastery,** at the beginning of the rewarding trek up to the summit of Sveti Ilija (see sidebar this page).

Regular car ferries make the short crossing to Korčula on the island of the same name opposite. Unless you are traveling by car,

---

EXPERIENCE:
Climb Sveti Ilija

Sveti Ilija (St. Elias), the dramatic, high peak facing Korčula toward the tip of the Pelješac Peninsula, has one of the best hiking routes anywhere along the Croatian coast. Starting from sea level, the trail climbs 3,153 feet (961 m) to reach the rocky summit, with amazing views along the twisted spine of the peninsula and out across the island of Korčula. The path is clearly marked, starting from **Orebić** and passing the **Franciscan monastery,** before ascending a steady, easy trail up to the top. Allow around five hours round-trip. There is no source of clean water on the route—the water from a small well on the way up needs purifying—and little or no shade on the initial part of the route. Contact the tourist office in Orebić *(tz-orebic.com)* for more information.

Cloister in the Franciscan monastery of Ston on the Pelješac Peninsula

however, you are better off taking one of the frequent small passenger boats, which go straight to Korčula's old town itself; the car ferry arrives at a larger jetty located a couple of miles (3 km) outside town.

West of Orebić

Around 4.5 miles (7 km) west of Orebić is the small town of **Viganj,** popular with campers and a favorite spot for windsurfing and other water sports. The Croatian windsurfing championships are regularly held here (see sidebar p. 261).

Inland from Viganj is the site of one of the area's most important archaeological finds of recent years, a cave near the village of Nakovana containing an **Illyrian shrine** that dates back more than 2,000 years. The cave entrance was sealed off after the discovery, so its artifacts have so far remained unplundered.

Wine Region

Just east of Orebić, a small area of the hillside around **Dingač** produces some of the best red wines in Croatia. Dingač wine is dark and rather concentrated, and made from the Plavac Mali grape. The terrain in this area is fairly steep, and in order to get to the vines, villagers eventually built a tunnel through the hillside in the 1970s to save having to struggle with their donkeys over the top. Several agencies offer wine tours in this area, from Orebić, Korčula, and Dubrovnik (see Travelwise p. 309). ■

The Islands

The southern Dalmatian islands are very popular destinations for travelers wishing to see an alternative side to Dalmatia after a few days in Dubrovnik. The islands offer a full range of activities, from water sports and beaches to the quiet refuge of the Elaphites, the unspoiled greenery of Mljet National Park, the stunning medieval town of Korčula, and the wonderfully remote Lastovo far out into the Adriatic.

Koločep island is a haven of quiet after the crowds of nearby Dubrovnik.

Elaphite Islands
🅰 239 B1–C1

Lopud
🅰 239 C1
Visitor Information
✉ Obala I. Kuljevana 12
☎ 020 759 086
🕐 Closed Fri.

Elaphite Islands

There are seven Elaphite Islands, stretching between the base of the Pelješac Peninsula in the west and Dubrovnik. The three largest islands are Lopud, Šipan, and Koločep, and most visitors choose one of these.

The Greeks, Romans, and southern Slavs all built settlements on the islands. Politically, the islands were under the rule of the Republic of Ragusa (Dubrovnik) from the 11th century until its fall in 1808. Lopud was the administrative center of the Elaphites

under Dubrovnik, boasting a sizable population, more than 30 churches, and a huge fleet of ships. The island of Koločep was a center of the local coral industry until the 18th century.

Nowadays people flock to the islands on day trips from nearby Dubrovnik during the hot summer, though outside the busy summer months, the islands are sparsely populated, and there is not necessarily much open.

Lopud: In Lopud, the main settlement on the island of the same name, you will find the ruined **Rector's Palace** near the small **Town Museum** and **Treasury.** The church that once formed part of the island's **Franciscan monastery** here has some fine Venetian paintings inside.

Inland you will find a ruined **fortress,** and on the opposite side of the island there is a particularly nice beach at **Šunj,** only around a 30-minute walk away. Above the beach there is the 15th-century **Church of Our Lady of Šunj** (Gospa od Šunja), with a 16th-century painted carved wooden altarpiece.

Šipan: Šipan, the largest of the Elaphite Islands, has two main settlements, **Šipanska Luka** and **Suđurađ,** about 5 miles (7 km) apart by road, and both on the ferry route from Dubrovnik. There are numerous ruined **palaces** at the two settlements, most dating from the 15th and 16th centuries, and on the road between them there is a ruined fortress and the interesting fortified **Church of the Holy Spirit** (Sv. Duh).

There are still uncleared land mines in some parts of Šipan, so stick to paved roads and keep an eye out for warning signs if you are heading away from the towns. At present the land mines prevent many of the island's numerous olive groves from being worked.

Koločep: The main settlement on Koločep is **Donje Čelo,** where the 13th-century parish

INSIDER TIP:

The public ferry system to the islands can be confusing; check schedules in advance, arrive early, and be flexible whenever possible.

—DAVID KENNEDY
National Geographic contributor

church has fragments of earlier buildings built into its walls.

Ferries run regularly between Dubrovnik and the three islands, arriving at Koločep first, then Lopud, and finally Suđurađ and Šipanska Luka, respectively, on Šipan. The service is slow and steady, with the ferry taking more than 90 minutes to reach the final port of call.

Šipan
🗺 239 B1
Visitor Information
✉ Luka bb, Lika Šipanska
☎ 020 758 084
🕐 Closed Tues.

EXPERIENCE:
Windsurf the Straits

The Dalmatian coast is a haven for sailboarders. The straits between **Korčula** and the **Pelješac Peninsula** (particularly at **Viganj,** just west of Orebić) attract the world's best boarders. It is common to see sailboarders skimming back and forth between the island and the sliver of mainland. There are sailboarding schools and rental shops in Viganj *(windsurfing-kite surfing-viganj.com).* Another good place for windsurfing is the strait between the islands of **Brač** and **Hvar** (see pp. 210–211). *(The current in the island straits can be very strong, particularly between Brač and Hvar, so only experienced sailboarders should venture this far out from the shore.)*

Korčula's fortified old town resembles a small version of Dubrovnik.

Korčula

🅰 239 B2

Visitor Information

✉ Obala dr. Franje Tuđmana 4, Korčula town

☎ 020 715 867

visitkorcula.eu

Blato

🅰 239 B1

Visitor Information

✉ Blato Tourist Office, Trg Dr. Franje Tuđmana 4

☎ 020 851 850

tzo-blato.hr

Korčula

This island was known by the Greeks as Korkyra Melaina (meaning "black Korčula")— a reference to the lush, dark pine forests on the island that distinguished it from the other Korkyra island, better known today as Corfu.

A Greek colony was founded in the fourth century B.C. on Korčula. It was then wrested from the Illyrians by the Romans in 33 B.C., passed to Byzantium in the sixth century A.D., then in turn to Venice, medieval Croatia, and Hungary, and back to Venice again. It received its own independent statute in 1214, one of the earliest of its kind in Dalmatia.

A huge naval battle took place off the island in 1298, in which Venice was defeated by Genoa, and following which Marco Polo (possibly a son of Korčula; see sidebar p. 265) was thrown into a Genoese prison.

Plague struck the island in the 16th century, and Korčula became an Austrian possession in 1797 along with the rest of the coast. It then had spells under Russian and British control, and was occupied by Italy during World War I and both Italy and Germany during World War II.

Korčula Town: The town of Korčula is a magical place, girdled by the remains of massive medieval walls, which surround a perfect herringbone pattern of narrow stone streets descending from the main axis. It sits on a small peninsula toward the eastern end of the island, opposite the towering crags of Sveti Ilija on the Pelješac Peninsula (see sidebar p. 258).

Remarkably, despite being one of the most beautiful towns on the Adriatic, it is far, far less crowded than Dubrovnik or Hvar town. The walls were built

EXPERIENCE: See *Moreška* Sword Dances

Korčula's *Moreška* sword dance, which continues a tradition stretching back almost a thousand years, is one of the few surviving examples of a type of dance that was once widespread across the Mediterranean and beyond. As such, it is linked to similar dances from Spain, Corsica, and southern Italy.

The Moreška may have arrived here from Italy or Spain, and a comedy by local playwright Marin Držić dating from 1548 mentions the dance being performed in Split. A performance in Korčula—its modern stronghold—is first mentioned in the 18th century.

The dance depicts the combat between two kings (the Black King, dressed in black, and the White King, ironically dressed in red) and their soldiers. The conflict is over a Muslim woman named Bula, who, despite the Black King's advances, refuses to betray her love for the White King.

Although sometimes described as representing a combat between Christians and Muslims—as was the case with a number of other versions of the dance—it is thought that in the Korčula version, the combatants actually represent the rivalry between the Turkish Ottomans and the Arabs. The name Moreška means "Moorish" and links the dance with traditional morris dancing from England, which is thought to have similar derivation.

The Moreška is performed regularly in **Korčula** during the summer months, usually in the old open-air cinema just to the left below the Revelin Tower as you enter the old town. You can buy tickets (*$$$*) from most agencies in town (such as Kantun Tours). The dance is preceded by a fine *klapa recital* (see sidebar p. 206). Performances last around 45 minutes (the full-length version can go on for two hours), and are performed with considerable vim and sparks flying; sword blades are often broken, and travelers with young children are advised not to sit in the front row.

Another version of the dance, the **Kumpanija,** also survives on Korčula. It is performed elsewhere on the island, such as **Blato** and **Vela Luka.** The Moreška was inscribed on the UNESCO List of Intangible Cultural Heritage in 2014.

Performers give their all during a *Moreška* dance in Korčula's old town.

Cathedral of St. Mark

 Statuta 1214, Korčula town

Daily July–Aug.; Mass only Sept.–June

between the 14th and 16th centuries, and were once more extensive. Sections were pulled down in the 19th century.

The town of Korčula preserves a centuries-old tradition in its *Moreška* sword dance (see p. 263), which is performed regularly during the summer and should on no account be missed.

Old Town: Entering the old town from the south, the visitor passes through the main **Land Gate** (Kopnena Vrata) beneath the 14th-century **Revelin Tower.** Note the Venetian Lion of St. Mark on the exterior. The tower houses a small **Moreška museum,** and it offers fine views from its roof of the Cathedral of St. Mark and the rest of the town, and Sveti Ilija beyond.

Just inside the gate, there is a **Loggia** on the left, and on the right stands the small **Church of St. Michael** (Sv. Mihovil), which dates from the early 17th century. Continue up the narrow main street (Ul. Korčulanskog Statuta) to **St. Mark's Square** (Trg Sv. Marka), in front of Korčula's magnificent cathedral.

Cathedral & Bishop's Palace: The **Cathedral of St. Mark** (Sv. Marko) is more accurately a church since it has long lost its bishopric, although, like many others in Croatia, it has maintained its popular title of cathedral. Mostly the work of local stonemasons, it was built in the early 15th century on the site of an older building. The extra chapel was added on

Actors put on a show in Korčula during Marco Polo's anniversary festivities.

the northern side in 1525.

The main entrance portal is richly carved with two lions and below these, the naked figures of Adam and Eve. In the arch above is the figure of St. Mark. Above the entrance is a particularly impressive **wheel window** carved with four heads, and above this the **cornice** is wildly decorated with the heads of lions, a staring human torso, a variety of monsters, and, to the left, a typically strange medieval interpretation of an elephant. It is a wonderful concoction, best appreciated in the early evening light as swallows swoop through the sky above. A niche on the lower right-hand side of the facade has a **figure of St. Theodore,** the town's other patron saint. Inside is a painting by Tintoretto (1518–1594) and, behind a door on the left backing onto the west front, a tiny chapel with a carved font surmounted by a bronze Christ.

Next to the cathedral is the **Bishop's Palace** (the baroque facade is later than the building itself), which houses the cathedral **treasury.** On the opposite side of the square, the **Town Museum** stands next to a handsome Gothic **palace.**

Just past the cathedral, in a small square on your right, is the small **Church of St. Peter** (Sv. Petar), the oldest church in Korčula. Originally Romanesque, it was rebuilt in 1338 and features 17th-century wooden figures of the Twelve Apostles.

Farther Afield: Beyond St. Mark's Square, still heading

Marco Polo

Korčula's most famous son is undoubtedly Marco Polo (ca 1254–1324), the celebrated Venetian traveler and author of *Il Milione* (now usually known as *The Travels of Marco Polo*), who may or may not have actually been born here. The so-called Marco Polo House near the cathedral appears to be later than Polo's lifetime. However, he was certainly imprisoned by the Genoese during the naval battle with Venice near the island in 1298 and went on to recount his fantastic tales of travel in Asia and the Mongol court of Kublai Khan to his fellow prisoners. The rest, as they say, is history.

along the main axis of the town, a narrow street on the right leads down to the much vaunted **Marco Polo House,** said to be—though it is far from proven—the erstwhile home of the famous Venetian traveler (see sidebar this page). There is not much here except a single tower (dating from later than Polo's lifetime), albeit one with an excellent view. Continuing along the main street, you'll pass some nice little boutique shops, selling Murano glass jewelry (a traditional Venetian craft) and other locally made crafts and souvenirs.

Near the southeast corner of the old town, just off the pleasant

Town Museum
 Trg Sv. Marka,
Korčula town
☎ 020 711 420
💲 $

gm-korcula.com

Icon Gallery

✉ Trg Svih Svetih, Korčula town

🕐 Closed Sun.

💲 $

promenade (Šetalište Petra Kana-velića), is the fascinating **Icon Gallery,** housed in the former guildhall. Inside you will find a small but outstanding collection of icons as well as a silver cross dating from 1430 and a large, painted cross dating from the 14th century. Adjoining the gallery and connected to it by a bridge is the small **Church of All Saints** (Svi Sveti), with a beautiful 18th-century carved

corner, the stout, massive **Kula Balbi.** Note the memorial plaque commemorating the local "victims of fascism" during World War II here. About halfway along the western side of the old town, a neo-baroque double stairway gives access to a terrace with the former **Sea Gate** (Morska Vrata), from which an alley leads back up to St. Mark's Square.

On the opposite side of the road from the old town are a

Lumbarda's beaches on the eastern side of Korčula are the best on the island.

wooden Pietà and an early 15th-century polyptych, a painted ceiling, and items relating to the various city guilds to which this church is still connected.

Walking around the outside of the old town, you will find some of the prominent towers and bastions from the original forti-fications, including the so-called **Kula Kanavelić** toward the far (north) end, and at the southwest

warren of café-lined streets, a part of Korčula town that grew up in the 16th century, when plague had struck in the old town. The district contains the baroque **Church of St. Justine** (Sv. Justina).

West of the old town along the waterfront is the late 15th-century **Church and Dominican Monastery of St. Nicholas** (Sv. Nikola), below which some

INSIDER TIP:

In Korčula town, be sure to visit Cukarin, a traditional cake and sweet shop selling sugared orange peel and other local specialties—perfect with a glass of local wine (try Pošip or Grk).

—HRVOJE PRCIC
*National Geographic Croatia
Editor in Chief*

rocky beaches provide a good spot for swimming without heading too far out of town. Heading up one of the flights of stone steps between the old town and the Dominican monastery brings you up through pine forest to a large hilltop tower *(kula);* allow 40 minutes for the return walk.

Getting There: Korčula town is connected by car ferry to Dubrovnik, Hvar, Split, and Rijeka (twice weekly) and by daily catamaran services to Split via Hvar. The ferries and catamarans use the quays on both sides of the old town, depending on the weather.

The car ferry to Orebić on the Pelješac Peninsula departs from a terminal a couple of miles (3 km) east of the old town, so if you are just traveling to Orebić as a foot passenger, you are much better off taking one of the frequent boats that leave from the quay (Obala dr Franje Tuđmana) that is located on the west side of the old town.

You will find the bus station on the southeast side of the old town. It offers regular services to Vela Luka and the car ferry port, as well as less-frequent services to several other places on the island.

Lumbarda: The small town of Lumbarda sits toward the eastern tip of Korčula island at the base of the Ražnjić Peninsula, around 4.5 miles (7 km) from Korčula town. Most people come here for the beaches, which are the best on the island (though correspondingly popular and fairly busy).

Lumbarda was the second Greek settlement on Korčula. The greatest local archaeological discovery was the **Psephisma of Lumbarda,** a stone tablet dating from the third century B.C. that records the organization of the settlement by its founders, Greek colonists on the island of Vis (see p. 221). The original stone is in the Archaeological Museum in Zagreb (see p. 73).

Lumbarda was the birthplace of Frano Kršenić (1897–1982), one of Croatia's most famous 20th-century sculptors, and there is also a local version of the *Moreška* that you can sometimes see performed here (see p. 263). You can catch performances of the sword dance in Vela Luka, too (see p. 268).

There are regular local buses between Korčula and Lumbarda during the week, with a less frequent service operating on weekends. Shared taxis operate from near the bus station in Korčula, and the fare is reasonable for a full car of passengers.

Lumbarda
 239 B2
Visitor Information
✉ Lumbarda Tourist Office, Prvi žal bb
☎ 020 712 042
lumbarda.hr

Vela Luka

◩ 239 A2

Visitor Information

✉ Obala 3 br. 19

☎ 020 813 619

tzvelaluka.hr

Town Museum

✉ Obala 3/9, Vela Luka

☎ 020 813 602

Vela Špila

✉ Ulica 26 br. 3

☎ 020 813 602

velaspila.hr

Mljet

◩ 239 B1

Visitor Information

✉ Zabrježe 2, Babino polje

☎ 020 744 186 (Polače office); 020 746 025 (Sobra office)

mljet.hr

Badija & Vrnik: A short boat trip from Korčula (taxi boats leave from the waterfront between the old town and the bus station) is the island of Badija with a late 14th-century **Franciscan monastery** (currently undergoing renovation), including an elaborately carved west entrance. There are plenty of spots for swimming near the spot where the boat moors, backed by shady pine trees with picnic tables, and you'll often see deer wandering freely here and elsewhere on the island.

The nearby island of **Vrnik** is where stone was quarried for the cathedral.

Vela Luka: Vela Luka lies at the head of a deep inlet at the western end of the island. It sees far fewer foreign visitors than the town of Korčula, apart from those who travel through briefly between the ferry to Split and the bus to Korčula. Nevertheless, it is a pleasant town, and there are some good but rocky beaches along the northern shore of the bay. The **Town Museum** (Centar za Kuttora Vela Luka) has finds from nearby Vela Špilja (see below), displays of the island's maritime history, and two sculptures by English artist Henry Moore.

Just outside Vela Luka is the large prehistoric cave **Vela Špilja,** which was inhabited during the Upper Paleolithic (around 20,000 B.C.). A road and a shorter marked footpath lead up to the cave from the northern side of town.

INSIDER TIP:

Inside Mljet National Park, take the hourly boat out to St. Mary's Island and the Benedictine monastery. While there, enjoy an espresso or sample the *prošek* (a sweet wine) at the café-restaurant.

—GRACE FIELDER
National Geographic contributor

The islands scattered through the bay are even better for swimming, especially **Proizd,** lying off the island's far western tip, and **Ošjak** (the self-styled "Island of Love"), only 10 minutes by boat from town. Tours head to these islands, or you can hire your own boat in town.

Vela Luka is connected by ferry and fast catamaran to Split, both stopping on Hvar and the latter continuing to remote Lastovo. Regular buses link Vela Luka with Korčula, at the other end of the island. A small taxi boat shuttles passengers over the bay from one side of town to the other.

Mljet

The island of Mljet was home to the Illyrians, the remains of whose hill forts can still be found on the island. The Romans arrived in 35 B.C. and called the island Melita. It has been suggested, quite plausibly, that it was here rather than on Malta that St. Paul was shipwrecked on his way to Rome. According to the story, while there Paul was bitten by a viper but suffered no ill effects. Malta famously has no dangerous snakes, while Mljet does. In fact, the island was so overrun with the reptiles at the turn of the 20th century that mongooses were introduced to tackle the problem (see sidebar p. 270). Early sources from the Republic of Ragusa (Dubrovnik) suggest that Mljet was sometimes used as a place of exile. The city of Dubrovnik bought the island in the 14th century.

Mljet National Park:

Running parallel to the Pelješac Peninsula, Mljet is around 20 miles (32 km) long. The main settlement is **Babino Polje,** at the center of the island, although the majority of visitors see only Mljet National Park in the west, arriving at either **Pomena** or **Polače.**

Declared a national park in 1960, the western half of the island includes the two saltwater lakes of **Malo Jezero** and **Veliko Jezero,** connected to one another by a narrow channel; the latter, larger body of water connects to the sea. Large areas of the island are covered with luxuriant Mediterranean forest, including some particularly large stands of Aleppo pine.

The 12th-century **Benedictine monastery** on the small island of **St. Mary** (Sv. Marija) in the larger of the two lakes was used as a hotel in the Tito era. Boats head over to the monastery from the shore of Veliko Jezero and are included in the national park's entrance ticket. Alternatively, for unsurpassed views of the lake and island, follow the road inland from the information office where the boats depart, turning right at the picnic area and taking a trail up to Veliki Gradac.

A ruined Roman palace is at Polace, dating probably from the third century B.C., while at Babino Polje there are two pre-Romanesque churches.

Mljet National Park

🏛 239 B1
✉ Pristanište 2, Goveđari
☎ 020 744 041
💲 $$$

np-mljet.hr

EXPERIENCE: Take a Mljet Lake Walk

Mljet has some lovely, very easy hiking trails. Head up along the road behind the national park office in Pomena, then turn right down a clearly marked woodland trail to the shore of **Malo Jezero,** the smaller of the two lakes. Following the footpath around either shore of the lake leads to the point where the two lakes join, the channel between them spanned by a small bridge (Mali Most). There's a small beach, and you can also rent canoes and bikes. The departure point for the boat over to the island of St. Mary (Sv. Marija) is along the northern shore of Veliko Jezero (30 minutes on from Mali Most), by the information kiosk. Alternatively, following the southern shore leads behind St. Mary, and on to the eastern end of the lake where it meets the oceans, but there is no bridge over to the opposite bank here. (*Do not attempt to swim the channel; the currents here are extremely powerful, and you will struggle to reach the other side.*) A new, longer walking route, the **Mljet Hiking Trail** (mljet.hr), covers more than half the length of the island.

Lastovo

🅰 239 A1

Visitor Information

✉ Dolac 3,
Lastovo town

☎ 020 801 023

lastovo.hr

Pomena is a new settlement, established during the 20th century. Most people come here to visit the national park, however, and stroll around its pine-encircled lakes (see sidebar p. 269).

Though it is possible to stay on the island, many people visit Mljet as a one-day boat trip from Dubrovnik or Korčula, which allows just enough time to walk over to the lakes from Pomena and spend a couple of hours there. If you want to stay longer, there are some private accommodations available in Pomena and other centers, as well as the large Hotel Odisej *(tel 020 300 300)*.

Ferries run between Sobra and Dubrovnik, and during the summer a faster catamaran service

---

Mljet Mongoose

Several Indian mongooses *(Herpestes edwardsii)* were introduced onto Mljet in 1910 to curb the island's large population of snakes. The 11 original individuals quickly adapted to their new habitat, bred rapidly, and their descendants are still here in numbers, preying on plenty of other species apart from snakes.

---

continues to Polače, inside the national park. Also during the summer months, a catamaran connects Polače with Trstenik on Pelješac. Local buses run between Sobra and Polače, or there's ample scope for exploring this part of the island by bike.

Lastovo

Lastovo, south of Korčula, remains the least visited of the major islands on the Croatian Adriatic. The two main towns on the island, Ubli near its western tip and Lastovo town on its northeast shore, are only around 6 miles (10 km) apart.

Lastovo (the Greek colony of Ladesta) was sacked by Venice in A.D. 998, when its inhabitants decided to move to the opposite end of the island and founded a new settlement at Ubli. During the 13th century, the island became a possession of the Republic of Ragusa, largely autonomous at first, though this was later lost. The island passed to Napoleon, and then briefly to the British, before becoming part of Austria. It was occupied by Italy from 1918 to 1943. Like equally remote Vis (see pp. 221–223), there was a Yugoslav military base on Lastovo until Croatia's independence in the 1990s.

In the town of **Lastovo,** the **Church of Sts. Cosmas and Damian** (Sv. Kuzma i Damjan) dates from the 15th century, with a carved 18th-century bell featuring the heads of lions and fantastic beasts mirroring those of the Cathedral of St. Mark in Korčula (see pp. 264–265). Look out for the old houses and palaces, some dating back to the 16th century, with their cylindrical chimneys, called *fumari.* Each chimney is topped with a conical cap that gives it the look of a miniature minaret. The **fortress** on the hill above the town (now a meteorological station) was built by the French in the early 1800s, on the site of an earlier fort built by Dubrovnik.

In **Ubli,** there is an early Christian basilica, the **Church of St. Peter** (Sv. Petar), which dates from the sixth century. A relief carving from the church is now in the Archaeological Museum in Zadar (see p. 173).

(see p. 173)

The islands of the **Lastovo archipelago,** to the east of the main island, were declared a nature park in 2006 (Croatia's newest reserve). The islands are home to a number of rare species and provide refuge for migrating birds, and the surrounding waters offer some great opportunities for scuba diving. Lastovo island has lovely hiking trails, and **Skrivena Luka** is a fine swimming spot on the southern coast, on one side of which stands the oldest lighthouse on the Croatian Adriatic, Struga.

Ubli is connected to Split by a fast catamaran, which calls at Vela Luka and Hvar; there's also a slower ferry. During the summer, a catamaran runs from Dubrovnik to Ubli via Mljet and Korčula.

Festivals: The annual **Lastovo Carnival,** or *Poklad,* is a colorful affair lasting three days during Lent. The carnival culminates in the humiliation, punishment, and burning of an effigy. The tradition commemorates the destruction of a fleet of Catalan pirates, on their way to plunder the island, by a miraculous storm. The effigy represents the pirates' messenger, Poklad, dispatched to demand the town's surrender. Much more mellow and sedate is the island's annual **Jazz Festival.** ■

Lastovo Archipelago Nature Park

✉ Trg Sv Petra 7, Ubli

☎ 020 801 250

pp-lastovo.hr

Visitors are few and far between on Lastovo.

TRAVELWISE

A Zagreb streetcar waits for pedestrians in the heart of Croatia's historic capital.

PLANNING YOUR TRIP

When to Go

Croatia can be divided into two climatic zones—Mediterranean on the coast and islands, and continental inland. Summers on the coast are hot and dry, with daytime temperatures averaging around 86°F (30°C), though frequently climbing quite a bit higher. The southern parts of the coast, from Split to Dubrovnik, are generally warmer than the north. Most of the rainfall on the coast falls during the winter, though temperatures remain relatively mild. Inland, summers are also hot and still relatively dry (Zagreb can be very humid during midsummer); however, winters are much colder, with heavy snowfall.

Most visitors come between early June and late September, with the peak season being July and August for both foreign and domestic vacations. Temperatures are at their highest then, the days at their sunniest, and the sea at its warmest. The heat, however, can be more than a little oppressive during August. At this time, the islands, where the heat is tempered by a slight breeze, are more pleasant than the mainland. Peak season can also get very busy, with crowded sites and beaches, and you will need to book hotels in advance. On balance, the most pleasant time to visit the coast is September, when the weather is still lovely but the crowds have thinned.

If you are hiking in the mountains, June through September

is the best time of year. In the winter, be prepared for deep snow and freezing temperatures. Most mountain huts are closed in winter, but unstaffed shelters remain year-round.

Some hotels close over the winter, and private rooms and apartments are sometimes open only from the beginning of June to the end of October. Ferries see reduced services on some routes during the winter months. Otherwise, opening hours and other services are the same throughout the country whatever time of year you visit.

What to Take

In the summer, bring light, breathable clothes. If you are visiting churches, more modest attire will be best—something with longer sleeves or a longer skirt. Otherwise, there is little reason to bring anything but the essentials since Croatia has plenty of well-stocked shops where you can buy most things you might need or have forgotten.

Inland in the winter, think thermal underwear, a warm jacket, and shoes that will be comfortable for trudging through the snow.

Beaches are generally rocky, and there are usually a few sea urchins lurking among the rocks, so think about a cheap pair of plastic beach shoes for getting into the water.

If you are an avid reader, English-language novels are limited to a few bookshops in some of the larger towns and cities.

Entry Formalities

In a policy that is rather at odds with Croatia's desire to present itself as a tourist-friendly country, all foreign visitors arriving in Croatia are required by law to register with the police within 48 hours. If you are staying in a hotel, private accommodations, hostel, or official campsite, this will be done automatically for you once they have taken your passport details. If you do not fit into the above categories, you are supposed to go and register yourself at the local police station. In reality, however, you are very unlikely as a tourist to encounter problems in this respect, unless you are stopped by the police for doing something you shouldn't, or if you've been in the country a comparatively long time.

Visas

Visas are not required for U.S., Canadian, and EU citizens arriving in Croatia for stays of up to 90 days. All you need to enter the country is a valid passport. The website of the **Ministry of Foreign Affairs** *(mvp.hr)* has details for

nationals requiring a visa to enter Croatia. If you want to stay longer than 90 days, you can simply cross the border to a neighboring country for a couple of days and then return to Croatia, where you will be entitled to stay for a further 90 days. For longer stays, apply for a Temporary Residence permit at the Croatian Embassy in your home country.

Croatian Embassies

United States

Embassy of the Republic of Croatia
2343 Massachusetts Ave. N.W.
Washington, DC 20008
Tel 202/588-5899
croatiaemb.org

United Kingdom

Embassy of the Republic of Croatia
21 Conway St.
London W1T 6BN
Tel 020 7387 1144
croatia.embassyhomepage.com

Canada

Embassy of the Republic of Croatia
229 Chapel St.
Ottawa
Ontario K1N 7Y6
Tel 613/562-7820
ca.mfa.hr

Customs

Although there are no restrictions on how much foreign currency you can bring into Croatia, you are required to declare amounts more than the equivalent of 40,000 kunas. The maximum Croatian currency you can import or export is 15,000 kunas. Customs allowances for Croatia are 2 liters (0.5 gallon) of wine; 2 liters (0.5 gallon) of liqueur, dessert, or sparkling wine; one bottle of spirits; 200 cigarettes; 50 cigars; and 250 ml (0.5 pint) of perfume per person.

Insurance

Croatia has reciprocal agreements with most European countries to cover emergency medical treatment. If you are covered by this agreement, it is a good idea to show your passport to make this clear from the outset. This does not cover private medical care or dentist bills; however, both are reasonable compared to those in the United Kingdom and North America.

If you are from a country not covered by a reciprocal agreement, such as the United States, you will need to pay for any medical treatment and then file a claim through your insurance company. Thus, travel insurance might be advisable.

Note that many basic travel insurance policies don't cover "dangerous" sports or activities such as hiking, climbing, and diving, so if you are planning to do any of these in Croatia, make sure you choose suitable coverage. In the event you need to make a claim, you will need to provide receipts or medical bills, or in order to prove theft, a police statement.

HOW TO GET TO CROATIA

By Airplane

Croatia Airlines *(croatiaairlines .com)* has direct flights to Zagreb from numerous European countries, and a number of direct flights to Dubrovnik. Other flights to the coast are routed via Zagreb. There are no direct flights to Croatia from the United States, so flights will be routed through a European hub. Some European airlines fly into smaller Croatian cities, notably Rijeka and Split.

Zagreb Airport (ZAG; *tel 01 45 62 222, zagreb-airport.hr*) is at Pleso, 10.5 miles (17 km) southwest of the city center. There are regular shuttle buses into town *($, run by Croatia Airlines)*. Taxis are also available *($$$$$)*.

Split Airport (SPU; *tel 21 203 555, split-airport.hr*) is at Kaštel, between the city and Trogir, and is connected to Split by shuttle bus *($, run by Croatia Airlines)* and taxi *($$$)*.

Dubrovnik Airport (DBV; *tel 020 773 100, airport-dubrovnik.hr*) is located some 12 miles (20 km) south of the city at Čilipi, close to Cavtat and connected to the city by Croatia Airlines shuttle bus *($)* and taxis *($$$)*.

Rijeka Airport (RJK; *tel 051 842 132, rijeka-airport.hr*) is actually on the nearby island of Krk. There are also small airports at **Pula** (PUY; *tel 052 530 105, airport-pula.com*) and **Zadar** (ZAD; *tel 023 205 800, zadar-airport.hr*).

By Bus
Zagreb's main bus station, **Autobusni Kolodvor Zagreb** *(tel 060 313 333, akz.hr)*, is about a 20-minute walk southeast of the main railroad station, connected by tram and taxi with the city center. International bus services run to Zagreb from all neighboring European countries.

By Ferry
Several international ferry and catamaran services operate between Croatia and Italy:

Jadrolinija *(tel 051 666 111, jadrolinija.hr)*, from Dubrovnik to Bari in Italy

Blue Line *(tel 45 3672 2001, blueline-ferries.com)*, from Ancona, Italy, to Split, Hvar, and Vis

Snav *(tel 39 71 207 6116, snav.it)*, from Ancona and Pescara in Italy to Split and Hvar

Emilia Romagna Lines *(tel 39 547 675157, emiliaromagnalines.it)*, from Ravenna, Italy, to Rovinj, and from Rimini and Pescara, Italy, to Mali Lošinj and Zadar

Venezia Lines *(venezialines.com)* from Venice, Italy, to Pore, Rovinj, Pula, and other ports in Istria, as well as to Mali Lošinj.

Some of these operate year-round (Jadrolinija and Blue Line to Split), while others (Blue Line to Hvar and Vis, Snav, Venezia Lines, Emilia Romagna Lines) operate only during the summer months.

By Train
Zagreb's main railway station, **Glavni Kolodvor** *(tel 01 378 2532, hznet.hr)* is connected by direct trains to Ljubljana in Slovenia; Graz and Vienna in Austria; Munich and other stations in Germany; Trieste and Venice in Italy; Budapest in Hungary; Belgrade and other stations in Serbia; and Sarajevo and other stations in Bosnia and Herzegovina.

InterRail *(raileurope.co.uk)* and **Eurail** *(eurail.com)* passes cover Croatia along with other countries in Europe. However, it is not really worth getting one just for Croatia, as train fares are inexpensive anyway, and not all of the country is covered by rail. In both cases, tickets need to be arranged before arriving in mainland Europe.

GETTING AROUND
By Airplane
Croatia Airlines *(Zagreb: tel 01 481 9633; Split: tel 021 362 997; Dubrovnik: tel 060 313 333; croatiaairlines.com)* operates domestic flights across the country, mostly from Zagreb but sometimes flying between points on the coast on the way to or from the capital.

Zagreb's is by far the largest and busiest airport, yet it is still comparatively small and very easy to negotiate by international standards.

By Bus
Try to buy bus tickets in advance if you can, at least on popular routes on the coast. When you buy a return ticket *(povratna karta)*, this usually includes a seat reservation *(rezervacija)* for the outward

though not for the return portion of the journey. It is worth getting a seat reservation for the return journey (which costs very little) when you arrive at your destination—even though you may well be told at the ticket office that you really don't need one.

Baggage *(prtljaga)* that is placed in the hold (effectively anything larger than hand luggage) is charged for *($)*, and you should always get a small ticket as receipt.

Most intercity buses have a toilet on board (though they're not always working), and all are nonsmoking. Journeys are usually broken by a refreshment stop of around 10 to 15 minutes.

Zagreb's bus station, **Autobusni Kolodvor Zagreb** *(tel 060 313 333, akz.hr)*, has luggage lockers *($)* and is accessible 24 hours a day.

By Ferry
Traveling by ferry can be one of the nicest ways of getting around the Croatian coast, completely bypassing summer traffic on the main coast road, and fares (at least for foot passengers) are very cheap. Ferry types range from large car and passenger vessels to smaller craft and speedy catamarans (foot passengers only).

Sailing routes and schedules are fairly comprehensive, and you can get to most (but not all) of the major islands—though not always from the place you want. For catamarans and some of the smaller boats, try to book your tickets a day in advance.

Most of the routes are operated by the state ferry company **Jadrolinija** *(tel 051 666 111; jadrolinija.hr /en/home)*.

A number of private companies also operate, in particular some of the catamaran services and shorter sailing routes.

Kapetan Luka *(tel 021 872 994, krilo.hr)* runs a catamaran between Split, Hvar, and Korčula.

Rapska Plovidba *(tel 051 724 122, rapska-plovidba.hr)* runs the ferry from Mišnjak on the island of Rab to Jablanac.

Mia Tours *(tel 023 254 300, miatours.hr)* provides the service between Zadar and Premuda, Silba, and Olib.

GV Lines *(Dubrovnik: tel 020 313 119; Zadar: tel 023 250 733; gv-line.hr)* runs the services between Zadar and Mali Iž and Dubrovnik and Šipan.

Venezia Lines *(tel 052 422 896, venezialines.com)*, an Italian company, also runs between several places in Istria (Poreč, Rovinj, Pula, Rabac).

In general, the private companies are slightly more expensive, though tickets are still very reasonable.

By Train

Croatia's rail network is reliable and efficient, fares reasonable, and over longer distances preferable to traveling by bus. From Zagreb there are trains east across Slavonia, west to Rijeka, and south to Split on the Dalmatian coast, with a high-speed service operating on the latter route as well as north toward the Slovenian and Hungarian borders—but note that there's no railway line along the coast itself.

Schedules are available at *hznet .hr*. Tickets (*karta*, singular; *karte*, plural) can be purchased as single (*u jednom smjeru*) or return (*povratna karta*), the latter working out slightly cheaper than two singles. Two or more people traveling together can be issued a single ticket (*na istu kartu*) covering all passengers, which is cheaper still, but you'll have to travel together as planned, including the return leg of the journey. Tickets do not necessarily include a seat reservation (*rezervacija*), particularly for the return trip, so ask for one if you want to be guaranteed a seat on a busy route like Zagreb–Split. Buy the seat reservation for the

return journey (*$*) when you arrive at your destination.

By Tram

Several cities in Croatia, including Zagreb (Zagrebački Električni Tramvaj: ZET; *tel 01 3651 555, zet.hr*), Osijek, Split, and Rijeka, have trams on routes through the city center and out into the suburbs. These are often the most straightforward way to get around. Tickets are very reasonably priced and can be bought on board from the driver or from newspaper kiosks, where they are slightly cheaper. In either case, the tickets need to be stamped in one of the ticket machines once on board in order to be valid.

By Rental Car

If you rent a car (and there are many car rental offices in Croatia, you will need your driver's license. The legal driving age is 18.

Croatians drive on the right and speed limits are 31 mph (50 km/h) in built-up areas, 55 mph (90 km/h) on open roads, 68 mph (110 km/h) on major highways, and 80 mph (130 km/h) on interstate-style roads. Speed cameras are fairly common, though that does not stop a fair amount of reckless driving.

Croatia has a very new set of freeways (*autocesta; hac.hr*) that make getting between places very quick—unless you get caught in the long backlog of traffic heading back into Zagreb or on the main coastal highway (the Jadranska Magistrala). These roads can get very congested during the summer.

Freeways operate on a toll system. Simply collect a ticket when you roll on and pay when you exit (*$*). A toll is also payable on the bridge to Krk.

The blood alcohol level is 0.05 percent (zero for drivers under the

age of 24), and it is illegal to drive while using a mobile phone.

Other things of note: If you witness an accident, you are legally obliged to stop. Chains should be carried during the winter. Drivers must have a reflective jacket in the car (not always supplied with a rental car), which must be worn if getting out of the vehicle by the roadside.

Driving in larger towns and cities usually entails negotiating a labyrinthine system of one-way streets, and finding a place to park can be difficult.

Fuel costs are high compared to North America, about $5–$6 per gallon ($1.4/liter). For a list of gas stations (*benzinska stanica*) and for route planning, see **Industrija Nafte** *(ina.hr)*. For traffic and road conditions, see **HAK** *(hak.hr)*.

By Sailboat

For those sailing on the Croatian Adriatic, most marinas in Croatia are owned by the Croatian Association of Nautical Tourism, and almost half of these are run by the **Adriatic Croatia International Club,** or ACI *(tel 051 271 288, aci-club.hr)*. The marinas are in general very well equipped, with fuel and water available. Weather forecasts are issued (in both Croatian and English) by harbor offices (Rijeka on VHF 69, Pula on VHF 73, Split on VHF 67, and Dubrovnik on VHF 73) and by Radio Rijeka's, Radio Split's, and Radio Dubrovnik's VHF channels. Do not underestimate the strength of the northeast wind known as the *bura*, which can blow at gale force.

By Taxi

Licensed taxis operate in all major towns and cities, and are fairly expensive by Croatian standards. Fares are charged according to the meter (though it always pays to have a quick glance to check this is switched on), except for some longer journeys (for example, to some airports), in which case a set fare might be the norm—check that you understand if this is the case. A new licensed taxi firm, Cammeo (taxi-cammeo .hr), started operating recently and introduced much lower fares—causing an uproar among other taxi firms. Cammeo now operates in Zagreb, Osijek, and Rijeka, and it might be worth calling them first if you're in one of these cities (they don't operate from ranks). Eko Taxi should be your second choice in Zagreb.

By Bike

While bike lanes have been introduced in some larger cities like Zagreb, Croatian roads remain slightly less bike friendly than one might hope. Nevertheless, there are some lovely areas for cycling, and a number of local tourist boards—most notably Istria (istria-bike.com)—are making stellar efforts to promote bike routes, both on- and off-road. There's also a "bed-and-bike" scheme with listings of cycle-friendly accommodation.

Consult **Pedala** (pedala.hr) for cycle routes and detailed maps.

PRACTICAL ADVICE
Addresses

Street addresses are written with the name of the street, followed by the number, a zip code, and the city (for example, Ilica 50, 10000, Zagreb). Many addresses include the abbreviation bb, which stands for bez broja and means "no number."

Communications
Internet

Internet cafés are fairly plentiful in Croatia, at least in larger towns and cities and tourist centers,

though connections can be slow in some places. Most hotels have free Wi-Fi, though private rooms generally do not offer this. Highly recommended in Zagreb is **Sublink** (Teslina 12, tel 01 481 9993), Croatia's first Internet café. It has been running since 1996.

Mail

Croatia's postal system, **Hrvatska Pošta** (posta.hr), is reliable and easy to use, though cards and letters sent from Croatia can sometimes be a little on the slow side. When buying stamps (marke) at the post office (pošta), it is normal to hand over the completed postcard or letter at the counter to be stamped and posted. "By airmail" in Croatian is avionom.

Telephone

The international dialing code for Croatia is 385, and area codes are two or three digits beginning with zero (for example, Zagreb is 01, Split is 021). Local numbers use both six- and seven-digit systems. If calling Croatia from overseas, start with the international access code and omit the initial zero from the area code. For example, to call Zagreb from overseas, dial 00 385 1 followed by the local number; to call Zagreb from within Croatia, dial 01 followed by the local number.

Croatia's blue public pay phones are found on streets and in post offices, and operate on either phone cards (available from newspaper kiosks) or coins. Call boxes are also found in post offices, and are the least expensive way of calling overseas.

Most cell phones work fine in Croatia. Those staying for a longer amount of time may find it worth buying a local SIM card ($$$). **VIP** (vip.hr) and **T-Mobile** (t-mobile.hr) are the main service providers.

To call overseas from Croatia, dial 00 followed by the country and area codes, and the local number. The international operator is 901.

Conversions

Croatia uses the metric system.

Electricity

Electricity in Croatia is 220V/ 50Hz, and the country uses the standard, two-pin European plug.

Etiquette & Local Customs

Croatians greet one another with a handshake or, when on familiar terms, a light kiss on both cheeks. The word bok! is used for an informal hello or goodbye in Zagreb; otherwise the correct greetings are dobro jutro (good morning), dobar dan (hello or good day), dobra veđer (good evening), and do viđenja (goodbye). When asking for something, begin with molim vas... (Please can I have...), though it should be added that Croats often don't bother with such niceties—not because they're being rude, but simply because it's common and perfectly acceptable to say "Give me..." rather than "Please can I have..."—but that needn't keep you from using such civilities. Croatians in general are very courteous.

Croatia remains fairly conservative, and when visiting churches, you should dress appropriately—no swimsuits, bare chests, or very short skirts.

Holidays

The following days are public holidays in Croatia, when some businesses (including museums and some shops and restaurants) will be closed:
January 1—New Year's Day
January 6—Epiphany

Easter Sunday & Easter Monday
May 1—Labor Day
Corpus Christi
June 22—Anti-Fascist
  Resistance Day
June 25—Independence Day
  (Dan Državnosti)
August 5—Victory Day &
  National Thanksgiving Day
August 15—Assumption Day
October 8—Independence Day
November 1—All Saints' Day
December 25–26—Christmas

Liquor Laws
The legal age for drinking or buying alcohol in Croatia is 18.

Media
The state TV company in Croatia is **HTV** (Hrvatska Televizija), with two channels, HTV1 and HTV2. Along with the main radio company, **HR** (Hrvatski Radio), it forms the state broadcasting company **HRT** (Hrvatska Radio-televizija; hrt.hr). There are also various cable networks.

The main national daily newspapers are *Jutarnji List* (literally, "Morning Leaf"), *Vearnji List* (Evening Leaf), and *Vjesnik*. On the coast you can buy *Slobodna Dalmacija* and *Novi List* (the latter in Rijeka). The magazines with the largest circulation are the weekly *Globus* and *Nacional*.

Money
The favored foreign exchange currency in Croatia is the euro, though you can just as easily change most other major currencies, including U.S. dollars and U.K. pounds sterling, throughout the country. Most prices are quoted in kunas, though some hotels quote in euros, which are converted according to the daily exchange rate. Having joined the EU in 2013, Croatia will probably adopt the euro as currency within the next few years.

Credit cards (including Visa, MasterCard, and American Express) are accepted widely in hotels, shops, and restaurants—though not usually for private accommodations or in smaller cafés. Exchange offices *(mjenjanica)* are common and should have daily rates posted.

ATMs *(bankomat)* are widespread in larger towns and cities. You can cash traveler's checks in banks, but be prepared to wait in line; American Express is still the most widely accepted.

With the exception of some old markets, bargaining is not acceptable in Croatia, any more than it would be in shops or markets in North America.

Opening Times
Shops and other businesses tend to open fairly early (7:30–8:30 a.m.), and most close around 8:30 p.m., with supermarkets and some pharmacies tending to keep longer hours in the evening. Many places, including some shops and tourist information offices, close for an hour or two at lunchtime. During the summer, this closed period lasts longer, often from midday to 4 or 5 p.m.

Banking hours are generally 8 a.m. to 6 p.m., Monday through Friday, with some banks opening on Saturday mornings, too. Office workers tend to work from 8:30 a.m. or earlier to 4:30 p.m. Most shops (except supermarkets) outside the tourist areas close on Sundays or at least work reduced hours. Museums are often closed on Mondays.

Religion
Croatia's population is predominantly Roman Catholic (87 percent), with smaller percentages of Orthodox (4.4), and Muslim (1.3). Check with your hotel for local service times and contact details for places of worship.

Restrooms
Restrooms are available at bus and train stations and at various central city locations, and usually cost 2 kunas (though some places charge up to 5 kunas). They are in general perfectly clean, with someone employed to keep them so and collect money from people as they go in or out. There are also restrooms in almost any café or restaurant.

Some restrooms at older bus stations may contain squatting rather than western (sitting) toilets, but this would never be the case in hotels, cafés, etc.

A restroom is known as a WC (pronounced ve-se) in Croatian. Men's rooms are marked *muškarci* or *muški*; ladies' rooms, *žene* or *ženski*—or sometimes just M and Ž, respectively.

Smoking
Croatia was, until quite recently, a staunch bastion of smoking, with cafés and restaurants often smoke-filled places that nonsmokers might find unpleasant, to say the least. In 2009, a smoking ban in public areas (including offices, cafés, bars, and restaurants) was introduced, though it caused such an uproar it is now under review. As it stands, buses are nonsmoking, but train compartments not always so. Restaurants and cafés are nonsmoking or have nonsmoking areas. Hotel rooms are usually nonsmoking, although you may still want to ask for a nonsmoking room, particularly in some of the older establishments.

Time Differences
Croatia is one hour ahead of Greenwich mean time (GMT+1). There is a 6-hour difference between New York and Zagreb. It operates daylight savings time in summer.

Tipping

Tipping in restaurants and cafés (in the vast majority of which a service charge is not automatically added to the bill) for good service is always appreciated, with 5 or 10 percent of the bill, or a few kunas, being sufficient. Tipping in cabs is not necessary.

Traveling With Kids

Croatia can be a great place to travel with kids, with plenty to keep them occupied to balance the amount of time Mom and Dad spend sightseeing. Safe, shallow, pebble beaches can be found in many places on the otherwise rocky coast, and most towns of any size have a playground (igralište) for kids, with bouncy castles and slides, easy to find, especially on the coast during summer. Good attractions for kids include Zagreb Zoo, Pula Aquarium, Blue World Institute in Veli Lošinj, Aquapark Istralandia in Poreč, the Falconry Center near Šibenik, and the Safari Park on the Brijuni Islands; the Children's Parade at the Rijeka Carnival and Zagreb's Cest is d'Best Festival are also enjoyable.

Travelers With Disabilities

Travelers with disabilities may not be quite as well catered to in Croatia as they might be in North America or Western Europe, at least in terms of special facilities on public transportation, at hotels, museums, etc. However, particularly in larger cities, authorities are doing a very good job of improving access, with ramps, lower pay phones, etc. The newer trams in Zagreb are much lower and step-free. Disabled travelers qualify for free city transport on buses and trams. Anyone perceived as needing assistance, whether aged or disabled, will usually be directed immediately to the front of a line.

Traveling With Pets

If traveling with a pet, you'll need to bring the animal's international health certificate, and you'll be restricted to certain border crossings.

Visitor Information

The Croatian National Tourist Board (croatia.hr) has lots of information on what to see and do in the country and some on accommodations. For more on accommodations and restaurants, check the websites of local tourist boards. Visit Croatia (visit-croatia .co.uk) is an excellent online independent source of information.

EMERGENCIES

Croatia is a relatively safe place to travel and its crime rate is comparatively low. Nevertheless, you should still take the usual precautions. Carry money and valuables in a money belt beneath your clothes, avoid ostentatious displays of wealth, don't leave your bags unattended, and avoid poorly lit backstreets at night. Carry photocopies of your passport or other documents (separately from the documents themselves), and use ATMs and traveler's checks to avoid carrying large quantities of cash. If you go swimming, leave valuables in the hotel safe rather than in your bag on the beach. Police are usually helpful and courteous.

Help!	U pomoć!
Police	policija
Policeman	policajac
Emergency	hitno

Embassies

United States Embassy
Ulica Thomasa Jeffersona 2
10010, Zagreb
Tel 01 661 2200
zagreb.usembassy.gov

British Embassy
Ivana Lučića 4
10000, Zagreb
Tel 01 600 9100
gov.uk/government
/world/organisations
/british-embassy-zagreb

Canadian Embassy
Prilaz Gjure Deželića 4
10000, Zagreb
Tel 01 488 1200
canadainternational.gc.ca/croatia
-croatie/index.aspx

Emergency Telephone Numbers

Police   192
Fire   193
Ambulance   194
Emergency services can also be reached on 112

Health

Croatia has a very good public health system. Dental fees are extremely reasonable compared to those in the United Kingdom and the United States. Should you need emergency medical treatment, this will need to be covered either by a reciprocal agreement with some EU countries, which grants free emergency medical treatment, or by your insurance (make sure you get a receipt in order to claim for this). Most prescription medicines are available through pharmacies, though some less common ones may take a while to get, and prescription costs are comparatively high.

Tap water is safe to drink in Croatia (if in doubt, bottled water is widely available).

Beware of ticks in forest areas; check exposed skin and scalp after hiking in forest or through long grass, wear a hat and long trousers, and pay particular attention to children. If you find a tick, remove it as soon as possible using tick tweezers (available from pharmacies), grasping the body close to the skin and pulling gently at right angles, taking care not to crush the abdomen. Seek medical attention.

Snakebite remains a possibility in the mountains, and the nose-horned viper is quite venomous. If bitten, immobilize the limb and get the victim to a hospital, where antivenom will be available, and if possible try to identify the snake. You can minimize the danger from sea urchins (the spines can be very difficult to remove) when getting into or out of the sea on rocky beaches by wearing plastic sandals.

There are no vaccinations required for entry into Croatia.

A little vocabulary:

hospital	bolnica
doctor	doktor
dentist	zubar
pharmacy	apoteka or ljekarna
medicine	lijek
ambulance	hitna pomoć

Lost Property
In the event of theft, you should get a police report within 24 hours in order to file an insurance claim. If your passport is lost or stolen, contact your embassy.

What to Do in Event of a Car Accident
If you're driving and have a car accident, you are required to stay at the scene and will be expected to give your details to the police and possibly attend a court hearing within 24 hours. An interpreter will be provided.

FURTHER READING
History & Archaeology
A Short History of the Yugoslav Peoples by Fred Singleton (1989)

Croatia: A History by Ivo Goldstein (1999)
Croatia: A Nation Forged in War by Marcus Tanner (1997)
Dubrovnik–A History by Robin Harris (2003)
Gorjanovi-Kramberger and Krapina Early Man by Jakov Radovčić (1988)
The Balkans, 1804–1999: Nationalism, War and the Great Powers by Misha Glenny (1999)
The Balkans: From the End of Byzantium to the Present Day by Mark Mazower (2001)
The Demise of Yugoslavia: A Political Memoir by Stipe Mesić (2004)
The Illyrians by John Wilkes (1992)
Southeastern Europe in the Middle Ages 500–1250 by Florin Curta (2006)
The Uskoks of Senj: Piracy, Banditry and Holy War in the Sixteenth-Century Adriatic by Catherine Wendy Bracewell (1992)
Zagreb–A Cultural and Literary History by Celia Hawkesworth (2007)

Arts, Culture & Language
Art Treasures of Croatia by Radovan Ivančević (1993)
Colloquial Croatian: The Complete Course for Beginners by Celia Hawkesworth with Ivana Jović (2005)
Croatia: Aspects of Art, Architecture and Cultural Heritage by John Julius Norwich, Stjepan Ćosić, and others (2009)
Early Christian and Byzantine Art by John Beckwith (1970)
From Home to Museum: Ivan Meštrović in Zagreb by Danica Plazibat (2004)
Moreška: The War Dance From Korčula by Zoran Palčok (1974)
The Art of the Hlebine School by Vladimir Crnković (2005)
The Best of Croatian Cooking by Liliana Pavičić and Gordana Pirker-Mosher (2000)

Outdoors & Nature
Birds of Europe by Lars Svensson, Peter J Grant, Killian Mullarney, and Dan Zetterström (1999)
Central and Eastern European Wildlife by Gerard Gorman (2008)
Flora Jadranska obali i otoka by Sanja Kovačić (2008)
Flowers of Greece and the Balkans: A Field Guide by Oleg Polunin (1987)
The Islands of Croatia by Rudolf Abraham (2014)
Krka National Park Natural Science Guide by Drago Marguš (2007)
Walking in Croatia by Rudolf Abraham (2010)

Travel
Black Lamb and Grey Falcon: A Journey Through Yugoslavia by Rebecca West (2007)
Eastern Approaches by Fitzroy Maclean (1949)
Istria by Rudolf Abraham and Thammy Evans (2013)
The Companion Guide to Jugoslavia by J. A. Cudden (1968)
Through the Embers of Chaos: Balkan Journeys by Dervla Murphy (2002)

Fiction
Café Europa by Slavenka Drakulić (1991)
Croatian Nights by Tony White and others (2005)
How We Survived Communism and Even Laughed by Slavenka Drakulić (1991)
In the Jaws of Life by Dubravka Ugrešić (1992)
On the Edge of Reason by Miroslav Krleža (1995)
The Banquet in Blitva by Miroslav Krleža (2003)
The Culture of Lies by Dubravka Ugrešić (1998)
The Return of Philip Latinowicz by Miroslav Krleža (1995)

Hotels & Restaurants

Accommodation in Croatia spans a huge range, from homey private rooms in someone's stone-built house to large, modern resort complexes and luxurious boutique hotels, not to mention a huge number of camping grounds along the coast. Restaurants range from simple snack bars to outstanding gourmet establishments and rustic taverns.

Hotels

Hotel accommodations in Croatia fall into two main categories, hotels (whether small boutique or large international chain) and the *pansion* (pensions, similar to a bed-and-breakfast). A predominance of large, brutalist hotel complexes from the 1970s, sometimes in need of a face-lift, are happily now increasingly supplemented by a new generation of boutique hotels, and many of the older places are being luxuriously renovated and rebranded. There are also a number of older, Austro-Hungarian hotels (particularly in Opatija) that ooze opulence. Many of the larger hotels have spa and health centers, and most of the more modern places now have free Wi-Fi access.

Prices for hotels tend to be comparatively high by Croatian standards, peaking in the high season (*July–Aug.*) and dropping slightly other times of the year. During the winter, those places that remain open—a number close, in particular the large resort-style places—often offer discounts of up to 50 percent.

Online booking is available for many of the larger hotels, often with special deals below the standard rates. Hotels and pensions usually include breakfast in the cost of a room, and half board is sometimes available for not much extra.

Village tourism is also on the increase, giving you the opportunity to stay in a traditional village home, eat home-cooked food (frequently including plenty of regional specialties), and experience a much more genuine slice of life in rural Croatia.

The following listings tend to concentrate on places within towns, rather than the larger (sometimes perfectly nice) complexes farther outside town.

Private rooms and apartments are one of the most common and popular forms of accommodation in Croatia (with the notable exception of Zagreb, where there is very little of this available), and in both cases are usually more intimate, and almost always cheaper, than hotels. However, private rooms and apartments are generally not included in the listings here. Exceptions are made where places have their own website and booking facilities, are in an exceptional location, or where few reasonable alternatives exist. This occurs in places where reservations are channeled through agencies or local tourist offices. The latter should be your first port of call for private accommodations.

It is also very common in Croatia for people to wait at bus and train stations offering *sobe* (rooms) or *apartmani* (apartments), which can vary in standards. If you turn up in town without a reservation and want to try your luck with one of these before going to the tourist information office, try to get a clear idea of how far out of the town center it is, and ask to see pictures of the room before taking a look.

Where no hotel is given for a location in the following listings, it implies that private accommodation is the better option. Like some of the resort-style hotels, many private rooms and apartments are unavailable during the winter.

A local tourist tax ($) is added to accommodation prices.

Restaurants

Croatian restaurants come in several guises, *restoran* (restaurant), *konoba* (a slightly more homey place, though this is absolutely no indication of a drop in quality), and *gostionica* (generally a more simple version of a konoba). If you feel like a "night in," the larger hotels generally have their own restaurants (often more than one), and even many of the smaller pansions have their own terrace restaurant or pizzeria. A handy resource for basic details on Croatian restaurants is *gastronaut.hr*.

It is difficult to give an exact figure for restaurant prices here. The cost of a main course in the same establishment often ranges dramatically from a cheap pasta dish to premium seafood charged per kilo, so these price categories should be taken only as a rule of thumb.

Organization & Abbreviations

Hotels and restaurants are listed by chapter and place-names, then arranged alphabetically by price. Hotels are listed first. The number of rooms indicated for hotels includes both rooms and suites. Restaurants are listed second. No smoking indicates either nonsmoking rooms or an entire nonsmoking policy in a hotel, and in restaurants a nonsmoking area or nonsmoking policy (this does not usually extend to a terrace or outdoor seating). Abbreviations used are AE (American Express), DC (Diner's Club), MC (MasterCard), and V (Visa).

⊞ Hotel 🍴 Restaurant 🛏 No. of Guest Rooms ✚ No. of Seats 🅿 Parking 🕐 Closed 🛗 Elevator

PRICES

HOTELS

The cost of a double room with private bathroom in peak season is given by **$** signs.

$$$$$	Over $315
$$$$	$191–$315
$$$	$126–$190
$$	$60–$125
$	Under $60

RESTAURANTS

The average cost of a two-course meal for one person, excluding tip or drinks, is given by **$** signs.

$$$$$	Over $40
$$$$	$31–$40
$$$	$21–$30
$$	$10–$20
$	Under $10

■ ZAGREB

ZAGREB

HOTELS

🏨 ESPLANADE
🍴 $$$–$$$$$

MIHANOVIČEVA 1
TEL 01 456 6666
esplanade.hr

The height of luxury in Zagreb, with plush furnishings, fluffy goose-down pillows, and enormous marble bathrooms. There are two restaurants, the top-notch **Zinfandel's** and **Le Bistro.** The hotel dates from the 1920s, when Zagreb was a stop on the *Orient Express,* and its guests have included the likes of Orson Welles, Woody Allen, Alfred Hitchcock, and Charles Lindbergh. It was reopened in 2004 after a makeover.

🛈 209 🅿 🚭 🕃 🛇 🔁 💦
🏧 All major cards

🏨 HOTEL INTERNATIONAL
🍴 ZAGREB
$–$$$$$

MIRAMARSKA 24
TEL 01 610 8800
hotel-international.hr

Located just outside the historic center, in Novi Zagreb, this comfortable hotel meets all the business traveler's needs—high speed Internet, conference center, and restaurant. The first floor corner bar has an outside patio that allows guests to enjoy a quiet drink or watch a soccer match. Complimentary breakfast.

🛈 207 🚭 🅿 🕃 🛇
🏧 AE, MC, V

SOMETHING SPECIAL

🏨 DOUBLETREE BY
🍴 HILTON
$$$–$$$$

ULICA GRADA VUKOVARA 269A
TEL 01 6001 900
doubletree.com

Excellent new four-star hotel in the Green Gold business district, a ten-minute walk southeast of the bus station. Stylish, spacious rooms (the corner rooms are the best) all with huge LCD TV screens and blisteringly fast free Wi-Fi; and the bathrooms are among the nicest you'll find anywhere in Croatia, with separate shower cubicle and bathtub. Tea- and coffeemaking facilities and ironing board in each room. The warm welcome includes a tasty chocolate chip cookie. Bar and top-notch restaurant, the **OXBO Urban Bar & Grill.**

🛈 152 🅿 🚭 🕃 🛇 🔁 🕃
🏧 All major cards

🏨 WESTIN ZAGREB
$$$–$$$$

KRSNJAVOGA 1
TEL 01 489 2000
starwoodhotels.com

The Westin is one of Zagreb's top five-star hotels, with a list of past guests including Presidents Putin and Bush and the Rolling Stones. Plush rooms, conveniently located near the Mimara Museum.

🛈 378 🅿 🚭 🕃 🛇 🔁 💦
🏧 All major cards

🏨 HOTEL AS
🍴 $$$

ZELENGAJ 2
TEL 01 460 9111
hotel-as.hr

Set amid the peaceful greenery of Zelengaj, just a short taxi or bus ride north of British Square, this excellent four-star hotel has spacious rooms with tasteful, antique-style furnishings and friendly service. There's also an award-winning seafood eatery, **Restaurant AS,** with an extensive wine list and an elegant café-bar.

🛈 23 🅿 🚭 🕃 🛇
🏧 AE, MC, V

🏨 HOTEL JÄGERHORN
$$$

ILICA 14
TEL 01 483 3877
hotel-jagerhorn.hr

Friendly family-run place, hidden away down an alley off Ilica just a few minutes' walk from the main square, with clean, comfortable rooms, a spacious lounge, and a terrace.

🛈 13 🛇 🕃 🕃 🏧 All major cards

SOMETHING SPECIAL

🏨 HOTEL PRESIDENT
🍴 $$$

PANTOVČAK 52
TEL 01 488 1480
president-zagreb.com

Stylish new four-star boutique hotel, just a short walk uphill from British Square, with light, spacious rooms with polished wooden floors, tastefully decorated with various pieces of art. All of the rooms have terraces with lovely views over the greenery of Zelengaj, and there's a light-flooded lounge bar and restaurant in the glass-paned rear of the building.

[i] 10 **[e] [s] [e]**
[s] All major cards

[h] HOTEL MAKSIMIR
$$
MAKSIMIRSKA 57/1
TEL 01 666 6160
hotel-maksimir.hr
Attractive new place out toward Maksimir, offering excellent-value, clean, and neatly furnished rooms. Breakfast is included. Only a few stops on the tram from the main square.

[i] 12 **[P] [s] [s]** AE, MC, V

[h] ZAGREB POINT APARTMENTS
$$
MAKSIMIRSKA 57A
TEL 099 5622 485
zagrebpoint.com
zagreb-apartment.net
Stylish, spacious modern apartments at several convenient locations across Zagreb provide a welcome addition to the choice of accommodation in the Croatian capital. Apartment 3, in a block behind the railway station, comes recommended—large, tastefully furnished, with a balcony. Efficient, friendly service.

[i] 9 **[s] [s]** All major cards

RESTAURANTS

SOMETHING SPECIAL

[r] OKRUGLJAK
$$$–$$$$
MLINOVI 28, ŠESTINE
TEL 01 467 4112
okrugljak.hr
Excellent traditional restaurant out near Šestine (bus number 102 from Kaptol), on the lower flanks of Medvednica,

which has been in business for around a century. Crisp white tablecloths, a wooden-beamed interior, and a huge open terrace are the setting for authentic, hearty dishes from the Zagreb region and northern Croatia, and there's a good wine list. Try the vast Croatian Platter or Mixed Grill, both for two, or the Zagreb steak. Reservations recommended on weekends.

[i] 500 **[s] [s]** All major cards

SOMETHING SPECIAL

[r] IVICA I MARICA
$$$
TKALČIĆEVA 70
TEL 01 482 8999
ivicaimarica.com
Excellent restaurant on café-lined Tkalčićeva, with a rustic interior, streetside tables outside, and an emphasis on fresh, locally grown, and organic produce. The menu includes a range of traditional Croatian dishes alongside vegetarian options—including excellent *štrukli*—and its celebrated bakery next door serves some of the finest cakes in Zagreb. The name is Croatian for "Hansel and Gretel."

[n] 100 **[s] [s]** All major cards

[r] KORČULA
$$$
TESLINA 17
TEL 020 487 2159
restoran-korcula.hr
Very good traditional seafood restaurant, which has been around for years. Top-notch grilled fish, *pašticada*, and other Dalmatian specialties, surrounded by pictures, a ship's wheel, and paraphernalia with a maritime theme.

[n] 60 **[c]** Closed Sun. **[s]**
[s] All major cards

[r] POD GRIČKIM TOPOM
$$$
ZAKMARDIJEVE STUBE 5
TEL 020 483 3607
restoran-pod-grickim-topom.hr
This excellent restaurant, with a lovely terrace and winter garden overlooking Zagreb's tiled roofs and secessionist facades, is perched on the side of Gornji Grad, just below the Lotrščak Tower. Dishes range from traditional Dalmatian fare and seafood to Zagreb steak. Try the *pašticada*–marinated beef or veal cooked with dried plums.

[n] 70 **[c]** Closed Sun. **[s]**
[s] All major cards

[r] SOFRA
$$–$$$
RADNICKA CESTA 52
TEL 01 4111 621
sofra.hr
Excellent Bosnian restaurant in this block near DoubleTree by Hilton—the best place in Zagreb to try *ćevapčići*, with a good range of Bosnian specialties such as *čobanac* (traditional meat and vegetable stew) and stuffed vegetables, in an atmospheric setting. Worth checking your bill though.

[n] 100 **[s]** All major cards

[r] KEREMPUH
$$
KAPTOL 3
TEL 020 481 9000
A true Zagreb institution and perennial favorite, perched on the corner of the upper terrace of Zagreb's huge open market, Dolac, with pink tablecloths inside and a terrace overlooking the stalls outside. The menu changes almost daily, but might include goulash, boiled ham with cabbage and potatoes, or meatloaf stuffed with cheese. Closes early on Sunday. Reservations recommended.

[n] 150 **[c]** Closed D Sun.
[s] [s] All major cards

PRICES

HOTELS
The cost of a double room
with private bathroom in
peak season is given by
$ signs.

$$$$$	Over $315
$$$$	$191–$315
$$$	$126–$190
$$	$60–$125
$	Under $60

RESTAURANTS
The average cost of a two-
course meal for one person,
excluding tip or drinks, is
given by $ signs.

$$$$$	Over $40
$$$$	$31–$40
$$$	$21–$30
$$	$10–$20
$	Under $10

🍴 VALLIS AUREA
$$
TOMIĆEVA 4
TEL 01 483 1305
vallis-aurea.com
Wonderful, unpretentious
restaurant just off Ilica near
the funicular, with a rustic,
tavernlike interior, a daily
changing menu, and friendly
service. Does some good
Slavonian dishes and tasty
stuffed squid. Excellent
value.
🔲 50 🕐 Closed Sun. 🚭
🔳 AE, DC, V

🍴 VEGE HOP
$$
VLAŠKA 79
TEL 01 4649 400
vegehop.hr
Excellent little vegetarian and
vegan option off Vlaška, a cou-
ple of tram stops east of Jelačić
Square. The tagliatelle made

of fine strips of marinated raw
vegetables, tossed in a mouth-
watering sauce, is particularly
good, and the daily set menus
are great value.
🔲 20 🚭 🔳 No credit cards

🍴 ZRNO
$$
MEDULIĆEVE 20
TEL 01 4847 540
zrnobiobistro.hr
The latest of an outstanding
new breed of vegetarian,
vegan, and macrobiotic res-
taurants to open in Zagreb,
Zrno dishes up deliciously
healthy appetizers, entrées,
and desserts that will prove
the perfect counterpoint to all
those seafood dinners, grilled
meats, and pizzas you have
been indulging in elsewhere.
Stylish, with friendly service
and very good value. Highly
recommended.
🔲 40 🚭 🔳 AE, MC, V

🍴 MRKI MEDO
$–$$
TKALČIĆEVA 36
TEL 01 4929 613
pivnica-medvedgrad.hr
Great pub with tables spilling out onto busy, café-lined
Tkalčićeva, serving a range of
its own excellent beers—Mrki
Medvjed (a dark ruby ale) and
Crna Kraljica (a thumpingly
good stout) are particularly
fine. Forget the "theme" pubs
elsewhere in the capital, this is
the place to try some fine locally
brewed ales.
🔲 80 🔳 All major cards

🍴 NOKTURNO
$–$$
SKALINSKA 4
TEL 01 481 3394
restoran.nokturno.hr
Perennially popular piz-
zeria on Skalinska, the
narrow cobbled street running up from Tkalčićeva to
Dolac. Great value, young
friendly staff, and excellent

pizzas—thin-based, crispy, and
still the best in Zagreb—as
well as various pasta dishes,
and there's an inviting
enclosed terrace on the street.
🔲 100 🚭 🔳 All major cards

🍴 VINCEK
$
ILICA 18
TEL 01 483 3612
vincek.com.hr
Zagreb's most famous ice-
cream shop *(slasti arnica)*, on
Ilica, with numerous flavors
to choose from and a good
selection of cakes.
🕐 Closed Sun. & daily after
6 p.m. 🚭 🔳 No credit cards

■ NORTHERN CROATIA

JASTREBARSKO & PLEŠIVICA WINE ROAD

🏨 VINSKA KUĆA JANA
🍴 $$
PRODIN DOL BB, GORICA
SVETOJANSKA
TEL 01 628 7372
A great place to stay, just off
the main wine road, offering
ten simple but newly refurbished rooms. The price of
the room includes breakfast.
The restaurant features a good
menu, including wild boar or
duck, grilled trout, and zuc-
chini and mushroom soup,
and of course wine from
the vineyard.
ⓘ 10 🔲 220 🅿 🚭
🔳 No credit cards

🍴 RESTORAN IVANČIĆ
$$
PLEŠIVICA 45, JASTREBARSKO
TEL 01 629 3303
restoran-ivancic.hr
Very popular place, with a
lovely terrace and a menu
that includes venison *paprikaš*,
Zagreb steak, *štrukli*, and a veg-
etarian platter. Wines include
zeleni silvanac (white) and

portugizac (red). Reservations are recommended.

🛏 110 🅿 Ⓢ
🔷 All major cards

KARLOVAC

🏨 **HOTEL KORANA-**
🍴 **SRAKOVCII**
$$$–$$$$$
PERIVOJ JOSIPA VRBANIĆA 8
TEL 047 609 090
hotelkorana.hr
Good four-star hotel right on the banks of the Korana, just a short walk from the town center and surrounded by parkland, with 15 spacious doubles and three suites, and two good restaurants, **Dobra** and **Kupa**. The hotel was origi-nally built in 1906 as a health resort and was completely renovated in 2003.

ⓘ 18 🅿 Ⓢ Ⓢ 🔷 📺
🔷 All major cards

🏨 **HOTEL CARLSTADT**
🍴 **$$**
AMBROZA VRANICZANYEVA 1
TEL 047 611 111
carlstadt.hr
Convenient, central three-star hotel with plain but functional rooms and its own restaurant.

ⓘ 40 🅿 Ⓢ
🔷 All major cards

PREGRADA

🏨 **DVORAC BEŽANEC**
🍴 **$$–$$$**
VALENTINOVO 55
TEL 049 376 800
hotel-dvorac-bezanec.hr
For those who want to stay in one of the castles of northern Croatia, the late 17th-century Bežanec has rooms with antique furniture (and some, apparently, their own ghosts) as well as its own restaurant and wine cellar. Its parkland accommodates bike rental, horseback riding, and archery.

ⓘ 30 Ⓢ 🔷 All major cards

SAMOBOR

🏨 **HOTEL LIVADIĆ**
$$
TRG KRALJA TOMISLAVA 1
TEL 01 336 5850
hotel-livadic.hr
An inviting hotel with attrac-tively furnished rooms with wooden floors, right on the main square. Breakfast is included, and there's a good café in the central courtyard.

ⓘ 12 Ⓢ 🔷 All major cards

🏨 **HOTEL LAVICA**
🍴 **$**
FERDE LIVADIĆA 5
TEL 01 336 8000
lavica-hotel.hr
Very good value, just across the river from the main square, with clean, tidy rooms and a brick-vaulted restaurant.

ⓘ 22 🅿 Ⓢ
🔷 All major cards

🍴 **SAMOBORSKA KLET**
$$
TRG KRAJA TOMISLAVA 7
TEL 01 332 6536
samoborska-klet.hr
Another great place, just off the northern side of the main square and reached by a small alley, serving a good range of traditional fare in a large, rustic interior.

🛏 100 Ⓢ 🔷 All major cards

VARAŽDIN

🏨 **HOTEL ISTRA**
🍴 **$$$**
ULICA IVANA KUKULJEVIĆA 6
TEL 042 659 659
istra-hotel.hr
Recently renovated four-star hotel, originally built in 1911, in the center of town, with smart rooms, its own restaurant, and a casino.

ⓘ 11 🅿 🔷 Ⓢ Ⓢ
🔷 All major cards

🏨 **HOTEL VARAŽDIN**
🍴 **$$**
KOLODVORSKA 19
042 290 720
hotelvarazdin.com
Recently opened three-star hotel near the railway station with fairly spacious, pastel-colored rooms and its own restaurant.

ⓘ 27 🅿 Ⓢ Ⓢ
🔷 All major cards

🏨 **PANSION MALTAR**
$$
PREŠERNOVA 1
TEL 042 311 100
maltar.hr
Friendly, family-run place just south of the town center, near the bus station, with simply furnished rooms. Breakfast is included.

ⓘ 25 🅿 Ⓢ Ⓢ
🔷 All major cards

🍴 **ZLATNE RUKE**
$$$
IVANA KUKULJEVIĆA 13
TEL 042 320 650
zlatneruke.com OR
zlatne-gorice.com
With a cavernous, vaulted stone interior slung with banners, and exposed wood and white cushions, this upscale place specializes in hearty local Zagorje fare. Reservations recommended.

🛏 210 Ⓢ 🔷 All major cards

◼ SLAVONIA

ĐAKOVO

🏨 **HOTEL ĐAKOVO**
🍴 **$$**
NIKOLE TESLE 52
TEL 031 840 570
hotel-djakovo.hr
New three-star hotel on the edge of town, with tidy, heavy-draped rooms and its own restaurant.

ⓘ 25 🅿 Ⓢ 🔷 All major cards

PRICES

HOTELS

The cost of a double room with private bathroom in peak season is given by $ signs.

$$$$$	Over $315
$$$$	$191–$315
$$$	$126–$190
$$	$60–$125
$	Under $60

RESTAURANTS

The average cost of a two-course meal for one person, excluding tip or drinks, is given by $ signs.

$$$$$	Over $40
$$$$	$31–$40
$$$	$21–$30
$$	$10–$20
$	Under $10

🏨 RESTORAN-PANSION
🍽 CROATIA-TURIST
$$

P PRERADOVIĆA 25
TEL 031 813 391
croatiaturist.hr
Attractive place to eat and stay located just south of the city center, with tidy if slightly kitsch rooms. It has its own highly regarded restaurant, where the menu includes grilled meat and fish and vegetarian options, and local specialties including homemade *kulen* and *grah* (bean stew) with homemade sausages.
🛈 8 🅿 🚭 ❄ 🅾 All major cards

ILOK

🏨 HOTEL DUNAV
🍽 $$

J BENEŠIĆA 62
TEL 032 596 500

hoteldunavilok.com
Fine peaceful three-star hotel on the Danube, surrounded by foliage. It has simple rooms with wooden furniture and its own restaurant serving fresh-water fish and other dishes.
🛈 16 🅿 🅾 All major cards

LONJSKO POLJE NATURE PARK

🏨 ETNO SELO STARA
🍽 LONJA
$$–$$$

LONJA 50
TEL 044 710 619
etnoselo-staralonja.com
Home-prepared food, accommodation (three rooms and one apartment), canoe rental, and other recreational facilities.
🛈 4 🅿 🅾 No credit cards

🏨 IŽA NA TREM
🍽 $$

ČIGOČ 57
TEL 044 715 167
iza-na-trem.hr
Cozy little place to stay in Čigoč, close to the information center, with homey wood-beamed rooms in a lovely, old wooden house. The friendly owners offer two apartments and one double room, with self-catering facilities and home-cooked food available.
🛈 3 🅿 🅾 No credit cards

🏨 TRADICIJE ČIGOČ
🍽 $$

ČIGOČ 7A
TEL 044 715 124
tradicije-cigoc.hr
A good place to stay or eat in the village of Čigoč. A traditional wooden house with a restaurant and breakfast included.
🅿 🚭 🅾 No credit cards

MARIJA BISTRICA

SOMETHING SPECIAL

🏨 HOTEL KAJ
🍽 $$$–$$$$

ZAGREBAČKA BB
TEL 049 326 600
hotelkaj.hr
Excellent, upmarket four-star hotel in the center of town. The restaurant is superb, serving exquisitely prepared local specialties, and has some outstanding Croatian wines. Book well ahead if you're planning to visit around August 15 (Assumption Day), when tens of thousands of pilgrims from all over Croatia converge on Marija Bistrica.
🛈 65 🅿 ❄ 🚭 🅾 All major cards

NAŠICE

🏨 HOTEL PARK
$–$$

PEJAČEVIĆEV SQUARE 4
TEL 85 31 613 822
hotel-park.hr
Located on the main street, this hotel provides the basic conveniences. Some of the comfortable rooms overlook the castle. Small, dark lobby but delightful outdoor seating. Breakfast included.
🛈 52 🅾 All major cards

OSIJEK

🏨 OSIJEK
$$$

ŠAMAČKA 4
TEL 031 230 333
hotelosijek.hr
Excellent modern four-star hotel overlooking the Drava, now completely renovated and boasting spacious, stylishly furnished rooms, impeccable service, and a phenomenally good breakfast. Hands down the best place to stay in Osijek.
🛈 147 🅿 ❄ 🚭 🅾 🏋 🅾 All major cards

🚭 Nonsmoking ❄ Air-conditioning 🏊 Indoor Pool 🏊 Outdoor Pool 🏋 Health Club 🅾 Credit Cards

WALDINGER
$$$
ŽUPANIJSKA ULICA 8
TEL 031 250 450
waldinger.hr
Good four-star hotel in an
art nouveau building near
the cathedral, with plush
red-carpeted rooms and
shiny new bathrooms com-
plete with Jacuzzis.

🛏 17 P S S S
S All major cards

CENTRAL
$$
TRG ANTE STARČEVIĆA 6
TEL 031 283 399
hotel-central-os.hr
The oldest hotel in Osijek,
opened in 1889, right on
the main square next to the
cathedral (which, as a down-
side, means you might get
some noise from the cathedral
bells), with nicely refurbished,
spacious rooms. Bike rental.
Guests receive a complimentary theater ticket to the Croatian National Theatre in Osijek.

🛏 32 P S S All major cards

KOD RUŽE
$$–$$$
FRANJO KUHAC 25
TEL 031 206 066
omnia-osijek.hr
Very good restaurant in the
heart of Tvrđa, serving hearty
Slavonian specialties such as
čobanac with game and *perkelt
od soma* (catfish stew) in a folk
art–style setting. Live traditional music.

🪑 120 🕐 Closed D Sun.
S S All major cards

ALAS
$$
REISNEROVA 12
TEL 031 213 032
restoranalasosijek.com
In the south of town near the
railway and bus stations, with
an emphasis on freshwater
fish (the name is local dialect
for fisherman). The house

specialty is a rich and spicy
perkelt od soma (catfish stew).

🪑 54 S S All major cards

SOMETHING SPECIAL

BARANJSKA KUĆA
$$
KOLODVORSKA 99, KARANAC
TEL 031 720 180
baranjska-kuca.com
Superb traditional Slavonian
restaurant about 12 miles
(20 km) north of Osijek, with
long, heavy wooden tables
in an atmospheric brick and
wood-beamed interior, outstanding food, and infectious
live traditional folk music.
The staff are friendly and
welcoming, and there are
plenty of local specialties on
the menu, including *kulen* and
kajmak, grilled carp, and excellent *fiš paprikaš*. Reservations
are recommended.

🪑 120 🕐 Closed Mon. S
S AE, MC, V

SLAVONSKA KUĆA
$$
KAMILA FIRINGER 26
TEL 031 369 955
slavonskakuca.com
Popular and very good value
restaurant in Tvrđa, with
rustic decor and Slavonian
specialties, including *čobanac*
(shepherd's stew), spicy *fiš
paprikaš*, venison stew served
with homemade noodles, fried
catfish, and *sarma* (stuffed
cabbage leaves). Live tradi-
tional music.

🪑 55 S S All major cards

PITOMAČA

ZLATNI KLAS
$$–$$$$
OTROVANEC 228
TEL 033 714 114
zlatni-klas.hr
A countryside restaurant with
class. Start by trying the nettle
dishes—either the bread, the
soup, or both—then move on

to the traditional meat and
fish dishes. Vegetarians should
ask the owner for recommen-
dations; he has been a non-
meat-eater for 25 years. After
eating, explore the property,
see the crafts and animals, and
perhaps spend the night at the
nearby eco-apartment.

🪑 300 S All major cards

SLAVONSKI BROD

CENTRAL
$$
ULICA PETRA KREŠIMIRA IV 45
TEL 035 492 030
hotelcentralsb.hr
A welcoming new family-run
three-star hotel right in the
center of town, with clean
modern rooms (some with
access for disabled). The
restaurant has a decent, well-
priced menu that includes a
number of vegetarian options.

🛏 15 P S S S
S All major cards

VUKOVAR

HOTEL LAV
$$$
J.J. STROSSMAYERA 18
TEL 032 445 100
hotel-lav.hr
Top-notch newly renovated
four-star hotel by the river,
with its own restaurant and
summer terrace and an
impressive wine list.

🛏 42 P S S S
S All major cards

VRŠKE
$$$
PAROBRODSKA 3
TEL 032 441 788
restoran-vrske.hr
Great restaurant in a beautiful
setting with a terrace by the
banks of the Danube River.
The creative menu specializes
in freshwater fish and grilled
meat dishes.

🪑 200 🕐 Closed Dec.–Jan.
S S All major cards

🏨 Hotel 🍽 Restaurant 🛏 No. of Guest Rooms 🪑 No. of Seats P Parking 🕐 Closed 🛗 Elevator

PRICES

HOTELS

The cost of a double room with private bathroom in peak season is given by $ signs.

$$$$$	Over $315
$$$$	$191–$315
$$$	$126–$190
$$	$60–$125
$	Under $60

RESTAURANTS

The average cost of a two-course meal for one person, excluding tip or drinks, is given by $ signs.

$$$$$	Over $40
$$$$	$31–$40
$$$	$21–$30
$$	$10–$20
$	Under $10

■ ISTRIA

BUJE

SOMETHING SPECIAL

🍴 KONOBA NONO

$$$

UMAŠKA 35, PETROVIJA

TEL 052 740 160

konoba-nono.com

Excellent local favorite serving an array of mouthwatering Istrian specialties, in many cases using ingredients from its own farm. On the road between Umag and Buje. Don't miss the delicious signature dessert, *torta nona*. Reservations recommended.

🍽 80 P 🚭
🏦 All major cards

BRTONIGLA

🏨 SAN ROCCO
🍴 $$$$

SREDNJA ULICA 2

TEL 052 725 000

san-rocco.hr/en/hotel

Award-winning boutique hotel with its own spa and top-notch San Rocco Restaurant.

🛏 12 P 🚭 ❄
🏦 All major cards

BUZET

SOMETHING SPECIAL

🏨 HOTEL VELA VRATA
🍴 $$$$

ŠETALIŠTE VLADIMIRA GORTANA 7

TEL 052 494 750

velavrata.net

Excellent new boutique hotel in Buzet's old town, with stylish rooms, great service, and its own outstandingly good restaurant serving exquisitely prepared Istrian dishes.

🛏 18 ❄ 🏦 All major cards

🍴 STARA OŠTARIJA

$$$

PETRA FLEGA 5

TEL 052 694 003

stara-ostarija.com.hr

Very good restaurant with an emphasis—as might be guessed in this part of Istria—on truffles, whether with gnocchi or locally caught trout. Lovely view.

🍽 80 🚭 🏦 All major cards

GROŽNJAN

🏨 PINTUR
🍴 $$

M GORJANA 9

TEL 052 776 397

Small, traditional, and friendly three-star hotel with four rooms and a small restaurant, the latter closed on Mondays. With the exception of private accommodations, this is Grožnjan's only hotel, so reservations need to be booked in advance.

🛏 4 🕐 Closed Jan.–March
🚭 ❄ No credit cards

HUM

🍴 KONOBA HUM

$$–$$$

HUM 2

TEL 052 660 005

hum.hr/humskakonoba

The only restaurant in sleepy Hum is this little *konoba*, with a lovely terrace from which to sit and watch the world go slowly by.

🍽 80 🕐 Closed Mon. 🚭
❄ No credit cards

LIVADE

🍴 ZIGANTE

$$$$$

LEVADE 7

TEL 052 664 302

restaurantzigante.com

Showcase restaurant owned by Giancarlo Zigante, who discovered what was at the time the world's largest white truffle in the woods of Istria in 1999. The menu includes dishes such as fish carpaccio with truffles, octopus with truffles, and sheep's cheese with honey and truffles, though there are some "truffle-free" dishes, too.

🍽 94 🚭 🏦 All major cards

🍴 KONOBA DOLINA

$$–$$$

GRADINJE 59

TEL 052 664 091

konobadolina.hr

Just outside Livade, this superb local favorite excels in freshly cooked Istrian dishes and is well off the tourist trail.

🍽 80 🕐 Closed Tues. 🚭
❄ No credit cards

MOTOVUN

SOMETHING SPECIAL

 KAŠTEL

$$–$$$

TRG ANDREA ANTICO 7

TEL 052 681 607

hotel-kastel-motovun.hr

Good value three-star hotel with simply furnished, comfortable rooms, some with air-conditioning, and two with balconies, set in a 17th-century palace—and, this being a hill town, almost every room has a decent view. It has a very good restaurant, the **Palladio,** serving various Istrian specialties such as *manestra* (a rustic corn soup) and truffle-infused *fuzi* (Istrian pasta) with venison stew, served on a lovely terrace shaded by tall trees. There is also a newly opened spa and wellness center, with large glass windows looking out onto the peaceful gardens, and an art gallery showcasing the work of local artists.

33 P All major cards

POD VOLTUM

$$

ŠETALIŠTA V NAZORA, MOTOVUN

TEL 052 681 923

Good, down-to-earth *konoba* by the old city gate, serving various Istrian dishes, with a blazing fire in winter.

60 Closed Wed. No credit cards

POREČ

RIVIERA HOTEL AND RESIDENCE

$$$$–$$$$$

OBALA MARŠALA TITA 15–18

TEL 052 465 130 OR 052 465 120

valamar.com

Opened in 2010, this luxurious four-star hotel (formerly the Parentino and Neptun hotels) has been completely renovated and occupies a prime waterfront location in the old town. The stylish, bright modern rooms (mostly doubles but there are also some suites) have polished wooden floors. Includes the **Spinnaker Restaurant** with an open-plan kitchen and a terrace.

105 P Closed Nov.–April All major cards

HOTEL JADRAN

$$–$$$

OBALA MARŠALA TITA 24

TEL 052 465 130 OR 052 465 120

valamar.com

Simply furnished rooms right on the waterfront, many of them with sea views. Guests receive complimentary boat trips out to the island of Sv. Nikola.

22 Closed Oct.–April All major cards

GOSTIONICA ISTRA

$$$

BOŽE MILANOVIĆA 30

TEL 052 434 636

This good restaurant near the bus station specializes in seafood and Istrian dishes.

120 Closed Jan.–March All major cards

PETEROKUTNA KULA

$$$

DECUMANUS 1

TEL 052 451 378

kula-porec.com.hr

Atmospheric restaurant in the old town, occupying a 15th-century stone tower and serving various Istrian dishes.

170 All major cards

PULA

HISTRIA

$$$–$$$$

VERUDELA BB

TEL 052 590 000

arenaturist.hr

The best of the large resort-style accommodations out on the Verudela Peninsula is this four-star hotel, a short bus or taxi ride from town, which has stylish and spacious rooms with balconies. There are two restaurants (one serving fine Istrian specialties, the other doing a really good buffet), a large terrace, as well as tennis courts and other facilities. Rates include breakfast, and half board costs only a fraction more.

233 P All major cards

GALIJA

$$$

EPULONOVA 3

TEL 052 383 802

hotelgalija.hr

Small, stylish family-run boutique three-star hotel right in the center of town near the Arch of the Sergii. The individually furnished rooms have eclectic, period-style furniture, some have exposed masonry on the walls, and the hotel has a restaurant with a nautical theme.

20 P All major cards

MILAN

$$$

STOJA 4, STOJA

TEL 052 300 200

milan1967.hr

Clean, spacious, simple three-star rooms out at Stoja, and a long-established and highly rated seafood eatery, **Milan 1967,** where the day's catch is displayed in an enormous iced display case. Crisp white tablecloths inside, wicker chairs on the terrace, and an extensive wine list.

12 120 P All major cards

SCALETTA

$$–$$$

FLAVIJENSKA 26

TEL 052 541 599

hotel-scaletta.com

PRICES

HOTELS

The cost of a double room with private bathroom in peak season is given by $ signs.

$$$$$	Over $315
$$$$	$191–$315
$$$	$126–$190
$$	$60–$125
$	Under $60

RESTAURANTS

The average cost of a two-course meal for one person, excluding tip or drinks, is given by $ signs.

$$$$$	Over $40
$$$$	$31–$40
$$$	$21–$30
$$	$10–$20
$	Under $10

Small, centrally located town house, just past the amphitheater, with clean, simple rooms, a summer terrace, and an award-winning restaurant. Good value, and breakfast is included.

🛏 12 🅿 🚭 🔲
🔲 All major cards

APARTMENTS ARENA PULA
$$
FLAVIJEVSKA 2
TEL 052 506 217
CELL 098 486 109
pula-apartments.com
Four very spacious, well-renovated apartments right next to the Roman amphitheater, sleeping between three and five people. Very good value.

🛏 4 🚭 🔲 No credit cards

SOMETHING SPECIAL

🍴 KONOBA BATELINA
$$$
ČIMULJE 25, BANJOLE
TEL 052 573 767
Wonderful seafood restaurant in the village of Banjole, with superb food and excellent wines served in a lovely, relaxed setting, run by the friendly and welcoming Skoko family. The menu is based on whatever is in that day's catch. Appetizers might include succulent scallops, a light mousse made from conger eel, lightly dressed crabmeat served in its shell, and variations on sardines and anchovies, while for entrées there could be grilled monkfish or sea bass. Delicious homemade desserts and a range of local spirits all add up to make this one of the best meals anywhere in Croatia.

🍴 50 🚭 🔲 All major cards

🍴 JUPITER
$–$$
CASTROPOLA 42
TEL 051 214 333
Good, low-key, friendly restaurant on the road leading up to the fort, serving great pizzas and a good range of other dishes.

🍴 80 🚭 🔲 All major cards

🍴 VINOTEKA HAFNE
$
ISTARSKA 11
TEL 051 214 333
Great little wine bar with something of a bohemian air. It also sells local wines by the bottle, making it a great place to shop for Istrian wine.

🍴 20 🔲 No credit cards

RABAC

🏨 VILLA ANNETTE
🍴 $$$$–$$$$$
RAŠKA 24
TEL 052 884 222

villa-annette.com
Boutique four-star hotel on the slopes overlooking the bay, with panoramic views to match, and clean, stylish suites, all of which have sea views. There's an infinity pool and a good restaurant, which also has gourmet slow-food weekends in the garden. There's a supplement for stays of fewer than three nights.

🛏 12 🅿 🚭 🔲 🔲
🔲 All major cards

🏨 HOTEL AMFORA
$$$
RABAC BB
TEL 052 872 222
hotel-amfora.com
Centrally located right on the waterfront, this modern, newly renovated building has clean, functional rooms, half of them with a sea view and balcony. The price includes half board.

🛏 52 🅿 🚭 🔲 🔲 🏊
🔲 All major cards

ROVINJ

🏨 HOTEL LONE
🍴 $$$$$
LUJE ADAMOVIĆA 31
TEL 052 632 000
lonehotel.com
Fabulously stylish boutique five-star designer hotel, just outside town, with its own spa and restaurant, sea views, and rooms with individual private infinity pools.

🛏 248 🅿 🚭 🔲
🔲 All major cards

🏨 ANGELO D'ORO
🍴 $$$$
V ŠVALBA 38–42
TEL 052 840 502
Restored 17th-century Venetian bishop's palace, right in the old town, with polished wooden floors and plush, antique or period-style furniture. Some of the rooms have sea views, others look over the

old town. The hotel also has an excellent restaurant with a stone-walled interior, a wine cellar where tastings can be arranged, and a lovely garden.

(i) 24 P Ⓢ Ⓢ 🏳
Ⓢ All major cards

🏨 VILLA VALDIBORA
$$$$
S CHIURCIO 8
TEL 052 845 040
valdibora.com
In the heart of the old town, this restored 18th-century town house has tasteful double rooms and studio apartments, with wooden floors and period furniture.

(i) 9 Ⓢ Ⓢ Ⓢ All major cards

🏨 ADRIATIC
$$$
TRG MARŠALA TITA 5
TEL 052 800 250
maistra.hr
Right on the waterfront, Rovinj's oldest hotel has plenty of character, with town-facing and larger (though possibly noisier) sea-view rooms, and a pleasant street-level terrace.

(i) 27 P Ⓢ Ⓢ ⚏
Ⓢ All major cards

🏨 CASA GARZOTTO
$$$
VIA GARZOTTO 8
TEL 052 811 884
casa-garzotto.com
Lovely little boutique hotel, with just four studio apartments, in a beautifully renovated old stone house, located on a narrow, cobbled street in the center of the old town. The individually decorated rooms have wood-beamed ceilings and polished wooden floors, wrought-iron beds, and original period furniture, and there are open fires in two of them. There's an atmospheric stone tavern downstairs, free bike rental,

and breakfast is included in the price.

(i) 4 P Ⓢ Ⓢ
Ⓢ All major cards

🍴 AL GASTALDO
$$$$
IZA KASARNE 14
TEL 052 814 109
Friendly family-run seafood restaurant, serving shellfish and other dishes as well as meat dishes, in a cozy interior filled with antiques and paintings.

⬛ 80 Ⓢ Ⓢ No credit cards

🍴 VELI JOŽE
$$$
SV. KRIŽA 1
TEL 052 816 337
velijoze.net
Good *konoba* near the harbor, with plenty of Istrian specialties such as shellfish lasagna and dishes infused with truffles, served in an antiques-filled interior and on a large terrace outside.

⬛ 100 Ⓢ Ⓢ All major cards

▦ KVARNER GULF & ISLANDS

BAŠKA

🏨 HOTEL ATRIUM
🍴 RESIDENCE
$$$$
EMILA GEISTLICHA 39
TEL 051 656 111
hotelibaska.hr
Luxurious new four- to five-star hotel in Baška, right on the beach, with elegant, spacious rooms and suites and balconies overlooking the water. There's a restaurant and free use of indoor and outdoor pools at the nearby Hotel Corinthia. Breakfast is included in the room price.

(i) 64 🕐 Closed Nov.–March
⬌ Ⓢ Ⓢ 🏳 ⚏ ⚏
Ⓢ All major cards

🍴 BISTRO FRANICA
$$$
RIBARSKA 39
TEL 051 860 023
franica.hr
An inviting, shaded restaurant with a fine terrace by the harbor, serving local specialties as well as seafood and Italian fare.

⬛ 75 🕐 Closed Nov.–March
Ⓢ No credit cards

CRES

🏨 HOTEL ZLATNI LAV
🍴 $$–$$$
MARTINŠĆICA 18, MARTINŠĆICA
TEL 051 574 020
hotel-zlatni-lav.com
A welcoming hotel in this seaside village south of Cres, with sea views and balconies for some of the rooms. Expect a 20 percent surcharge for stays of fewer than three nights (five nights in July and Aug.). There's a restaurant, and an infrequent local bus service runs between Martinšćica and Cres.

(i) 29 P Ⓢ Ⓢ Ⓢ
Ⓢ AE, MC, V

🏨 HOTEL KIMEN
$$
MELIN I/16
TEL 051 573 305
hotel-kimen.com
Large resort-style complex a little over half a mile (0.8 km) west of Cres, close to the beach and consisting of the main building (three-star) as well as the smaller and slightly cheaper **Hotel Dependence** (two-star) and **Villa Kimen** (three-star).

(i) 223 P Ⓢ Ⓢ
Ⓢ AE, MC, V

🍴 KONOBA BONACA
$$–$$$
ULICA CRESKOG
STATUCA 13
TEL 051 572 215

🏨 Hotel   🍴 Restaurant   (i) No. of Guest Rooms   ⬛ No. of Seats   P Parking   🕐 Closed   ⬌ Elevator

PRICES

HOTELS

The cost of a double room with private bathroom in peak season is given by $ signs.

$$$$$	Over $315
$$$$	$191–$315
$$$	$126–$190
$$	$60–$125
$	Under $60

RESTAURANTS

The average cost of a two-course meal for one person, excluding tip or drinks, is given by $ signs.

$$$$$	Over $40
$$$$	$31–$40
$$$	$21–$30
$$	$10–$20
$	Under $10

Fine low-key eatery next to the fish market, with stone walls, wood-beamed ceiling, and simple wooden tables and chairs. Seafood, fresh from the market, features prominently on the menu, along with other local dishes such as Cres lamb with roast potatoes.

🛏 70 🚭 🆑 No credit cards

🍴 AL BUON GUSTO
$$

SV SIDAR 14
TEL 051 571 878

An alluring little spaghetteria hidden away in the narrow streets of the old town; friendly and much better value than many of the places on the waterfront.

🛏 20 🚭 🆑 All major cards

GORSKI KOTAR

🏨 HOTEL FRANKOPAN
🍴 $$$–$$$$

IVANA GORANA KOVAČIĆA 1, OGULIN
TEL 047 525 509
hotel-frankopan.hr

Excellent, recently renovated four-star hotel, in an 18th-century building converted in the late 19th century, right next to Ogulin's 16th-century castle. The rooms (including four suites) are tastefully furnished and named after characters from the works of Ivana Brlić-Mažuranić, Croatia's most famous writer of fairy tales, who was from Ogulin. The restaurant serves game and other local specialties, and an atmospheric, brick-vaulted wine cellar features wine tastings.

🛏 21 Ⓟ 🚭 🆑 🍷 🆑 All major cards

🏨 HOTEL BITORAJ
🍴 $$–$$$

SVETI KRIŽ 1, FUŽINE
TEL 051 830 005
bitoraj.hr

Lovely boutique four-star hotel in the center of Fužine, recently renovated, with comfortable, stylish rooms and friendly service. There's a good restaurant with plenty of game and other hearty local specialties on the menu, including goulash, wild boar steak, grilled trout, and home-made sausages and black pudding with pickled cabbage, as well as a decent selection of vegetarian options.

🛈 20 🛏 105 Ⓟ 🚭 🆑 🆑 All major cards

KRK

🏨 HOTEL MARINA
🍴 $$$–$$$$

OBALA HRVATSKE MORNARICE BB
TEL 051 221 128 OR 051 655 755

hotelikrk.hr

Newly renovated boutique four-star hotel, right in the center of Krk, with stylish, luxurious rooms and suites and a restaurant with an outside terrace for summer dining.

🛈 10 🚭 🆑 🆑 All major cards

LOŠINJ

SOMETHING SPECIAL

🏨 WELLNESS HOTEL
🍴 AURORA
$$$–$$$$

SUNČANA UVALA BB, MALI LOŠINJ
TEL 051 667 200 OR 051 661 111
losinj-hotels.com

Perfect hotel, great location out by the beach at Sunčana Uvala, perfect for families, with a super pool, stylish rooms, and probably the best buffet breakfast of any hotel in Croatia. The meals are excellent, so the half board is definitely worth going for. There's a shuttle bus running into town (it's cheaper to buy all day tickets at the hotel reception, otherwise buy individual tickets on the bus). Highly recommended.

🛏 393 Ⓟ 🚭 🏊 🆑 All major cards

🏨 FAMILY HOTEL
🍴 VESPERA
$$$$

SUNČANA UVALA BB, MALI LOŠINJ
TEL 051 661 111
kinderhotel-vespera.com

Part of the Kinderhotels portfolio, this excellent family hotel is located next to the Aurora (see above), just 55 yards (50 m) from the sea and surrounded by lush pine forest. Smart rooms with balconies, swimming pools, outstanding breakfasts and half-board buffet dinner, kids activities and entertainment, and some

🚭 Nonsmoking ❄ Air-conditioning 🏊 Indoor Pool 🏊 Outdoor Pool 🍷 Health Club 🆑 Credit Cards

lovely swimming beaches, either the pebbly Sunčana Uvala or (better) the level rock terraces just below the hotel itself, complete with steps into the clear, clean water. Only a 1.2-mile (2 km) walk from Mali Lošinj, and there's a regular shuttle bus.

🛈 404 🅿 🚻 ⛵
💳 All major cards

🏨 HOTEL APOKSIOMEN
🍴 $$$

RIVA LOŠINJSKIH KAPETANA 1, MALI LOŠINJ
TEL 051 520 820
vi-hotels.com
Small, recently renovated boutique four-star hotel, right on the Riva, with attractive, spacious rooms, most of them with sea views. The hotel has its own restaurant and a fine terrace out on the waterfront where you can greet the day over breakfast (included).

🛈 25 🅿 🕐 Closed Nov.–Feb.
🛗 🚻 🛗 💳 All major cards

🏨 MARE MARE SUITES
$$$

RIVA LOŠINJSKIH KAPETANA 36, MALI LOŠINJ
TEL 051 232 010
mare-mare.com
Small four-star boutique hotel on the waterfront, with brightly painted rooms and suites, all of them sea-facing, and a lovely rooftop terrace with great views. Breakfast is included.

🛈 16 🅿 🚻 🛗
💳 All major cards

LOVRAN

🏨 LOVRAN
🍴 $$$

ŠETALIŠTE MARŠALA TITA 19/2
TEL 051 291 222
hotel-lovran.hr
The three-star Lovran has clean, pleasant rooms in two renovated old villas, as well as

a small (concrete) beach and its own restaurant. Sea-view rooms cost slightly more.

🛈 56 🅿 🛗
💳 All major cards

OPATIJA

🏨 HOTEL KVARNER
$$$$

PAVA TOMAŠIĆA 2
TEL 051 710 444
remisens.com/en /hotel-kvarner
The oldest hotel in Opatija, the four-star Hotel Kvarner maintains its late 19th-century grandeur, with sea-view balconies in some rooms, a newly restored terrace, and a huge crystal ballroom.

🛈 58 🛗 🚻 🛗 ⛵
💳 All major cards

🏨 HOTEL MOZART
$$$–$$$$

OBALA MARŠALA TITA 138
TEL 051 718 260
hotel-mozart.hr
Plush five-star hotel located in a beautiful art nouveau building built in 1894. Rooms have polished wooden floors and heavy drapes and period-style or antique furniture. Standard rooms come with views over the gardens and inland; deluxe rooms have balconies overlooking the sea.

🛈 26 🅿 🚻 🛗 🛗
💳 All major cards

SOMETHING SPECIAL

🏨 VILLA KAPETANOVIĆ
🍴 $$$–$$$$

NOVA CESTA 12A
TEL 051 741 355
villa-kapetanovic.hr
Lovely family-run four-star boutique hotel on the hillside above the gourmet enclave of Volosko, with panoramic views out over the Kvarner Gulf and islands. Spacious, stylish rooms with balconies. Spa, pool, delicious breakfast, and free

shuttle service to the town (and in summer, to the beach). The highly rated restaurant, **Laurus,** uses fresh, locally sourced ingredients. Go for the excellent Tasting Menu, with several courses each paired with an apt wine, and dine on such exquisite dishes as tuna carpaccio, sea bass fillet filled with cream cheese, and ravioli with prawns and truffles. The owners plan to open a new property on the waterfront in Volosko in 2015.

🛈 27 🛗 14 🅿 🚻 🛗 🛗 ⛵
💳 All major cards

🏨 DESIGN HOTEL
🍴 ASTORIA
$$$

OBALA MARŠALA TITA 174
TEL 051 706 350
vi-hotels.com/en/astoria
Slick, recently renovated four-star hotel offering stylish rooms with modern conveniences within an early 20th-century exterior. It has its own restaurant and terrace, and guests get use of the nearby gym.

🛈 50 🅿 🚻 🛗 🛗
💳 All major cards

RAB

🏨 ARBIANA
$$$–$$$$

OBALA KRALJA KREŠIMIRA IV
TEL 051 725 563
arbianahotel.com
Beautifully renovated old villa in the heart of the old town, with spacious four-star rooms, tastefully decorated with antique-style furniture and with views of the sea or the town's Romanesque bell towers.

🛈 28 🅿 🚻 🛗 💳 AE, MC, V

🏨 HOTEL INTERNATIONAL
🍴 $$$

OBALA P KREŠIMIROVA 4
TEL 051 602 000

🏨 Hotel 🍴 Restaurant 🛈 No. of Guest Rooms 🛗 No. of Seats 🅿 Parking 🕐 Closed 🛗 Elevator

PRICES

HOTELS
The cost of a double room
with private bathroom in
peak season is given by
$ signs.

$$$$$	Over $315
$$$$	$191–$315
$$$	$126–$190
$$	$60–$125
$	Under $60

RESTAURANTS
The average cost of a two-
course meal for one person,
excluding tip or drinks, is
given by $ signs.

$$$$$	Over $40
$$$$	$31–$40
$$$	$21–$30
$$	$10–$20
$	Under $10

hotelrab.com
Formerly the Ros Maris, the
International was recently
downgraded from four to
three stars, with reduced prices
but no loss in quality. Spacious
rooms, all recently renovated,
right in the old town, with a
terrace, restaurant, and spa
center. Breakfast is included.
 140 ⬆ Ⓢ Ⓢ ⬛ 🐾 🏆
🁢 All major cards

🍴 **ASTORIA**
🏨 **$$$**
DINKA DOKULE 2
TEL 051 774 844
astoria-rab.com
Right in the center of town is
this excellent restaurant set in
a Venetian palace with a great
terrace overlooking the main
square and attached to a small
hotel with five apartments.
ⓘ 5 60 🕒 Closed Dec.–
April Ⓢ 🁢 AE, V

🍴 **GOSTIONICA LABIRINT**
$$$
SREDNJA ULICA
TEL 051 771 145
An attractive eatery in the old
town, serving local island specialties such as Rab fish soup
with potatoes and rice, with a
pleasant roof terrace.
⯐ 60 Ⓢ 🁢 No credit cards

RIJEKA

🏨 **GRAND HOTEL**
🍴 **BONAVIA**
$$$–$$$$$
DOLAC 4
TEL 051 357 100
bonavia.hr
Plush four-star hotel in a cen-
tral location just off the Korzo,
with stylish rooms (including
half a dozen suites), two highly
rated restaurants and a roof
terrace, and a new spa and
wellness center. The Bonavia
is Rijeka's oldest hotel, having
opened its doors in 1876, and
was completely renovated
in 2000.
ⓘ 121 Ⓟ ⬆ Ⓢ Ⓢ 🏆
🁢 All major cards

🏨 **CONTINENTAL**
🍴 **$$–$$$**
ŠETALIŠTE ANDRIJE
KAČIĆA-MIOŠIĆA 1
TEL 051 372 008
jadran-hoteli.hr
Renovated in 2008 and
upgraded to three stars, the
Continental (built in the late
19th century) now has taste-
fully furnished rooms, many
of them with views across
the Rječina River to the old
town, as well as four spacious
suites. There's also an inviting
terrace restaurant.
ⓘ 69 Ⓟ Ⓢ Ⓢ
🁢 All major cards

🍴 **ZLATNA ŠKOLJKA**
$$$–$$$$
KRUČINA 12A
TEL 051 213 782

zlatna-skoljka.hr
Popular cellar restaurant just
off the Korzo with good sea-
food as well as generous salads
and friendly service.
⯐ 90 Ⓢ 🁢 All major cards

🍴 **KONOBA FERAL**
$$–$$$
MATIJE GUPCA 5B
TEL 051 212 274
konoba-feral.com
Excellent traditional seafood
restaurant. A local favorite
with friendly service and very
reasonable prices.
⯐ 60 Ⓢ 🁢 All major cards

VOLOSKO

🏨 **VILLA ARISTON**
🍴 **$$$–$$$$$**
OBALA MARŠALA TITA 179
TEL 051 271 379
villa-ariston.hr
Lovely three-star hotel in a
restored late 19th-century
mansion a short walk along
the Lungomare, right by the
water and surrounded by
trees and peaceful gardens.
The immaculate rooms have
polished wooden floors and
balconies, and there's a huge
presidential suite. There's also
the fine **Restaurant Villa
Ariston** with terrace and
garden tables.
ⓘ 10 Ⓟ Ⓢ Ⓢ
🁢 All major cards

🍴 **LE MANDRAĆ**
$$$$–$$$$$
FRANA SUPILA 10
TEL 051 701 357
lemandrac.com
Top-notch gourmet establishment in Volosko, where the
freshest seafood and other
locally sourced ingredients are
prepared with an inventive
modern twist, in a glass-
fronted modern building
overlooking the water.
Reservations recommended.
⯐ 80 Ⓢ 🁢 All major cards

Ⓢ Nonsmoking Ⓢ Air-conditioning ⬛ Indoor Pool 🌊 Outdoor Pool 🏆 Health Club 🁢 Credit Cards

SOMETHING SPECIAL

🍴 PLAVI PODRUM
$$$$–$$$$$
FRANA SUPILA 4
TEL 051 701 223
plavipodrum.com
Impeccable traditional seafood restaurant that has been around for about a century, where the menu includes a five-course degustation and (perhaps not surprisingly since the owner, Daniela Kramari, is an award-winning sommelier) a fantastic wine cellar. Rated as one of the finest tables in Croatia. Reservations recommended.
🔳 140 🚫 💳 All major cards

■ NORTHERN DALMATIA

DUGI OTOK

🏨 HOTEL SALI
🍴 $$
SALI
TEL 023 377 049
hotel-sali.hr
Three-star hotel set in pine-woods near the beach, with simple, comfortable rooms, a restaurant, and its own scuba diving center.
ⓘ 52 🅿 🚫 💳
💳 All major cards

KRKA NATIONAL PARK

🏨 HOTEL SKRADINSKI
🍴 BUK
$$
BURINOVAC BB, SKRADIN
TEL 022 771 771
skradinskibuk.hr
Conveniently located three-star hotel in the small town of Skradin, where the boats leave for Krka National Park, with simply furnished rooms, a garden, and its own restaurant with pleasant covered

terrace. Breakfast is included in the price.
ⓘ 29 🅿 🚫 💳 All major cards

PAG

🏨 LUNA ISLAND HOTEL
🍴 $$$$–$$$$$
JAKŠNICA BB, LUN
TEL 053 654 700
lunaislandhotel.com
Brand-new four-star hotel a short drive from Novalja, near the ferry port of Žigljen and right on the beach, part of the Valamar chain, with bright, spacious rooms, many with sea views, and some with balconies. The hotel has its own restaurant, the **Oleaster.**
ⓘ 93 🅿 🕐 Closed Nov.–March 💳 🚫 💳 🏊 🎾
💳 All major cards

🏨 BOŠKINAC
🍴 $$$$
NOVALJA POLJE, NOVALJA
TEL 053 663 500
boskinac.com
Lovely four-star hotel in peaceful surroundings in the countryside beyond Novalja, with its own vineyard, spacious, tastefully furnished rooms, a tavern in the wine cellar, and an excellent restaurant.
ⓘ 11 🅿 🚫 💳
💳 All major cards

🏨 PLAŽA
$$$
MARKA MARULIĆA 14, PAG TOWN
TEL 023 600 855
plaza-croatia.com
Modern four-star hotel on the beach, with simple but comfortable rooms and views across the bay to the old town. Expect to pay a supplement of 30 percent for stays of fewer than three nights.
ⓘ 29 🅿 🕐 Closed Oct.–May 🚫 💳 🏊 🎾 💳 All major cards

🏨 HOTEL TONY
🍴 $$
DUBROVAČKA 39, PAG TOWN
TEL 023 611 370
hotel-tony.com
Small family-run place out around the northern side of the bay, with clean, comfortable rooms, a garden, and a traditional Dalmatian seafood restaurant.
ⓘ 20 🅿 🚫 💳
💳 All major cards

🏨 PANSION TAMARIS
🍴 $$
KRIŽEVAČKA, PAG TOWN
TEL 023 611 277
tamaris-pag.com.hr
Small family-run three-star establishment with clean, simply furnished rooms, a great location on the northern edge of the old town, and its own restaurant.
ⓘ 14 🅿 🚫
💳 No credit cards

🍴 KONOBA BILE
$$$
JURJA DALMATINCA 35, PAG TOWN
TEL 023 611 127
Small, low-key place serving light meals, hams, and cheeses in a stone cellar.
🔳 40 🚫 💳 No credit cards

ŠIBENIK

🏨 JADRAN
🍴 $$$
OBALA DR FRANJE TUĐMANA 52
TEL 022 242 2000
rivijera.hr
Centrally located three-star hotel, in a modern concrete block in need of a face-lift, with small, functional rooms (ask for one with a sea view—same price) and a fish restaurant.
ⓘ 57 🅿 💳 🚫
💳 All major cards

🏨 Hotel 🍴 Restaurant ⓘ No. of Guest Rooms 🔳 No. of Seats 🅿 Parking 🕐 Closed 💳 Elevator

PRICES

HOTELS

The cost of a double room with private bathroom in peak season is given by $ signs.

$$$$$	Over $315
$$$$	$191–$315
$$$	$126–$190
$$	$60–$125
$	Under $60

RESTAURANTS

The average cost of a two-course meal for one person, excluding tip or drinks, is given by $ signs.

$$$$$	Over $40
$$$$	$31–$40
$$$	$21–$30
$$	$10–$20
$	Under $10

🏨 HOTEL PANORAMA
🍴 $$–$$$

ŠIBENSKI MOST 1
TEL 022 213 398
hotel-panorama.hr

As an alternative to the rather drab Jadran or private rooms in Šibenik itself, this modern three-star hotel out at Šibenski Most (the bridge over the Krka) has fantastic views over the Krka gorge. The simply furnished rooms have air-conditioning and balconies. There is a restaurant-pizzeria with a large terrace, as well as (if you really fancy it) bungee jumping from the nearby bridge.

🛈 20 🅿 🚭 🅢 🅢
🅢 All major cards

🍴 GRADSKA VIJEĆ NICA
$$$

TRG REPUBLIKE HRVATSKE 3
TEL 022 213 605

Good food in Šibenik's old 16th-century Venetian town hall, with a great terrace and right on the main square.

🍴 120 🕐 Closed 2nd half Jun. 🅢 All major cards

SOMETHING SPECIAL

🍴 KONOBA-VINOTEKA PELEGRINI
$$$

JURJA DALMATINCA 1
TEL 022 213 701
pelegrini.hr

Lovely stone-walled restaurant with a great terrace on the roof, in a renovated medieval palace opposite the cathedral, with an interesting menu, including ravioli stuffed with prawns, fish with truffles and pine nuts, as well as homemade bread, and a decent wine list.

🍴 105 🕐 Closed Mon. 🅢
🅢 All major cards

STARIGRAD-PAKLENICA

🏨 HOTEL ALAN
🍴 $$$$–$$$$$

DR. FRANJE TUĐMANA 14
TEL 023 209 050
hotel-alan.hr

Late 1960s resort-style three-star hotel, recently modernized and renovated, right on the beach, and close to the entrance to Paklenica National Park. All rooms have balconies, and there are several suites.

🛈 162 🅿 🚭 🅢 🅢 🏊 🛡
🅢 AE, MC, V

ZADAR

🏨 FALKENSTEINER CLUB
🍴 FUNIMATION BORIK
$$$$

MAJSTORA RADOVANA 7, BORIK
TEL 023 555 600
falkensteiner.com

Large, resort-style hotel at Borik, a short distance from central Zadar (bus number 5 or 8). Great for families—pools galore, an enormous water slide, own beach, plenty of kids' entertainment, and child care available. Spa, restaurant, bar. Rates in high season are all inclusive, covering full board.

🛈 258 🅿 🚭 🅢 🏊
🅢 All major cards

SOMETHING SPECIAL

🏨 HOTEL BASTION
🍴 $$$$

BEDEMI ZADARSKIH POBUNA 13
TEL 023 494 950
hotel-bastion.hr

Stylish new four-star boutique hotel near Three Wells Square in the old town, with spacious rooms, exposed stone walls, polished wooden floors, and efficient service. There's a terrace, and the hotel has its own spa center and restaurant, **Kaštel**, with fine fish and homemade pasta dishes.

🛈 28 🅢 🅢 🛡
🅢 All major cards

🏨 ART HOTEL
🍴 KALELARGA
$$$

MAJKE MARGARITE 3
TEL 023 233 000
arthotel-kalelarga.com

This stylish new four-star boutique hotel is located right in the center of the old town, just off Kalelarga (Široka Ulica), and has its own upmarket restaurant, **Gourmet Kalelarga.**

🛈 10 🅢 🅢 All major cards

🏨 BOUTIQUE HOSTEL FORUM
$$$

KALELARGA
TEL 023 250 705
en.hostelforumzadar.com

Falling somewhere between boutique hostel and boutique hotel, this supremely stylish little place has the best location (and views) of any accommodation in Zadar's old town. Double rooms overlook the Roman

🅢 Nonsmoking 🅢 Air-conditioning 🅢 Indoor Pool 🏊 Outdoor Pool 🛡 Health Club 🅢 Credit Cards

forum, Sv. Donat, and the
cathedral bell tower. Friendly
service, and good breakfast.

🛈 26 🔲 🔷 All major cards

🏨 NIKO
🍴 $$$
OBALA KNEZA DOMOGOJA 9,
BORIK
TEL 023 337 880 (HOTEL)
TEL 023 337 888 (RESTAURANT)
hotel-niko.hr
Local favorite near Borik, with
an austere exterior disguising a
hotel upstairs offering several
spacious, attractive rooms. The
Nico Restaurant, with fresh
seafood, a good wine list, and
a terrace overlooking the water,
is superb.

🛈 11 🍴 120 🅿 🔲
🔷 All major cards

🏨 ZADAR APARTMENTS
$$
UL. IVANA ZAJCA
TEL 091 535 4557
apartmentszadar.eu
Beautiful, and very stylishly
furnished, apartments in
several locations across central
Zadar. Spotlessly clean, effi-
ciently managed. A very welcome addition to the range of
accommodation choices in this
city. Highly recommended.

🛈 9 🔄 🔲 🔷 AE, MC, V

🍴 DVA RIBARA
$$$
BLAŽA JURJEVA 1
TEL 023 213 445
Elegant dining in the heart of
the old town, and not all seafood—various other dishes, and
they also do pizzas.

🍴 44 🔲 🔷 All major cards

🍴 KORNAT
$$$
LIBURNSKA OBALA
TEL 023 254 501
restaurant-kornat.com
One of the best restaurants in
Zadar, near the ferry terminal,
with a covered terrace looking
out across Luka Jazine (the

marina). Top-notch seafood
and other more unexpected
dishes, including steak with
truffles, and an extensive wine
list. Friendly staff.

🍴 90 🔲 🔷 All major cards

🍴 THE GARDEN
$$
LIBURNSKA 6
TEL 023 364 320
thegardenzadar.com
Very hip lounge bar on the
waterfront, owned by Jimmy
Brown (drummer of the British band UB40), perfect for
sipping coffee or cocktails.

🔲 🏖 🔷 No credit cards

🍴 PIZZERIA TRI BUNARA
$$
TRG TRI BUNARA
Great little pizzeria, hidden
away off the main thorough-
fares on this square behind
Hotel Bastion (see p. 295).
Unpretentious, friendly service
(in stark contrast to the popular Nico in Borik), good value,
and the best pizzas in Zadar.

🍴 10 🔲 🔷 All major cards

ZATON

🏨 ZATON HOLIDAY
🍴 RESORT
$$$–$$$$
DRAŽNIKOVA 76T
TEL 023 205 588
zaton.hr
Zadar region's most luxurious
resort and its most desirable
beach, a lovely mile-long
stretch of sand and pebbles,
backed by 247 acres (100 ha)
of pine forest. Accommodation
comes in the form of beautiful,
spacious, and stylish apartments, all with balconies, and
each equipped with a small
kitchen. Go for the four-star
ones with air-conditioning.
Pools, restaurants, and bars,
activities including horseback
riding, diving, and tennis. Great
for families, with entertainment aimed at youngsters and

teens, and a good playground.

🛈 600 🅿 🔲 🏖
🔷 All major cards

■ CENTRAL DALMATIA

BOL

🏨 HOTEL KAŠTIL
🍴 $$$
FRANE RADIĆA
TEL 021 635 995
kastil.hr
Newly renovated stone building down near the waterfront,
many of the rooms with sea
views. Has its own restaurant,
the Topolino Restaurant, and
pizzeria, Terrace Pizzeria.

🛈 32 🕐 Closed Nov.–March
🔲 🔷 🔷 All major cards

🏨 KONOBA TOMIĆ
🍴 $$
GORNJI HUMAC
TEL 021 647 228 OR 091 225 1199
konobatomic.com
Located in the center of
Brač island, in a rustic setting
around 7.5 miles (12 km) from
Bol, is this excellent konoba.
The delicious food is prepared
using fresh ingredients from
their own farm, and wines
and spirits are from their own
vineyard. There are nine simple, reasonably priced rooms,
two with balconies.

🅿 🕐 Closed Nov.–April 🔲
🔷 No credit cards

HVAR

🏨 AMFORA GRAND
🍴 BEACH RESORT
$$$$$
UL. BISKUPA JURJA
DUBOKOVICA 5
MAJEROVICA BB
TEL 021 750 300
suncanihvar.com
A ten-minute walk from Hvar's
old town, the newly renovated
Amfora has an exclusive beach
club, a cascading pool, three

restaurants, and a beach bar. Most of the stylish rooms have balconies and views of the Pakleni Islands, and some have access for the disabled.

[i] 324 🛇 🄴 🄴 🏊 🖤
🄴 All major cards

HOTEL PARK
$$$$$
BANKETE
TEL 021 718 337
hotelparkhvar.com
Boutique four-star hotel in the center of town, stylishly decorated, with sea views.
[i] 15 🛇 🄴 🄴 MC, V

PALACE
$$$$
TRG SV. STJEPANA BB
TEL 021 741 966
suncanihvar.com
Newly renovated in 2008, Hvar's oldest hotel (the Palace was opened in 1903) incorporates a Venetian loggia, and its rooms have views over the Pakleni Islands. Centrally located, just across from the famous Arsenal, with a restaurant and good terrace.
[i] 73 🕐 Closed Nov.–March
🄴 🛇 🄴 🏊 🖤
🄴 All major cards

LUNA
$$$
PETRA HEKTOROVIĆA
TEL 021 741 400
Good seafood restaurant serving wonderful dishes, with an open-roof terrace.
🍴 84 🕐 Closed Oct.–April
🛇 🄴 AE, DC, V

ZLATNA ŠKOLJKA
$$$
PETRA HEKTOROVIĆA 8
TEL 098 168 8797
zlatna.skoljka.com
Set in a 13th-century house with a fine terrace, the excellent Zlatna Školjka (Golden Shell) has typical seafood dishes alongside more

inventive fare, some tasty gnocchi entrées, and opulent lamb and rabbit dishes, all prepared with an emphasis on "slow food." There are also four- and six-course "challenge" menus. Reservations recommended.
🍴 25 🕐 Closed Nov.–April
🛇 🄴 No credit cards

KOMIŽA

HOTEL BIŠEVO
$$
RIBARSKA 72
TEL 021 713 279
hotel-bisevo.com.hr
Modern, somewhat blocky resort-style hotel, but with sea-facing balconies and close to center of town. Not all the rooms have air-conditioning (ask for a suite to ensure AC).
[i] 131 🄿 🄴 🄴 🖤
🄴 AE, DC, V

KONOBA BAKO
$$$
GUNDULIĆEVA 1
TEL 021 713 742
konobabako.hr
Excellent seafood restaurant right on the waterfront, surrounded by amphorae and other archaeological finds plucked from the seabed, with a good wine list. Some local dishes, such as yellowtail cooked with capers, bay leaves, and rosemary, as well as plenty of grilled meats.
🍴 60 🕐 Closed until 5 p.m.
🄴 All major cards

MAKARSKA

HOTEL PORIN
$$–$$$
MARINETA 2
TEL 021 613 744
hotel-porin.hr
Once the town library, this renovated 19th-century palace has a central location and its own restaurant, and it is right on the waterfront. Expect

some noise from the nearby bars during peak season.
[i] 8 🛇 🄴 🄴 All major cards

OMIŠ

HOTEL VILLA DVOR
$$$
MOSORSKA CESTA 13
TEL 021 863 444
hotel-villadvor.hr
New boutique three-star hotel with large, modern rooms (four with balcony) and views of the Cetina Gorge or of the sea. There's a terrace with a Jacuzzi offering panoramic views, and Restaurant Knez. Access from the town is by a long flight of stone steps.
[i] 23 🄿 🄴 🄴 🄴
🄴 AE, MC, V

SPLIT

HOTEL VESTIBUL
PALACE
$$$$$
IZA VESTIBULA 4
TEL 021 329 329
vestibulpalace.com
Sleek, stylish rooms nestle into the ancient walls of Diocletian's Palace, incorporating Roman, Gothic, and Renaissance details into the hotel's streamlined design. Be sure to ask for the main building and not the annex. Diocles restaurant serves Mediterranean dishes with strong Dalmatian flair.
[i] 7 🄿 🄴 🄴 All major cards

LE MERIDIEN LAV
$$$$–$$$$$
GRLJEVAČKA 2A, PODSTRANA
TEL 021 500 500
lemeridien.com/split
Split's premier hotel, this luxurious five-star establishment with a pleasantly relaxed atmosphere is located right on the waterfront, 5 miles (8 km) outside the town center at Podstrana. You'll find everything here from a

---

marina and beach to an infinity pool, a great restaurant, a casino, conference facilities, and a spa and beauty center, not to mention a great old-style *pivnica* (beer hall) and a sparkling champagne bar.

🛏 380 🛌 420 🅿 🔄 📶 ♿
🍽 🏊 📺 ♿ All major cards

🏨 HOTEL PRESIDENT
🍽 $$$$

STARČEVIĆA 1
TEL 021 305 222
hotelpresident.hr
Four-star establishment in central location, a short walk north from the palace near the National Theatre, with plush, period-style furnishings. The hotel also has ten suites. The hotel restaurant offers classic-style dining in a stylish atmosphere, as well as live entertainment and dancing in the evening.

🛏 63 🅿 🔄 📶 ♿
♿ AE, MC, V

🏨 MARMONT HOTEL
$$$$

ZADARSKA 13
TEL 021 308 060
marmonthotel.com
Very smart new four-star hotel, centrally located within the palace walls, with light rooms and wooden floors, exposed stone in the dining room and lounge bar, and a good terrace.

🛏 21 📶 ♿
♿ All major cards

🏨 HOTEL ADRIANA
$$$–$$$$

OBALA HRVATSKOG NAROD-
NOG PREPORODA 8 (RIVA)
TEL 021 340 000
hotel-adriana.com
Recently opened three-star hotel with central location, above restaurant on the Riva, with carpeted rooms and modern bathrooms. Some rooms are smaller than others.

🛏 14 📶 ♿ ♿ All major cards

🏨 HOTEL B&B VILLA KAŠTEL
$$

MIHOVILOVA ŠIRINA 5
TEL 021 343 912
kastelsplit.com
Best-value place in the palace, with lovely three-star rooms and one four-star suite, exposed stone walls, and polished wooden floors.

🛏 20 📶 ♿ ♿ All major cards

🏨 APARTMENTS SIMONI
$

ZLODRINA POLJANA BB
TEL 021 488 780
sobesimoni.com
apartments-simoni.com
An excellent budget choice, with clean, simple three-star rooms in a modern building and efficient, welcoming service. Conveniently located on a quiet backstreet just behind the railway station. The owner can meet you at or drive you to the airport for slightly less than a taxi. The best bargain accommodations in Split.

🛏 7 🅿 📶 ♿
♿ All major cards

🍽 NOŠTROMO
$$$$$

KRAJ SV. MARIJE 10
restoran-nostromo.hr
Excellent seafood restaurant right next to the fish market, serving top-notch fresh, grilled fish as well as less common dishes such as fish kebabs and traditional pan-fried sea anemones. The interior is hung with paintings by various Croatian artists. Reservations advised.

🛌 40 📶 ♿ No credit cards

🍽 KONOBA HVARANIN
$$$

BAN MLADENOVA 9
TEL 091 767 5891
Small, busy family-run place with good traditional homemade fare.

🛌 30 📶 ♿ No credit cards

🍽 KONOBA KOD JOŽE
$$$

SREDMANUŠKA 4
TEL 021 347 397
Good-value *konoba*, across the park behind the palace, with great food and a fine terrace.

🛌 100 📶 ♿ MC, V

🍽 MAKROVEGA
$$

LEŠTINA 2
TEL 021 394 440
makrovega.hr
Vegetarian, vegan, and macrobiotic restaurant off Bana Jelačića, with good-value daily combination menus and a modern interior. The place to go for vegetarians in Split.

📶 ♿ No credit cards

🍽 PIZZERIA GRGUR
$$

KOD ZLATNIH VRATA 1
TEL 021 348 799
Hidden away down an alley near the Golden Gate, Grgur has good, well-priced pizzas, pasta, and Dalmatian dishes, and a decent terrace. A favorite pizzeria in Split for several years.

🛌 32 🕐 Closed Nov.–March
📶 ♿ AE, DC, V

STARI GRAD

🏨 LAVANDA
$$$

NASELJE HELIOS 6
TEL 021 306 330
heliosfaros.eu
Formerly the Adriatic, this resort-style three-star hotel on one side of the bay has balconies and sea views.

🛏 94 📶 🍽 ♿ AE, DC, V

🍽 ANTIKA
$$

DONJA KOLA
TEL 021 765 479
In a 16th-century house with wood-beamed ceilings and eclectic tables and chairs, the

---

🏨 Hotel   🍽 Restaurant   🛏 No. of Guest Rooms   🛌 No. of Seats   🅿 Parking   🕐 Closed   🔄 Elevator

PRICES

HOTELS
The cost of a double room with private bathroom in peak season is given by $ signs.

$$$$$	Over $315
$$$$	$191–$315
$$$	$126–$190
$$	$60–$125
$	Under $60

RESTAURANTS
The average cost of a two-course meal for one person, excluding tip or drinks, is given by $ signs.

$$$$$	Over $40
$$$$	$31–$40
$$$	$21–$30
$$	$10–$20
$	Under $10

slightly bohemian Antika has a broad, well-priced menu and a roof terrace. It also does a good breakfast.
🔲 80 🕐 Closed Dec.–Jan. 🅢 🅢 No credit cards

TROGIR

🏨 HOTEL CONCORDIA
🍴 $$–$$$
BANA BERISLAVIĆA 22
TEL 021 885 400
concordia-hotel.net
Situated right on the old town's waterfront near the Kamerlengo Fortress, in a 300-year-old building. Most of the rooms have a sea view, and there's a small restaurant downstairs.
ⓘ 11 🅿 🅢 🅢 🅢 AE, MC

🏨 HOTEL FONTANA
🍴 $$–$$$
OBROV 1
TEL 021 885 744
fontana-commerce.htnet.hr
Three-star hotel in the old town with good-value rooms and its own restaurant, where you can enjoy breakfast on the terraces.
ⓘ 13 🅢 🅢 All major cards

🏨 HOTEL PALACE
$$
PUT GRADINE
TEL 021 685 555
hotel-palace.net
Luxurious new four-star hotel, about a five-minute walk from the old town on Čiovo. Rooms have dark, polished wooden floors and sea-view balconies, and several have access for the disabled. A spa is planned to open in the near future.
ⓘ 38 🅿 🅢 🅢 🅢 All major cards

VIS

🏨 HOTEL SAN GIORGIO
🍴 $$$–$$$$
PETRA HEKTOROVIĆA 2
TEL 021 711 362
hotelsangiorgiovis.com
Small family-run boutique hotel, recently renovated (it was previously the Hotel Paula), in Kut, a suburb of Vis town. The stone building has individually decorated rooms, and there is a good seafood restaurant, the **Bocadoro.** They can also arrange accommodation in a lighthouse on a nearby islet.
ⓘ 10 🅢 🅢 🅢 All major cards

🏨 KUĆA VISOKA
$$$
VIS
TEL 44 (0)203 2870015 (U.K.)
thisisvis.com
Beautifully renovated old stone house in the center of Vis town, restored and run by

a young English couple who've now pursued a similar venture near Lake Skadar in Montenegro. Minimum four-night stay in season.
ⓘ 3 🅢 🅢 All major cards

🏨 HOTEL TAMARIS
🍴 $$–$$$
OBALA SV. JURAJ 30
TEL 021 711 350
hotelsvis.com
The nicer of the large hotels in town, in a central location, with a terrace restaurant.
ⓘ 25 🕐 Closed Nov.–April
🅢 🅢 🅢 All major cards

🏨 PANSION DIONIS
🍴 $$
MATIJE GUBCA 1
TEL 021 711 963
dionis.hr
Small family-run place, centrally located, with clean, simple rooms and a pizzeria downstairs. Rooms at the front have a joint terrace overlooking the sea; those at the back, separate terraces overlooking the garden.
ⓘ 8 🅢 🅢 🅢 AE, MC, V

🍴 RESTORAN SENKO
$$$
MALA TRAVNA
TEL 098 352 5803
Set in a small, beautiful bay on the south coast of the island, Senko is run by well-known local writer Senko Karuza, who does all the cooking himself, from locally grown ingredients. Expect a long, entertaining evening in informal surroundings, with several courses, served by Senko himself. Reservations essential.
🕐 Closed in winter
🅢 No credit cards

SOMETHING SPECIAL

🍴 POJODA
$$–$$$
DON CVJETKA MARASOVIĆA 8
TEL 021 711 575

Truly lovely seafood restaurant in Kut, the small suburb along the southeast side of the bay, served in a beautifully atmospheric setting—choose between the peaceful central courtyard, or the stone-walled interior. Exquisitely prepared dishes, from octopus salad to succulent prawn risotto and glisteningly fresh fish. Very reasonably priced, very friendly and attentive service. Hands down one of the best restaurants anywhere in Croatia.

🛈 60 🅢 🕸 All major cards

🍴 KARIJOLA
$$
ŠETALIŠTE VIŠKI BOJ 4
TEL 021 711 433
Best pizza in Vis (and maybe in Croatia), with a crisp thin base, served on a splendid terrace overlooking the sea.

🛟 60 🅢 🕸 All major cards

■ THE DALMATIAN HINTERLAND

PLITVICE LAKES NATIONAL PARK

🏨 HOTEL JEZERO
🍴 $$$–$$$$
ULAZ 2
TEL 053 751 500
np-plitvicka-jezera.hr
The best of the several large hotels at the Ulaz 2 entrance to the park, old style but comfortable, with a restaurant, and right at the start of the trail down to the lakes. Five of the rooms have access for the disabled.

🛈 229 🅿 🛗 📺
🕸 All major cards

SINJ

🏨 HOTEL ALKAR
🍴 $$
VRLIČKA 50
TEL 021 824 474

hotel-alkar.hr
Good, modern three-star hotel, with a restaurant and café offering a mix of traditional local meals, Dalmatian specialties, and Croatian dishes.

🛟 50 🅿 🅢 🕸 All major cards

🍴 KONOBA ISPOD URE
$$
ISTARSKA 2
TEL 021 822 229
Excellent and popular traditional restaurant, with a stone-walled interior, serving delicious local signature dishes such as *arambašići* (cabbage leaves stuffed with finely chopped meat cooked in spices).

🛟 20 🅢 🕸 All major cards

■ SOUTHERN DALMATIA

CAVTAT

🏨 HOTEL CAVTAT
$$$
PUT TIHE 8
TEL 020 202 000
hotel-cavtat.hr
Right on the waterfront, with rather functional rooms, but most have sea views.

🛈 94 🅢 🅢 🕸 All major cards

🏨 VILLA KVATERNIK
$$$
KVATERNIKOVA 3
TEL 020 479 800
hotelvillakvaternik.com
Good, centrally located choice in an old converted 15th-century villa.

🛈 178 🅢 🅢
🕸 No credit cards

🍴 TAVERNA GALIJA
$$$
VULČEĆEVA 1
TEL 020 478 566
galija.hr
Attractive, stone-walled place with wood-beamed ceilings

and a great terrace. The menu is good, though the service can be rather offhand.

🛟 150 🅢 🕸 All major cards

DUBROVNIK

HOTELS

🏨 HILTON IMPERIAL
🍴 DUBROVNIK
$$$$$
MARIJANA BLAŽIĆA 2
TEL 020 320 220
hilton.com
Just outside the Pile Gate, elegantly restored after the Homeland War, with some rooms looking across to the Lovrijenac tower, a pleasant terrace, and its own restaurant, the **Porat.**

🛈 147 🅿 🛗 🅢 🅢 🌊
🕸 All major cards

🏨 HOTEL VILLA ORSULA
$$$$$
FRANA SUPILA 14, PLOČE
TEL 020 430 830
adriaticluxuryhotels.com
Part of the Villa Argentina complex of luxury villas in Ploče, less than a 15-minute walk from the old town, this one was built in the 1930s, with sea-view rooms, luxurious, period-style furniture, and the use of a private beach.

🛈 12 🅿 🅢 🅢 🌊 🌊
🕸 All major cards

🏨 PUČIĆ PALACE
🍴 $$$$$
OD PUĆA 1
TEL 020 326 222
thepucicpalace.com
Sumptuous five-star boutique hotel in the center of the old town, in a restored Renaissance palace on one side of Gunduli Poljana. Period-style furnishings, mosaic-tiled bathrooms, and views over the adjacent square.

🛈 17 🛗 🅢 🅢
🕸 All major cards

🏨 Hotel 🍴 Restaurant 🛈 No. of Guest Rooms 🛟 No. of Seats 🅿 Parking 🕐 Closed 🛗 Elevator

PRICES

HOTELS

The cost of a double room with private bathroom in peak season is given by $ signs.

$$$$$	Over $315
$$$$	$191–$315
$$$	$126–$190
$$	$60–$125
$	Under $60

RESTAURANTS

The average cost of a two-course meal for one person, excluding tip or drinks, is given by $ signs.

$$$$$	Over $40
$$$$	$31–$40
$$$	$21–$30
$$	$10–$20
$	Under $10

🏨 HOTEL STARI GRAD
$$$–$$$$
OD SIGURATE 4
TEL 020 322 244
hotelstarigrad.com
In a side street just off Stradun, the three-star rooms (four single, four double) in this renovated old building have tiled floors and elegant, old-style furnishings. There's no view, but they're quiet, and there's a good roof terrace.

🚪 8 🛏 🚭 💳
💳 All major cards

🏨 BERKELEY HOTEL
$$–$$$
ANDRIJE HEBRANGA 116A, GRUŽ
TEL 020 494 160
berkeleyhotel.hr
Excellent new boutique hotel in Gruž, only five minutes from the ferry terminal, with stylish, comfortable doubles

and apartments, as well as a great breakfast

🚪 24 🅿 🚭 💳
💳 All major cards

🏨 KARMEN APARTMENTS
$$–$$$
BANDUREVA 1
TEL 020 323 433
karmendu.com
Absolutely lovely place in Pustijerne, the southeast corner of the medieval city right next to the old port, and only a few minutes' walk from the cathedral. Four homey, self-contained apartments in an old stone house, each sleeping two to three people, with wooden floors, kitchen, and views over the old port, the cathedral, or the adjacent courtyard, one with a balcony. There's a surcharge for stays of less than three nights. One of the nicest places you could hope to stay in the old town.

🚪 4 💳 No credit cards

RESTAURANTS

🍴 PROTO
$$$$$
ŠIROKA 1
TEL 020 323 234
esculaprestaurants.com
One of Dubrovnik's most famous restaurants, just off Stradun. The upscale Proto has been serving up premium fare since 1886, its guests including such dignitaries as Edward VIII. Fine seafood and other dishes, and a lovely terrace upstairs. Reservations recommended.

🍽 200 🚭 💳 All major cards

🍴 GVEROVIĆ ORSAN
$$$$
STILKOVIĆA 43, ZATON MALI
TEL 020 891 267
gverovic-orsan.hr
Located 4.5 miles (7 km) northwest of Dubrovnik, this highly respected, family-run place has been serving

outstanding food in a converted old boathouse since 1966. Features fine seafood and organic or local produce, and a wine list including one made exclusively for the restaurant by a vineyard on Hvar. The specialty is a legendary black risotto.

🍽 160 🕐 Closed Jan.–Feb. 🚭
💳 AE, MC, V

🍴 KLARISA
$$$
PASKA MILEČEVIĆA 1
TEL 020 413 100
klarisa-dubrovnik.com
Worth going to for the setting alone—located in the 13th-century cloisters of the former Convent of St. Claire. Good rather than outstanding food.

🚭 💳 All major cards

🍴 KAMENICE
$$
GUNDULIĆEVA POLJANA 8
TEL 020 323 682
Kamenice (which means oyster in Croatian) serves up excellent, good-value shellfish and other seafood. Always busy, it remains a favorite with locals as well as foreign visitors.

🍽 60 🕐 Closed D in winter
🚭 💳 No credit cards

🍴 LOKANDA PESKARIJA
$$
NA PONTI
TEL 020 324 750
mea-culpa.hr
Tiny local favorite right on the old port, with tables spread across the waterfront, serving well-priced seafood and other dishes from a succinct menu. Packed to overflowing in the summer, and perhaps at its best out of season.

💳 No credit cards

🚭 Nonsmoking 🛏 Air-conditioning 🏊 Indoor Pool 🏊 Outdoor Pool 🏋 Health Club 💳 Credit Cards

NISHTA
$$
PRIJEKO BB
TEL 020 867 440
nishtarestaurant.com
Great vegetarian restaurant, owned by the same people who own the nearby (also good) Smuuti Bar (see below), with a variety of soups, snacks, and main dishes, and vegan as well as gluten-free options in colorful surroundings.
Closed Mon. L & all Sun.
MC, V

SMUUTI BAR
$$
PALMOTIĆEVA 5
TEL 020 867 440
nishtarestaurant.com
This café-bar serves excellent breakfasts and is one of the few places in Dubrovnik where you can get smoothies. You can choose your own blend from an extensive list of delicious, and some even rather unusual, ingredients.
MC, V

KORČULA

LEŠIĆ DIMITRI PALACE
$$$$$
DON PAVLE POŠE
TEL 020 715 560
lesic-dimitri.com
If money is no object, this newly opened five-star hotel has luxurious themed rooms in an 18th-century bishop's palace along with five medieval cottages.
13
All major cards

HOTEL MARKO POLO
$$$$
ŠETALIŠTE FRANA KRŠINICA
TEL 020 726 100
korcula-hotels.com
Newly renovated four-star

hotel, now one of the better places among the large resort-style complexes on the edge of town, with clean, comfortable rooms, and fine views out toward Pelješac.
94
All major cards

HOTEL KORSAL
$$$
ŠETALIŠTE FRANA KRŠINIĆA 80
TEL 020 715 722
hotel-korsal.com
An attractive new boutique hotel with spacious rooms, right on the waterfront just outside the old town.
10
All major cards

ROYAL APARTMENTS
$$
TRG PETRA SEGEDINA 4
TEL 098 184 0444
korcularoyalapartments.com
Good alternative to the hotel accommodations offered in Korčula, which generally consist of large, resort-type complexes some distance from the old town, while those within the old town are either in need of renovation or are luxurious but considerably more expensive. There are a number of other good rooms and apartments along the stretch of road to the west of the old town.
5 Closed Nov.–May
No credit cards

KONOBA GAJETA
$$
ŠETALIŠTE PETRA KANAVELIĆA
TEL 020 716 359
Fine unpretentious restaurant serving up a good range of reasonably priced dishes, with tables along both sides of the pleasant waterfront promenade on the east

side of the old town. The tables overlooking the water tend to fill up fast.
100
No credit cards

PIZZERIA CAENAZZO
$$
TRG SV. MARKA
TEL 098 244 012
Excellent, well-priced pizzeria in a wonderful setting, with tables spilling out across the square in front of the cathedral. Come in the evening when the light from the setting sun hits the cathedral facade and swallows swoop through the sky above.
60
No credit cards

LASTOVO

HOTEL SOLITUDO
$$$
UVALA PASADUR BB, UBLI
TEL 020 802 100
hotel-solitudo.com
Situated on a remote bay, right by the water and surrounded by pine trees, this three-star hotel with two restaurants is currently the only hotel on the island. A bit cut off from the rest of Lastovo island though: You might do better to look for a private room in Lastovo town through the tourist office, and experience more of the island.
73
All major cards

KONOBA AUGUSTA INSULA
$$$
ZAKLOPATICA 21, LASTOVO TOWN
TEL 020 801 167
augustainsula.com
Friendly family-run *konoba* serving excellent dishes at Zaklopatica, in the north of the island, around 2 miles (3 km) west of Lastovo town, with an emphasis on

fresh seafood and wines from its own vineyard. Local dishes include a sea-grass salad, lobster with spaghetti, and Lastovo-style *brodet*.
🛏 160 🕐 Closed Nov.–May
🚭 🚫 No credit cards

🍴 KONOBA BAČVARA
$$
LASTOVO TOWN
TEL 020 801 131
Lovely, welcoming, homely, family-run *konoba*, serving great seafood and other local specialties such as chickpea stew. You'll find it toward the bottom of the rambling flights of stone steps leading down through Lastovo town. Highly recommended.
🛏 40 🚭 🚫 No credit cards

LOPUD

🏨 VILLA VILINA
$$$$
IVA KULJEVANA 5
TEL 020 759 333
villa-vilina.hr
Upscale four-star hotel in a restored 18th-century mansion with sea views.
🛏 17 🚭 🚫
🚫 All major cards

LUMBARDA

🏨 HOTEL BORIK
🍴 **$$–$$$**
PRVI ŽAL BB
TEL 020 712 215
hotelborik.hr
Renovated stone mansion in central location, with simple but stylish rooms, as well as its own restaurant, pizzeria, and lounge bar, and only 650 feet (200 m) from the beach.
🛏 80 🚫 No credit cards

🏨 VILLA VESNA/ PANSION BEBIĆ
$$
TEL 020 712 505
bebic.hr
Just outside of Lumbarda, in a stone-front building. Offers simple rooms with balconies, sea views, and its own terrace restaurant.
🛏 12 🅿 🚭
🚫 No credit cards

MALI STON

🏨 HOTEL OSTREA
🍴 **$$$**
MALI STON
TEL 020 754 555
ostrea.hr
Family-run place in restored old stone house, with beautifully kept rooms and its own restaurant, the **Mlinica.**
🛏 14 🅿 🚭 🚫
🚫 All major cards

🏨 VILA KORUNA
🍴 **$$**
MALI STON
020 754 999
vila-koruna.hr
A good option, open year-round, with simple sea-view rooms for two to four people, and a great restaurant downstairs on a covered terrace by the water.
🛏 6 🅿 🚭 🚫
🚫 No credit cards

🍴 KAPETANOVA KUĆA
$$$
MALI STON
TEL 020 754 555
ostrea.hr
Popular place owned by the same family as the Hotel Ostrea. Right on the waterfront, it serves shellfish and other local specialties, with a good selection of wines from the Pelješac Peninsula.
🚭 🚫 All major cards

MLJET

🏨 HOTEL ODISEJ
🍴 **$$–$$$**
POMENA BB, POMENA
TEL 020 362 111
adriaticluxuryhotels.com
Large three-star hotel, with boat moorings and a small beach, standard and sea-view rooms, a restaurant, and a pizzeria.
🛏 157 🕐 Closed Nov.–April
🚭 🎖 🚫 All major cards

OREBIĆ

🏨 GRAND HOTEL OREBIĆ
🍴 **$$$**
KRALJ PETRA KRESIMIRA IV 107
TEL 020 798 000
adriaticluxuryhotels.com
New four-star hotel, a ten-minute walk along the beach from town, with its own restaurant and bar.
🛏 173 🅿 🚭 🚫 🏊
🚫 No credit cards

VELA LUKA

🏨 HOTEL KORKYRA
🍴 **$$$**
OBALA 3
TEL 020 601 000
hotel-korkyra.com
Newly renovated hotel in the center of town with stylish, spacious rooms and its own restaurant, swimming pool, and spa.
🛏 58 🚭 🚫 🏊
🚫 All major cards

🏨 DALMACIJA
🍴 **$$**
ULICA 62 BR 2
TEL 020 812 042
humhotels.hr
Simple, central two-star hotel with clean, functional doubles right on the waterfront, all with sea view and balcony.
🛏 14 🚭 🚫 No credit cards

Shopping

Though many Croats regularly leave the country on shopping trips to Trieste in Italy or Graz in Austria, you will find plenty to shop for in Croatia, from attractively packaged local foodstuffs, wine, and spirits to art, jewelry, and local designer clothes, and there are some wonderful open markets in which to browse.

Bargaining

Haggling is not acceptable when buying goods in shops and markets in Croatia; the price quoted, whether for a Murano glass ring or a kilo of zucchinis, is the price you'll be expected to pay. The only exception is antiques markets, where some friendly bargaining may (but not always) be in order. Bear in mind that the amount in question may be trivial in your own currency, but Croatia is by no means a third-world economy. If you feel that the suggested price for an antique is too high, remain polite and suggest a slightly lower figure by saying, "*Može za...?*" which means "Would...be OK?"

Payment

Boutique souvenir shops will almost always accept payment by credit card. The same does not apply to markets, which are strictly a cash-only environment. Try to carry a reasonable amount of small-denomination notes and coins when shopping in markets; stallholders quite often have only a limited amount of change at their outlet, and payment with something close to the correct amount in notes/coins rather than a large denomination banknote is always very much appreciated. Needless to say, for such purchases, you will be paying in kunas. One of the few occasions when foreign currency is accepted (normally the euro) is as payment for some private rooms and apartments.

Tax

Sales tax in Croatia (called PDV) is 22 percent and is already included in the prices displayed in shops.

What to Buy

There is a huge range of attractive souvenirs available in Croatia, including foodstuffs such as local olive oil, wine, *rakija*, truffles, cheeses, *pršut*, olives, and anchovies, as well as handmade soaps and natural cosmetics. Locally made jewelry, including items made from Murano glass and objects with shapes deriving from folk themes, can also be found fairly widely. Textiles include the exquisite lace *(čipka)* from Pag (see p. 179), among the finest handmade products you could hope to find anywhere in Croatia, and the beautiful Konavle embroidery from the region south of Dubrovnik. Small bags of lavender are a traditional product of Hvar, while particularly evocative of Zagreb are *licitarsko srce* (colored, heart-shaped ornaments) or *šestinski kišobrani* (miniature umbrellas). Artwork by local Croatian artists can be found in street stalls and galleries, ranging from local prints and drawings that might cost a few dollars, to works by well-known Croatian artists that might set you back thousands.

Art

You can buy local artwork all over Croatia, from street stalls to large galleries. In Zagreb there are frequently stalls selling local art and crafts in the pedestrian streets leading between Bogovićeva and Ilica, and in Jelačić Square, especially around Easter. For antiques, browse the Sunday market on Zagreb's British Square and the various stalls just inside the main gate to the old town in Zadar.

Art Shop Klovičevi Dvori
Jezuitski Trg 4, Zagreb
Tel 01 4851 926
galerijaklovic.hr
Art shop attached to this excellent gallery in Zagreb's Gornji Grad.

Fonticus
Trg lođe 3, Grožnjan
Tel 052 776 131
Gallery specializing in contemporary local artists.

Gallery Deči
Radićeva 19, Zagreb
galerijadeci.hr
Small, well-established gallery selling work by some of Croatia's best known artists. Closed Sun.

Pharos
Gorjana 8, Grožnjan
Just one of numerous establishments in Grožnjan selling art and souvenirs. Closed Oct.–March.

Podrumi
Diocletian's Palace, Split
The brick-vaulted underground halls *(podrumi)* at the southern entrance to Diocletian's Palace have plenty of well-priced local paintings, prints, and drawings for sale, both framed and unframed.

Studio Lik
Don Ive Prodana 7, Zadar
Tel 098 273 473
Various arts and crafts, including

traditional lace from Pag and Lepoglava. Closed Sun.

Books

Algoritam
Gajeva 1, Zagreb
Tel 01 2359 333
algoritam.hr
Bookstore chain with large stock of English-language titles, from novels to travel guides, as well as foreign newspapers. Also has branches in a number of other Croatian cities:

> Placa 1, Dubrovnik
> Tel 020 322 044

> Trg Slobode 8, Osijek
> Tel 031 214 310

> Prolaz Kod Kažališta 1, Pula
> Tel 052 393 987

> Bajamontijeva 2, Split
> Tel 021 348 030

Jesenski i Turk
Preradovićeva 5, Zagreb
jesenski-turk.hr
Small, well-known bookshop with new and secondhand titles.

Profil
Bogovićeva 7, Zagreb
Tel 01 4877 300
profil.hr
Excellent bookshop, with the best range of English-language titles in Zagreb, and also a good selection of Croatian films on DVD. Additional branches can be found at the following locations:

> Tower Centar Rijeka, IV Kat, Rijeka
> Tel 051 614 901

> Šubićeva 7, Split
> Tel 021 332 675

Trgovački Centar City Galleria
Murvička 1, Zadar
Tel 023 493 050

Chocolate

Kras
kras.hr
Zagreb's most famous confectioner and chocolatier, with several stores across the capital (there's one on Ilica and another on Jelačić Square). Their most celebrated products are Bajadera, made with almond and hazelnut nougat, and Griotte, a wickedly rich cherry liqueur. Widely available, including in supermarkets and airport shops.

Milenij Choco World
Hotel Continental, Opatija
milenijhoteli.com
Artisan chocolates and other sweet things in the basement of the Hotel Continental.

Clothes

I-GLE
Dežmanov 4, Zagreb
Tel 01 4846 508
i-gle.com
Cult local designer label run by Martina Vrdoljak Ranilović and Nataša Mihaljčišin.

Mak
Kopilica 58, Split
Tel 021 389 628
mak-modna-kuca.hr
Another cult designer label, run by Neda Makjanić-Kunić from Split. There are other stores in Split and Zadar:

> R Boškovića 9, Split
> Tel 021 470 005

> Cro-a-Porter, Široka Ulica 18, Zadar
> Tel 023 204 902

Cosmetics

Aromateka
Heinzelova 2, Zagreb
Tel 01 4651 309
aromateka.hr

Store selling natural and organic Croatian cosmetics and beauty products. Closed Sun.

Jewelry

Jewellery Garden
Boškovićeva Poljana bb, Dubrovnik
Tel 091 5084 850
Jewelry shop with pieces by well-known Croatian jewelry designers; some pieces displayed in the garden.

Seba Dizajn
Korčula
Tel 091 5084 850
sebasilver.com
Beautiful handmade filigree silver jewelry made by Ruth Seba in Korčula.

Markets
Croatia has some wonderful markets, selling fruits and vegetables, meat and fish, cheeses, flowers, and antiques.

British Square market
Britanski Trg, Zagreb
A fruit and vegetable market most mornings of the week, and an interesting antiques market on Sunday mornings, with all sorts of things from furniture to bric-a-brac.

Dolac
Dolac, Zagreb
Zagreb's huge open market is a must-see, even if you don't intend to buy anything—meat and dairy produce downstairs, fruits and vegetables (and a separate fish market) upstairs. Open mornings until 2 p.m. (3 p.m. on Sun.).

Gundulićeva Poljana Market
Gundulićeva Poljana, Dubrovnik
Good place to buy fresh fruit and vegetables in Dubrovnik, as well as other local produce such as

olive oil and honey. You can also usually find handmade lace here.

Hrelić Market
Sajmišna cesta 8, Jakuševac, Zagreb
Huge Sunday market on the southern fringe of Zagreb, something between a flea market and a garage sale, with an enormous and wonderfully eclectic range of goods on sale. Open Sunday morning until around midday.

Music

Aquarius
Varšavska 13, Zagreb
Tel 01 492 0380
aquarius-records.com

Dinaton
Ulica Petra Preradovića 12, Zagreb
Tel 01 4855 281
CD shop with a decent selection of classical, jazz, and world music. There's another branch at Trg Petra Preradovića 5 with Croatian and international rock and pop.

Shopping Malls

There are several large shopping centers in Zagreb and other major cities—though nothing on the scale of a U.S. mall—stocking local and international brands.

Avenue Mall
Avenija Dubrovnik 16, Zagreb
avenuemall.com.hr

Kaptol Centar
Nova Ves 17, Zagreb
centarkaptol.hr

West Gate
Zaprešićka 2, Jablanovec, Donja Bistra, Zagreb
westgate.com.hr
Vast shopping center north of Zagreb on the road to Maribor.

Traditional Products & Souvenirs

Aqua
aquamaritime.hr
Distinctive, well-made blue and white clothing, towels, bathrobes, and souvenirs. Stores in major towns on the coast and islands.

Bakina Kuća
Strossmayerov Trg 7, Zagreb
bakina-kuca.hr
Shop in central Zagreb selling a wide range of traditional and attractive Croatian products. Closed Sun.

Medusa
Prijeko 18, Dubrovnik
Tel 020 322 004
medusa.hr
Decent local craft and souvenir shop on café-lined Prijeko, selling a range of items from handmade jewelry, paintings, and Konavle embroidery to olive oil, natural soaps, and cosmetics. You can also buy CDs of local folk music.

Natura Croatica
Petra Preradovića 8, Zagreb
Tel 01 485 5076
naturacroatica.com
This shop, which also has a branch in the Westin Zagreb, sells a range of traditional Croatian products, from olive oil and spirits to lavender and natural soaps. Closed Sun.

Tilda
Zlatarska 1, Dubrovnik
Tel 020 321 554
Local Konavle embroidery. Closed Sun.

Zeleno i Plavo
Trpimirova 1a, Rijeka
Tel 052 322 598
zelenoiplavo.hr
An excellent place to shop for a wide range of locally made souvenirs as well as local wine, olive oil, and other products.

Truffles

Zigante Tartufi
zigantetartufi.com
Truffle pastes, oils, and other products. Several stores across Istria.

Wine

Wine can often be purchased direct from vineyards. Alternatively, try the following stores:

Bornstein
Kaptol 19, Zagreb
Tel 01 481 2361
bornstein.hr
Wine boutique with a huge range of local and international wines and helpful staff. Come here for a nice bottle of Dingać (a powerful red from the Pelješac Peninsula) or a crisp white from eastern Slavonia. There's another branch on Pantovčak. Closed Sun.

Kuća Hrvatskih Vina Vinoteka (House of Croatian Wines)
Zastavnica 13C, Hrvatski Leskovac, Lučko, Zagreb
Tel 01 6557 555
Boutique Croatian wine cellar east of Zagreb near the beginning of the Zagreb County wine road. Closed Sun.

The Wine Shop
Pred Dvorom 1, Dubrovnik
Tel 020 321 202
mea-culpa.hr
Located inside the popular Gradska Kavana, with one of the best wine selections in Dubrovnik—some 250 different varieties, mostly Croatian but also some imported, as well as various local liqueurs and brandies. If you want to try a good range of wines by the glass first while in Dubrovnik, head for D'Vino Wine Bar on Palmotićeva.

Entertainment

The range of entertainment offered in Croatia runs the gamut from jazz and film to theater and opera, carnivals, and traditional folk festivals.

Carnival

Almost any town of any size in Croatia has its own Carnival in the days immediately before Lent (usually February). The largest by far is the **Rijeka Carnival** *(ri-karn eval.com.hr)*, a spectacular parade of floats, dancing, and wild costumes (see p. 18 & sidebar p. 143). Much smaller but equally memorable is the **Poklad Festival** on Lastovo (see pp. 18 & 271).

Needless to say, accommodations need to be booked way in advance if staying in town during Carnival, or any other festival.

Cinema

Croatia has a number of film festivals, foremost among these being the world-class **Pula Film Festival** *(pulafilmfestival.hr)* and the **Motovun Film Festival** *(motovunfilmfestival.com)*, both in Istria and held in July (see p. 129). There's also the **Zagreb Film Festival** *(zagrebfilmfestival.com)* in October and **Animafest** (World Festival of Animated Film; *anima fest.hr*) in June, also in Zagreb.

If you just want to go see a film in Croatia, you will find plenty of cinemas around, from large multiplexes showing new international releases to small repertory cinemas showing classics and world cinema (though increasingly rarely—hence the introduction of the Motovun Film Festival). Movie tickets are very cheap *($)*, and films are shown with Croatian subtitles rather than dubbed, meaning you will be watching in the original language, be that English, French, or whatever. For a good, non-multiplex cinema in Zagreb, head for **Kino Europa** *(Varšavska 3, Zagreb, tel 01 4872 888, kinoeuropa.hr)* on the Flower Square.

Dance

The *Moreška* (see p. 263), a spectacular type of traditional sword dance, is performed in July and August on the island of Korčula.

The biggest folk dancing festival is the **Brodsko Kolo** *(brodsko-kolo .com)*, held in Slavonski Brod in June (see p. 18).

Music

Croatia has a thriving music scene, encompassing folk, jazz, pop, and classical, with lots of live concerts by local as well as international artists. There are first-rate music festivals, from Zagreb's **Biennale** *(mbz.hr)*, the **Dubrovnik Summer Festival** *(dubrovnik-festival.hr)*, and Varaždin's **Festival of Baroque Music** to huge dance, electronica, and pop events such as the annual **Garden Festival** *(thegardenfestival .eu)* near Zadar (see p. 171). Major Croatian pop acts to keep an eye open for include Oliver Dragojević and Nina Badrić.

Folk

The most familiar form of traditional folk music is the haunting *klapa*, Dalmatian a cappella song (see sidebar p. 206). You can hear klapa in many places along the coast during the summer, and Omiš holds an annual **Festival of Dalmatian Klapa** *(fdk.hr)* in July (see p. 18).

Jazz

The Croatian capital has a particularly fertile underground music scene, from cool jazz clubs to grungy alternative venues and dance clubs. The BP Club (see below) organizes several jazz festivals in Zagreb, the largest in October. Other places to catch live jazz performances include festivals in Grožnjan, Poreč, and on the island of Lastovo. Further jazz concerts are listed on *jazz.hr*.

Bacchus Jazz Bar
Trg Kraja Tomislava 16, Zagreb
Tel 01 4922 218
Popular new laid-back hangout, with live jazz Thurs.–Sat.

BP Club
Teslina 7, Zagreb
Tel 01 4814 444
Zagreb's premier jazz club, run by Croatian vibraphone player and jazz composer Boško Petrović, with live acts (both local and international) on a small stage in an intimate basement setting, and jazz festivals in February, March, and October. Past guests have included the likes of legendary jazz guitarist Joe Pass.

Jazz Club
Gundulićeva 11, Zagreb
New jazz club below street level in central Zagreb. Closed Sun.

Sax
Palmotićeva 22/2, Zagreb
Tel 01 4872 836
sax-zg.hr
One of Zagreb's best live music venues, with regular performances of jazz, blues, and pop in its cavernous interior. Closed Sun.

Troubadour Hard Jazz Cafe
Bunićeva Poljana 2, Dubrovnik
Tel 020 32 34 76
Jazz hangout (albeit a slightly pricey one) with live acts and views of Dubrovnik's cathedral.

Nightclubs
Aquarius
Aleja Matije Ljubeka, Zagreb

Tel 01 3640 231
aquarius.hr
Huge lakeside dance club at
Jarun. During the summer, Aquarius's other venue at Novalja, on
the island of Pag, becomes the
clubbing capital of Croatia.

Jabuka
Jabukovac 28, Zagreb
Tel 01 4834 397
Legendary club just off Tuškanac,
caters to slightly older local crowd
in search of 1980s nostalgia.
Closed Sun.–Thurs.

Theater & Opera

Tickets for theater, opera, and
ballet in Croatia are very cheap in
comparison with the United States
and Britain ($$–$$$$), and the
standards of performance generally excellent. While in Zagreb, try
to catch a concert, opera, or ballet
in the grand **Croatian National
Theatre** (Hrvatsko Narodno
Kazelište, or HNK for short). The
HNK also has theaters in Osijek
and Split. Classical performances
can also be seen in the more modern **Lisinski Theater** in Zagreb.

**Croatian National Theatre
(Hrvatsko Narodno Kazelište)**
Trg Maršala Tita, Zagreb
Tel 01 4888 418
hnk.hr

**Croatian National Theatre
Osijek**
Županijska 9, Osijek
Tel 031 220 700
hnk-osijek.hr

Croatian National Theatre, Split
Trg Gaje Bulata 1, Split
Tel 021 344 999
hnk-split.hr

**Lisinski Theater (Koncertna
dvorana Vatroslava Lisinskog)**
Trg Stjepana Radića 4, Zagreb
Tel 01 6121 111
lisinski.hr

Festivals

There's a huge range of festivals
in Croatia. Many of them take
place during the summer. Some
of the best are listed below.

Animafest
animafest.hr
Excellent festival of animated film
in Zagreb in June.

Brodsko Kolo
brodsko-kolo.com
Held in Slavonski Brod in June,
this is Croatia's premier folk-
dance festival.

Cest is d'Best
cestisdbest.com
Fantastic festival of street theater
in Zagreb in June.

Dubrovnik Summer Festival
dubrovnik-festival.hr
45 days in July and August, with
Croatian and international music,
opera, theater, and dance.

**Embroidery Festival
(Đakovački Vezovi)**
Held in Đakovo in July and featuring traditional embroidery,
as well as concerts, parades, and
displays by the Lipizzaner horses
for which this area is famous.

Festival of Dalmatian Klapa
fdk.hr
Held in July in Omiš, this is the
premier event for traditional
Dalmatian *klapa*.

International Folk Festival
msf.hr
Croatia's largest folk festival, held
in Zagreb in July.

Motovun Film Festival
motovunfilmfestival.com
Held over five days in July in this
stunning medieval Istria hill town.

**Poklad Festival (Lastovo
Carnival)**
The island of Lastovo holds its
own, highly individual Carnival for
three days during Lent.

Pula Film Festival
pulafilmfestival.hr
Croatia's premier film festival,
held over two weeks in July, with
some screenings in the magnificent Roman arena.

**Procession of the Cross
(Za Križen)**
Takes place on the last Thursday
before Easter (Maundy Thursday)
on the island of Hvar, between
the villages of Jelsa, Pitve, Vrisnik,
Svirče, Vrbanj, and Vrboska.

Rab Crossbow Festival
Held in May, July, and August in
the town of the same name, and
marking its apparently miraculous
deliverance from a siege in 1358.

Rijeka Carnival
ri-karneval.com.hr
The second largest carnival in
Europe after Venice, held just
before Lent (usually February).

Sinjska Alka
Jousting tournament in August
commemorating a victory over
the Ottomans in 1715 in Sinj.

Spancirfest
spancirfest.com
Ten days of music, dance, comedy,
and street theater in Varaždin, in
late August.

Split Summer Festival
splitsko-ljeto.hr
Split's largest festival takes place
in July and August.

**Tilting at the Ring (Trka na
prstenac)**
Held in Barban, in Istria, in
August, this festival dates back
to 1696, and sees horsemen
competing to spear a large
metal ring.

Tours, Classes, & Outdoor Activities

Croatia has plenty of scope for outdoor activities, from hiking and cycling to kayaking, while the Adriatic acts as a magnet for sailing holidays, and there's also some good scuba diving. The wide range of special interest tours available includes wildlife tours and bird-watching, and culinary and wine tours. Agencies may offer several different activities, but are listed here under one heading.

Vineyards & Wine Tours

A number of vineyards offer tastings, and cellar and vineyard tours, generally with prior notice. Many also offer private rooms and meals. For a greater concentration of vineyards than can be visited in one area, consider traveling along one of Croatia's established "wine roads," such as Plešivica (see pp. 96–97) or Ilok (*vinailok.hr, turizamilok.hr*; see p. 119). A good online source of information on wine regions and grape varieties in Croatia is *hrvatska-vina.com*.

Bartulović
Prizdrina, Pelješac
Tel 020 742 506
vinarijabartulovic.hr

Boškinac Winery
Novaljsko polje bb, Pag
Tel 053 663 500
boskinac.com

Enjingi
Hrnjevac 87, Vetovo
Tel 034 267 200
enjingi.hr
One of the most respected vineyards, with tastings and tours.

Franc Arman
Narduči 5, Vižinada
Tel 052 446 226 or 091 4462 266
francarman.hr
Friendly, family-run vineyard in central Istria producing excellent, crisp Malvazija as well as Teran. Tastings available.

Iločki Podrumi
Dr. Franje Tuđmana 72, Ilok
Tel 032 590 003

ilocki-podrumi.hr
Ilok's most famous wine cellar.

Korak
Plešivica 34, Jastrebarsko
Tel 01 6293 088
vino-korak.hr
Vineyard on the Plešivica Wine Road.

Krešimir Režek
Plešivica 39, Jastrebarsko
Tel 01 6294 836
rezek.hr
Vineyard on the Plešivica Wine Road.

Nada
Glavaca 22, Vrbnik, Krk
Tel 051 857 065
nada-vrbnik.hr
A good place to sample the local Žlahtina on Krk.

Trapan
Veruda 10, Pula
Tel 098 244 457
trapan.hr
Excellent (and award-winning) examples of what can be achieved with Istria's signature grape.

Zlatan Otok
Sveta Nedjelja, Hvar
Tel 021 745 709
zlatanotok.hr
Well-known vineyard on Hvar.

The following agencies also offer wine tours in Croatia:

Arblaster & Clarke Wine Tours Ltd.
Cedar Court, 5 College St., Petersfield, Hampshire
GU31 4AE, UK

Tel 44 (0)1730 263111 (U.K.)
winetours.co.uk
U.K.-based operator offering luxury wine tours and cruises in Istria and Dalmatia.

Culinary Croatia
culinary-croatia.com
Wine tours of the Dingać region on Pelješac, Hvar, Skradin (near Šibenik), and Dalmatia.

Culinary Tours & Cooking Courses

Croatia has some truly delicious food, making it a great place for culinary tours and cooking workshops. For some Croatian recipes, see **Maninas Food Matters** (*maninas.wordpress.com*).

Croatia Culinary Tours
Tel 01 48 81 807
croatiaculinarytours.com
Zagreb-based outfit offering interesting culinary tours throughout Croatia.

Culinary Croatia
culinary-croatia.com
Croatian company offering unique culinary tours, olive oil tours, and cooking courses, with plenty of information and interesting links on its blog.

Secret Dalmatia
Offices in Zadar, Split, and Dubrovnik
Tel 091 567 1604
secretdalmatia.com
Company offering custom tours and small group programs—food, heritage, and more—with an active commitment to raising awareness of issues like illegal hunting and

threats to Croatia's natural environment and cultural heritage.

Wildlife Tours

Falco Tours
Zrnovnička 11, Split
Tel 021 548 646
falco-tours.com
Combined sea kayaking and bird-watching tours.

Pro Birder
gerard@probirder.com
probirder.com
Tours arranged by respected birder and author Gerard Gorman, with local guides.

Val Tours
Trg Hrvatskih Velikana bb, Biograd
Tel 023 386 479
val-tours.hr
One-week bird-watching tours with an itinerary including the Zrmanje River, Paklenica, Velebit, and Vrana Lake. Also kayaking, rafting, diving, and sailing courses.

Outdoor Activities

Cycling & Mountain Biking
Croatia has some great opportunities for cycling, and some local tourist boards have made a particular effort to promote cycling in their region, especially the **Istria Tourist Board** (istria-bike .com and istra.hr) and the **Zagreb County Tourist Board** (tzzz.hr), with lists of routes and detailed maps available online. Other good online resources are pedala .hr and takeadventure.com.

Freedom Treks
Tel 44 (0)12 732 24 066 (U.K.)
freedomtreks.co.uk
U.K.-based company with multi-day cycling itineraries in Istria, with accommodation, bike and equipment rental, and maps and

transfers, as well as "cruise and cycle" holidays in Istria, Kvarner, and Dalmatia.

Exodus
Tel 44 (0)20 8772 3936 or 44 (0)845 863 9600 (U.K.)
sales@exodus.co.uk
exodus.co.uk
Eight-day bike tours on the Dalmatian Islands, connected by ferry transfers.

Meridien Ten
Split
meridien.hr
Split-based agency offering cycle tours and bike rentals, as well as hiking, kayaking, and windsurfing.

Neilson Adventures
Tel 44 (0)844 879 8152 (U.K.)
neilsonadventures.co.uk
U.K.-based company offering eight-day Istria self-guided tours.

Pedal and Sea Adventures
Tel 877/777-5699 (U.S./Can.)
pedalandseaadventures.com
Canadian-based company offering one-week itineraries in southern Dalmatia.

Blue Bike Zagreb
Tel 098 188 3344
zagrebbybike.com
Cycle tours of the Croatian capital.

Diving

Croatia Divers
Obala 1 Br 42, Vela Luka, Korčula
Tel 020 813 508 (April–Oct.) or 091 256 7803
croatiadivers.com
PADI IDC accredited dive center in Vela Luka, with English and Dutch management and multilingual staff.

Diving Lastovo
Pasadur bb, Lastovo
Tel 020 805 179
diving-lastovo.com

Kornati Diving Center
Zaglav, Dugi Otok
Tel 091 3679 506
kornati-diving.com
Scuba diving center based in Zaglav.

General
Several companies offer a range of outdoor and adventure packages to cover most interests.

Gral Putovanja
Trg Fontana 7/1, Buzet
Tel 052 662 959
gral-putovanja.eu
Excellent Buzet-based agency specializing in outdoor and active travel—for which Istria has plenty of opportunities on offer. Cycling (road and off-road), canoeing, hiking, hot-air ballooning (listed among the top 10 balloon flights in the world), and more, as well as wine, gastro, and cultural tours. Very good English spoken. Highly recommended.

Kayaking
Kayaking is becoming increasingly popular, with a number of possible itineraries now run by small local Croatian operators. Spring and summer are the best times of year for river kayaking and rafting, while summer is better for sea kayaking.

Adria Adventure
Dubrovnik
Tel 020 311 545
adriaadventure.hr
Dubrovnik-based company specializing in minimum-impact itineraries, including the Elaphites and Lokrum, local guides, and small groups.

Adriatic Kayak Tours
Zrinsko Frankopanska 6,
Dubrovnik
Tel 020 312 770
adriatickayaktours.com
Small company in Dubrovnik
founded by U.S. kayaker, with
local guides leading single- and
multiday itineraries, including
Lokrum, the Elaphites, and Tara
Canyon in Montenegro. Small
groups and an emphasis on
minimum impact travel.

Adventure Dalmatia
Matije Gupca 26, Split
Tel 021 540 642
adventuredalmatia.com
Split-based company run by
the founders of Cro Challenge,
Croatia's biggest adventure race,
offering one-day and multiday
itineraries, including Elaphite
Islands, Hvar, and the Cetina
River; also mountain biking,
rafting, and hiking.

Sailing
With more than 3,400 miles
(5,500 km) of highly indented
coastline, including some 1,200
islands and islets, Croatia is an
idyllic place to sail, either as a
novice learning the ropes on
a sailing course or as an experienced skipper. Marinas are
mostly owned by the Croatian
Association of Nautical Tourism,
and almost half of these are
run by the **Adriatic Croatia
International Club,** or ACI
(aci-club.hr). A useful site for
sailing on the Croatian Adriatic
is sailingcroatia.net.

Croatia Charter
Hrvatske Mornarice 1d, Split
Tel 021 474 464
croatiacharter.com

Croatia Yachting
Split
Tel 021 332 332
croatia-yachting1
-charter.com

Naulitus Yachting
Tel 44 (0)1732 867 445 (U.K.)
nautilus-yachting.com
Well-established U.K.-based
company.

Sail Croatia
Kralja Zvonimira 35, Split
Tel 44 (0)800 193 8289 (U.K.)
sail-croatia.com
U.K.-based company, with
traditional cruises as well as
"navigator cruises" catering
to under 35s, also cycling and
adventure tours.

SailCroatia
Šetalište kralja Tomislava bb,
Kaštel Gomilica, Split
Tel 021 494 885
sailcroatia.net
Split-based company
offering high-quality yacht
charters, repairs, and
technical backup.

Sailing Europe
Savska cesta 23a, Zagreb
Tel 385 1 488 2200 or
44 (0)122 385 8423 (U.K.) or
567/248-9698 (U.S.)
sailingeurope.com
Zagreb-based fleet, including
Cyclades 39.3, 43.4, and 50.5.

Walking
Croatia offers some great
hiking, much of it hardly ever
seen by foreign visitors, with
well-marked paths, good local
maps, and a network of mountain huts. For further information, see Walking in Croatia by
Rudolf Abraham (2010).

Freedom Treks
Tel 44 (0)12 732 24 066 (U.K.)
freedomtreks.co.uk
Guided or self-guided walking,
cycling, and cruising holidays
from a small U.K. operator.

Headwater Holidays
Tel 016 0682 8344
headwater.com
Company based in northern U.K.
offering walking, cycling, canoeing, and winter snow holidays.

Windsurfing & Kiteboarding
The top spots for windsurfing
in Croatia are the straits
between Korčula and the
Pelješac Peninsula (particularly
Viganj, just north of Orebić)
and between the islands of Brač
and Hvar (although beware that
the current in the straits can be
quite strong). Istria is also popular for windsurfing.

Windsurf Station
Creska 22, Pula
windsurfstation.com
Courses to suit all levels.

Yellow Cat Kiteboarding
Bol, Brač
Tel 01 4880 610 (Zagreb agency)
zutimacak.hr
Kiteboarding school and
equipment rental.

Menu Reader

General

Food	hrana
Breakfast	doručak
Lunch	ručak
Dinner	večera
Appetizer	predjelo
Entrée	glavno jelo
Dessert	desert
Grilled	na žaru
Boiled	kuhano
Fried	prženo
Pasta	tjestenina
Risotto	rižoto
Rice	riža
Eggs	jaje
Brown bread	
	crni kruh
White bread	
	bijeli kruh
Vegetarian (food)	
	vegetarijanska (hrana)

Appetizers

Soup	juha
Fish soup	riblja juha
Vegetable soup	
	juha od povrća
Dalmatian dried ham (prosciutto)	
	pršut
Olives	masline
Cheese from Pag	
	Paški sir
Slavonian dried sausage	
	kulen

Seafood

Fish	riba
Shellfish	školjke
Scampi	škampi
Scampi cooked with white wine, garlic, and olive oil	
	škampi na buzaru
Octopus	hobotnica
Roasted octopus with potatoes and onions and olive oil	
	hobotnica na žaru
Squid	lignje
Fried squid	
	pržene lignje

Stuffed squid	
	punjene lignje
Cuttlefish	sipa
Cuttlefish risotto (cooked in its own ink)	
	crni rižoto
Mussels	dagnje
Oysters	kamenice
Gray mullet	
	cipal
John Dory	kovač
Sea bass	brancin
Mackerel	skuša
Trout	pastrva
Carp	šaran
Fish stew (similar to Italian brodetto)	
	brodet
Carp and pepper stew	
	fiš paprikaš

Meat

Meat	meso
Beef	govedina
Veal	teletina
Pork	svinjetina
Lamb	janjetina
Chicken	piletina
Turkey	puretina
Turkey with mlinci (baked noodles)	
	puretina s mlincima
Venison	srnetina
Wild boar	divlja svinja
Steak	odrezak
Zagreb steak (veal stuffed with ham and cheese, fried in breadcrumbs)	
	Zagrebački odrezak
Beef (or veal) marinated and cooked with dried plums	
	pašticada
Mixed grill or barbecue	
	roštilj
Cabbage leaves stuffed with meat and rice	
	sarma
Grilled meatballs	
	ćevapčići
Sausages	kobasice

Vegetables

Vegetables	povrće
Potatoes	krumpir
French fries	pomfrit
Swiss chard	blitva
Beans	grah
Carrot	mrkva
Cabbage	kupus
Corn	kukuruz

Salads

Salad	salata
Seasonal salad	sezonska salata
Mixed salad	miješana salata
Green salad	zelena salata
Tomato salad	salata od paradajza / rajčica
Cabbage salad	kupus salata
Octopus and potato salad	salata od hobotnice

Fruits

Fruit	voće
Orange	naranča
Apple	jabuka
Strawberry	jagoda
Plum	šljiva
Grapes	grožđe

Desserts

Ice cream	sladoled
Pancakes	palačinke
Flan	rožata
Cake	kolač

Drinks

Drinks	piće
Water	voda
Mineral water (still / sparkling)	
	mineralna voda (negazirana / gazirana)
Red wine	crno vino
White wine	bijelo vino
Beer	pivo
Draught beer	točeno pivo
Tea	čaj
Coffee	kava
Milk	mlijeko

Language Guide

Greetings

Hello	*Dobar dan*
Hi/bye! (informal, in Zagreb only)	*Bok!*
Good morning	*Dobro jutro*
Good evening	*Dobra večer*
Good night	*Laku noć*
	Do viČenja
Yes	*Da*
No	*Ne*
Please	*Molim*
Thank you	*Hvala*
I beg your pardon?	*Molim?*
Sorry!	*Oprostite!/Pardon!*
Excuse me (when about to request something)	*Oprostite*
Here you are! (when offering something)	*Izvolite!*
Cheers! (as a toast)	*Živjeli!*
Do you speak English?	*Govorite li engleski?*
I'm sorry, I don't speak Croatian	*Oprostite, ne znam hrvatski*
I don't understand	*Ne razumijem*
How are you?	*Kako ste?*
Fine, thank you	*Dobro, hvala*
Pleased to meet you!	*Drago mi je!*
Where are you from?	*Odakle ste?*
I'm from the United States / England	*Ja sam iz Amerike / Engleske*
Mr.	*Gospodin*
Mrs.	*Gospođa*

Accommodation

Hotel	*hotel*
Apartment	*apartman*
Room	*soba*
Do you have a single / double room?	*Imate li jednokrevetnu sobu / dvokrevetnu sobu?*
For tonight / tomorrow	*Za večeras / sutra*
For one night / three nights	*Za jednu noć / tri noći*
With private bathroom	*S kupaonicom*
Is breakfast included?	*Je li uključen doručak*

Shopping

Please could I have...	*Molim vas...*
Do you have...?	*Imate li...?*
How much does it cost?	*Koliko košta?*
Can I pay by credit card?	*Mogu li platiti s kredit nom karticom?*
Can I help you?	*Mogu li pomoći?*
I'm just looking, thanks	*Samo gledam, hvala*

Restaurants

Do you have a table for two?	*Imate li stol za dvoje?*
Can we sit outside / on the terrace?	*Možemo li sjesti vani / na terasi?*
Can I have an English menu, please?	*Mogu li dobiti meni na engleskom molim?*
Can I order, please?	*Mogu li naručiti?*
I've already ordered, thank you	*Već sam naručio, hvala*
Can I have the bill, please?	*Molim vas račun?*
I've finished, thank you	*Gotov sam, hvala*
It was very good	*Bilo je vrlo dobro*

Travel & Directions

Excuse me, where is the bus station?	*Oprostite, gdje je autobusni kolodvor?*
Train	*vlak*
Bus	*autobus*
Car	*auto*
Ferry	*trajekt*
Gas station	*benzinska stanica*
One ticket to..., please	*Jednu kartu do..., molim*
Which platform?	*Koji peron?*
Which number?	*Koji broj?*

Sightseeing

Museum	*muzej*
Gallery	*galerija*
Castle	*dvorac*
Old town	*stari grad*
Tour guide	*vodič*

Money

ATM	*bankomat*
Bank	*banka*
Exchange office	*mjenjačnica*
Credit card	*kreditna kartica*

Times & Dates

Excuse me, what time is it?	*Oprostite, koliko je sati?*
11:00	*jedanaest sati*
1:30	*jedan i pol (or pola dva)*
8:45	*petnaest do devet*
Today	*danas*
Tomorrow	*sutra*
Yesterday	*jučer*
Morning	*jutro*
Afternoon	*popodne*
Evening	*večer*

INDEX

ILLUSTRATIONS CREDITS

Cover, Phant/Shutterstock; Spine, imageBROKER/
Alamy; 2-3, Gavn Helier/Jon Arnold/Photolibrary;
4, Gavin Helier/Alamy; 8, Jon Arnold/Alamy; 10,
pics721/Shutterstock; 12 John Miller/Robert Harding
World Imagery/Photolibrary; 14-15, Guido Alberto
Rossi/Tips Italia/Photolibrary; 17, David Lomax/
Robert Harding World Imagery/Photolibrary; 19, JTB
Photo/Photolibrary; 20, STR/Reuters/Corbis; 21,
Bloomberg via Getty Images; 22-23, Philippe Body/
Hemis/Photolibrary; 25, Jean-Pierre Lescourret/
Corbis; 26, Cameraphoto Arte Venezia/Bridgeman
Art Library; 28, Jean-Pierre Lescourret/Corbis; 31,
Rainer Hackenberg/Corbis; 33, Interfoto/Alamy; 34,
Ed Kashi/Corbis; 37, Walter Bibikow/age fotostock/
Photolibrary; 38, Alexander Poschel/Imagebroker/
Photolibrary; 40, Jevgenija Pigozne/Imagebroker/
Photolibrary; 42, Rudolf Abraham/Alamy; 45, A
demoes/Photononstop/Photolibrary; 46-47, Jevgenija
Pigozne/Imagebroker/Photolibrary; 49, Dennis Dono-
hue/Shutterstock; 50-51, Bodo Muller/Imagebroker/
Photolibrary; 52, Philip Kieran/Alamy; 55, Lightworks
Media/Alamy; 56, Walter Bibikow/age fotostock/Pho-
tolibrary; 58, Mark Bassett/Alamy; 60, Ken Gillham/
Robert Harding World Imagery/Photolibrary; 63, Dallas
and John Heaton/Photolibrary; 64, Walter Bibikow/
Jon Arnold Travel/Photolibrary; 66 JTB Photo/Alamy;
68, William Manning/Alamy; 71, JTB Photo/
Photolibrary; 73, Philippe Body/Hemis/Photolibrary;
74, Peter Fosberg/Alamy; 76, Pjr Travel/Alamy; 79,
Christan Kober/John Warburton-Lee/Photolibrary; 82,
Pete Hill/Alamy; 84, xbrchx/Shutterstock; 86, Rudolf
Abraham; 88, SVIP/Shutterstock; 90, John Elk III/
Alamy; 92, iStockphoto; 93, Ingolf Pompe/Alamy; 95,
Nikola Solic/Reuters/Corbis; 96; Rudolf Abraham; 98,
Pat Behnke/Alamy; 100, Ingolf Pompe/Look-foto/
Photolibrary; 104, Ivica Jandrijevic/Shutterstock; 106,
Tim Draper/Dorling Kindersley/Getty Images; 108,
Aleksandar Plavšić/500px Prime; 110, Jasenka Luksa/
Shutterstock; 112, Svabo/Alamy; 115, Steven Stefa-
novic/OSF/Photolibrary; 116, University of Oxford/
Bridgeman Art Library; 117, Mark Bassett/Alamy; 120,
Hemis/Alamy; 122, Ivica Jandrijevic/Shutterstock; 125,
Jevgenija Pigozne/Imagebroker/Photolibrary; 126,
Christian Kober/Robert Harding World Imagery/Pho-
tolibrary; 129, Christian Kober/Alamy; 131, Zvonimir

Atletic/Shutterstock; 132, Nick Biemans/Shutterstock;
134 Rudolf Abraham; 136, Bahnmueller/Imagebroker/
Photolibrary; 138, Movemantway/Imagebroker/
Photolibrary; 142, Frank Fell / Tips Italia / Photolibrary;
145, Grand Tour/Corbis; 146, Gordana Sermek/Shut-
terstock; 149, Alan Copson/Jon Arnold Travel/Pho-
tolibrary; 150, mida/Alamy; 152, Martin Siepmann/
Imagebroker/Alamy; 154, Konrad Wothe/Look-foto/
Photolibrary; 157, Bernd Zoller/Imagebroker/Photo-
library; 158, Katia Kreder/Imagebroker/Photolibrary;
163, Wolfgang Poetzer/Waterframe/Photolibrary; 165,
Krkr/Shutterstock; 166 Nick Gregory/Alamy; 170, Wal-
ter Bibikow/Jon Arnold Travel/Photolibrary; 173, Frank
Guiziou/Hemis/Photolibrary; 174, Frank Guiziou/
Alamy; 177, Rudolf Abraham; 181, Peter Arnold/Pho-
tolibrary; 184, Kevin Galvin/Alamy; 186, Powered by
Light/Alan Spencer/Alamy; 188, Frederic Soreau/Pho-
tononstop/Photolibrary; 191, Kuttig-Travel/Alamy; 192,
Nik Wheeler/Alamy; 196, JTB Photo/Photolibrary;
198, Sheldon Lewis/Ticket/Photolibrary; 199 Jozef
Sedmak/Shutterstock; 201, Bertrand Gardel/Hemis/
Photolibrary; 202, Kuttig-Travel/Alamy; 204, Torino/
Photolibrary; 208, Wolfgang Weinhapi/Photolibrary;
210, Konrad Wothe/Look-foto/Photolibrary; 213,
John Harper/Alamy; 214, Bertrand Gardel/Hemis/
Photolibrary; 216, Funkyfood London - Paul Williams/
Alamy; 218; Frederic Soreau/Photononstop/Photo-
library; 220, Borut Furlan/Waterframe/Photolibrary;
223, Jen-Daniel Sudre/Hemis/Alamy; 224, Damir
Sago/Reuters/Corbis; 228, Kuttig-Travel/Alamy; 230,
Rudolf Abraham; 232, Ivan Hateren/Shutterstock; 234,
Pat Behnke/Alamy; 236, Keren Su/Corbis; 238, Alan
Copson/Jon Arnold Travel/Photolibrary; 239, Robin
McKelvie; 242, Gunter Flegan/Imagebroker/Photo-
library; 244, Ivan Zupic/age fotostock/Photolibrary;
246, Robin McKelvie; 247, Gavin Helier/Robert Harding World Imagery; 250, Kevin O'Hara/age fotostock;
251, Christian Kober/John Warburton-Lee/Photoli-
brary; 255, Photolibrary; 256, Wolfgang Thieme/dpa/
Corbis; 259, TOPIC Media/Bodo Muller/Alamy; 260,
Lightworks Media/Alamy; 262, Robin McKelvie; 263,
Rudolf Abraham/Alamy; 264, Robin McKelvie; 266,
Peter Higgins/Robert Harding World Imagery/Alamy;
271, Frank Guiziou/Hemis/Photolibrary; 272, Dallas
and John Heaton/Photolibrary.

National Geographic
TRAVELER
Croatia
Rudolf Abraham

Published by the National Geographic Society
Gary E. Knell, *President and Chief Executive Officer*
John M. Fahey, *Chairman of the Board*
Declan Moore, *Chief Media Officer*
Chris Johns, *Chief Content Officer*
Keith Bellows, *Senior Vice President and Editor in Chief,
   National Geographic Travel Media*

Prepared by the Book Division
Hector Sierra, *Senior Vice President and General Manager*
Janet Goldstein, *Senior Vice President and
   Editorial Director*
Jonathan Halling, *Creative Director*
Marianne R. Koszorus, *Design Director*
Barbara A. Noe, *Senior Editor*
R. Gary Colbert, *Production Director*
Jennifer A. Thornton, *Director of Managing Editorial*
Susan S. Blair, *Director of Photography*
Meredith C. Wilcox, *Director, Administration and
   Rights Clearance*

Staff for This Book
Justin Kavanagh, *Project Editor*
Elisa Gibson, *Art Director*
Ruth Ann Thompson, *Designer*
Carl Mehler, *Director of Maps*
Mike McNey & Mapping Specialists, *Map Production*
Marshall Kiker, *Associate Managing Editor*
Michael O'Connor, *Production Editor*
Galen Young, *Rights Clearance Specialist*
Katie Olsen, *Design Production Specialist*
Nicole Miller, *Design Production Assistant*
Robert L. Barr, *Manager Production Services*
Marlena Serviss, *Contributor*

The information in this book has been carefully
checked and to the best of our knowledge is
accurate. However, details are subject to change,
and the National Geographic Society cannot be
responsible for such changes, or for errors or omissions.
Assessments of sites, hotels, and restaurants are based
on the author's subjective opinions, which do not
necessarily reflect the publisher's opinion.

The National Geographic Society is one of the
world's largest nonprofit scientific and educational
organizations. Founded in 1888 to "increase and dif-
fuse geographic knowledge," the member-supported
Society works to inspire people to care about the planet.
Through its online community, members can get closer
to explorers and photographers, connect with other
members around the world, and help make a difference.
National Geographic reflects the world through its
magazines, television programs, films, music and radio,
books, DVDs, maps, exhibitions, live events, school
publishing programs, interactive media, and merchandise.
National Geographic magazine, the Society's official
journal, published in English and 38 local-language
editions, is read by more than 60 million people each
month. The National Geographic Channel reaches
440 million households in 171 countries in 38 languages.
National Geographic Digital Media receives more than
25 million visitors a month. National Geographic has
funded more than 10,000 scientific research, conservation, and exploration projects and supports an education
program promoting geography literacy. For more
information, visit nationalgeographic.com.

For more information, please call 1-800-NGS LINE
(647-5463) or write to the following address:

National Geographic Society
1145 17th Street N.W.
Washington, D.C. 20036-4688 U.S.A.

For information about special discounts for bulk
purchases, please contact National Geographic Books
Special Sales: ngspecsales@ngs.org

For rights or permissions inquiries, please contact
National Geographic Books Subsidiary Rights:
ngbookrights@ngs.org

Copyright © 2011, 2015 National Geographic Society
All rights reserved. Reproduction of the whole or any
part of the contents without written permission from
the publisher is prohibited.

National Geographic Traveler: Croatia
(Second Edition)
ISBN: 978-1-4262-1469-1

Printed in Hong Kong
14/THK/1

EXPERIENCE TOTAL IMMERSION

Now, with more than 75 destinations,
the National Geographic Traveler guidebooks
are available wherever books are sold or visit us online at

www.shopng.com/travelerguides

NATIONAL GEOGRAPHIC **TRAVEL**

THE COMPLETE TRAVEL EXPERIENCE

 for iPhone®, iPod touch®, and iPad®

EXPEDITIONS   MAGAZINE   APPS

Like us on Facebook: Nat Geo Books

Follow us on Twitter: @NatGeoBooks

© 2014 National Geographic Society